EUROLEGALISM

R. DANIEL KELEMEN

Eurolegalism

The Transformation of Law and Regulation in the European Union

HARVARD UNIVERSITY PRESS
Cambridge, Massachusetts
London, England
2011

Printed in the United States of America

Library of Congress Cataloging-in-Publication Data

Kelemen, R. Daniel.
Eurolegalism : the transformation of law and regulation in the European Union/ R. Daniel Kelemen.
p. cm.
Includes bibliographical references and index.
ISBN 978-0-674-04694-8 (alk. paper)
1. Law–European Union countries. I. Title.

KJE947.K45 2011
341.242'2—dc22 2010039552

For Tasha and Zara

Contents

Figures

EUROLEGALISM

CHAPTER 1

The Juris Touch

In crowded airport terminals from Brussels to Bratislava, the European Union (EU) reaches out to weary travelers. Posters sponsored by the European Commission and adorned with the blue and yellow European flag remind disgruntled passengers that they have rights. Have you been denied boarding on an overbooked flight? Has your flight been delayed by several hours or canceled? Has the airline lost your baggage? If so, the Commission would like to remind you that European law gives you a legally enforceable right to compensation. (See Figure 1.1.)

The EU's call to arms resonated with many frustrated passengers. After the EU adopted a passenger rights regulation in February 2004,[1] airlines were hit with a dramatic upsurge in claims—with a total of twenty-two thousand complaints during the first eight months the regulation was in force. The International Air Transport Association (IATA) estimated that new compensation claims could cost the typical midsized European airline €40 million annually, approximately 20 percent of its annual operating profit (Minder 2006). Easyjet, Ryanair, and other low-cost carriers were particularly threatened by the compensation requirements, because compensation payments are linked to the length of the flight, not to the ticket price. As a result, passengers who pay pocket change for one of Ryanair's celebrated discount tickets could be owed compensation of €600 should they be bumped from their flight.

Ten of these discount airlines from nine countries formed a trade association, the European Low Fares Airline Association (ELFAA), for the

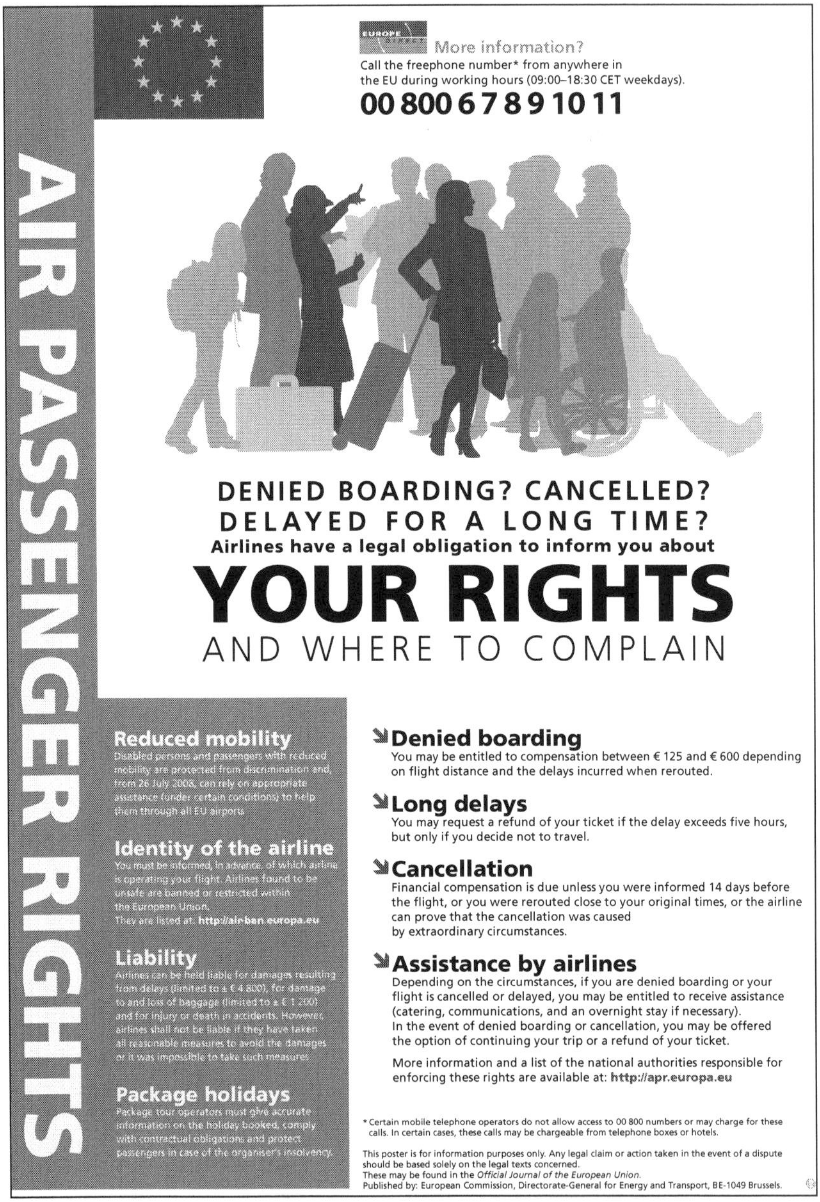

Figure 1.1. Air passenger rights poster sponsored by the European Commission.

express purpose of combating the passenger rights regulation. In a case of "legal turnabout is fair play," the airlines sought to have their own day in court. IATA and the newly created ELFAA challenged the UK's implementation of the EU regulation before the High Court of Justice of England and Wales (Queen's Bench Division). The airlines argued that the regulation was invalid on a number of grounds, including that its penalties were disproportionately high, that it violated the principle of "equal treatment" of different transport sectors, and that it violated the EU's international obligations under the Montreal Convention on air transport. As the airlines' challenge raised questions concerning the validity of the EU regulation, the High Court decided to invoke the EU's preliminary ruling procedure, whereby the court ordered a stay in its proceedings and referred a set of questions to the European Court of Justice (ECJ). Essentially, the High Court wanted the ECJ to rule on whether the airlines' arguments against the validity of the EU regulation were well founded. Ultimately, the ECJ rejected all of the airlines' arguments and upheld the new EU passenger rights established in the regulation.[2] The airline association IATA said that the ruling marked "a sad day for Europe," while the European Commission retorted that the ruling was "good news for consumers" (Minder 2006).

Meanwhile, the Commission continued its efforts to bring legal pressure to bear on reluctant member states—forcing them to strengthen their enforcement of the passenger rights regulation. Beginning in July 2005, the European Commission had initiated a number of infringement proceedings against member states (initially Austria, Belgium, Italy, Luxembourg, Malta, and Sweden and later the UK) for failure to meet all their obligations under the regulation (Commission 2005a), and the Commission filed formal infringement proceedings before the ECJ against Austria, Sweden, and Luxembourg in 2006.[3] In April 2007, the Commission issued a new report (Commission 2007a) criticizing member states for inadequate enforcement of EU passenger rights and threatened to initiate a new round of infringement proceedings after six months against any states that had not taken necessary steps to strengthen enforcement (Commission 2007b).

Meanwhile, disgruntled passengers have continued to pursue claims. A niche industry of passenger compensation–claim legal advisors has sprung up to assist passengers with claims. Firms such as Aviaclaim, EUclaim, and Ticketclaim advertise widely on the Web, soliciting clients to bring compensation claims against airlines.[4] Aviaclaim advertises that they work on a "no-cure, no-pay" (in American parlance, no-win, no-fee) basis and charge only a modest 22 percent success fee. EUclaim, whose Web site claimed (as of December 2009) that over seventeen thousand passengers had used their services, also works on a no-win, no-fee basis, charging clients 27 percent, plus an administrative fee. EUclaim maintains an office in Amsterdam's Schiphol Airport, where passengers can stop by to make claims. After all, if their flights are canceled, they may have time on their hands.

National courts have continued to refer questions concerning the application of the regulation to the ECJ, with a total of eight references from national courts concerning the regulation reaching the ECJ by the end of 2009.[5] ECJ rulings have bolstered passenger rights. In December 2008, the ECJ ruled that technical problems with an aircraft are not covered by the concept of "extraordinary circumstances" that airlines could use to exonerate themselves from paying compensation for cancellations.[6] In a November 2009 ruling, the ECJ extended the compensation provisions dramatically. The regulation had provided for compensation payments (ranging from €250 to €600) for denied boarding and canceled flights, but for long flight delays the regulation had only required airlines to reimburse passengers tickets or reroute them and provide free food and accommodation. However, in its November 2009 ruling,[7] the ECJ held that because the damage sustained by air passengers in cases of long delays is comparable to the damage they sustain from cancellations, requiring compensation for cancellations but not for delayed flights would violate the fundamental principle of "equal treatment." Therefore, the Court concluded that when flights are delayed more than three hours, passengers have the right to compensation payments as outlined in the directive—up to €600 per passenger.

* * *

This chain of events would have been unimaginable thirty years ago. The European Union publicly calling on citizens to enforce their EU rights? Businesses forming pan-European interest groups to bring legal challenges against EU rights? The Commission threatening coercive legal action against member states that do not enforce consumer rights? Legal service firms springing up that widely advertise and solicit clients to bring EU rights claims? Well into the 1980s, such practices would have seemed highly out of place in Europe. The emphasis on the language of rights—EU rights no less—and the courtroom battles between regulators and the regulated would have been out of step with the more cooperative and decidedly less judicialized approaches to regulation that prevailed across Europe. Indeed, the entire episode would have had a distinctly American air about it.

And yet, in today's Europe, the passenger rights saga chronicled above is hardly unusual. There are increasing indications that a European variant of American regulatory style is spreading across the European Union. Across policy areas ranging from employment discrimination to consumer protection to antitrust to securities regulation to the free movement rights of workers, students, and even medical patients, we can observe more coercive legal enforcement, more rights claims, and a growing judicial role in shaping policy. Such developments have not gone unnoticed in the European media, with major papers running articles with titles such as "Business Warns EU against Class Actions" (Parker, Buck, and Tait 2007), "Investors Win Powers to Sue" (Adams, Tait, and Jopson 2005), "Brussels Wins Right to Force EU Countries to Jail Polluters" (Watt 2005), "Watchdog Calls in Lawyers over Equality Directive" (Turner 2005), "France Fined €20 Million over Fish Stocks" (Minder 2005b), "Microsoft to Appeal against €900m EC Fine" (Tait 2008b), "European Court Paves Way for Health Tourism" (Laurance 2006), "ECJ Tax Ruling Threatens London Stock Markets" (Herman 2008), "European Student Had Right to UK Loan" (Rennie 2005), "Business Groups Hit Out at 'Compensation Culture'" (Brunsden 2009), "Les consommateurs favorables à l' 'action de groupe' à la française" (Consumers in Favor of Class Actions à la *française*) (*Le Monde* 2007)," "Furcht vor Sammelklagen und Erfolgshonoraren" (Fear of Group Actions and Success Fees)" (Jahn 2007), "Megaclaims in Holland: 'Hebzucht is toch prima?'" (Megaclaims in Holland: "Greed Is Good, Isn't It?") (Volkskrant 2005), "La UE concluye que una empresa puede jubilar de manera forzosa a los 65 años" (The EU Concludes That a Business Can Force 65-Year-Olds to Retire)" (Manzano 2007).

Seeking to make sense of such developments, an emerging literature explores the increasing role of lawyers, courts, and litigation in regulatory and administrative processes across Europe. Some scholars argue that this judicialization is pushing patterns of law and regulation across Europe toward something akin to an "American legal style" (Wiegand 1991; Shapiro 1993; Trubek 1994; Galanter 1992; Shapiro and Stone 1994; Kelemen and Sibbitt 2004; Kelemen 2006, 2008; Van Waarden and Hildebrand 2009; Rehder 2009). Other scholars disagree, maintaining that entrenched national legal institutions and cultures will block such convergence (Kagan 1997, 2007, 2008; Van Waarden 1995; Legrand 1996; Cioffi 2009). Not all authors engaged in these debates mean precisely the same thing when they invoke the notion of American law or American legal and regulatory style. Some focus more on growing judicial power, others on adversarial relations between government and regulated entities, and still others on a growing proclivity to sue, or "compensation culture," among the public at large. While no concept can capture all of these understandings of American legal and regulatory style, Robert A. Kagan's notion of "adversarial legalism" comes close.[8]

In a series of publications and in his landmark book *Adversarial Legalism: The American Way of Law,* Kagan (2001) notes that between the 1970s and 1990s a substantial body of literature in the field of comparative law and public policy demonstrated that the predominant approach to regulation in the United States differed substantially from the approaches to regulation—or modes of governance—that prevailed across western Europe. Kagan labeled this distinctive American approach to governance "adversarial legalism." Distilling the findings of dozens of studies,[9] Kagan (2001, 2007) explains that compared with the approaches that prevailed across western Europe, American regulatory style was (and still is) characterized by (1) detailed, prescriptive rules often containing strict transparency and disclosure requirements, (2) legalistic and adversarial approaches to regulatory enforcement and dispute resolution, (3) costly legal contestation and multifaceted megalawyering techniques, (4) active judicial review of administrative decisions and practices, and frequent judicial intervention, (5) frequent private litigation concerning regulatory policies. Above all, American-style adversarial legalism is distinguished by its emphasis on enforcing legal norms through transparent legal rules and procedures and broad access to justice, empowering private actors to assert their legal rights (Kelemen and Sibbitt 2004, 2005). Importantly, it is a mistake simply to equate adversarial legalism with large volumes of litigation. As I discuss in Chapter 3, countries such as Germany, Sweden, and Austria, where policymaking was not traditionally characterized by adversarial legalism, nevertheless have long had higher civil litigation rates than the United States. Adversarial legalism is a mode of governance that manifests itself in a variety of ways and not simply—and not necessarily—in more frequent litigation.

Compared with American-style adversarial legalism, the various approaches to regulation that long predominated across western Europe were more informal, cooperative, and opaque and relied less on the involvement of lawyers, courts, and private enforcement actions. As I discuss below, these systems typically relied on opaque networks of bureaucrats and regulated interests developing and implementing regulatory policies in close concertation. Regulators could rely on more flexible, informal means of achieving regulatory objectives, with courts rarely challenging regulators' decisions. As a result, while "regulation through litigation" (Viscusi 2002) was central to American regulatory governance and while the threat of potential litigation stimulated a wide range of behavioral changes among actors in the regulatory arena, these dynamics were largely absent in Europe.

Nor was American adversarial legalism something many Europeans hoped to import to their shores. Most Europeans have long viewed American legal and regulatory style with a mixture of amusement and horror—and perhaps a touch of Schadenfreude. Ambulance-chasing lawyers, class action lawsuits, massive punitive damage awards, and, more generally, adversarial, litigious relationships among government, industry, and interest groups were and still are viewed as part of the fabric of "American exceptionalism" (Lipset 1996)—symptoms of an American disease,[10] against which European countries were shielded, thankfully, by the Atlantic and by virtue of the sobriety of their legal cultures. And certainly most Europeans—even those who admire particular American laws or legal practices—would be horrified at the prospect of American-style adversarial legalism spreading across Europe. While most Europeans may continue to feel secure in their immunity to this "American disease," this book suggests that theirs is a false sense of security.

* * *

The central argument of this book is that the process of European integration is encouraging the spread of a European variant of adversarial legalism, which we can call Eurolegalism. Eurolegalism shares the same defining characteristics as American-style adversarial legalism, but due to the moderating influence of entrenched national legal institutions and norms, the version of adversarial legalism that is spreading in Europe is more restrained and sedate than that found in America.[11] European integration is encouraging the spread of Eurolegalism as a mode of governance through two linked causal mechanisms, which I explore in greater detail in Chapter 2. The first mechanism involves the process of deregulation and juridical reregulation linked to the creation of the EU's single market. The economic liberalization associated with the creation of the single market has undermined traditionally cooperative, informal, and opaque approaches to regulation at the national level. Deregulation at the national level has been linked to reregulation at the European level, as national regulations that impeded the operation of the single market are replaced with pan-European frameworks. However, most new EU regulations do not resemble the national ones they replaced. The increased volume and diversity of players in the liberalized single market and the demands from market participants and governments alike to ensure a "level playing field" pressure EU policy makers to rely on a more formal, transparent approach to regulation backed by vigorous enforcement, often by private parties.

The second mechanism stems from the EU's fragmented institutional structure and its impact on EU policymaking. When policy makers seek to reregulate at the EU level, they do so in the context of a highly fragmented regulatory state with a powerful judicial system and a weak administrative apparatus. The vertical fragmentation between the EU and the member states and the horizontal fragmentation of power between institutions at the EU level (i.e., the Council, the Parliament, and the Commission) generate principal-agent problems that encourage the adoption of laws with strict, judicially enforceable goals, deadlines, and transparent procedural requirements. Also, given the EU's extremely limited implementation and enforcement capacities, EU lawmakers have an incentive to create justiciable rights and to empower private parties to serve as the enforcers of EU law. In the absence of a Eurocracy powerful enough to enforce EU law from Brussels (Kelemen 2005), the EU is encouraging the spread of adversarial legalism as a mode of governance that can harness private litigants and national courts for the decentralized enforcement of European law.

Eurolegalism is emerging as a quite unexpected—and in many circles unwanted—stepchild of European integration. Together, the EU's institutional structure and its ongoing project of market integration generate political incentives and functional pressures that have led policy makers to enact transparent, justiciable regulations backed by strict public enforcement and increased opportunities for private enforcement. In other words, adversarial legalism is emerging in Europe for much the same reason it emerged decades earlier in the United States. As Kagan has emphasized (2001, pp. 40–54), in the US case, the combination of "fragmented governmental authority" and "fragmented economic power" was crucial to the emergence of adversarial legalism. In the United States, regulation through litigation emerged as a tool of a weak, highly fragmented state attempting to regulate an expansive and highly liberalized economy. So too in Europe.

The argument set out above challenges prevailing orthodoxies concerning EU governance. EU policy makers regularly—one might say ritualistically—profess their commitment to adopting flexible, informal approaches to governance (Commission 2001a, p. 428; Kelemen and Menon 2007). Likewise, many scholars (Héritier 2002; Radaelli 2003; Trubek and Trubek 2002; Falkner et al. 2005) emphasize the EU's role in promoting new, flexible modes of governance that rely on voluntary agreements, framework directives, soft law, self-regulation, and the Open Method of Coordination. In contrast, this book suggests these flexible new modes of governance are red herring (Idema and Kelemen 2006). The impact of the EU's dalliance with such flexible new modes of governance is overshadowed by the EU's far more pervasive role in promoting the spread of Eurolegalism across a wide range of policy areas.[12]

My argument also challenges prominent arguments concerning the resilience of national legal styles and patterns of policy diffusion. A number of scholars have suggested that impediments to litigation entrenched in national institutions and legal cultures across the EU will block the spread of adversarial legalism in general (Kagan 1997) and of EU rights litigation specifically (Conant 2002; Harlow 1999; Alter and Vargas 2000, Burke 2004; Vanhala 2009a, 2009b; Slepcevic 2009). These arguments identify a variety of institutional impediments to litigation—such as restrictive rules of standing, inadequate financial support and incentives, the absence of class actions—and deeply embedded norms concerning the role of law and lawyers that all seem to make Europe inhospitable terrain for the growth of adversarial legalism. I demonstrate that many of these barriers are gradually eroding as a result of pressures unleashed by European integration and that while these barriers will continue to channel and constrain the development of adversarial legalism in Europe, they will not halt it.

Importantly, my argument does not rely on the sorts of diffusion processes typically found in studies of the spread of regulatory norms or techniques across jurisdictions (Kelemen and Sibbitt 2005). Studies of policy diffusion typically emphasize the role of coercion, regulatory competition, learning, or emulation in spreading policies across jurisdictions (Simmons, Dobbin, and Garrett 2008). American influences have played some role in the spread of adversarial legalism to Europe, as I will discuss further below. The American legal system has become the most influential national legal system in the world, and many US legal norms have spread to other jurisdictions through a variety of diffusion processes (Mattei 1994; Wiegand 1991; De Lisle 1999; Lester 1988; Ajani 1995; Dezalay and Garth 1995; Kelemen and Sibbitt 2005; Garth 2008). US law firms active in the EU have also played an important role as transmission belts, accelerating the spread of models of US legal practice to jurisdictions across Europe (Kelemen and Sibbitt 2004, 2005). Certainly, American regulatory style provides a salient model that is familiar to EU policy makers and interest groups in many issue areas. However, American-style adversarial legalism typically is viewed with revulsion in Europe. US regulatory style is referred to far more often as an example of what must be avoided than as a model to be emulated. One of the central puzzles addressed by this study is why a legal style that almost no one explicitly advocates is spreading so widely. Ultimately, the primary underlying cause of the spread of adversarial legalism in the EU does not involve being coerced by, competing with, learning from, or emulating the United States. Rather, the explanation for the spread of adversarial legalism is to be found in shifts within the political economy of Europe.

* * *

I elaborate my argument and review opposing arguments in Chapter 2, but first it is important that I emphasize what I am *not* arguing. First, the argument here is not that we should expect European approaches to governance to converge rapidly or completely on an American model. The rise of Eurolegalism involves an increasing reliance on formal law, lawyers, and litigation in policymaking and dispute resolution, not a complete convergence with American practices. Indeed, one could hardly expect total convergence when American regulatory style itself is a moving target—as evidenced by the alternating waves of tort reform, regulatory reform, and access-to-justice initiatives in the United States—and when US legal regulatory style varies substantially across policy areas and states. And more importantly, as Kagan and other scholars discussed below suggest, entrenched national legal institutions and norms will limit the spread of some American practices in Europe. While the existing institutional and cultural landscape of European legal systems will not block the spread of adversarial legalism, this landscape will surely channel and moderate these developments. Likewise, differences in national legal institutions and regulatory styles will modify the impact of adversarial legalism across member states. Thus, to say that something akin to American adversarial legalism is taking root in the EU is not to suggest that European jurisdictions will soon or ever experience the most notorious excesses, real or imagined, of the US legal system. For Europe, then, there will be no cavalcades of personal injury lawyers at accident scenes and no charmed circle of class action lawyers jurisdiction-hopping in their Learjets. The Eurolegalism that is spreading across the EU is a rather subdued variant of American adversarial legalism.

Second, the argument is not that every policy undertaken by the EU has the characteristics of adversarial legalism. To argue that adversarial legalism is emerging as a dominant mode of governance in the European Union is not to deny that the EU deploys other modes of governance. As Jeremy Richardson (1982) recognized, policy style can vary within a political system across different issue areas (see also Howlett and Ramesh 2003 and Pollack 2008). US experience is instructive in this regard. While scholars agree that US regulatory governance is dominated by adversarial legalism, the prevalence of adversarial legalism varies across policy areas and across states, and regulators frequently adopt rules and practices that do not fit the model of adversarial legalism.[13] The EU has a wide range of instruments and approaches in its regulatory repertoire and certainly does occasionally deploy flexible, informal approaches to regulation. Eurolegalism is not the EU's only mode of governance, but it is emerging as its dominant mode of governance—a regulatory leitmotif to which the EU returns again and again across a wide range of policy areas.

Finally, forces associated with European integration are not the only causes of the spread of adversarial legalism. In the post–World War II era, democracies in Europe and around the world have experienced a profound, multifaceted judicialization of politics. For some sociologists and social theorists drawing on the work of Durkheim (1893/1964) or Weber (1914/1978), the judicialization of politics is a manifestation of the broader juridification of social relationships in increasingly complex, heterogenous modern societies (see Black 1976; Luhmann 1985; Habermas 1987, pp. 318–331, 359; Teubner 1987; Hirschl 2008, p. 121). An extensive literature in law and political science explores this judicialization of politics and identifies a number of factors that have encouraged it, including declining support for the principle of parliamentary sovereignty, increasing emphasis on citizens' rights, and the expanding scope of public regulation (Henkin 1990; Shapiro and Stone 1994; Tate and Vallinder 1995; Stone Sweet 2000; Guarnieri and Pederzoli 2001; Shapiro and Stone Sweet 2002; Ferejohn 2002; Ginsburg 2003; Hirschl 2004b, 2008b).

There is overlap between some of the arguments found in the judicialization literature and the argument developed in this book, for instance, arguments concerning the influence of political fragmentation on judicial power (Ginsburg 2003). However, while the shifts in approaches to regulation that are the focus of this book are related to the broader judicialization of politics, they are not synonymous with it. Most scholarly literature on judicialization has focused on the strengthening of courts' constitutional review powers (Holland 1991; Tate and Vallinder 1995; Stone 1992; Volcansek 1992; Shapiro and Stone 1994; Stone Sweet 2000; Ferejohn 2002; Guarnieri and Pederzoli 2001; Ginsburg 2003; Hirschl 2004b) or of the role of courts in what Ran Hirschl (2008a) terms "mega-politics." This book focuses on the less dramatic but equally important judicialization of day-to-day regulatory and administrative processes in the European Union. Polities can and do develop expansive constitutional review without adopting anything akin to adversarial legalism in the regulatory arena (Rose-Ackerman 1995; Blankenburg 1996, p. 303). Broader processes of the judicialization of politics have certainly supported the developments described in this book, but these broad processes do not provide an adequate explanation for the spread of Eurolegalism.

This book builds on the rich literature on EU law and politics, but the focus here differs. Much of the leading scholarship on EU law and politics analyzes how and to what extent the ECJ has propelled the process of European integration (Weiler 1991; Stone Sweet 2000, 2004; Burley and Mattli 1993; Mattli and Slaughter 1995, 2003; Alter 1998; Garrett, Kelemen, and Schulz 1998) and highlights the role of private enforcement litigation in the construction of a European legal order (Harlow and Rawlings 1992; Rawlings 1993; Alter 2001; Conant 2002; Stone Sweet 2004; Cichowski 2007). While this book shares those concerns, it does not concentrate on questions of how the EU legal system was constructed or how the ECJ affected the pace of European integration. Rather, this is a book about how the EU uses a particular approach to regulation—Eurolegalism—to pursue its policy objectives and how its style of governance affects traditional national patterns of regulation. Thus, this study links research on European legal integration with research on European policy styles (Richardson 1982; D. Vogel 1986) or modes of governance (Kohler-Koch and Eising 1999; Héritier 2001; Kohler-Koch and Rittberger 2006; Majone 2008).[14]

Comparing Regulatory Styles: What Exactly Is Changing?

"Concept formation" is a crucial first step in social science research (Sartori 1970; Collier and Mahon 1993; Collier and Levitsky 1997; Gerring 1999; Collier and Adcock 1999; Adcock 2005; Goertz 2006). Before we can proceed with our analysis of changing patterns of governance in the EU, we need to be confident that the concepts we are using to identify and express those changes are well suited to our purposes. Regulatory style is what social scientists term a "thick" concept (Coppedge 1999). Like other thick concepts, such as democracy or varieties of capitalism, regulatory style is multidimensional and cannot be reduced to a single indicator. A polity's regulatory style has many components, including the nature of the polity's legal norms, prevailing approaches to rule enforcement and dispute resolution, scope and frequency of judicial review, and the role of private litigants in enforcing policies and even challenging government.[15] This study focuses on shifts toward a European variant of adversarial legalism, a regulatory style distinguished, above all, by its emphasis on strict enforcement of detailed legal norms through a combination of transparency requirements and the broad empowerment of private actors to assert their legal rights (i.e., access to justice) (Kelemen and Sibbitt 2005).

Is adversarial legalism or Eurolegalism the right concept to use in studying the phenomena of interest to us in this study? Is it too specific or too abstract?[16] Some critics might suggest that to understand the phenomena of interest to this study we should instead be studying the broader phenomenon of judicialization. Though the spread of adversarial legalism is related to judicialization, the latter is a far broader concept, which encompasses many phenomena unrelated to regulatory policy. And, as noted above, polities can experience significant forms of judicialization in other domains without adopting some form of adversarial legalism as a regulatory style. Other critics might suggest that we disaggregate adversarial legalism and study particular components of that regulatory style, such as transparency or access to justice, in isolation (Levi-Faur 2005). Such "conceptual splitting" would be ill advised. A political system's regulatory style is more than merely the sum of its parts: the various institutions and practices that comprise a regulatory style are often highly interdependent and complementary.[17] We can learn more about law and regulation by studying such interactive patterns of policy style than by disaggregating.[18] For us to understand emerging patterns of EU regulation, the concept of Eurolegalism is neither too big nor too small but just right.

To appreciate how the spread of this variant of adversarial legalism is changing the nature of governance across the EU, we must clarify how it differs from the traditional European regulatory styles that it is supplanting. An obvious challenge in doing so is that the traditional national regulatory styles in EU member states varied from one another in many very significant ways (Richardson 1982). Frans Van Waarden (MS, University of Utrecht) warns against accounts that lump together European legal and regulatory systems, explaining, "Even close neighbors have rather different political, administrative and legal institutions, in particular in Europe where state formation set in early on, and where different nation-states followed quite different paths of institution building." Recognizing this rich diversity, one can nevertheless identify a number of common attributes that distinguished European legal styles—in broad terms—from American-style adversarial legalism (Kagan 2001). The approaches to regulation that long predominated across western Europe were more informal, cooperative, and opaque and relied less on the involvement of lawyers and courts than those that predominated in the United States. Across the variety of systems of regulation found in EU member states, closed networks of bureaucrats and regulated interests developed and implemented policies in concertation. Regulators were free to pursue more informal means of achieving regulatory objectives, with courts rarely challenging their decisions. In a number of states, particularly Austria, Sweden, Germany, and the Netherlands, corporatist patterns of interest intermediation predominated (Lehmbruch and Schmitter 1982; Goldthorpe 1984; Kitschelt et al. 1999; Van Waarden 1995, 1999). In France, elite government technocrats traditionally dominated regulatory policymaking (Hayward 1982; Suleiman 1978). In the UK, a pattern of cooperative, informal, "chummy" relationships between regulators and regulated entities prevailed (D. Vogel 1986; S. Vogel 1996). In the Netherlands, consociationalism and corporatism were intertwined such that organized interests and government officials engaged in consensual policymaking across a wide range of policy fields (Daalder 1966; Lijphart 1975; Van Waarden 2002b, 2003).

Traditionally, these systems of regulation relied on closed policymaking networks and delegated wide discretion to regulators to pursue informal means of achieving regulatory objectives. Regulators, regulated industries, and other network insiders resolved conflicts informally, without resorting to judicial processes. Network insiders had no need to resort to litigation. Outsiders had greater incentives to do so but typically found courts unwilling to block policy initiatives developed within elite networks.[19] Law firms in Europe played a limited role in business affairs and in the regulatory process. Law firms tended to be small, and they focused on litigation, playing little role as intermediaries between business and government or as advisors on general business affairs (Trubek et al 1994, p. 422; Morgan and Quack 2005). Law firms did not engage extensively in the "mega-lawyering" (Galanter 1983, 1992) techniques associated with large American law firms, techniques such as multi-jurisdictional litigation strategies, lobbying, and other nonjudicial forms of advocacy.

A host of comparative, cross-national, and cross-sectoral studies confirmed that European approaches differed from American-style adversarial legalism. Such findings were replicated in areas as diverse as environmental regulation (D. Vogel 1986), chemicals and hazardous waste regulation (Brickman, Jasanoff, and Ilgen 1985; Badarraco 1985; Church and Nakamura 1994), product liability (Schwartz 1991), labor relations regulation (Bok 1971), workplace safety (Kelman 1981; Braithewaite 1985), corporate governance (Charkham 1994), and securities regulation (S. Vogel 1996). In study after study, in countries including France, Germany, the United Kingdom, the Netherlands, and other EU member states, European approaches to regulation were found to be less judicialized and litigious, less driven by legal formalities, less unpredictable, and less adversarial than the US approach to the policy area in question. Thus, if European integration is encouraging the spread of a regulatory style similar to American-style adversarial legalism, this style would indeed represent a profound departure from traditional modes of governance across Europe. As I discuss in the concluding chapter, this shift in regulatory style has important implications for economic performance and approaches to economic management and for European models of democracy.

Research Design and Road Map

In describing his approach to research design in his classic *Making Democracy Work,* Robert Putnam writes (1992, p. 12), "The prudent social scientist, like the wise investor, must rely on diversification to magnify the strengths, and to offset the weaknesses, of any single instrument." This sensibility has informed the research design of this book. Such prudent diversification is particularly valuable when, as in this study, the dependent variable under investigation is an inherently thick concept that does not lend itself to a simple operationalization (Coppedge 1999). No single measure can capture broad changes in regulatory style. Also, variation in regulatory style across areas of law within any polity poses a challenge to attempts to generalize about trends. This book's approach to operationalization and to assessment of the spread of Eurolegalism relies on pulling together a number of indicators—both qualitative and quantitative—which together can form a composite picture of the trend. The analysis is longitudinal, taking the mid-1980s as a baseline for all measures and assessing shifts in regulatory style over the next two decades. It was in the mid-1980s that the launch of the single market initiative and reforms to the structure and authority of EU institutions began to generate economic pressures and political incentives that would encourage the rise of Eurolegalism.

After elaborating the theoretical argument in Chapter 2, I begin my empirical account in Chapter 3, examining overarching indicators of the spread of adversarial legalism in the EU, indicators that cut across policy areas. I look both at aggregate data on legal activity, such as litigation and the size of the legal services industry, and at qualitative changes in the law, such as the spread of class action lawsuits and conditional fee arrangements. Many of the reforms and trends discussed in Chapter 3 must be understood as both products of the spread of Eurolegalism and catalysts for its further growth. Some indicators can be taken as evidence of Eurolegalism; others simply show that changes in the European "legal field" (Vauchez 2008)[20] necessary to underpin the future growth of adversarial legalism are falling into place. For instance, data showing that the European legal services industry is growing rapidly and transforming its forms of organization both reflect the growth of Eurolegalism and will further accelerate its spread. Likewise, procedural reforms, such as the spread of class actions, reflect political pressure to increase access to justice and will in time open the way for more private enforcement of EU law.

Analysis of these general trends underscores the broad scope of the transformation of legal and regulatory systems across the EU. While such aggregate indicators are revealing, they have inherent limitations. First, much of the aggregate data will capture the effects of developments that have nothing to do with European integration. For instance, legal reforms or social or cultural developments having nothing to do with European integration may spawn increased (or decreased) rates of civil litigation. While indicative of broad trends, aggregate data cannot definitively establish a causal link between European integration and shifts in regulatory style.[21] Even taken together, the quantitative and qualitative indicators presented in Chapter 3 cannot adequately capture changes in regulatory style. To explore and understand the causal pathways linking European integration and adversarial legalism, we must turn to detailed case studies of particular policy areas.

Chapters 4 through 6 present comparative case studies of the spread of adversarial legalism in three policy areas—securities regulation, competition policy, and disability policy. These policy area case studies were selected on the basis of a "most different systems" research design (Przeworski and Teune 1970), which approximates the "method of agreement" of John Stuart Mill (1843/2002).[22] Generally, this approach calls on the researcher to select cases that differ as much as possible with regard to potential causal factors, except that the cases are all exposed to the one causal factor that the researcher assumes to be significant. If one can show that these very different cases, which shared only one potential causal factor in common, experienced a similar outcome, this suggests that that factor was indeed the cause of the outcome.

In line with this research design, I examine disparate areas of policy-making in different national legal contexts, all of which have been affected by EU regulation. As policy areas, competition policy, securities regulation, and disability policy vary in myriad ways. Of greatest theoretical relevance, the nature of the potential litigants involved in each field and the resources and legal opportunities available to them differs significantly. The firms and shareholders who are the principal litigants in the fields of competition policy and securities regulation have far more resources and legal expertise at their disposal than do victims of disability discrimination or the associations that represent them.[23] In discussing developments in these policy areas, I look both at developments at the EU level and at their impact in the UK, Germany, France, and the Netherlands, all of which were already EU member states in the mid-1980s and which had well-established national regulatory styles that were—as discussed above—well documented in the social science literature (see Richardson 1982).

The aim of these case studies is not to systematically compare the impact of various national legal institutions and traditions or the impact of the characteristics of particular policy areas. Rather, I seek to demonstrate that European integration is inducing shifts toward adversarial legalism across a wide range of policy areas and member states and to trace the process through which European integration encourages adversarial legalism. Through careful process tracing (George and Bennett 2005), I explore the means through which and the extent to which European integration encourages moves toward a more adversarial legalistic regulatory style. In each case I begin by describing the dominant regulatory style in a particular issue area in the early to mid-1980s and then assess how and to what extent European integration and increasing EU involvement in the issue area after the mid-1980s encouraged a shift toward Eurolegalism.[24] Many scholars who doubt the central claim of this book emphasize that entrenched institutional impediments and barriers to rights litigation at the national level will stop adversarial legalism from taking root in European jurisdictions. While I agree that such impediments at the national level will certainly constrain and channel the spread of adversarial legalism, the case studies presented below demonstrate that a European variant of this regulatory style—Eurolegalism—is taking root across diverse countries and policy areas despite such impediments. The selection of diverse policy areas not only comports with the most different systems research design but also enables me to demonstrate the broad range of policy areas affected by the spread of Eurolegalism.

Finally, in Chapter 7, I conclude by summarizing the study's central findings and considering the normative implications of the spread of Eurolegalism.

Conclusion

In Greek mythology, Dionysus, the god of wine and fertility, grants King Midas's wish for the power to turn everything he touches into gold. Quickly, the blessing of the Midas touch turns out to be a curse. Midas nearly starves as he watches any food or drink he touches turn to gold, and he accidentally kills his daughter when his touch turns her into a golden statue. The EU certainly does not have a Midas touch—if it did, the budget crises facing Greece and other member states might quickly be resolved. But the EU does have a special touch of its own, which we might call "the juris touch." It seems that nearly everything the European Union touches turns into law. This is of course an exaggeration: there is a limited role for law or adversarial legalism in important areas of EU activity, such as monetary policy or common defense.[25] However, regularly, and across a broad range of areas of social and economic regulation connected with the single market, EU involvement encourages the rise of modes of governance based on adversarial legalism. Where the EU exerts its authority, prescriptive regulations, judicial controls, and legions of lawyers follow. And like Midas's touch, the EU's juris touch is both a blessing and a curse.

The juris touch is a blessing in that it enables the EU to govern. The EU is a community built on the rule of law, and it is above all the strength of the EU's legal system that distinguishes it from all less powerful supranational entities. With an executive comprising less than twenty-five thousand Eurocrats facing a Union with a population of nearly half a billion souls, the EU could not hope to achieve much in the regulatory arena without the tools of adversarial legalism. If the EU is any kind of state, it is a weak one with an extremely limited administrative capacity. And like some other weak states, the EU relies on courts and private litigants to function as substitutes for a more robust administrative apparatus (Skowronek 1982, Dobbin and Sutton 1998; Kagan 2001).

The EU's juris touch is also a curse in that it threatens to bring to Europe some of the vices of adversarial legalism so well known and lamented in the United States: high costs, protracted regulatory procedures, excessive litigation, and rapacious lawyers. Moreover, it risks provoking a backlash against the EU. British Eurosceptics regularly rail against the inflexible regulations emanating from Brussels and denounced the Charter of Fundamental Rights, claiming that it would open the door to a flood of bogus rights claims. As Eurolegalism becomes more widespread and visible, the EU risks becoming a target for those burdened by its costs and pathologies.

CHAPTER 2

The Political Economy of Eurolegalism

This chapter elaborates this book's explanation for the spread of Eurolegalism and contends with counterarguments and alternative explanations. This study focuses on the sort of big, slow-moving causal processes that Paul Pierson (2004, p. 98) argues contemporary political science often overlooks. As Pierson explains, while most contemporary political science focuses on processes that involve short term causes and short term outcomes, many of the outcomes of greatest interest to political scientists actually unfold slowly as the result of cumulative, macrosocial causal processes.[1] Similarly, Wolfgang Streeck and Kathleen Thelen (2005, p. 9) emphasize the importance of causal processes that involve incremental change with transformative results.

The rise of adversarial legalism in Europe is based on a multifaceted, incremental causal process. The political institutions and economic institutions that have encouraged the spread of Eurolegalism emerged as the result of gradual political and economic reforms. Likewise, the outcome examined in this study—a shift in patterns of legal and regulatory style—did not appear suddenly after a critical juncture occurred (Capoccia and Kelemen 2007) or when causal factors had pushed past a tipping point. Rather, the version of adversarial legalism in the European Union (EU) continues to emerge gradually through a cumulative, multifaceted, slow-moving process of institutional change (Mahoney and Thelen 2010).

This chapter elaborates my explanation for the spread of Eurolegalism and contends with counterarguments and alternative explanations. I begin by elaborating the central argument presented in Chapter 1. I explain how the economic liberalization and political fragmentation associated with European integration have encouraged policy makers to rely on adversarial legalism as a mode of governance. I then address alternative perspectives on the EU's legal and regulatory style, examining three counterarguments to my explanation. Finally, I highlight some qualifications and limitations to the argument and conclude.

The Argument

European integration is encouraging the rise of Eurolegalism through two closely intertwined causal mechanisms. First, the EU's drive to create a single European market has led to the dismantling of many traditional, national regulatory regimes and to their replacement with far more formal and judicialized regulatory regimes at the EU level. In other words, economic liberalization and deregulation at the national level have been coupled with juridical reregulation at the EU level. Second, the high degree of political fragmentation that is so deeply embedded in the EU's institutional structure has generated powerful political incentives for policy makers to rely on adversarial legalism as a mode of governance. The confluence of causal processes related to economic liberalization and political fragmentation has both undermined traditional styles of regulation and encouraged the rise of Eurolegalism.

Economic Liberalization

The economic liberalization resulting from the 1992 Single Market initiative and ongoing efforts to complete the Single Market have undermined traditional approaches to regulation at the national level, through both direct and indirect means. Many national regulations have been struck down outright by the European Court of Justice (ECJ) as illegal nontariff barriers to trade, and other informal, flexible regulatory practices are regularly attacked for their lack of transparency and legal certainty. In addition to such direct forms of deregulation, or "negative integration" (Scharpf 1996), economic liberalization has also undermined traditional approaches to regulation by introducing new actors, both foreign and domestic, into previously sheltered domestic markets. The growing number and diversity of players in these liberalized markets has subverted informal, opaque systems of regulation, which relied on closed insider networks and trust. For these outsiders, opaque systems of regulation that relied on insider networks could not help but skew the playing field in favor of domestic players. These new actors, their state sponsors, and the European Commission and Parliament all attacked informal, flexible regulatory practices at the national level for their lack of transparency and legal certainty.

As traditional approaches break down, national and EU regulators seek new means by which to pursue their regulatory goals—means which are better suited to the liberalized environment. Therefore, liberalization leads to more than simple deregulation; it also creates pressure for reregulation to enable government to enforce regulatory norms in a liberalized environment (S. Vogel 1996; Moran 1991). However, the new approaches to regulation differ greatly from the old. Following a fundamental insight of the sociology of law, as the social distance and distrust between regulators and regulated actors in liberalized markets increases, laws and regulatory processes tend to become more formal, transparent, and legalistic (Black 1976). In a dynamic that Steven Vogel (1996, 2007) has identified in a number of political systems, "freer markets" actually require "more rules" and deregulation is often followed by "juridical reregulation."[2] This cycle of market liberalization followed by juridical reregulation creates greater demand for lawyers to protect the interest of their clients through guidance, advocacy, and dispute resolution, as contracts replace handshakes and courtrooms replace smoke-filled rooms.

The EU has followed this pattern. Flexible, informal, and rather opaque systems of regulation have proven largely incompatible with European integration. They are dismantled at the national level because they threaten the operation of the single market, and such systems cannot be resurrected at the EU level. With a greater volume and diversity of players and demands for evenhanded regulation, the EU cannot rely on informal systems based on closed insider networks and trust. To be effective and legitimate, EU regulation must ensure equal treatment for new entrants and foreign actors. Thus, traditional approaches to regulation at the national level are replaced with pan-European regulatory frameworks that are more formal, inflexible, and judicialized.

Political Fragmentation

A predisposition toward adversarial legalism is programmed into the very institutional foundations of the European Union. Political fragmentation was programmed into the EU's institutional structure from its founding, and the EU has grown more fragmented over time as a consequence of EU enlargement and the growing legislative power of the European Parliament. In George Tsebelis' (2002) terms, the EU is a polity replete with veto players. Authority is divided vertically between the EU and member state governments and horizontally at the EU level between the Council, the Parliament, the Commission, and the ECJ. The EU has a powerful judiciary but is otherwise a weak state with extremely limited implementation and enforcement capacity. This fragmented institutional structure has generated strong political incentives to rely on adversarial legalism as a mode of governance across a wide range of policy areas.

Democracies vary considerably and systematically in terms of the specificity of the legal obligations they produce, such as statutes, contracts, and court rulings (Cooter and Ginsburg 2003), and in their reliance on litigation as a means of enforcement (Kagan 2001). Comparative research suggests that the fragmentation of political power is a primary cause of judicial empowerment in general (Shapiro 1981; Ferejohn 2002; Ginsburg 2003; Vanberg 2001, 2007) and of adversarial legalism as a policy style in particular (Kagan 2001; Kelemen and Sibbitt 2004). In contrast, systems of informal, nonjudicialized regulation are most likely to be found only in political systems in which political authority is concentrated in the hands of a small number of like-minded veto players (Tsebelis 2002, pp. 235–239). Where political authority is concentrated, political leaders (the principals) need not resort to codified, legalistic means to control their regulatory bureaucracy or private self-regulatory bodies (the agents) and to achieve their regulatory aims. Instead, they can establish less formal incentive structures backed by monitoring mechanisms that encourage the bureaucracy to pursue their goals faithfully (Ramseyer and Rosenbluth 1993, pp. 107–119). If political leaders are unhappy with actions undertaken by the bureaucracy, they can readily rein them in. Moreover, where political authority is concentrated, courts tend to play a weak role in oversight of the bureaucracy; therefore, recourse to judicialization as a means of controlling the bureaucracy would be futile (Shapiro 1981; Moe and Caldwell 1994; Ferejohn 1995; Cooter and Ginsburg 1996).

In contrast, as political authority becomes more fragmented, adversarial legalism becomes a more attractive mode of governance for lawmakers. Political fragmentation creates agency problems and simultaneously offers a tempting solution to them. As fragmentation increases (i.e., as the number of veto players increases), lawmakers will have greater difficulty assembling the political coalitions necessary to pass new legislation or to otherwise rein in bureaucratic agents to whom they have delegated power. Recognizing the likelihood of political gridlock and the durability of legislation, lawmakers have an incentive to draft legislation in a manner that will insulate their policies against potential manipulation by the bureaucracy (bureaucratic drift) or by political forces that may come to power later (political drift) (Moe 1990; Horn 1995; McCubbins, Noll, and Weingast 1999).

Lawmakers also recognize that the fragmentation of power insulates the judiciary against easy legislative overrides and other forms of political backlash (Shapiro 1981; Ferejohn 1995; Whittington 2003; Vanberg 2001, 2008) and that courts may therefore be willing to play an active role in constraining bureaucratic discretion (Moe and Caldwell 1994; Cooter and Ginsburg 1996). Lawmakers draft statutes that specify in great detail the goals that bureaucratic agencies must achieve, the deadlines they must meet, and the administrative procedures they must follow. Lawmakers create legally enforceable rights for private individuals and legal persons (i.e., firms or interest groups), assuring that the lawmakers' allies will have access to the courts to hold the executive accountable (McCubbins, Noll and Weingast 1987, pp. 243–277; Moe 1990). Also, in the context of a federal-type system like the EU's, framing federal (or supranational) legal norms as individual rights guaranteed to all members of the federation can have dramatic centralizing effects, justifying the extension of the power of the federal (supranational) level government vis-à-vis state governments (Cappelletti 1989, p. 395; Sunstein 1990; Epp 1998; Melnick 1996; Katz and Tarr 1996; Baar 1991; Manfredi 2001). By relying on such a judicialization strategy as a means to control bureaucratic agents and state governments, lawmakers encourage the development of an inflexible, adversarial, and litigious approach to the implementation and enforcement of regulatory policy.

Finally, fragmentation of political authority also encourages adversarial legalism by creating multiple openings through which interest groups can access political power. The existence of multiple access points encourages groups to engage in political and legal forum shopping and multipronged lobbying and litigation strategies (Weaver and Rockman 1993, pp. 445–461). In a fragmented system, if one political authority does not accede to a group's demands, the group need not necessarily reach a negotiated compromise; instead, it can shift its efforts to another source of political or judicial authority.

As in other polities, the fragmentation of power between lawmakers in the EU encourages them to adopt laws with strict goals, deadlines, and transparent procedural requirements and to rely on a judicialized approach to enforcement (Prechal 1995, pp. 109–113; Franchino 2004, pp. 339–476; Kelemen 2004a). The European Parliament is generally the strongest backer of this approach. It recognizes that member states will have incentives to shirk their EU commitments and therefore demands legislation that includes detailed, legally enforceable provisions and individual rights that will encourage the Commission or private parties to take enforcement actions against laggard states (Kelemen 2004a; Franchino 2004). The Commission too favors this approach, in particular the emphasis on encouraging private enforcement of European Union law, as the Commission recognizes its limited capacity to enforce EU law from Brussels. Even member state governments regularly favor this approach, willingly tying their own hands and exposing themselves to enforcement litigation as a commitment device. Member states support this approach because they doubt one another's commitment to implementation and fear becoming the "sucker" that implements costly EU policies while others shirk (Majone 1995). To make their commitments more credible, member states regularly support strict EU laws that create justiciable rights that can be monitored and enforced by the Commission and private parties before European and national courts. More generally, all players in the EU's legislative process recognize the difficulty of adopting or amending EU legislation and anticipate the difficulty in exercising political control of (other) member states' administrations after an EU law is adopted. Therefore, member states try to program controls into the EU laws they draft and invite the ECJ, national courts, and private litigants to play a central role in the implementation process. Finally, the fragmentation of power has enhanced the power of the ECJ, emboldening it to make expansive interpretations of EU rights, to stand up to laggard member states, and to play an active role in the policy process more generally. Divisions between the Council, the Parliament, and the Commission make it difficult for these political branches to act in concert to rein in the ECJ. The European Court of Justice can take an assertive stance in expanding the scope of EU law and enforcing EU law against noncompliant member states, with little fear of political backlash (Pollack 1997; Alter 1998; Garrett, Kelemen, and Schulz 1998).

The European Union's weak administrative capacity also encourages EU policy makers to rely on adversarial legalism. The EU's budget is capped at roughly 1.25 percent of the collective gross domestic product (GDP) of the member states. Also, for all the criticisms of the EU's supposedly burgeoning bureaucracy, with roughly twenty-five thousand employees the Commission actually employs approximately the same number of bureaucrats as the administration of a midsized European city. With its modest budget and diminutive bureaucracy, the EU cannot hope to adopt significant distributive policies or to establish large-scale programs implemented by Eurocrats (Majone 1993). Moreover, EU policy makers recognize that they lack even the capacity necessary to enforce EU laws and regulations from Brussels and that member states will never permit them to establish an EU-level bureaucracy of the size necessary to implement and enforce EU law effectively. Working within the confines of this weak state, EU policy makers that wish to affect outcomes on the ground within member states have an incentive to create rights for private parties and to enlist national courts to apply them. Though the times and context differ greatly, the judicialization of contemporary EU governance echoes the approach taken by the early builders of the American state. As Stephen Skowronek explains in his pathbreaking study of state building in the late nineteenth- and early twentieth-century United States, "The courts had become the American surrogate for a more fully developed administrative apparatus"(1982, p. 28). And scholars of contemporary US regulatory politics continue to find that judicialization of the policy process acts as a substitute for a strong and centralized administrative state in the United States (Kagan 2001; Dobbin and Sutton 1998; Burke 2004).

Likewise, recognizing the limits on centralized enforcement from Brussels, EU policy makers in various fields have actively sought to promote private enforcement of EU law, encouraging citizens and economic actors (e.g., firms) to bring litigation to enforce their EU rights before national courts and to access the EU judicial system via the preliminary ruling procedure. By presenting policy goals as individual rights that private actors and state governments are obliged to respect and that national courts are obliged to enforce, the EU can readily shift the costs of compliance to the private sector and state governments.

Finally, in addition to the impact of the structural features of the EU polity discussed above, mounting criticism of the EU's supposed democratic deficit and public distrust of so-called faceless Eurocrats has further encouraged the spread of adversarial legalism. Critics of the democratic deficit have called for increasing transparency and public participation in the EU's regulatory processes (Harlow 1999; Shapiro 2001; Bignami 2003; D. Vogel 2003; Hartnell 2004, p. 81; Schepel and Blankenburg 2001).[3] While citizens long seemed willing to tolerate, or at least to ignore, the opacity of regulatory processes at the national level in their own countries, they demand far more transparency from the European Union today. EU policy makers have responded by enhancing transparency, formalizing procedures for public participation, and increasing access to justice for aggrieved parties (Shapiro 2001; Kelemen 2006).

Counterarguments

There are three primary counterarguments to the explanation for the spread of Eurolegalism detailed above. First, there are those who argue that EU regulation is moving in a direction nearly opposite to what I suggest; they posit that with the advent of new modes of governance, EU regulation is becoming more flexible, voluntary, cooperative, and informal. Second, other scholars might agree that there is some impetus for adversarial legalism and rights litigation but argue that entrenched institutions and legal cultures will stymie the development of adversarial legalism in Europe. Finally, there are those who agree that a European variant of adversarial legalism may be taking root but offer alternative explanations grounded in the international relations literature on policy diffusion. I examine and rebut each argument in turn.

New Modes of Governance

A series of European Commission publications and an extensive literature on new modes of governance in the EU offers a stark challenge to the arguments put forward in this book. Over the past decade, Commission officials have trumpeted initiatives promising to introduce "new modes of governance" into the EU's policymaking repertoire (Commission 2001a). Included among these supposedly new modes of governance are framework directives, soft law, coregulation, self-regulation, voluntary agreements, economic instruments, and, above all, the open method of coordination. The Commission's initiatives concerning these new modes of governance have attracted considerable scholarly attention, which the EU has actively encouraged by funding a pan-European academic research network on new modes of governance.[4] Recent scholarly work on the European Union has emphasized the growing importance of these new modes of governance (Zeitlin and Pochet 2005; Borrás and Jacobsson 2004; Scott and Trubek 2001; Trubek and Mosher 2003; Radaelli 2003; Jacobsson 2004; Eberlein and Kerwer 2004; Falkner et al. 2005), sometimes referring to them as "network governance" (Kohler-Koch and Eising 1999), "new governance architecture" (Radaelli 2003), or simply "new governance" (Trubek and Trubek 2007).

Authors in this field refer to *governance,* as opposed to *government,* as they claim that authoritative allocation increasingly takes place without or outside government. J. Scott and David M. Trubek (2001) highlight a number of characteristics of new modes of governance that distinguish these modes from traditional governance, including a greater degree of deliberation among and power sharing with stakeholders, coordination of multiple levels of government while permitting diversity and increased reliance on informal, flexible guidelines. Beate Kohler-Koch and Rainer Eising (1999) emphasize the purported absence of central authority and hierarchy, explaining that, "in essence, 'governance' is about the structured ways and means in which the divergent preferences of interdependent actors are translated into policy choices 'to allocate values,' so that the plurality of interests is transformed into co-ordinated action and the compliance of actors is achieved" (p. 5). In other words, through deliberation and voluntary cooperation, relevant stakeholders can agree on rules that everyone can support and adhere to.

If new modes of governance following this pattern were growing in significance and coming to predominate the EU's approach to policymaking, then it would be very difficult to sustain the case made in this book, namely, that a mode of governance based on coercive, judicialized enforcement of detailed legal norms is growing in significance. Of course, there is room in any political system for multiple modes of governance varying in significance across issue areas. But the contradiction between the arguments is more intractable than that: both in its underlying premises and in its predictions about the essential character and trajectory of EU regulation, the literature on new modes of governance is fundamentally at odds with the analysis presented in this book.

What does the evidence suggest? As for the spread of Eurolegalism, readers can judge the evidence presented in subsequent chapters. As for the significance and growth of new modes of governance, the literature provides very little evidence.[5] The literature is dominated by normative analyses that trumpet the supposed virtues and future promise of the open method of coordination (OMC) and other new modes of governance. However, most detailed empirical studies—even by some of the leading advocates of these approaches—have found that new modes of governance have had limited discernable impact and remain a decidedly peripheral element of the EU's policymaking repertoire.

In 2004, the High Level Group on the Lisbon Strategy concluded that "the open method of coordination has fallen far short of expectations" (Commission 2004, p. 42). Contributors to a 2005 comprehensive evaluation of the OMC came to similar conclusions (Zeitlin and Pochet 2005). As Jonathan Zeitlin suggests in his conclusion (Zeitlin and Pochet 2005, p. 483), there seems to be a growing consensus in the literature that the empirical results of applications of the OMC thus far remain rather limited (see also Hodson 2004; Idema and Kelemen 2006; Smismans 2008). Similarly, quantitative studies of the prevalence of new modes of governance in EU environmental policy find that despite the rhetorical emphasis placed on new modes in this field, hierarchical, command-and-control regulation continues to dominate, accounting for roughly 80 percent of all EU environmental policy (Holzinger, Knill, Schäfer 2006; Holzinger, Knill, Lenschow 2009).

The current significance and likely future impact of such modes of governance have been greatly exaggerated. The limited introduction of such flexible, informal, nonbinding measures does not herald the transformation of EU governance. Quite to the contrary, the OMC and new modes of governance more generally are fashionable red herrings (Idema and Kelemen 2006), which distract attention from the more significant and pervasive spread of adversarial legalism in EU policymaking.

Many policy makers may sincerely wish to pursue informal, flexible "new" modes of governance, such as the OMC. However, the EU does not provide an institutional environment conducive to the use of such policy instruments. For the reasons discussed above, the underlying structure of EU institutions generates incentives for policy makers that make it unlikely that experiments with new modes of governance will ever amount to more than just that—experiments.[6] Policy makers in peripheral areas, such as social policy, where the EU has no legal basis for issuing binding regulation, may continue to rely on the OMC and other similar instruments (Falkner et al. 2005). Indeed, they have little choice but to do so. But in core areas of EU competence, such new modes of governance will remain of little significance. They will be overshadowed by the persistent tendency of the EU to rely on judicial enforcement of strict legal norms.

Given their questionable effectiveness and the limited significance of new modes of governance, why have policy makers placed so much emphasis on the OMC and other forms of new, informal modes of governance? Policy makers have done so largely for rhetorical reasons. The European Commission's professed commitment to flexible informal governance is part of a public relations campaign aimed at dispelling the widely held view that the EU is an incorrigible producer of burdensome, inflexible, and occasionally absurd regulations. At least since Jacques Delors's drive to revitalize the single market with a "new approach" to regulation, EU leaders have been promising to make EU regulation more flexible. Since the early 1990s, successive Commission presidents Jacques Santer (Commission 1996a), Romano Prodi (Commission 2002a), and José Manuel Barroso (Commission 2005b) have all launched better regulation initiatives promising to simplify and improve the quality of EU legislation. The repeated emphasis of EU policy makers on new modes of governance, better regulation, soft law, and the OMC should all be seen as parts of an ongoing effort to improve the EU's reputation as a regulator. Policy makers professed commitment to new modes of governance may be entirely sincere and the EU's repertoire of policy instruments has surely expanded as a result of these initiatives. Nevertheless, on the whole EU regulation remains highly formal, prescriptive, and judicialized.

Entrenched Legal Cultures and Institutions

A second set of counterarguments posits that entrenched legal institutions and legal cultures in Europe will forestall the development of adversarial legalism. The most prominent exponent of this view is Robert A. Kagan, the very scholar who coined the term "adversarial legalism" in reference to the distinctive US legal style. In a 1997 article, Kagan posed the question, "Should Europe worry about adversarial legalism?" He answered largely in the negative. He noted that some economic and political changes were encouraging the spread of adversarial legalism in Europe but concluded that entrenched legal cultures and institutions would limit any such developments. Ten years later he revisited this question, elaborating on his argument and concluding again that a series of entrenched cultural and institutional differences—including the lower degree of politicization of European judiciaries; the absence of jury trials, contingency fees, and massive damage awards in European systems of tort law; and the existence across Europe of more generous public social and medical services—make European soil infertile terrain for the growth of adversarial legalism (Kagan 2007). Similarly, specialists in comparative law and public policy have identified institutional impediments to legal convergence in Europe (Van Waarden 1995; Legrand 1996), while EU scholars have identified barriers that prevent EU citizens from enforcing their rights under European law (Conant 2002; Harlow 1999; Alter and Vargas 2000; Burke 2004; Bignami 2007).

Together, this literature quite rightly identifies a variety of institutional impediments to litigation—such as restrictive rules of standing, inadequate financial support and incentives, the absence of class actions—and deeply embedded norms concerning the role of law and lawyers that all seem to make Europe inhospitable terrain for the growth of adversarial legalism. These entrenched institutions do matter. And because of differences in the legal institutions entrenched in various member states, the impact of EU law and the extent to which it will encourage adversarial legalism will vary (Bignami 2007; Hilson 2002; Van Waarden 2009). But path dependence is not destiny. Even long-entrenched institutions can experience transformative change through slow-moving, incremental processes (Streeck and Thelen 2005; Mahoney and Thelen 2010). On the whole, these authors have overestimated the strength and resilience of these barriers to adversarial legalism. As the coming chapters will demonstrate, many of these walls are already crumbling under the pressures unleashed by the economic liberalization and political fragmentation associated with the process of European integration. National differences will of course remain, but legal systems across the EU are changing in ways that will encourage adversarial legalism. Reforms of civil justice systems that facilitate access to justice, increasing activism among European judiciaries, the explosive growth of the legal services industry across Europe, the spread of a rights-based approach to many areas of social and economic regulation are all opening the door to adversarial legalism. Nevertheless, to the extent that these entrenched impediments remain in place, they will certainly lead to variations in the impact of adversarial legalism across member states and policy areas and, more generally, will ensure that the scope of the European variant—Eurolegalism—never matches that of adversarial legalism in the United States.

Diffusion

Finally, there are those who agree that adversarial legalism, or something quite like it, is spreading in Europe but who attribute this phenomenon to different causes than those identified above. Indeed, my initial research on this topic (Kelemen and Sibbitt 2004, 2005; Kelemen 2006) was inspired in part by earlier work of scholars who argued that patterns of law and regulation across Europe were converging on an American model (Wiegand 1991; Shapiro 1993; Trubek 1994; Galanter 1992; Shapiro and Stone 1994; Dezalay 1996). These important works identified a number of factors that played a role in encouraging the spread of American legal style in Europe, including economic globalization, growing distrust of bureaucrats, heightened judicial activism, and the international influence of US legal education and law firms. However, on the whole, these contributions did not offer a parsimonious, theoretically grounded explanation and failed to specify the relative causal weight of the various factors they highlighted (Kelemen and Sibbitt 2004). Perhaps the strongest theoretical implication of this literature is that the spread of a European variant of adversarial legalism should be viewed as a form of policy diffusion. Indeed, more recently, David Levi-Faur (2005) has suggested that theoretical models associated with international policy diffusion and the convergence of regulatory policies may explain the developments described in this book.

However, the leading arguments in the literature on diffusion and policy convergence do not provide a convincing explanation for the spread of Eurolegalism. The causal mechanisms behind policy diffusion may include coercion, competition, learning, or emulation (Simmons and Elkins 2004; Simmons, Dobbin, and Garrett 2008). Perhaps the most common explanations for policy convergence focus on the impact of regulatory competition. First, the logic of the well-known "race-to-the-bottom," or competition in laxity (see Swire 1996; Drezner 2001) argument suggests that competition between jurisdictions to attract and retain mobile targets of regulation (e.g., firms) may lead governments to reduce the stringency of their regulations. David Vogel (1995) has offered a contrasting explanation, arguing that economic liberalization and regulatory competition may lead to a "race to the top," or competition in strictness. By this logic, if a jurisdiction with a large market chooses to adopt strict regulatory standards and makes access to its market contingent on meeting those standards, foreign producers who wish to access the market will be pressured to adopt those standards. Once foreign producers adjust to these higher standards, they will be more willing to accept the introduction of these standards in their home jurisdictions and may even actively support them as a way of disadvantaging competitors that would have more difficulty adjusting to the new standards. Finally, regulatory competition of either variety may be coupled with political coercion by powerful states. For instance, governments of high-standard states may pressure governments of lax states to raise their standards, in order to prevent these lower-standard states from deriving competitive benefits from their regulatory laxity (Drezner 2001, p. 77; L. Martin 1992, p. 778).

Neither of these forms of regulatory competition provides a convincing explanation for the spread of adversarial legalism in Europe. A race-to-the-bottom explanation would require that the European

Union was adopting US-style laws in an effort to make itself more attractive to mobile targets of regulation. This argument presumes that the United States has lower-cost regulatory processes and standards, which is clearly not true in many areas (Kagan and Axelrad 2000; Nivola 1997). Rather, many critics argue that American adversarial legalism is excessively costly, conflictual, and slow and that the absence of this American disease in western Europe—where more cooperative and inexpensive approaches to regulation prevail—provides the latter with a competitive advantage (Epp 1992; Galanter 1996; Kagan 1997). In short, one would hardly expect foreign jurisdictions to promote adversarial legalism as a mode of governance in an effort to compete for mobile targets of regulation.

As for the race-to-the-top argument, European firms forced to meet US legal or regulatory requirements stricter than EU standards in order to access the US market might encourage the adoption of US regulations at home. This dynamic may explain the EU's adoption of particular US laws or regulatory standards (Simmons 2001, pp. 609–611; D. Vogel 1995). However, race-to-the-top dynamics are likely to be limited to standards for traded goods and services, in which case a high-standard state can threaten to block market access (Swire 1996, p. 85). Thus, the race-to-the-top argument cannot explain why the EU would promote something akin to adversarial legalism as a mode of governance in regulatory areas having nothing to do with product standards. Finally, as the case studies in this book will show, even when there is evidence that the United States attempted to promote the adoption of specific American legal norms, there is no evidence that the US government has tried to promote American-style adversarial legalism in Europe.[7]

Another set of explanations for policy convergence focuses on policy emulation among nations. Rooted in sociological institutionalism, emulation arguments suggest that convergence may occur as governments model their policies after those of salient global leaders or those advocated by international governmental organizations (Meyer et al. 1997; Finnemore 1996; Drezner 2001; Simmons and Elkins 2004). Emulation arguments do not provide a convincing explanation for the spread of adversarial legalism in Europe. Certainly, US policies serve as a salient reference point in many EU policy debates, and emulation of US policies has occurred to some extent in some policy areas, most prominently perhaps in the case of disability rights, which are discussed in Chapter 6. However, more often than not, the US model is highlighted as one to avoid rather than as one to emulate. As noted above, there is a widespread view in Europe that America suffers from a plague of lawyers and litigiousness and that Europeans must safeguard themselves against—rather than emulate—this American disease. Thus, even those who advocate reforms that would shift EU regulation in the direction of adversarial legalism emphasize without fail that any such reforms must be crafted in such a way as to avoid the supposed excesses of the American model (Fleming 2005; Parker, Buck, and Tait 2007).

Processes associated with policy diffusion—such as regulatory competition and emulation—are not the primary cause of the spread of Eurolegalism. Nevertheless, diffusion processes have certainly played some role in accelerating the trend. Various forms of diffusion do play an important role in the spread of particular legal norms. Indeed, the comparative law literature is so replete with examples of "legal transplants" (Watson 1978, 1993; Kahn-Freund 1974; Mattei 1994; Ewald 1995) over the past thousand years that it would be implausible to suggest that emulation and related diffusion mechanisms played no role. W. Wiegand (1991) has drawn parallels between the "reception" of American law in Europe in the twentieth century and the "reception" of Roman law across Europe between the fifteenth and seventeenth centuries. Since the post–World War II era, the US legal system has become the most influential national legal system in the world, and many aspects of American law have spread to European countries through diffusion processes (Mattei 1994; Wiegand 1991; DeLisle 1999; Lester 1988; Ajani 1995; Dezalay and Garth 1995; Kelemen and Sibbitt 2005; Garth 2008). Through diffusion processes, US laws and legal practices have influenced constitutional rules concerning the role of the judiciary (such as judicial review), substantive developments in a wide range of areas of law (such as constitutional law, corporate law, securities law, criminal law, and patent law), and models of legal education and legal practice (Langer 2004). As Eric Sibbitt and I argue (Kelemen and Sibbitt 2004, 2005), American law firms have played an important role as catalysts, spurring the reorganization of the legal profession in Europe and accelerating the spread of adversarial legalism in policy areas where US law firms are active.

While diffusion has certainly played a role in the spread of Eurolegalism, the impact of any such diffusion processes is overshadowed by the pressures generated by economic liberalization and political fragmentation within the EU. Neither regulatory competition between governments nor policy emulation provide adequate explanations. EU policy makers are moving toward adversarial legalism not in order to better compete with the United States, nor out of a desire to emulate the US system. Rather, they are doing so because—like their US counterparts decades earlier—EU policy makers confront a liberalized economy and a set of fragmented political institutions that generate functional pressures and political incentives to rely on adversarial legalism as a mode of governance.

Conclusion

The political incentives and functional pressures generated by the ongoing effort to establish a single market and by the very structure of the European Union's political institutions have both undermined more informal national styles of regulation and encouraged policy makers to rely on adversarial legalism as a mode of governance. A variety of entrenched legal institutions and norms across EU member states will continue to discourage and mediate this trend, and as a result, adversarial legalism will not take root in Europe quickly, easily, or evenly. As Max Weber famously put it, "Politics is a strong and slow boring of hard boards." (1918/1958, p. 128) The politics of transforming the "legal field" (Vauchez 2008) in Europe will involve very slow boring and very hard boards. But time and time again, promoters of European integration have proven adept at pursuing just such long term, slow-moving projects. It took decades to create the single market, the single currency, and the European Security and Defense Policy. So too will it take decades and the accumulation of hundreds of piecemeal changes to create a "European area of justice." But day by day and month by month a subtle legal war of attrition is eroding bulwarks of traditional national legal styles and opening the door to Eurolegalism—a new European legal style that bears a strong "family resemblance"[8] to adversarial legalism.

CHAPTER 3

Europe's Shifting Legal Landscape

At least since Montesquieu published his *The Spirit of Laws* in 1748, scholars of comparative law have used metaphors relating to climate and soil when explaining differences in national legal systems (Watson 2003, p. 293). The law is described as a sensitive plant that reflects the *terroir*—the combined effects of the local soil, climate, and topography—in which it is grown. As a result, transfers, or "transplants," of legal norms and practices from one country to another may not produce intended effects, as the plants wither or mutate in foreign climes. Robert Kagan (2006) invokes the same imagery, explaining that "certain features of the American way of law are too exotic to be transplanted successfully into European legal soil" (p. 4). Adversarial legalism, in this account, cannot take root in Europe because the "climactic" conditions necessary for it to thrive are absent. In Europe, litigation-funding mechanisms, civil and administrative procedures, the organization of the legal profession, and the prevailing legal culture—to name but a few key elements—provide a hostile environment for adversarial legalism.

It is certainly true that many of the legal norms and institutions that prevail in European Union (EU) member states discourage the spread of adversarial legalism—and that differences in such institutions across member states help explain differences in the degree to which aspects of adversarial legalism do spread. But across Europe, the legal landscape is changing. Slowly and subtly, the reform of civil justice systems, the development of the legal services industry, and the adoption of new legal norms are changing the legal *terroir* in ways that both reflect and will further encourage the spread of a European variety of adversarial legalism—Eurolegalism.

In this chapter, I provide a panorama of overarching indicators of the spread of adversarial legalism across Europe and an overview of the role of the EU in this process. Ultimately, the most convincing evidence of the spread of Eurolegalism is likely to come from the accumulation of careful studies documenting the transformation of regulatory style across a range of policy areas. Because adversarial legalism manifests itself in different ways in different policy areas, only fine-grained case studies can capture its spread and recognize the role European integration plays in the process. The case studies in the chapters that follow—along with a handful of earlier policy area case studies in fields as diverse as competition policy, environmental policy, securities regulation, consumer protection, antidiscrimination policy, contract law, and administrative law—have presented evidence that the EU encourages reliance on adversarial legalism as a mode of governance (Kelemen 2003, 2004, 2006; Hodges 2006; Wils 2003; Djelic 2002; Riley 2002; Shapiro 1998, 2001; Mabbett 2005).[1]

However, case studies have their own blind spots and limitations. Many of the changes observed in the case studies in the following chapters are not unique to those policy areas but have their roots in overarching reforms and developments that have effects across policy areas. Focusing myopically on case studies, we could easily overlook these connections—missing the forest for the trees. Thus, before turning our focus to case studies, we must step back to analyze general, crosscutting trends. Analysis of these trends underscores the broad scope of the transformation of legal and regulatory systems across the EU and suggests the potential generalizability of this book's argument beyond the policy areas discussed in the following chapters.

While there is a widely held view that countries across Europe are experiencing a dramatic growth of all things legal (Blankenburg 2001), existing research on judicialization suffers from a data deficit. There have of course been many important studies of judicialization at the EU level and within particular member states (Stone 1992, Stone Sweet 2000, 2004; Guarnieri and Pederzoli 2001, Nicol 2001; Cichowski 2007). However, very little comparable aggregate, longitudinal data is available on litigation rates, amounts spent on legal services, and other potential measures of Eurolegalism. Moreover, the data that does exist—and new data I present in this chapter—must be interpreted with caution. No single measure can capture the spread of adversarial legalism, and some measures that one might assume provide revealing indicators can be very misleading. This chapter attempts to interpret and synthesize a wide range of qualitative and quantitative indicators—some of which might not seem at first glance to be linked—and to explain how all of them relate to the spread of adversarial legalism.

Most of the indicators discussed in this chapter cannot be neatly divided into independent and dependent variables. Some of the reforms and trends discussed below can be taken as evidence of Eurolegalism; others simply show that changes in the European "legal field" (Vauchez 2008) that encourage the spread of Eurolegalism are taking root. Most of these reforms and trends are best understood as both products of the spread of Europe's variant of adversarial legalism and catalysts for its further growth. For instance, the European legal services industry is growing rapidly and transforming its forms of organization in ways that both reflect the growth of adversarial legalism and further accelerate its spread. Likewise, procedural reforms such as the spread of collective redress procedures reflect political pressure to increase access to justice, and these reforms will in time open the way for more private enforcement of EU law.

Though many of the developments discussed in this study are closely intertwined, we can divide them into three broad categories. First, we can look to the growing catalog of EU rights and other detailed, judicially enforceable legal norms. For the private enforcement of legal norms, which is so central to adversarial legalism, to play a meaningful role, private parties must enjoy effective access to justice. The second category of indicators includes policies, procedures, and institutions that support access to justice. We shall see that the EU has encouraged a host of civil justice initiatives and procedural reforms designed to enable and encourage private actors to vindicate their rights in court. Third, we can turn to indicators of legal activity. The spread of adversarial legalism should stimulate increased legal activity. Litigation itself is of course the most obvious form of legal activity, and adversarial legalism should certainly encourage increased litigation in the policy areas it affects, both at the EU level and across EU member states' legal systems. More importantly, however, the increased potential for litigation should cast a long shadow, stimulating a range of behavioral changes that involve "legal activity" in a broader sense. To gauge this shadow, we must move beyond apparent measures, such as aggregate litigation rates, and examine less direct and less self-evident measures of activity in the European legal field (Vauchez 2008).

Detailed, Enforceable Legal Norms and Rights

Before turning to EU law in action, we should look at EU law on the books. If policy makers are to rely on adversarial legalism as a mode of governance, they need to put in place laws that public officials and private actors can readily enforce in court. In his analysis of the United States, Kagan identifies legal norms characterized by detailed prescriptive rules, often containing strict transparency and disclosure requirements, as a defining feature of adversarial legalism. To encourage enforcement litigation, laws need to establish detailed substantive and procedural requirements, the violation of which can serve as the basis for legal claims. Laws also need to include transparency provisions that make it easier for potential litigants to identify breaches of the law. Finally, laws that establish individual rights and that are clearly framed in the language of rights will be particularly conducive to adversarial legalism.

Detailed Legal Norms

European Union regulation is replete with detailed, highly constraining, judicially enforceable provisions, and EU treaties and secondary legislation establish a host of rights that individuals are empowered to enforce before national courts. For decades, critics have attacked EU regulation for its excessive detail, formality, and inflexibility. These tendencies are evident in the character of EU directives. Directives and regulations are the two main legal instruments used by EU lawmakers. While regulations are intended to establish specific, uniform rules directly applicable in all member states, directives are intended—at least in principle—to establish common policy objectives but to allow member states considerable flexibility with regard to implementation. As Sacha Prechal (2005) one of the leading legal authorities on EU directives, explains, "Directives themselves have become quite detailed, sometimes even amounting to *lois uniformes* (cf. uniform laws). Often little is left of the freedom to choose form and method. Member states can only comply by transcribing the text of the directive at issue into their national law, a tendency which has been reinforced by the ECJ [European Court of Justice], notably where the Court requires an accurate reproduction of the directive's terminology in national implementing legislation" (pp. 484–485). Likewise Linda Senden (2004, p. 12) notes the high level of detail in EU directives and argues that the distinction between EU directives and EU regulations has been blurred.

As mentioned in Chapter 2, EU policy makers have responded to critiques of the inflexibility and coerciveness of EU regulation by repeatedly promising to make EU governance simpler, more flexible, and less formal. Since the 1980s, successive European Commission presidents have engaged "ceremonial self-flagellation concerning the inflexibility of EC [European Community] regulation" (Kelemen and Menon 2007, p. 183) and launched reform initiatives promising to simplify it and to embrace "new," more flexible modes of governance. In the mid-1980s, the Delors Commission announced that its Single Market program would be based on a "new approach" to regulation and would be moving away from total harmonization and instead allowing for greater flexibility and national discretion. In 1996, the Santer Commission launched a regulatory simplification initiative (SLIM), promising to "do less in order to do it better" (Commission 1996a). The Prodi Commission made its 2002 regulatory reform action plan, Simplifying and Improving the Regulatory Environment, a key element of its drive to enhance the competitiveness of the European economy (Commission 2002a). In 2005, the Barroso Commission embraced a high profile "better regulation" initiative, promising to slash red tape and simplify EU regulation (Commission 2005b; Kelemen and Menon 2007).

And yet, for all the public pronouncements and scholarly attention concerning such flexible, new modes of governance, the bulk of EU regulation continues to be characterized by highly detailed, legally enforceable requirements (Kelemen 2006; Senden 2004; Prechal 2005; Dehousse 2008, pp. 95–97). Developments in the field of environmental policy underscore this trend. Since the early 1990s, EU policy makers have singled out environmental policy as a field in which they were strongly committed to replacing detailed, inflexible command-and-control regulation with a mixture of economic instruments and flexible new modes of governance. The Fifth Environmental Action Program,[2] set to run from 1993 to 2000, promised a major shift toward such new modes of governance. Nevertheless, in a recent study, Katharina Holzinger, Christoph Knill, and Ansgar Schäfer (2006) find that traditional command-and-control–style regulation clearly remains the dominant form of environmental governance in the EU, comprising roughly 79 percent of policy instruments adopted between 1993 and 2000. Indeed, many of the major pieces of environmental legislation adopted in recent years could serve as archetypes of the very sort of highly detailed, prescriptive, inflexible legislation that reform advocates were promising to move away from two decades ago. For instance, REACH (Regulation 1907/2006/EC), the EU's landmark chemicals regulation adopted in 2006, came in at an impressive 849 pages and is replete with detailed requirements, deadlines, and legally enforceable provisions. REACH will unquestionably create a new basis for legal battles over the authorization of chemicals. The threat of litigation has even affected the EU's emissions-trading scheme, the most important example of a market-based alternative to command-and-control regulation: the Commission threatened infringement proceedings against four member states for failure to submit national allocation plans (NAPs) under the scheme (Commission 2006a), and the United Kingdom threatened legal action against the Commission if it failed to approve raising the UK's allowed CO_2 emissions (Harvey 2005).[3]

The persistent tendency of the EU to produce detailed, legally enforceable regulatory measures is a direct result of the dynamics described in Chapter 2. The fragmentation of power at the EU level generates political incentives for EU policy makers to craft detailed, action-forcing legislation and to put in place provisions that can readily be enforced in court. The EU has limited administrative capacity but strong courts. EU lawmakers (the principals) rely primarily on national administrations (their agents) to implement EU policy, but lawmakers recognize that these agents often will have incentives to shirk. Therefore, EU lawmakers seek to craft detailed, judicially enforceable laws that will limit discretion in implementation. The inclination of lawmakers, particularly those in the European Parliament (EP), to draft transparent, legally enforceable directives and regulations is further enhanced by their concern over criticisms of the EU's supposed democratic deficit. To allay such criticisms, they seek to ensure that laws require transparent processes of implementation and afford ample opportunities for the public to participate in regulatory processes and enforce their rights (Harlow 1999; Shapiro 2001; Bignami 2005; D. Vogel 2003; Hartnell 2004, p. 81; Schepel and Blankenburg 2001).

Fabio Franchino's detailed study (2007) of a large data set of EU directives adopted under the codecision procedure provides clear evidence of these dynamics. For instance, Franchino shows that as the legislative power of the European Parliament has grown, it has used its authority to make EU directives more precise, constraining, and judicially enforceable, with the aim of reducing the discretion of the national authorities in charge of policy implementation. Explaining why the European Parliament's amendments consistently added greater detail and precision to directives, Franchino concludes (2007, p. 255), "It is clear that the language inserted by the Parliament is designed to provide more detailed instructions for policy execution. It reveals a desire to describe with greater accuracy and precision the scope and objectives of the relevant act and the specific policy measures that have to be taken. Therefore, it shows the need to exercise greater control on the actions of national administrations." Parliament engages in "ongoing and relentless activity of specifying policy instructions in greater detail and precision, revealing the systematic desire of the Parliament to reduce discretion" (Franchino 2007, p. 264).

The desire of the Parliament and European Court of Justice to limit member state discretion also leads them to resist the spread of flexible, new modes of governance. For instance, the EP and the ECJ have expressed great reservations regarding the open method of coordination, or OMC (Scott and Trubek 2002). In a recent report on the OMC, the European Parliament (2003) was scathing:

> As things stand, the OMC is, in many cases, a process conducted between and on behalf of elites, the outcome of intergovernmental negotiation and consultation. The European Parliament and the ECJ are the traditional guardians of democratic debate in Europe. Parliament is either excluded as a formal or informal partner from all the various manifestations of the OMC, or marginalised as in the case of the em-

> ployment strategy. Parliament must force its way into these closed processes in order to exercise democratic control. . . . It is only in this way that the OMC can retain its legitimacy and its effectiveness as a means of achieving important objectives by a "soft" (as opposed to "hard law") approach. (p. 13)

The Parliament and the ECJ have expressed similar reservations concerning the democratic and judicial accountability of other new modes of governance, such as the use of voluntary agreements in the field of environmental protection (Kelemen 2004b, p. 215). In many cases, new modes of governance permit "end runs" around the increasingly stringent transparency and accountability requirements of the "traditional" Community Method of lawmaking (Dehousse 2008; Smismans 2008). This explains the appeal of new modes to some member states but also explains why the Parliament and ECJ will limit their use and why member states who want to ensure a truly level playing field may oppose them.

Rights in Community Law

One of the most striking and significant manifestations of the European Union's reliance on strict, judicially enforceable legal norms is the EU's tendency to pursue policy objectives through "rights-based" approaches. Repeatedly, and in a diverse range of policy areas, EU policy makers have created individual rights, framed policies in the language of rights, and encouraged private parties to enforce their rights. Policy makers have relied on this individual rights model even in areas where rights-based approaches were clearly not the norm at the national level.

Community law has long provided individuals with a wide variety of economic, social, and political rights (De Búrca 1995; Geddes 1995; Aziz 2004; Maas 2005). These rights have taken three principal forms: (1) rights established in the treaties, such as the rights to free movement of goods, capital, services, and labor; equal treatment of the sexes; and, later, EU citizenship rights, (2) fundamental rights that the ECJ divined in its case law from the common constitutional traditions of the member states, (3) statutory rights created in EU secondary legislation (regulations and directives), such as various consumer rights, shareholder rights, worker rights, and social rights. Both EU legislative actors and the ECJ have played active roles in the expansion of EU rights, and the 1990s in particular witnessed a marked increase in the salience of "rights talk" at the EU level and a dramatic expansion of the range of rights protected under Community law. Through information campaigns, glossy brochures, and training sessions for civil society groups and lawyers on issues such as citizenship rights, single market rights, passenger rights, antidiscrimination rights, and consumer rights, the EU has sought again and again to promote awareness of rights for individuals under European law.[4] The thrust of these initiatives is captured in a brochure (see Figure 3.1) that the European Commission produced for European Consumer Day: as the brochure states in bold letters superimposed on a European shopper—who rather curiously has a bag over her head—"Know your rights: Use your rights."

Why has "the language of rights" (De Búrca 1995) attained such prominence in so many areas of Community law since the 1990s? To some extent, increasing demand from social actors for EU rights and the increasing willingness of policy makers to supply EU rights can be understood simply as part of growing awareness and political salience of human rights across Europe and the rest of the Western world in the post–World War II era (Henkin 1990; Cappelletti 1989; Stone Sweet 2000; Shapiro 2005). However, the fact that we are living in an "age of rights" (Henkin 1990) does not provide an adequate explanation for the proliferation of rights-based policies at the EU level since the 1990s. Indeed, during the first few decades of European integration, the EU was viewed—at least by nonlawyers—as an institution focused on regional economic integration, with at most a marginal interest in or impact on fundamental rights. The EU's founding treaties contained no reference to fundamental rights, and where the treaties did establish individual rights, these were almost exclusively negative, economic rights, such as the right of free movement within the single market (the so-called four freedoms).[5] Likewise, very few policies in the early decades of European integration were framed in terms of positive, individual rights. The ECJ initially ruled in *Stork v. High Authority* that it had no power to review Community acts to ensure respect for fundamental rights,[6] and early ECJ rights jurisprudence focused almost exclusively on protecting the negative economic rights

Figure 3.1. Brochure produced by the European Commission for European Consumer Day.

(liberties) of economic operators against interference by member state governments (Kelemen 2006; Shapiro 2005, 2006).

Why then did the EU turn so decisively to a rights agenda in the 1990s? To understand these developments, we can begin by tracing the forces that led to the "constitutionalization" of fundamental rights in the EU (Schimmelfennig 2006) and the drafting of the Charter of Fundamental Rights and then consider the broader, underlying factors that encouraged framing other policies in the language of rights.

Two streams of demands for EU rights—one focusing on fundamental civil rights and the other focusing on fundamental social and economic rights—converged powerfully in the 1990s. First, with the expansion of EU power under the Single European Act (1986) and

Treaty of Maastricht (1992), member state governments and EU policy makers realized that they could no longer rely solely on ECJ case law as the basis for the EU's fundamental rights protections. Beginning in 1969, responding to concerns raised by the German and Italian constitutional courts regarding the failure of the EU's founding treaties to guarantee the protection of fundamental rights, the ECJ had affirmed that it would uphold fundamental rights—those based on the collective constitutional traditions of the member states—as general principles of Community law.[7] The European Commission and European Parliament had pressed for the EU to strengthen its role in protecting fundamental rights beginning in the mid-1970s.[8] However, these initiatives produced few concrete results, and the EU continued to rely on makeshift, judicially constructed rights guarantees into the mid-1980s (McCrudden 2001).

After the mid-1980s, as critics questioned the legitimacy of the EU extending its authority to new, more politically sensitive policy areas, EU policy makers responded by moving to put in place stronger, more visible, politically backed guarantees that the EU would protect fundamental rights. A first step came in the Single European Act, which included language affirming that EU member states would protect fundamental rights. The Maastricht Treaty went a step further, establishing the notion of European citizenship (Article 8) and affirming that the EU would protect the fundamental rights of European citizens (Article 6 and Article 2) (Shaw 1998; Jacobs 2007; Besson and Utzinger 2007).

Meanwhile, a second stream of criticism suggested that the Single Market Program threatened to undermine the European Social Model and that the EU needed to do more to protect social and economic rights. This argument, voiced most trenchantly by Fritz W. Scharpf (1999, 2003), suggests that there is an asymmetry between "negative integration" and "positive integration" in the EU: relying on the ECJ, the EU is capable of eliminating national social rights and protections in the name of the common market, but the fragmentation of power among EU legislative actors limits their ability to adopt new positive social rights and policies at the European level. This produces a neoliberal bias, with the EU being better at deregulating than at reregulating. European Commission President Jacques Delors was highly sensitive to such critiques from the Left and sought to couple the

Single Market Program with a drive to create "Social Europe." Given the lack of fiscal resources necessary to support traditional redistributive social policies, Social Europe in practice came to mean social regulations and social rights (Majone 1994, 1996). To that end, in 1988 Delors, with the strong backing of the European Parliament, proposed the Community Charter of Fundamental Social Rights for Workers, which was signed by all member states except the UK in the following year. The Charter then formed the basis for the Social Protocol, which was appended to the Maastricht Treaty, with the UK again opting out.

These two streams of rights demands—one focusing on fundamental human rights and one focusing on social rights—converged powerfully in the period leading up to the Treaty of Amsterdam negotiations. Neither the social rights charter and subsequent Social Protocol nor the fundamental rights language in the Maastricht Treaty constituted an enforceable European bill of rights. These measures had failed to satisfy critics who argued that in light of the dramatic expansion of its powers, the EU needed to greatly strengthen its commitment to rights protection. A broad coalition of rights campaigners and their allies in the European Parliament called for a unified approach to rights, arguing that the treaties should not distinguish between civil and social rights (McCrudden 2001; Menéndez 2002; Mabbett 2005, p. 100). Member states were increasingly open to these demands for new EU rights, first because they recognized the need to enhance the legitimacy of the EU in the eyes of skeptical citizens, and second because concerns over racism and xenophobia in east European applicant states made member states anxious to strengthen EU rights protections before proceeding with enlargement. Ultimately, member states agreed to include a broad provision on antidiscrimination rights (Article 13) and provisions concerning the role of human rights in the process of acceding to—or being suspended from—the European Union in the 1997 Amsterdam Treaty (McCrudden 2001).

The impetus to strengthen the EU's rights guarantees continued after Amsterdam, and in 1999 the member states tasked a body (the European Convention) with preparing a Charter of Fundamental Rights for the EU (Menéndez 2002; De Búrca 2001). The Convention agreed to a lengthy catalog of EU rights, including classic civil liberties as well as social, economic, and political rights. Member states were unwilling to incorporate the Charter into the 2000 Treaty of Nice, but the presidents of the European Parliament, Council, and Commission recognized and solemnly proclaimed the Charter on 7 December 2000. That proclamation put the Charter in a kind of legal limbo, recognizing it as a statement of legal principles but not as enforceable law.[9] The Constitutional Treaty would have put an end to that limbo, incorporating the text of the Charter and making it legally enforceable. After the Constitutional Treaty was rejected by French and Dutch voters in 2005, the status of the Charter of Fundamental Rights became a major source of contention in the negotiation of the Treaty of Lisbon (i.e., Reform Treaty) in 2007.[10] Ultimately, negotiators crafted a compromise whereby the actual text of the Charter was removed from the Treaties, but an article was included stating that the Charter "shall have the same legal value as the Treaties" (Article 6, para. 1). To assuage member states fearful that the Charter could serve as the basis for a flood of rights claims and for a dramatic expansion of EU power, negotiators also included in the treaty language stating that the Charter did not in any way extend EU powers (Article 51). However, the EU's own experience, along with that of federal polities, suggests that such legal text will not corral the impact of the Charter or restrain the ECJ from interpreting it expansively.[11]

Far beneath the rarified air of constitutional deliberations focusing on broad questions of fundamental rights, EU lawmakers have quietly continued to adopt directives and regulations that expand the catalog of substantive EU rights in particular policy areas. In many instances, the ECJ has expanded these statutory rights further still through its expansive interpretations (Cichowski 2007; Stone Sweet 2004). Perhaps the most dramatic recent expansion of substantive EU rights has come in the area of antidiscrimination rights. Article 13 of the Amsterdam Treaty empowered the EU to "combat discrimination based on . . . racial or ethnic origin, religion or belief, disability, age or sexual orientation" (Flynn 1999,1132). Secondary legislation enacted pursuant to Article 13—such as the Race Directive and the Framework Equal Treatment Directive[12]—established a number of directly effective provisions. Thus, today the right to equal treatment in the employment sphere, which was pioneered in the field of sex equality, has been extended to a number of other classes of persons, such as aged and disabled people (Mabbett 2005; Vanhala 2006; Jans 2007). Moreover, existing antidiscrimination rights, such as the right to equal treatment of the sexes, have been extended by secondary legislation and ECJ interpretations (Cichowski 2007). Likewise, the scope of consumer rights protected by EU secondary legislation is expanding; in addition to an array of general, horizontal rights guaranteed to all consumers, rights concerning issues such as product liability, advertising, and unfair commercial practices (Weatherill 2005; Weatherill and Bernitz 2007), there are a number of sector-specific rights, for instance, for air passengers (Karsten 2007) or consumers of medical services (Kaczorowska 2006). And the scope of social rights protected by EU law has grown similarly, both through secondary legislation and ECJ case law (Falkner 1998; De Búrca and De Witte 2005; Hervey and Kenner 2003; Fredman 2006; Conant 2006, 2007; Shaw 2000; Caporaso and Tarrow 2009). In the field of securities regulation, EU secondary legislation has established for shareholders a wide range of rights they can enforce in the case of corporate malfeasance (Kelemen 2006). In the field of competition policy, the Modernization Program launched in 2004 was premised largely on encouraging private parties—both competitors and consumers—to take legal action in national courts against firms that violated EU competition law (Riley 2003; Wigger and Nölke 2007).

Summing up the developments described above, we can observe that a tendency to expand individual rights and to explicitly frame policies in the language of rights has cropped up again and again across a wide range of policy areas in the EU in recent years. In part, EU lawmakers put in place individual rights for the same reasons (discussed above) that they put in place other detailed, enforceable legal norms, namely, to limit the discretion of the national authorities who implement EU law and to encourage private parties to play a role in enforcement. But framing legal norms as rights has distinct advantages for promoting deeper integration and greater legitimacy. First, for supporters of deeper European integration, framing legal norms as rights provides a compelling justification to expand EU power vis-à-vis the member states (De Búrca 1995; Weiler 2006). The experience of federal polities demonstrates how the creation of individual rights at the federal level can have dramatic centralizing effects, justifying federal intrusions into state affairs and sparking "rights revolutions" in which enforcement litigation extends the impact of federal law and the power of the center vis-à-vis the states (Cappelletti 1989, p. 395; Sunstein 1990; Epp 1998; Melnick 1996; Katz and Tarr 1996; Baar 1991;

Manfredi 2001). Crucially, for an administratively weak and fragmented union, the establishment of individual rights enables private parties to act as enforcers of EU law, minimizing the costs of monitoring and enforcement and helping to avoid head-to-head conflicts with and between governments (Alter, 2001; Cichowski 2007; Shapiro 2005).

Second, as noted above, with the resurgence of European integration in the mid-1980s, EU policy makers in the Commission and European Parliament and other advocates of deeper European integration saw the language of EU rights as a means to enhance the EU's legitimacy and to demonstrate that it was delivering concrete benefits for citizens (De Búrca 1995; Mabbett 2005, p. 103).[13] This held true not only with regard to fundamental rights but also with regard to more prosaic rights—such as rights to on-time flights, accurate financial statements, and safe consumer products. Finally, EU rights have also proliferated as a result of what William Eskridge and John Ferejohn (1996) term "virtual logrolling": the fragmented structure of EU institutions encourages the legislature (the European Parliament and Council of Ministers) and the judiciary (the ECJ) to defer to one another's rights-creating preferences.[14] Many rights are created, and few, if any, are rescinded. Compared with other types of legal norms, rights, once created, are highly resilient. Rights create new constituencies of beneficiaries, who work to defend their rights from attack (Pierson 1993), and rights are insulated against attempts to repeal them because they so often come to be seen as social obligations rather than simply as policy choices (Burke 2001, p. 1272).

Administrative Law and Procedural Rights

The European Union not only has established substantive rights but also has established a host of procedural rights and remedies, through the development of EU administrative law. For more than thirty years, the ECJ has emphasized that member state legal systems enjoy "procedural autonomy" when implementing acts of Community law, with regard both to the procedures involved in enforcement and to the remedies available to citizens.[15] And yet the EU has developed an extensive body of administrative law guaranteeing European citizens a host of procedural rights and increasingly forcing national authorities to respect common rules of administrative procedure. The direction of the EU's influence on national administrative law is unmistakable: EU law is encouraging greater transparency, accountability, and judicial intervention in administrative affairs. In short, the EU is promoting principles of administrative law that underpin adversarial legalism. Or, as Carol Harlow (2000) puts it, EU administrative law, "creates pressure for judicial resolution of every problem and denies its rightful place to the extra legal tradition" (p. 74). She and other critics worry that this tendency will undermine national administrative traditions that relied on more informal approaches to redress and will place unsustainable burdens on national judiciaries.[16]

EU administrative law is, for the most part, judge-made law, crafted through the case law of the ECJ.[17] The ECJ did not divine the principles of EU administrative law from the ether; rather, the court borrowed principles from the administrative law traditions of EU member states, above all, Germany and France (Harlow 1998; Bignami 2005; Schwarze 2000). But as Jürgen Schwarze (1996, 2000), one of the leading authorities on the Europeanization of administrative law, notes, this process of development has undergone an ironic reversal (see also Harlow 1998). EU administrative law, which was itself distilled from national traditions, is now reshaping those very traditions, imposing new constraints on national systems of administrative law and encouraging convergence from above (Schwarze 2000, pp. 164–165). As Harlow (1998) puts it, "In a number of highly publicised cases, rules of national administrative law have been forced to give way before the 'superior' legal order" (p. 8). Francesca Bignami (2005) notes that while many of the procedural rights enshrined in EU administrative law have their origins in the national legal traditions of the member states, once transferred to the EU level, these rights "display one striking common characteristic: they afford citizens a greater set of entitlements against European government than in their place of origin" (p. 351).

Two legal principles—the principles of equivalence (which requires that national systems of administrative law cannot make it harder to exercise EU rights than purely domestic rights) and effectiveness (which demands that domestic administrative procedures must not make it excessively difficult or practically impossible to exercise EU rights)—together provide the foundation stones upon which the edifice of EU administrative law is built (Kilpatrick 2000, p. 3; Harlow

2000; Hartnell 2002, pp. 120–121). These seemingly minor exceptions to the general rule that states should have procedural autonomy have opened the door to significant ECJ influence over national administrative procedures and remedies. In the 1980s and 1990s, the European Court of Justice and Court of First Instance (CFI) asserted an interventionist interpretation of effectiveness when they ruled that national courts were obliged to ensure the full and effective protection of EU rights by altering national rules on administrative procedure and remedies when necessary to ensure this protection (see, for instance, Van Gerven 1995; Ward 2000, p. 216; Eilmansberger 2004; Tridimas 2000; Curtin and Mortelmans 1994; Szyszczak 1996; Kilpatrick, Novitz, and Skidmore 2000). For instance, the ECJ restricted or outlawed national rules that limited the availability of judicial review of administrative acts *(Johnston*[18]*)*, that imposed time limits for instituting judicial proceedings *(Emmott* and *Levez*[19]*)*, that restricted interim relief for plaintiffs *(Factortame*[20]*)*, or that limited state liability *(Francovich*[21]*)*. And as we discuss below, a series of ECJ decisions has increased the level and range of damages that litigants can claim under Community law.

Also, the ECJ has extended one of the few administrative law provisions explicitly mentioned in the EU treaties—the "giving-reasons requirement." Article 253 (ex Article 190) of the EU treaties requires that organs of the European communities "give reasons" for their rule-making decisions.[22] This requirement is a powerful tool of judicial oversight, strengthening both the transparency and accountability of the administrative process. By the mid-1990s, the ECJ and CFI had moved to a strict reading of the giving-reasons requirement, engaging in detailed analysis of the reasons given by the Commission for its decisions and rejecting those it found inadequate (Shapiro 2001, pp. 103–104). Likewise, the ECJ has extended the giving-reasons requirement to national administrations on matters that affect EU law (Schwarze 2000, p. 170). The ECJ has also encouraged the spread across Europe of a "proportionality test" for discretionary administrative decisions—demanding that national courts assess whether an administrative measure imposed a burden on the individual suitable, necessary, and *proportional* to the objective sought (Craig and De Búrca 2008, p. 322–323, 545). By spreading the principle of proportionality across the EU, the ECJ has invited courts to engage in stricter judicial scrutiny of discretionary administrative decisions.

How can we explain the development of EU administrative law and its impact on national legal systems? Certainly, there is a clear line of legal reasoning behind the trajectory of ECJ jurisprudence. In a sense, the very notion that one level of government (the EU level) could establish and guarantee substantive rights while another level of government (the national level) maintained exclusive control over procedures and remedies was implausible from the outset.[23] However, if we move beyond a hermetically sealed legal account and consider the political context, we can see that the direction of EU administrative law is consistent with the explanation of the spread of adversarial legalism in the EU presented in Chapter 2. Martin Shapiro (2001, 2004) has offered an analysis of the development of EU administrative law that is entirely consistent with this argument. Shapiro explains that the development of EU administrative law in the 1980s and 1990s was driven by the confluence of two crosscutting phenomena: (1) a need to adopt a "huge apparatus of European-wide regulations" (2004, p. 14) to complete the common market and (2) a growing distrust of technocracy and a growing demand for transparency and participation. He argues that in the EU of the 1980s and 1990s, as in the United States of the 1960s and 1970s, the judiciary interposed itself in the administrative process of market building and addressed public concerns over the regulatory process and business demands for a level playing field by developing principles of administrative law that emphasize transparency and accountability.

Shapiro (2001, pp. 97–98) specifically links these trends to the fragmented structure of the European Union and its "distance" from citizens and regulated entities. The reregulation necessary for the creation of the Single Market, the fragmented nature of EU institutions, and the public distrust of Eurocrats all encouraged the development of an administrative law that would ensure transparency, accountability, enhanced access to justice, and the uniform application of Community law. This trend has encouraged placing increasing limits on administrative discretion at the national level and juridifying administrative procedures (See Harlow 1998).

Arguably, it is the role of individual rights that distinguishes the EU legal system from other international or supranational legal orders and that gives the EU legal system its unique quasi-federal character. Having established a host of individual rights under Community law, EU policy makers and the ECJ then have relied on the need to ensure effective judicial protection of those rights to justify the EU's incursion into the legal systems of its member states (Ward 2007, pp. 1–15; Burley and Mattli 1993). The ECJ justified the landmark doctrines of the supremacy and direct effect of Community law that it established in *Costa v. ENEL*[24] and *Van Gend*[25] by arguing that the doctrines were necessary to ensure the legal protection of individual rights. To put it plainly, the ECJ justifies telling national courts that they must change national administrative procedures or remedies by saying that doing so is necessary to protect the individual rights enshrined in EU law.[26] As we will see below, in the name of protecting individual rights and ensuring adequate judicial protection, the EU has launched a number of initiatives designed to enhance access to justice for private parties before national courts.

Access to Justice and the European Judicial Space

For a system of governance based on adversarial legalism to take root, it is not enough for legislators and judges simply to establish enforceable legal norms and rights. For law on the books to translate into law in action, litigants must have both opportunities and incentives to bring legal claims. Private parties must enjoy access to justice that is affordable, timely, and effective. For wealthy individuals and large corporations, financing litigation may present little difficulty. However, for most potential litigants—whether they be individuals, small businesses, or diffuse collective actors such as consumers or environmental groups—costs may present a significant deterrent.

Traditionally, many of the rules and institutions that prevailed in European civil justice systems have discouraged litigation. The prevalence of the "loser pays" rule made the potential cost of litigation (should the litigant lose) very high. The absence of American-style contingency fee arrangements kept the up-front costs of litigation high. The weakness, or in some cases the absence, of procedures for collective actions made it difficult for diffuse groups of litigants, such as consumers, to band together to take legal action.[27] Even if litigants were able to access the courts and prevail in their legal action, the remedies and damage awards they could secure were often quite limited. Despite these hurdles and disincentives, the volume of litigation exceeded the capacity of many inefficient national civil justice systems. In the 1990s, there was a widespread view that systems of civil justice across Europe were in crisis, wracked by extensive delays and high costs that limited access to justice for citizens (Zuckerman 1999). To be sure, legal aid systems financed litigation by some lower-income litigants in all EU countries, and legal costs were kept in check by fixed fee scales in some countries, such as Germany (Blankenburg 1992). However, legal aid coverage was limited, and costs and other procedural hurdles remained a significant deterrent for many potential litigants across Europe. In short, European civil justice systems discouraged adversarial legalism because litigation costs were high, delays were protracted, potential benefits tended to be low, and procedural devices that might have facilitated litigation were weak or absent. Such obstacles are precisely what many scholars have in mind when they suggest that European legal systems provide inhospitable soil for adversarial legalism to take root.

But the *terroir* is changing. Gradually and subtly, national justice systems are being transformed in ways that are creating a "new litigation landscape" (Willett 2005, p. 23). These changes have attracted little attention from scholars of European politics and governance. Topics like the harmonization of civil procedure and changes in rules concerning litigation finance elicit little more than a polite nod and a disguised yawn from most political scientists. The legal scholars who do focus on these issues typically examine particular developments—for instance, in class actions, contingency fee arrangements, or legal aid—in isolation and largely ignore their political dimensions (for important exceptions, see Hodges 2007; Hartnell 2004). The perspective advanced here suggests that access-to-justice initiatives and changes in civil procedure should be understood as part of a broad restructuring of the "legal field" (Vauchez 2008) closely linked to the process of European integration—a restructuring that both reflects and will encourage the spread of Eurolegalism.[28]

Certainly, not all these changes originate at the EU level. Given mounting domestic frustrations with the inefficiency and high cost of their civil justice systems, during the past decade many EU member states launched reform efforts, which they would have pursued absent any EU involvement (Zuckerman 1999; Commission 1993a). And yet it is no mere coincidence that so many EU member states have taken major steps—in many cases very similar steps—to reform their civil justice systems in recent years. Specific EU initiatives and general pressures associated with European integration have significantly contributed to most of these developments, encouraging member states to undertake reforms designed to facilitate access to justice.

Creating a "Genuine European Area of Justice"

The EU is leading a sustained, multifaceted effort to expand access to justice for citizens across the EU and to promote the harmonization of procedural law (Hartnell 2002; Hodges 2007, p. 97). Today, this broad agenda is being pursued under the banner of creating a "genuine European area of justice," a goal enunciated by the European Council at its 1999 summit in Tampere, Finland (Council of the European Union 1999). But the EU's efforts to expand access to justice can be traced further back, at least to the mid-1980s.[29] To put the flurry of initiatives launched since 1999 in context, we must first review these earlier developments and the motivations behind the drive to harmonize national systems of civil justice.

The intellectual vision behind these developments lies in the work of European legal scholars who, beginning in the 1980s, promoted the reestablishment of a European *ius commune.* The *ius commune,* or European common law, derived mainly from Roman law and prevailed across Europe between the twelfth and eighteenth centuries, until nation-states introduced civil and administrative codes that fragmented the European legal order. Inspired by the various efforts to promote European integration in post–World War II Europe, a network of legal scholars emerged that hoped to resurrect the *ius commune* and perhaps even to craft a European civil code (Van Dam 2007, pp. 106–113; Hartnell 2002, p. 131).

For many policy makers that support deeper European integration, the harmonization of national systems of civil procedure and the expansion of access to justice are seen as vital long-term objectives (Hodges 2007; Hartnell 2002). They favor the harmonization of civil justice systems for largely the same reasons they favor the harmonization of administrative procedures: uneven and inadequate national procedural rules undermine the rule of law in the EU and threaten to render EU rights dead letters. Also, variations in national civil justice systems may invite objectionable forms of "forum shopping" by litigants, such as the notorious "Italian torpedo."[30] Assuring legal certainty and the rule of law requires uniform and effective access to justice across the European Union.

These concerns have led advocates of deeper integration to conclude that economic and political integration require the establishment of an integrated "European judicial space." From this perspective, the Treaty of Rome contained a glaring omission: it called for the progressive establishment of a single market, while paying scant attention to the national (and cross-national) legal settings in which firms were expected to operate (Basedow 2000, p. 687).[31] Not until the late 1980s did civil justice harmonization emerge onto the political agenda in a sustained way. Although the 1986 Single European Act (SEA) did not specifically address judicial cooperation or harmonization of civil procedure, an intergovernmental working party on the topic was established in 1986. The member states addressed issues of judicial cooperation outside the formal framework of the European Community, in a series of treaties they concluded on specific issues in civil law (Hartnell 2002). In 1990, the European Commission convened an expert group to prepare a study on "the approximation of the laws of procedure of the twelve Member States" (Himsworth 1997). The group published its report—the Storme Report—in 1994. Two passages concerning the role of procedural law in market integration capture the report's central conclusions:

> If a market is to flourish, disputes arising out of business conducted in the market must be resolved consistently with one another, and that requires more than a uniform substantive law. Distortion is bound to occur if the mode of litigation, with all that that implies both by way of procedural techniques and by way of their implications for costs, delays, appeals, enforcement of judgments and so on, varies substantially from one place to another. The idea of a single "internal market" requires for its complete realization a single system for the judicial resolution of disputes. (T. Jolowicz 1994, p. xiii)

And, similarly, the report concludes that the legal certainty necessary for the market to function will only emerge

> if the citizen is fully aware that throughout Europe there exist equal, analogous and/or equivalent judicial procedures which give citizen and enterprise alike equal access to a system of procedural law which

> operates as straightforwardly, swiftly, efficiently and economically as possible. Fundamental confidence in European justice must be gradually built up by setting the Community's sights, as from 1993, on approximation of procedural law. (Storme 1994, p. 44)

In short, market integration requires legal certainty and equal access to justice. That certainty and equality in turn requires harmonization of some aspects of national systems of civil justice. The European Parliament has long shared this view, acting as a constant advocate of enhancing access to justice for citizens and ensuring the uniform application of Community law.[32] Whatever the merits of these arguments, the vision behind them is clear. It was not, however, a vision member states were eager to accept immediately. National systems of civil and administrative law have long been considered core aspects of national sovereignty, and overt efforts to harmonize them in the name of European integration were, and remain, highly controversial.

An opening came in the 1992 Treaty of Maastricht, when the member states included "justice and home affairs" as the "third pillar" in the restructured European Union (the first, "Community" pillar dealing with economic and social matters and the second pillar addressing Common Foreign and Security Policy). Though the most salient issues in the third pillar were asylum, immigration, and policing, it also created a less-noticed basis for the EU to address issues of judicial cooperation on civil matters (Hartnell 2002, p. 79). However, the Maastricht Treaty required that these third pillar policies be based on unanimous intergovernmental decision-making processes, which impeded progress through the mid-1990s.

Another major step for civil justice came with the 1997 Amsterdam Treaty. As discussed above, in the Amsterdam Treaty the member states sought to enhance the EU's legitimacy and bring it "closer to the people" (Council of the European Union 1998) by emphasizing and expanding the EU's role in promoting human rights, access to justice, and the rule of law. Beyond adding substantive rights, such as the antidiscrimination rights mentioned above, the Amsterdam Treaty also sought to accelerate cooperation on justice and home affairs issues and set the goal of developing the EU as "an area of freedom, security and justice," or AFSJ (Treaty of Amsterdam, Arr. 1, Art K.1). To facilitate this, member states agreed to shift civil justice issues from intergovernmental decision making (in the third pillar) to Community decision-making methods, to lower the hurdles for policymaking.

In 1998, the Council and Commission published an action plan—the Vienna Action Plan (Commission 1999)—detailing their plans for implementing the justice-related provisions of the Amsterdam Treaty. This effort accelerated after the Amsterdam Treaty took effect in 1999, when the European Council held a summit in Tampere, Finland, focused on implementing the provisions of the treaty relating to "freedom, security and justice" (see, for instance, Commission 2001a). The Council agreed to a set of three goals, or "Tampere milestones," that had to be met to establish a "genuine European area of justice": improved access to justice, mutual recognition of judicial decisions, and greater convergence in civil law (Council of the European Union 1999). To achieve these goals, the European Commission set up a series of "scoreboards" to measure and motivate progress. EU lawmakers then established legal networks, such as the European Judicial Network for Civil and Commercial Matters, to promote dispute settlement and to provide for training of and cooperation between national judiciaries (Claes and De Visser 2008).[33] Lawmakers also adopted a series of regulations designed to promote judicial cooperation and convergence of civil law, including regulations on the transmission of judicial documents (Regulation 1393/2007/EC), debt collection (Regulation 1896/2006/EC), small claims procedures (Regulation 861/2007/EC), the taking of evidence (Regulation 1206/2001/EC), the recognition and enforcement of judgments (Regulation 44/2001/EC, Regulation 805/2004/EC, Regulation 2201/2003/EC), and the harmonization of rules on "conflict of laws" for contractual (Rome I—Regulation 593/2008/EC) and noncontractual (Rome II—Regulation 864/2007/EC) obligations.[34]

Taken individually, these measures appear to be modest, technical exercises designed to facilitate resolution of cross-border disputes. But taken collectively, they represent an ambitious project. The drive to create a European area of justice has served as a basis for EU incursions into core aspects of national legal systems, such as contract, tort, and civil procedure, which are every bit as sacrosanct for judges and lawyers as control of taxation and the military are for government ministers (Hartnell 2002, p. 118). This initiative reflects concerns and goals highlighted more than a decade before in the Storme Report:

Opaque, costly and ineffective national civil procedures discourage cross-border movement of persons and commerce, as citizens and businesses fear they will not enjoy adequate legal protection abroad. Therefore, free movement in the internal market requires equal and effective access to justice across EU member states, and this can only be achieved through a substantial harmonization of national civil justice systems. The EU's civil justice initiatives also clearly aim to ensure the ability of EU citizens to realize their rights under Community law anywhere in the EU (Hartnell 2002, pp. 82–86; Hodges 2007, p. 110). Leaders envisioned a European area of justice in which citizens could seek justice on equal terms anywhere in the EU and in which "individuals and businesses should not be prevented or discouraged from exercising their rights by the incompatibility or complexity of the legal and administrative systems in the Member States" (Council of the European Union 1999, section 28).

The EU's supranational institutions, quite predictably, have embraced and sought to expand on this vision. For its part, the European Parliament has consistently supported greater cooperation between and harmonization of national justice systems, arguing that this is crucial for "deepening European integration" (European Parliament 1999a) and for making "European citizenship" a reality in people's everyday lives (European Parliament 1999b). The Commission's ambitions, though often expressed in understated language, are perhaps the grandest. In a 1998 Communication, the Commission called on member states to address "the substance of the problem of litigation in Europe, not just in terms of cooperation between courts but in much broader terms of equal access to rapid efficient and inexpensive justice" (Commission 1997a, para. 11). The Commission emphasized that this was necessary not only to make the internal market function but to ensure the equality of European citizens (ibid., para. 30). Again, after the Tampere summit the Commission emphasized, "The European Union faces the challenge of ensuring that in a genuine European Area of Justice individuals and businesses are not prevented or discouraged from exercising their rights by the incompatibility or complexity of the legal and judicial systems in the Member States" (Commission 2002c, p. 49). Examining the totality of the Commission's policy initiatives in this field, Christopher Hodges concludes that the Commission's unstated policy objective is to harmonize member states' rules of civil procedure (Hodges 2007, pp. 110–113).

The EU's efforts to promote the harmonization of civil justice systems are designed to expand access to justice so as to strengthen the ability of private litigants and national courts to serve as agents of European governance. A large body of scholarship has demonstrated the crucial role that national courts have played in supporting the process of European integration (Alter 2001; Burley and Mattli 1993; Weiler 1994). However, it is clear that a model of governance that relies heavily on private parties asserting EU rights before national courts cannot succeed if potential litigants cannot afford to bring claims, if they face procedural obstacles that prevent them from doing so, or if they are simply forced to wait years for judgments. Without effective access to justice, governance through litigation—and indeed the rule of law in the EU—will break down. Thus, the EU's civil justice initiatives represent, as Helen E. Hartnell puts it (2002, p. 130), an effort to enhance "the capacity of Member State Courts to participate in generating European governance through the process of judicialization."

The civil justice reforms associated with EU's drive to create a "genuine European area of justice" are certainly not the only initiatives encouraging an expansion of access to justice in European jurisdictions today. Impetus for reform also emanates from pressures associated with economic liberalization in the single market as well as from the national level in many jurisdictions and from other international and European institutions (such as the Council of Europe and its European Court of Human Rights, or ECHR). As a result of EU initiatives and these broader pressures for reform, the legal landscape in Europe is changing, with profound implications for issues ranging from legal aid, to conditional fee arrangements and other private funding mechanisms, to rules governing collective actions. Taken together, such reforms are improving the financial perspectives and lowering the procedural hurdles for potential litigants—thereby preparing the terrain for Eurolegalism to take root.

Legal Aid

For persons with low incomes, publicly funded legal aid has long been a significant source of litigation finance in many European Unon countries (Cappelletti 1981; Blankenburg 1992, 1999; Cousins 1994; Flood and Whyte 2006). Legal aid for civil matters expanded dramatically across the EU between the 1960s and 1980s, as many member states expanded their legal aid programs in an effort to enhance access to justice (Cappelleti and Garth 1978; Cappelletti 1981; Zuckerman 1999). But by the 1990s these programs had become, in a sense, too popular. The increasing cost of popular legal aid schemes clashed with governments' mounting fiscal pressures, leading policy makers to introduce various reforms designed to cut spending on legal aid and to promote alternative, privatized means of facilitating access to justice. The EU's efforts to promote access to justice have reflected these changes, in that while the EU has pressed laggard member states to strengthen their legal aid systems, it increasingly focuses on encouraging private forms of litigation finance. To understand the current wave of reforms that are spreading privatized litigation funding mechanisms across Europe, we need to look back briefly at the development of publicly funded legal aid in Europe since the 1960s.

Across the EU, legal aid in civil cases for low-income citizens is framed by its proponents as a matter of basic human rights and social justice. Though legal aid to the poor has a long history in many EU member states,[35] modern legal aid systems took shape beginning in the 1970s as a legal aid movement that originated in the United States, spread across the common law world and eventually to the civil law systems of continental Europe (Cappelletti, Gordley and Johnson 1975). In many European jurisdictions, legal aid was widely viewed as a natural extension of the growth of the welfare state in this period, and the right to counsel in civil cases was established by statute and/or by constitutional interpretation in a number of EU member states (Johnson 2000). Between 1970 and 1989, spending on legal aid increased twentyfold in England and Wales, seventeenfold in the Netherlands, and ninefold in Germany (Blankenburg 1992, p. 112). By the 1990s, funding for legal aid in civil matters in a number of EU member states by far exceeded that in the United States.[36]

And while the legal aid movement touched all EU member states, support for legal aid in civil matters remained very uneven. The United Kingdom and the Netherlands developed the most expansive schemes for civil legal aid.[37] For instance, in the 1980s, roughly 60 percent of Dutch households were eligible to receive legal aid, and 16 percent of lawyers worked predominantly on a legal aid basis (Blankenburg 1999, p. 125). Germany and France expanded their systems later and more modestly, with Germany adopting is most significant access-to-justice reforms in 1980, and France doing so in 1992. Some southern states, such as Italy and Greece, remain clearly far behind. For instance, as of 2006, legal aid in civil cases was granted twenty-eight times as often in the UK and twenty-three times as often in the Netherlands (on a per capita basis) as in Italy. Even Germany and France granted legal aid in civil cases ten and eleven times as often as Italy (CEPEJ 2008, pp. 50–51; also see Flood and Whyte 2006, p. 83; Chiarloni 1999).

At the European level, first the European Court of Human Rights and later the EU sought to pressure laggards to strengthen their legal aid systems. The ECHR ruled as early as 1979 that the right to a "fair hearing" guaranteed in Article 6 of the European Convention on Human Rights requires governments to provide legal aid to the poor in civil cases, when this is necessary for effective access to justice.[38] The Council of Europe then pressured member states to strengthen their legal aid systems and issued a number of resolutions on legal aid.[39] The EU itself entered the fray later. The Commission began by sponsoring studies concerning the problems that cross-border litigants faced in accessing legal aid, and after its authority to address issues of civil justice was expanded in the Amsterdam Treaty, the Commission launched its drive to establish some common standards on legal aid with a green paper (Commission 2000).

In 2002, the Commission proposed an access-to-justice directive (Commission 2002d) that would have required member states to provide legal aid to individuals who could not meet the cost of litigation in cross-border disputes and to fund litigation by public interest organizations (such as consumer groups). The Parliament strongly supported the proposal and called for the guarantee of legal aid to be extended to all civil and commercial cases, not just those with a cross-border dimension, though the Council of Ministers ultimately adopted a watered-down legal aid directive (Council Directive 2002/8 EC) that was limited to cross-border disputes and only guaranteed aid for "natural persons" (not for public interest groups). Nevertheless, the directive did pressure laggard member states to strengthen their legal aid systems by requiring them to achieve "effective" access to justice. Though the directive was restricted to legal aid for cross-border disputes, it would of course be politically difficult for member states to provide lower levels of legal aid support for domestic cases than they did for cross-border cases.

Ultimately, however, the EU's effort to strengthen national legal aid systems is likely to prove one of its least significant access-to-justice initiatives. Any success the EU has in pressuring laggard member states to strengthen their legal aid systems is likely to be overshadowed by its influence on the development of novel, privatized forms of litigation finance, such as conditional fee arrangements (Flood and Whyte 2006; Hodges 2007, p. 98). The heyday of legal aid is past. Since the 1990s, member states, such as the UK and the Netherlands, that pioneered expansive legal aid systems have been working to roll them back and cut their cost by turning to privatized, budget-neutral ways to facilitate access to justice, such as legal expenses insurance and conditional fee arrangements (Blankenburg 1992, p. 112, 1999, pp. 129–130). Given the ongoing austerity pressures facing governments, the major growth areas in terms of financing for litigation will come from such budget-neutral forms of private litigation finance (Flood and Whyte 2006; Hodges 2007, p. 98).

Conditional Fee Arrangements

Historically, contingency fee arrangements—referred to formally in European legal circles as a *pactum de quota litis*—have been prohibited by statute or by bar associations' codes of self-regulation across Europe. Even the Code of Conduct for European Lawyers drawn up by the Council of Bars and Law Societies of Europe (CCBE 2006) prohibits contingency fees. However, such prohibitions are increasingly being challenged and circumvented.

Governments across the EU have been caught in a crosscurrent: they face political pressure from domestic groups and supranational bodies to increase access to justice for their citizens, while simultaneously facing fiscal pressures to keep the costs of publicly funded legal aid in check. Conditional fee arrangements present an attractive means to escape this conundrum. They offer a privatized alternative to legal aid, which allows governments to increase access to justice for their citizens without footing the bill.

This shift is illustrated most dramatically in the case of England and Wales (Zander 2002; Hodges 2007). Throughout the 1990s, England and Wales had maintained the most generous legal aid system in the EU, and the ready availability of legal aid for civil matters had spawned a litigation industry and what critics suggested was a growing "compensation culture" among the public at large (Williams 2005; Department of Constitutional Affairs 2004; House of Commons, Constitutional Affairs Committee 2006). Enterprising lawyers had eagerly taken on cases on behalf of low-income plaintiffs, safe in the knowledge that lawyers would be paid by the legal aid system (and that the loser-pays rule would be waived for those on legal aid). As a result, the costs of the legal aid system in England and Wales spiraled ever higher in the 1990s, overwhelming efforts to contain costs.

Eventually the government turned to an entirely new, privatized approach. With the 1999 Access to Justice Act (and the subsequent Conditional Fees Agreements Regulations of 2000), legal aid was cut back drastically. As a substitute for legal aid, the 1999 act significantly expanded the scope for plaintiffs to rely on conditional fee agreements (CFAs) with lawyers. CFAs, which had been introduced on a limited scale with the Courts and Legal Services Act of 1990, were essentially a tempered, British version of American contingency fees. CFAs fall short of fully fledged contingency fees in that lawyers cannot set their fee as a percentage of the judgment or settlement, but CFAs do allow lawyers and litigants to enter into "no win, no fee" arrangements and permit lawyers to levy a "success fee" (typically, twice their normal fee) should they prevail. CFAs have proved popular with plaintiffs, too popular in the view of critics who suggest these agreements have encouraged ambulance chasing claims (Sherwood 2005) and heightened insurance premiums.[40] However, CFAs have generated confusion and difficulties for many litigants, leading some consumer advocates and legal experts in the UK to call for the introduction of fully fledged contingency fee arrangements in England and Wales (ibid.; Hodges 2007; Jackson 2010).

Looking beyond the English case, Scotland and Ireland have permitted "no win, no fee" arrangements for years. The Dutch Bar lifted its ban on "no win, no fee" (aka "no cure, no pay") arrangements in 2004. In July 2006, the Italian government adopted the Bersani Decree, a package of reforms of rules governing the professions, that for the first time allow lawyers to work on a contingency fee basis and to advertise their services. Calls for the introduction of contingency fees have also been made by prominent law reform commissions in Sweden and Ireland, though these have been rejected to date (Hodges 2007).

Even where formal prohibitions on contingency fees remain in place, lawyers and plaintiffs have found creative ways to circumvent them. For instance, in Germany and the Netherlands, a practice has emerged in which an organization promoting litigation (such as a consumer group) acts as an intermediary between individual plaintiffs and lawyers: the organization enters into a contingency fee arrangement with the individual claimants and simultaneously enters into a normal fee contract with the lawyer (which would typically not be enforced if the plaintiffs lose). Through this chain, the claimants enjoy the benefits of contingency fee arrangements, while the lawyer never formally violates the ban on entering contingency fee arrangements with clients (Hodges 2007). In France, even though American-style contingency fees are strictly prohibited, since the early 1990s many lawyers have started to accept lower billing rates in exchange for a "success fee" or "complementary fee" to be paid depending on the outcome of the case (Fleming 2004; Kritzer 2004, p. 259; Magnier 2009).[41] Across the new member states in east central Europe, formal bans on contingency fees are routinely violated. Legal aid systems across the post-Communist world are underdeveloped and poorly funded, and authorities have turned a blind eye as lawyers and litigants resort to contingency fee arrangements as an alternative means to finance litigation (Hodges 2007). More generally, a variety of creative third-party litigation-funding arrangements have emerged across Europe, arrangements that may act as a substitute for contingency fees. Financiers in Europe have become involved in bankrolling high-risk litigation that normal insurance policies would not cover, in exchange for a percent of any damage award (Lloyd's 2008b, pp. 7–10). Likewise, as discussed in Chapter 5, a Belgian company, Cartel Damage Claims, has developed a similar business model by acting as an intermediary in antitrust claims to circumvent bans on contingency fees.

Loser-Pays Rule and Legal Expenses Insurance

Another traditional disincentive to litigation in Europe was the loser-pays rule, which has long existed, in some form, in every European jurisdiction. The risk of having to pay the defendants' legal costs and court fees dissuaded many potential plaintiffs from bringing forward claims. However, exceptions to the loser-pays rule are proliferating, and increasingly plaintiffs have access to legal expenses insurance that may cover the costs of litigation. Generally, loser-pays rules are waived for plaintiffs who are supported by legal aid (and, in any case, the beneficiary of legal aid would not cover the costs themselves). Thus, as the scope of legal aid schemes grew in recent decades, so too did the number of plaintiffs exempt from loser-pays rules (Willett 2005, pp. 11–12). More recently, a new form of exemption has been introduced in the UK, as British courts have allowed plaintiffs who are not relying on legal aid to request "protective cost orders." In this procedure, plaintiffs—often public interest groups—can request during an early stage of legal proceedings that the court issue an order relieving them of the duty to pay the legal costs of the defendant should they lose.[42]

Legal expenses insurance provides another important counter to the dissuasive effects of loser-pays rules. In many EU countries, such as Germany, Austria, and Sweden, it has long been common for households to have legal expenses insurance, which can be used to cover the costs of civil litigation, including paying the other side's legal fees if the plaintiff loses. Germany has long been the largest market for legal expenses insurance and not just because of the size of its economy: fixed lawyers' fee scales in Germany have made it far simpler for insurers to calculate risks, and the government has quite consciously limited legal aid to very-low-income persons (Flood and Whyte 2006, p. 92; Kilian 2003; Kilian and Regan 2004). Recent estimates find that approximately 44 percent of households in Germany are covered by legal expenses insurance and that such insurance funds 3.6 million cases per year (Kilian and Regan 2004). The market for legal expenses insurance has grown steadily across Europe in recent decades, spreading to countries where it was nearly nonexistent twenty years ago (CEPEJ 2008, pp. 54–59). Between 1986 and 2007, the total value of legal expenses insurance premiums grew at a compound annual growth rate (CAGR) of 5.07 percent, or an inflation-adjusted CAGR of 2.08 percent. To put it another way, if we convert the size of the legal expenses insurance industry into euros and adjust for inflation, the industry increased by more than 50 percent in the last twenty, years from €3.1 billion to €4.7 billion (See Figure 3.2.).

The growth of legal expenses insurance, which is used primarily to cover costs associated with bringing litigation, may reflect a growing sense among consumers that they may become embroiled in legal disputes. Likewise, the growth of general liability insurance, which covers both legal expenses and any liability payments imposed on losing defendants, reflects to some extent fear of litigation. Between 1992 and 2006, the total value of general liability insurance premiums issued in Eurozone countries has grown from €12.9 billion to €19.4, a 50 percent increase (See Figure 3.3).[43]

Rightly or wrongly, European business leaders expect an increase in litigation and in the costs associated with litigation in the coming years (Peel 2007; Lloyd's 2008a, 2008b; Fleming 2004; Darcourt 2009). For instance, in a 2009 report on legal trends in Europe that affect the insurance industry, reinsurance intermediary Guy Carpenter and Company highlighted "the continuing pressure of the European and national parliaments to institute new laws to grant power of remedy to public interest groups" and emphasized that "these laws . . . expand casualty insurers' fields of exposure and call for new insurance products" (Guy Carpenter 2009, p. 21). Thus, we should expect firms to seek greater insurance cover for these perceived litigation risks. Changes in insurance coverage will interact with other institutional rules and practices affecting litigation. For instance, when both sides in a dispute

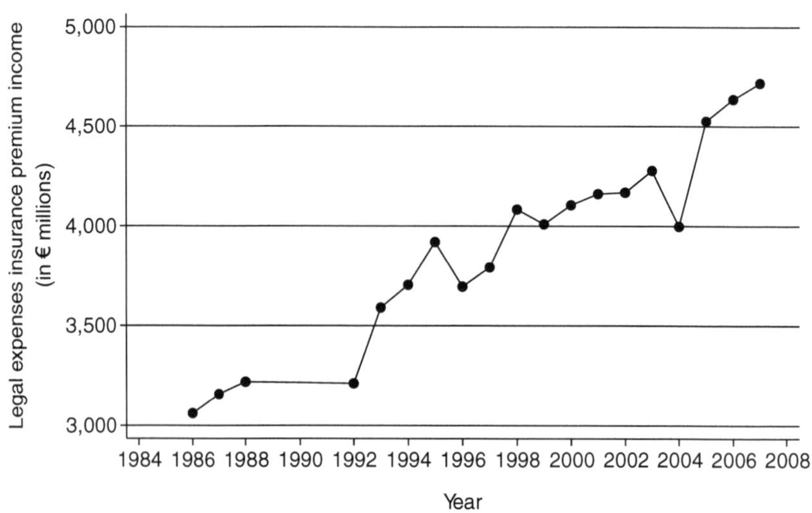

Figure 3.2. Legal expenses insurance in Eurozone countries, 1986–2007. (*Source:* Comité européen des assurances 1990, 1993, 1994, 1995, 1998a, 2001, 2002, 2003, 2006, 2008.)

have insurance that will cover their legal costs, loser-pays rules will have less dissuasive effects on litigation.[44]

Damages

Ultimately, questions concerning the costs of litigation cannot be separated from questions concerning damages and remedies. For any potential litigant weighing the potential costs and benefits of launching an action, the issues affecting litigation costs discussed above make up only half of the balance sheet and must be balanced against the damages, remedies, or other policy victories that courts may award them. Costs and benefits can be directly intertwined, in that lawyers, insurers, and other third-party financers will be more likely to finance litigation when they foresee high potential payouts. Across Europe, traditionally the high costs of litigation discussed above were coupled with limited potential benefits. Among the most renowned features of American adversarial legalism were the astronomically high damages awarded by juries in tort cases in fields such as consumer protection law (Kagan 2001, pp. 126–155). In contrast, compensatory damage awards tended

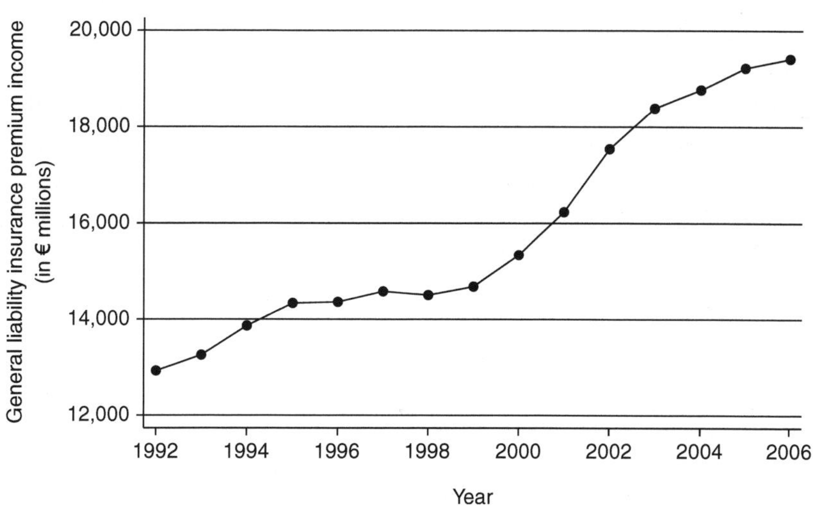

Figure 3.3. General liability insurance in Eurozone countries, 1992–2006. (*Source:* Comité européen des assurances 1998b, 2001, 2002, 2003, 2006, 2008.)

to be far lower in European jurisdictions than in the United States, and punitive damages were generally not available.[45] But currently, just as the up-front costs to litigants in Europe appear to be decreasing, the potential "returns" on litigation appear to be increasing.

In line with its broader insistence on effective judicial remedies, the ECJ has played a powerful role in increasing the level and range of damages that litigants can claim under Community law; the ECJ has pressed national courts to lift damage caps and other restrictions on damages that had been imposed by national legal systems and has established the principle of member state liability for violations of Community law. In *Von Colson, Dorit Harz,* and later in *Johnston,*[46] the ECJ ruled that when enforcing directives, national courts must provide for effective remedies. (For further discussion, see Craig and De Búrca 2008, pp. 309–320; Ward 2007, pp. 39–41.) In *Von Colson,* the court emphasized that damages must function not only as a form of redress but also as a deterrent to future harm. In *Marshall II,*[47] the ECJ ruled that member states must provide full compensation for damages concerning violations of the Equal Treatment Directive and therefore could not impose statutory ceilings on damage awards.[48] In a referral from an Austrian court in *Simone Leitner,*[49] the ECJ went so far as to "discover" in an EU directive a form of damages—psychological "loss of enjoyment of a holiday"—that had not been mentioned in the text and to impose it on a national legal system in which no such form of damages existed. Famously, in a series of decisions beginning with *Francovich,*[50] the ECJ established the principle that member state governments could be held liable for damages that private parties suffer as a result of the member state's breach of European law—and that member state courts must provide for that remedy (Craig and De Búrca 2008, pp. 329).

More recently, ECJ rulings in the field of competition policy, which I discuss in more detail in Chapter 5, have opened up new possibilities for damages claims. In *Courage* the ECJ established that at least in the field of competition policy, not only governments but private actors too could be held liable for damages resulting from their breach of EC competition law and that any individual who suffers from illegal conduct has a right to claim damages.[51] In *Schneider* the Court of First Instance turned the tables on the European Commission, establishing the precedent that when Commission merger or antitrust decisions are later overturned by European courts, the Commission may be forced to compensate firms for losses caused by those wrongful decisions (Bailey 2007).[52] Without question, these decisions increase incentives for litigation, and in fact they were crafted with precisely that aim in mind.

The concept of punitive damages seems to be gaining legitimacy in Europe (Gotanda 2007; Cavalier and Quéguiner 2007; Rouhette 2007). When the ECJ ruled in *Von Colson* that damages function as a deterrent to future harm, the court came close, conceptually, to endorsing the standard argument for punitive damages. Likewise, when the European Commission (Commission 2005c) suggested the introduction of double damages for violations of competition law, the Commission was in effect endorsing a form of punitive damages. And even proposals that would seem to denounce the notion of punitive damages may open the way for subtle alternatives to them. The Commission's *Green Paper on Collective Redress* emphasizes the need to avoid measures "which are said to encourage a litigation culture such as is said to exist in some non-European countries, such as punitive damages, contingency fees and other elements" (Commission 2008b, p. 12). However, on the same page, the green paper discusses the option of allowing courts to "skim-off the profit from traders who have committed an intra-Community infringement" and to put this money collected toward some "consumer-related purposes" (ibid.). Though such "skimming off" is intended as to act as a deterrent of such violations, some business groups see it as a backdoor route to punitive damages (Tait 2008a).

Within the member states, some national courts are indicating greater receptivity to punitive damages. In France in 2005, a commission formed by President Jacques Chirac to draft reforms to the Code of Obligations proposed adding a provision allowing the awarding of punitive damages (Gotanda 2007; Cavalier and Quéguiner 2007). And already, in recent years, French courts have imposed large nonpecuniary damage awards that French legal commentators suggest signal the court's disapproval of defendants' conduct and serve a punitive and preventive function (Van Dam 2006, p. 306). In Germany, though punitive damages in civil actions are still formally prohibited, in cases involving EU sex discrimination and employment discrimination directives, courts regularly award damages that go beyond simply compensating the plaintiff and clearly aim to have a deterrent effect (Behr 2003, pp. 130–145; Van Dam 2006, p. 305). Such developments suggest a blurring of the line between compensatory and punitive or deterrent functions of damages awards, potentially paving the way for larger awards.

Though there is anecdotal evidence of a general trend toward increased damage awards across the EU, systematic data is unavailable (Hodges 2007). It is clear, however, that damage award amounts and available heads of damage vary considerably between EU member states and that calls from some legal experts for greater harmonization of damages have as yet not been heeded by policy makers (Hodges 2007, p. 106; McIntosh and Holmes 2003; Van Dam 2006). It is also clear that damage awards in Europe are today far lower than those in the United States (Sugarman 2006) and that, with the possible exception of antitrust damages,[53] they are sure to remain far lower. Thus, we should expect neither total harmonization across Europe nor convergence on a US-style tort regime with massive punitive damage awards. What we can observe already and can expect to continue, however, is a gradual increase in the level and range of damages that can be awarded by European courts. Likewise, the direction—if not the magnitude—of the EU's impact on this trend is clear: EU law is creating pressure for increases in both the amount and the range of damages recognized by national courts.

Those who doubt the significance of these developments might argue that any EU influence is limited to instances in which member states and their courts are enforcing EU law. In practice, however, national courts and national governments find it difficult to quarantine these effects. It is difficult to imagine a national government or a national court justifying a situation in which citizens enjoy greater rights to compensation for legal injuries under European law than they enjoy under national law. Thus, we should expect that any expansion of damage awards under European law will leak into national legal systems.[54] Over the long term, such legal developments will tend to increase incentives for litigation.

Collective Actions

In December 2007, a conference held at Oxford University on the "globalization of class actions" attracted approximately two hundred participants, most of them from Europe.[55] They did not attend simply for the English food and medieval ambiance. They were drawn together, rather, by the growing understanding that moves are under way across a number of European jurisdictions, and at the EU level, to introduce some form of class actions. In the United States, class actions have long played a crucial role in facilitating litigation involving diffuse interests, such as those of investors, consumers, or victims of discrimination (Hensler 2000, 2001; Dickerson 1997). Many EU member states have long permitted forms of "representative" or "collective" actions in some policy areas (most often consumer protection), but these mechanisms fell short of US class actions in important ways (Hodges 2001; Hensler 2000, p. 10). Representative or collective actions typically allow government-authorized public interest groups (e.g., a consumer group) to bring legal action on behalf of the collective interests that they represent (in this instance consumers). In some cases, statutes give an ombudsman or a public regulator the authority to initiate legal proceedings on behalf of the collective interest of a diffuse group, such as consumers (Hodges 2009b, p. 79). In such actions, the interest group or regulator bringing litigation cannot seek a damage award but can obtain only injunctive relief forcing the offending firm to end their illegal practice.

This situation is changing. Governments across Europe and the EU itself are taking steps to strengthen collective redress mechanisms (Tait and Sherwood 2005; Hodges 2008, 2009c), and the spread of class action rules across the EU promises to increase litigation opportunities for diffuse interests and other plaintiffs who might otherwise lack the resources necessary to litigate. Thirteen of the twenty-seven EU member states currently have some form of collective redress in place (Commission 2008b, p. 4; Stuyck 2007). Laws establishing new procedures for multiparty (class or representative) actions have been adopted across Europe in recent years (Hodges 2009c; Tait and Sherwood 2005; Tait 2008a). New class action–type laws were adopted in England and Wales in 1999 (Hodges 2009a), in Spain in 2000 (Gutiérrez de Cabiedes 2009), in Sweden in 2003 (Lindblom 2009), in the Netherlands (for settlements only) in 2005 (Tzankova and Scheurleer 2009), in Germany (for investors only) in 2005 (Baetge 2009), in Italy (for consumers only) in 2009 (Silvestri 2009; and, more generally, see Hodges 2009c and Fleming 2004). In France, while approved groups have long been able to bring joint representative actions *(l'action en représentation conjointe)* on behalf of their members, American-style, lawyer-driven class actions have not been permitted. However, in 2005 President Chirac announced his support for the introduction of consumer class actions in France, and in 2007 newly elected President Nicolas Sarkozy also came out in support of class actions. These proposals have sparked heated debate over the possible introduction of "class actions *à la française*." While legislation introducing some form of class actions has not been adopted yet, a consensus is emerging that such legislation will be adopted soon (Thornhill 2005; Hollinger 2005; Tait and Sherwood 2005; Magnier 2009, p. 120).[56]

At the EU level, the Commission has been exploring the idea of introducing collective action mechanisms in consumer and competition policy. In the consumer policy field, a number of specific directives on issues—including misleading advertising (Directive 84/450 EEC, Article 4.1), unfair contract terms (Directive 93/13 EEC, Article 7.1), and unfair commercial practices (Directive 2005/29 EC, Article 11)—enable consumer organizations approved by member state governments to bring representative actions on behalf of consumers. The 1998 Injunctions Directive (Directive 98/27 EC) permits "qualified entities," such as consumer groups that are recognized in one member state, to bring group litigation on behalf of consumers before the courts of another member state. The Commission has launched a discussion on introducing a general, harmonized collective redress mechanism for consumers across Europe. In 2006 and 2007, the Commission launched an extensive comparative study of collective redress mechanisms across EU member states, and in 2008 it began a series of forums on the issue with stakeholders (Stuyck et al. 2007; Hodges 2007; Parker 2007; Euractiv 2008; Tait 2008a).[57] In November 2008 the Commission (Commission 2008a) published the *Green Paper on Consumer Collective Redress* (Commission 2008b), which outlined various options for establishing a collective redress mechanism at the EU level. The Commission received dozens of responses to the green paper from consumer groups, business associations, law firms, and national regulators, among others. The European Parliament strongly endorsed the idea, calling on the Commission to find a "coherent solution at European level, providing all consumers with access to collective redress" (European Parliament 2008, p. 8). In the competition field, the Commission introduced a white paper in 2008 (Commission 2008d) that proposed the introduction of representative claims by approved groups and a new opt-in collective action mechanism. Outside the fields of consumer protection and competition, the EU has empowered approved nongovernmental organizations to bring representative litigation in fields including intellectual property, data privacy, and environmental liability (Hodges 2009b, pp. 80–81).

These reforms are not being made in order to emulate the United States.[58] The US class action model is viewed as "unseemly and vaguely scandalous" (Jacoby 2005, p. A7) by most stakeholders in Europe. Not only have business groups warned against the dangers of importing American-style class actions (Parker, Buck, and Tait 2007), but even groups representing consumers and shareholders are at pains to emphasize that they want to avoid importing the American model (Hollinger 2005).[59] As for politicians, Hodges (2009c) explains that "politicians like to claim that they have increased access to justice, but are sensitive to accusations that they have harmed voters by harming the economy. In this context, 'class actions' and 'contingency fees' are inflammatory words in Europe" (p. 55). To avoid their being associated too closely with American-style class actions, policy makers have developed a new vocabulary to describe and frame their proposals, using the term collective redress rather than class action (Hodges 2009b, 2009c).

Rather than resulting from emulation of an American model, the spread of class actions in Europe results primarily from political and economic developments within Europe—many of them linked to the process of European integration. The introduction of new collective action mechanisms has been a response in part to increasing calls to facilitate access to justice for consumers and other diffuse groups, such as shareholders, who often confront legal systems ill equipped to handle multiple claims concerning the same issue. This became evident in some of the first major shareholder actions attempting to enforce EU securities regulations. The German legal system was overwhelmed when nearly 16,000 plaintiffs represented by 754 lawyers filed separate claims against Deutsche Telekom between 2001 and 2003, alleging that the company had provided wrongful information in prospectuses. German lawmakers responded by introducing a new collective action procedure, the Capital Markets Model Case Act (Gesetz über Musterverfahren in kapitalmarktrechtlichen Streitigkeiten, or KapMuG) designed to speed up the proceedings (Baetge 2009).[60]

For the EU, promoting collective redress for consumers and other diffuse public interests accords with its effort to demonstrate that it supports vulnerable citizens and not simply corporate interests—and thus to address its "legitimacy deficit" (Tait 2008a). Moreover, promoting collective actions is a budget-neutral, privatized means to encourage access to justice for diffuse groups. The drive to strengthen collective actions has also been linked to the process of economic liberalization. The European Commission has pressed an argument that facilitating collective redress is necessary to enhance economic competitiveness, because the inefficiency of national civil justice systems distorts the operation of the single market and undermines competitiveness (Hodges 2009c). Finally, economic integration is increasing opportunities for forum shopping. Generally, courts will hear a case if the claimant can establish a sufficient link with the jurisdiction. In an increasingly integrated European economy, it becomes easier, particularly in multiparty cases, for litigants to establish such links in a variety of jurisdictions (Lloyd's 2008b). This will encourage forum shopping, which many governments and the European Commission are eager to avoid (Tait 2008a; Lloyd's 2008b, p. 20).

Though these factors originating within the European context, rather than emulation of the US model, account for the reform of collective action procedures across the EU, there is one respect in which direct American influence may prove significant. The impact of the new collective action mechanisms may be heightened by contagion from across the Atlantic, as leading US class action firms are expanding their European operations in anticipation of litigation opportunities opened up by the reforms (Peel 2007; Jacoby 2005; Ewing and Matlack 2001; Thornhill 2005). Legislative efforts to discourage class action litigation in the United States, by capping damages and making it more difficult to engage in forum shopping, have created new obstacles for US firms specializing in class actions. As a result, a number of them—such as Milberg Weiss Bershad and Schulman LLP; Cohen, Milstein, Hausfeld, and Toll PLLC; Schiffrin and Barroway; Murray, Frank and Sailer LLP; and Bryan Cave LLP—sought to develop European class action practices and develop partnerships with European firms in recent years (Jacoby 2005; Freedman 2004; Peel 2007; Parker, Buck, and Tait 2007). Some of these firms have gone beyond simply exploiting new opportunities and become active voices in reform debates, "encouraging European countries to revamp their legal codes and move towards U.S.-style lawsuits" (Jacoby 2005, p. A1).

*   *   *

Viewed separately, the developments described above might appear as relatively modest reforms. Taken together, these changes reveal a legal landscape experiencing profound change. Civil justice systems must be understood as complex mechanisms composed of many interconnected parts (Hodges 2009c). In recent years, policy makers and judges have been introducing reforms to many aspects of the complex civil justice systems across Europe. There is an increasing variety of means through which potential litigants can fund legal action, and the potential returns on litigation—in terms of damage awards and remedies—appear to be increasing. As Hodges (2009d) observes, "If one looks at the set of factors that made the US litigation scene overheat some decades ago (class actions, unregulated contingency fees, punitive damages, juries), one can see significant developments in every category except juries in many Member States. No single Member State yet has achieved a full set of the other three factors, but some are very close" (p. 72).

Indicators of Legal Activity: Lawyers, Legal Services, and Litigation

If the argument advanced in this book is correct and adversarial legalism is spreading in Europe, this should be manifest in measurable indicators of increased legal activity. Not only should we expect the nature of legal norms and legal procedures to change, but also we should expect to see evidence that Eurolegalism is stimulating more legal activity. But what sort of legal activity? It might be tempting simply to look for evidence of "more litigation." While we should certainly consider data on litigation at the EU and national level, aggregate national statistics on national civil litigation rates actually conceal more than they reveal. Aggregate data on litigation reflect patterns and trends that have little or nothing to do with adversarial legalism, and—surprising as it may sound—some countries with famously corporatist approaches to public policy have higher aggregate litigation rates than that epitome of adversarial legalism, the United States, has. More generally, we must recognize that the legal activity associated with adversarial legalism involves far more than litigation. Where adversarial legalism takes hold, actual litigation is dwarfed by the shadow that the risk of litigation casts. Heightened concern over the potential for costly litigation will encourage public authorities and social actors to make behavioral changes that involve "legal activity" in some sense, even if they are never involved in litigation. Thus, we must look beyond apparent indicators of adversarial legalism and search for more obscure measures of legal activity in the shadows.

We can begin by looking for changes in the legal profession. While lawyers do not generate adversarial legalism by themselves (Kagan 1994), they are necessary for its operation and encourage its development. To date, the literature on European legal integration has largely ignored the role that legal professionals have played in structuring the European legal arena (Cohen and Vauchez 2007, p. 78). The European legal services industry is growing rapidly and transforming its forms of organization in ways that both reflect and will further accelerate the growth of adversarial legalism. The growth and reorganization of the legal services industry in Europe reflects the spread of adversarial legalism, in that shifts in regulatory and legal style have led to increased demand for new forms of legal services. Over time, through a positive feedback process, the providers of these legal services will themselves seek to increase demand for the services they offer, thereby encouraging the further spread of adversarial legalism. For example, after the growth of the EU competition law bar in the 1980s, law firms active in EU competition law became advocates of "modernizing" the EU competition law regime in ways that would increase demand for their legal services (Wigger and Nölke 2007). In essence, we observe here an example of the common phenomenon whereby new policies stimulate the emergence of new political actors and interests, who then influence the politics in the issue area in question (Pierson 1993).

As Figure 3.4 shows, the number of registered attorneys per capita has increased dramatically across EU member states over the past quarter century. Between 1980 and 2006, the number of attorneys across eight EU member states for which I have been able to gather data has increased by an (unweighted) average of just under 300 percent. All of these countries have seen the number of attorneys per capita increase substantially, with France and Austria, on the lower end, more than doubling the number of attorneys per capita (with increases of 211 percent and 227 percent, respectively) and Italy and Portugal, on the high end, experiencing a quadrupling of attorneys per capita (with increases of 397 percent and 421 percent, respectively).

Not only are there more lawyers, but they now organize themselves in different ways. European integration has stimulated dramatic changes in the organization of law firms across the EU. First, the EU opened the door to such reorganization by liberalizing the legal services industry in Europe. Beginning in the 1970s, through a combination of legislation and ECJ case law, the European Community forced open what had been highly sheltered national legal services markets and enabled lawyers and law firms to provide legal services across the Community (Goebel 1991, 2002).[61]

One consequence of this liberalization was to enable American law firms to enter the European market and to operate across the single market. American firms saw opportunities in the European Economic Community (EEC) from the outset, in connection with the Community's emerging competition policy and in terms of serving the interests of multinationals in the common market more generally (Spar

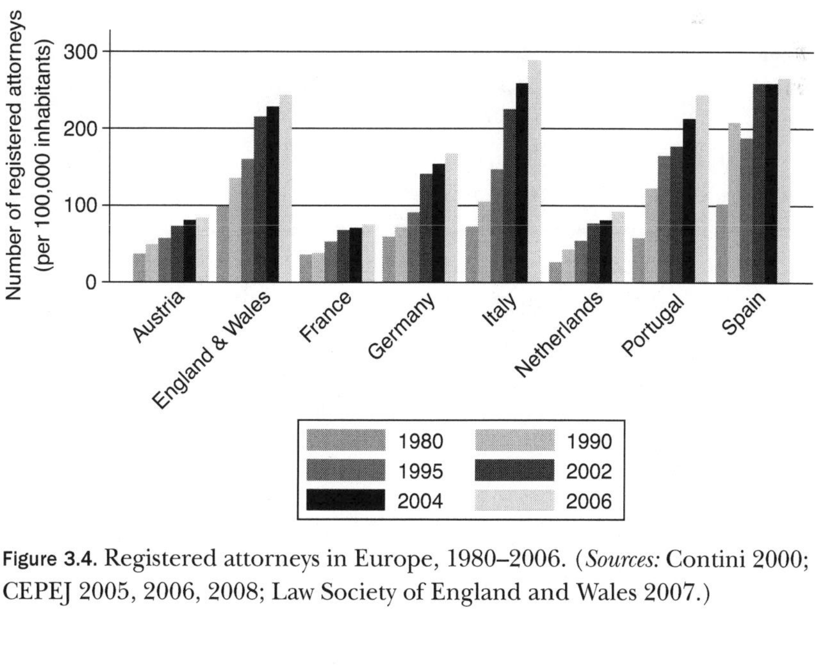

Figure 3.4. Registered attorneys in Europe, 1980–2006. (*Sources:* Contini 2000; CEPEJ 2005, 2006, 2008; Law Society of England and Wales 2007.)

1997; Flood 1996; Trubek et al. 1994; Silver 2000). In 1960, Jean Monnet's close friend and confidante George Ball led the way for his American firm, Cleary, Gottlieb, to open an office in Brussels (Bill 1997, p. 41). Throughout the 1960s and 1970s, other US firms followed their multinational corporate clients and established offices in Europe, primarily in London, Paris, and Brussels. American firms expanded in Europe dramatically after the mid-1980s, as they found that the EC's single market initiative created new opportunities for lucrative legal and advocacy work in which US firms possess an advantage relative to smaller European law firms. Once allowed entry into the European market, American law firms—and the British firms who first emulated aspects of American-style legal practice—thrived because they offered expertise and forms of organization and legal practice that were particularly well suited to the EU's emerging regulatory environment. First, American firms had considerable expertise in fields such as mergers and acquisitions, and securities regulation that became crucial with the liberalization of the internal market (Kelemen and Sibbitt 2004). Second, unlike smaller European firms, which typically provided a narrow range of legal services focused on one jurisdiction, American firms offered a host of what Marc Galanter (1983) has termed mega-lawyering techniques for their corporate clients, including multijurisdictional litigation strategies, advocacy, and lobbying (Kelemen and Sibbitt 2004; Morgan and Quack 2005; Trubek et al., 1994; Spar 1997). American firms were very commercially oriented and had experience in the "strategic use of law in business relations" (Silver 2000, p. 1096) that appealed to corporate clients in Europe.

Figures 3.5 and 3.6 demonstrate the dramatic growth of American law firms in Europe over the past two decades. Between 1985 and 2005, the number of offices of American law firms in western Europe (see Figure 3.5) more than tripled, rising from 57 to 282. The total number of lawyers employed by American firms in western Europe (see Figure 3.6) increased nearly twentyfold, rising from 437 to 8,254.[62] These figures demonstrate a dramatic growth in the US presence in European legal services markets, but they actually drastically underestimate that presence. Much of the legal work done by US firms for clients in Europe is actually performed in the law firms' home offices in the United States (Silver 2000, p. 1101). Also, the data ignores the legal services of US accounting firms, who emerged as major players in jurisdictions,

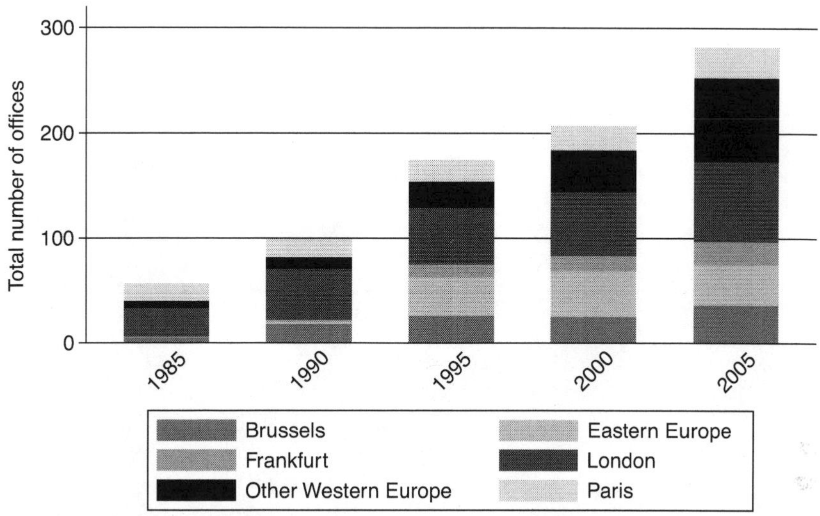

Figure 3.5. American law firm offices in Europe, 1985–2005. (*Source: National Law Journal* 1985, 1990, 1995, 2000, 2005.)

such as France, where they were permitted to provide legal services (Trubek et al. 1994, pp. 434–435).

The growing presence of American law firms in Europe was more a product than a cause of the spread of Eurolegalism. The success of these firms in Europe reflected the fact that the forms of organization and legal practice the firms employed—ones associated with adversarial legalism—were increasingly in demand in the political and economic environment in Europe. But clearly these firms did act as a catalyst, accelerating the spread of adversarial legalism that was taking place as a result of underlying political and economic conditions. They did so not only through the direct impact of their legal practice but also through their role in stimulating changes in the forms of organization and legal practice employed by European firms.

The entry of American law firms in Europe, along with more general competitive forces unleashed by liberalizing the market for legal services, pressured European law firms to change their forms of organization and legal practice in order to compete for lucrative corporate business. The British firms were the first to emulate the US firms, increasing their size and scope in order to defend their home market

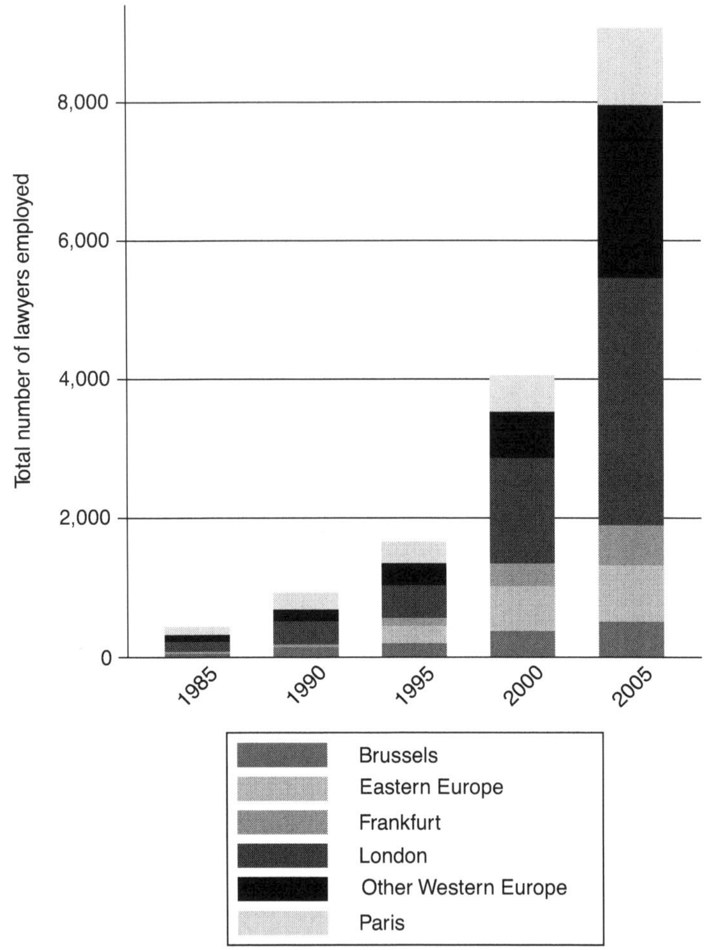

Figure 3.6. Number of lawyers employed by American law firms in Europe, 1985–2005. (*Source: National Law Journal* 1985, 1990, 1995, 2000, 2005.)

and to enter Continental markets (Morgan and Quack 2005, p. 1771). Over the past ten to fifteen years, the organization of the legal services industry across Europe has changed profoundly. European law firms are consolidating and growing rapidly, through the establishment of tight, formal networks, through mergers between firms from different countries and more generally through the expansion of their operations across jurisdictions. In Germany, for instance, as of the mid-1980s few firms had more than a handful of lawyers. The federal statute regulating the legal profession (the Bundesrechtsanwaltsordnung, BRAO) prohibited firms from opening branch offices or establishing national partnerships, such that legal practices typically operated in only one *Land.* The arrival of American and British firms who deployed mega–lawyering techniques stimulated a dramatic reorganization of the legal services industry in Germany, as local firms developed their own mega-lawyering techniques to compete with the Anglo-American intruders (Morgan and Quack 2005; E. Martin 2007; Flood 1996). By the late 1990s, observers spoke of a "merger mania" *(Fusionsfieber)* in the legal services industry (Ferguson 1999; Henssler and Terry 2001), and in 2000 mergers between leading German firms, giant English and American firms, and other European partners created some of the largest law firms in the world.[63] Such patterns were repeated across Europe, as the upper echelon of law firms reorganized, expanded, and engaged in mergers and acquisitions in order to better compete with large British and American firms by being able to offer the kind of one-stop shop—with multiple legal specialties, advocacy, and lobbying services, strategic advising, and the ability to plan and execute multijurisdictional litigation strategies—that American firms have long offered. One can see some of the results of this trend in Figure 3.7, which shows

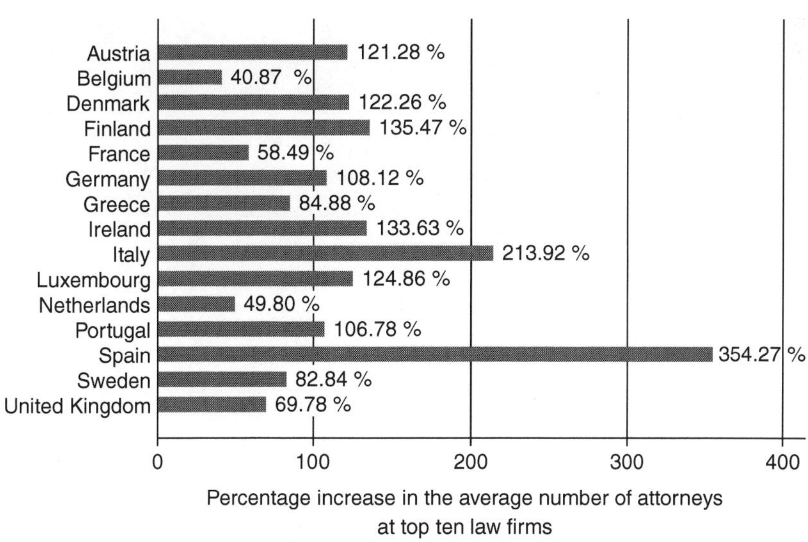

Figure 3.7. Growth in top ten law firms, 1997–2004. (*Source:* Pritchard 1997, 2000, 2004.)

the growing size of the top ten law firms between 1997 and 2004 in the then fifteen EU member states.

Not only are there more lawyers and larger firms across Europe today, but the legal services industry has become much larger overall. Unfortunately, systematic, longitudinal data on the gross revenues of the legal services industries of European states are unavailable.[64] However, market intelligence firms such as Datamonitor have gathered data on the legal services industries of a few large European states and find that the market value of the legal services industry in these states is increasing rapidly (See Figure 3.8.). Between 2002 and 2008, the market value of the legal services industries in France, Germany, and the United Kingdom grew, respectively, by 80 percent, 32 percent, and 27 percent, and in all three countries the legal services industry is forecast to continue growing substantially in the coming years (Datamonitor 2007a, 2007b, 2007c, 2009a, 2009b, 2009c).

The growth and reorganization of the legal profession across Europe is strengthening the "legal support structure" (Epp 1998) for many forms of litigation. However, those who question the breadth of the impact of these changes might emphasize that many of these devel-

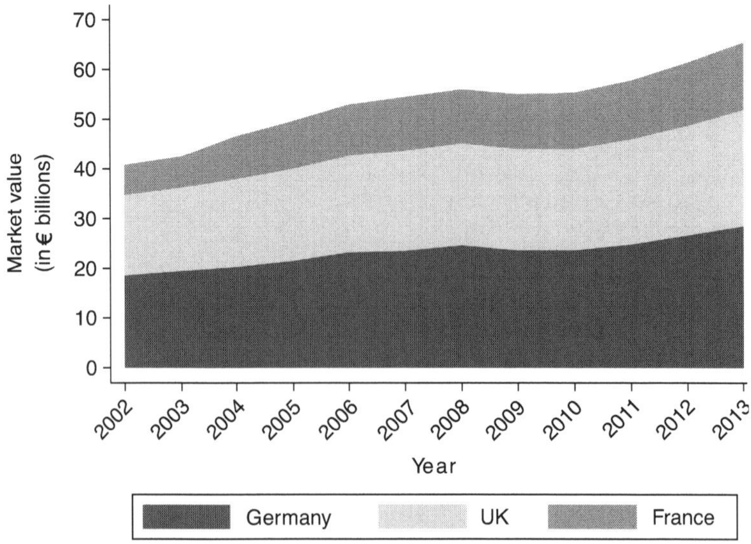

Figure 3.8. Market value of legal services industries in Germany, France, and the UK, 2002–2013. (*Source:* Datamonitor 2007a, 2007b, 2007c, 2009a, 2009b, 2009c.)

opments are limited primarily to the realm of corporate interests. For instance, Lisa Conant (2002, pp. 6, 20, 31) argues that there is inadequate financial or institutional support for individuals or vulnerable groups to pursue EU rights claims (see also Hilson 2002). This is a significant objection. As Marc Galanter (1974) and others (Harlow and Rawlings 1992; Conant 2002) have emphasized, repeat players, such as interest groups, play a central role in using litigation to promote policy reform. For diffuse public interests to be able to use the strategies associated with adversarial legalism to promote policy reform, the changes in litigation finance arrangements and civil procedures discussed above may be inadequate without the support of litigation-oriented NGOs or "public interest" law firms that focus on litigating on behalf of less-privileged interests.

Do such legal actors exist and are their ranks growing? Some important recent studies do suggest that EU civil society associations are increasingly relying on litigation (Fligstein and Stone Sweet 2002; Cichowski 1998, 2004, 2007; Börzel 2006; Alter and Vargas 2000; Caporaso and Jupille 1998; Barnard 1995). However, such studies focus overwhelmingly on the areas of gender equality and environmental policy, and some scholars have questioned the generalizability of these findings to other policy areas (Chalmers 2000).[65]

Findings of a survey of EU interest groups conducted in 2001, which included both business associations and public interest groups, suggested that a large majority of EU interest associations remain reluctant to rely on litigation strategies in pursuit of their policy objectives.[66] Only 28.9 percent of respondent groups reported ever having been involved in litigation related to their policy activities, either directly or indirectly by supporting litigation brought by their members.[67] The reluctance of so many interest associations to employ litigation strategies may constitute a substantial deterrent to the spread of adversarial legalism (Morag-Levine 2003). Likewise, across policy areas and across national legal cultures differences in terms of how receptive groups are to litigation strategies will mediate the impact of adversarial legalism (Vanhala 2009a; Hilson 2002).

But such attitudes and inclinations can change—sometimes quite rapidly. Many studies in the literature on repertoires or tool kits of collective action (Tilly 1978; Swidler 1986) that are employed by interest groups demonstrate that group strategies can and do change—

sometimes slowly through generational change (Morag-Levine 2003) but sometimes very rapidly in transformative "moments" (Zolberg 1972; Tarrow 1993). The US case is instructive in this regard. The legal practices that became hallmarks of adversarial legalism in the United States developed first in the corporate sector among well-resourced actors that enjoyed access to major law firms, and these practices only later spread to various areas of public interest law and policy advocacy (Kelemen 2003; Galanter and Palay 1991, pp. 41–52; Epp 1998, pp. 44–48). However, the practices spread very rapidly in the 1960s, in what has come to be known as the "rights revolution" (Epp 1998; Sunstein 1990; Melnick 1996; Burke 2001), as lawmakers and courts expanded the scope of federal rights and as litigation strategies emerged among civil society organizations (Handler 1978; Snow and Benford 1988) and new "public interest" law firms (Weisbrod, Handler, and Komesar 1978).

With the proliferation of EU rights and the changes in litigation finance and procedural rules discussed above, interest groups now have a stronger basis for and more opportunity for adopting litigation strategies in many policy areas across many member states. Already there is evidence that the sustained litigation strategies pioneered by business interests and employed later by women's rights groups are now expanding among civil society groups in other fields, such as environmental protection (Cichowski 2007) and disability rights (Vanhala 2006, 2009b). Movement in this direction is all the more likely because of the active role the EU plays in promoting it. The EU does not simply create new rights and inform citizens of their rights. In some areas, the Commission actively trains activists how to bring test cases and mount litigation strategies designed to enforce EU antidiscrimination rights.[68]

* * *

Finally, we can turn to aggregate data on litigation. As many scholars of EU law and politics have shown, the volume of litigation at the EU level has increased dramatically over the past two decades (Stone Sweet and Brunnel 1998; Alter 2001; Fligstein and Stone Sweet 2001; Cichowski 2007; Kelemen 2006; Börzel 2003). The volume of both enforcement actions brought by the Commission against member states (see Figure 3.9) and references for preliminary rulings brought by national courts to the ECJ (see Figure 3.10) have increased markedly. If we take

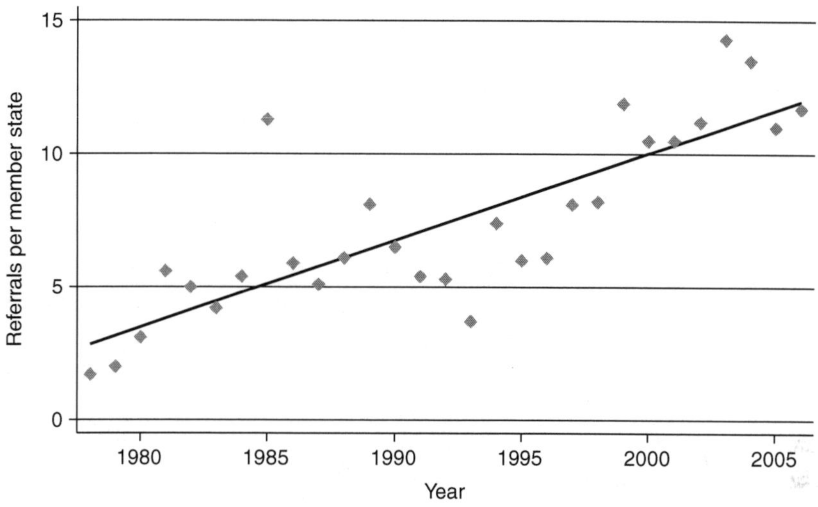

Figure 3.9. Average number of Article 226 Referrals to the ECJ, per member state, 1978–2006. (*Source:* European Commission Annual Reports on Monitoring the Application of Community Law. Available at http://ec.europa.eu/community_law/infringements/infringments_eu.htm.)

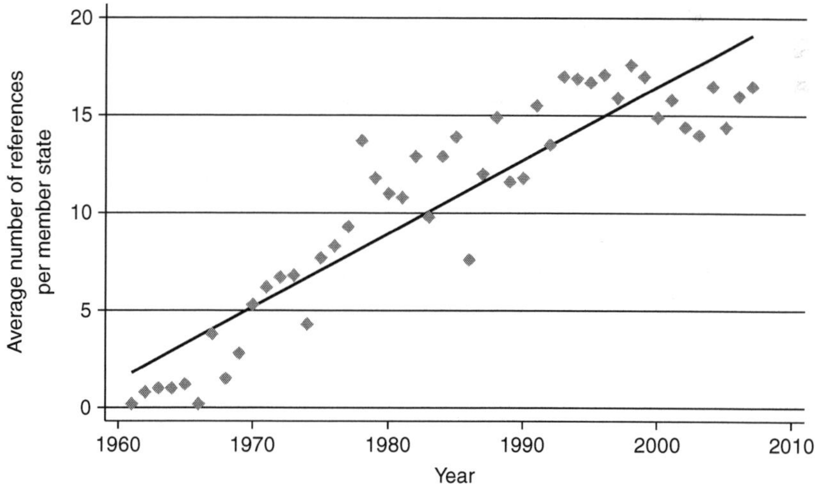

Figure 3.10. New references from national courts to the ECJ: preliminary rulings, 1961–2007. (*Source:* Statistics concerning the judicial activity of the Court of Justice, available at http://curia.europa.eu.)

all types of cases brought before the ECJ and CFI into account, the total volume has more than tripled since the 1980s (see Figure 3.11).

Is the growth of litigation at the EU level reflected in similar increases in litigation at the national level? If we take the broadest sorts of measures of aggregate litigation rates at the national level, the answer would seem to be no. As Figure 3.12 shows, we are not witnessing a consistent, cross-national increase in civil litigation rates. While the data on litigation rates is informative, we cannot take it as a reliable indicator of the spread of adversarial legalism as a mode of governance. Much of what is distinctive about adversarial legalism in the United States, and the Eurolegalism that is spreading to the EU, involves not litigation per se but behavioral changes in the shadow of potential litigation, such as the increases in spending on legal services and legal expenses insurance discussed above.

As Kagan (2001) himself points out, aggregate data on civil litigation cannot capture many manifestations of adversarial legalism, such as lengthy product safety warning labels, exhaustive due diligence in corporate transactions, high medical malpractice insurance premiums,

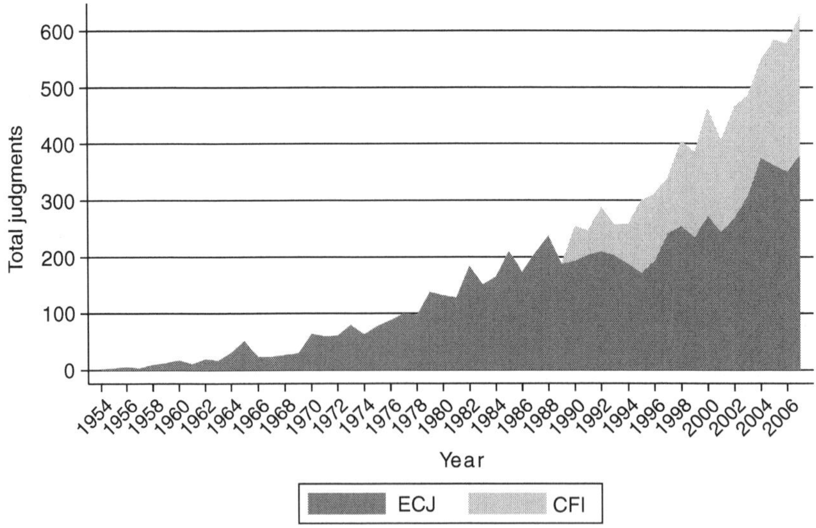

Figure 3.11. Total judgments delivered by the ECJ and the CFI, 1954–2007. (*Source:* Statistics concerning the judicial activity of the Court of Justice, available at http://curia.europa.eu.)

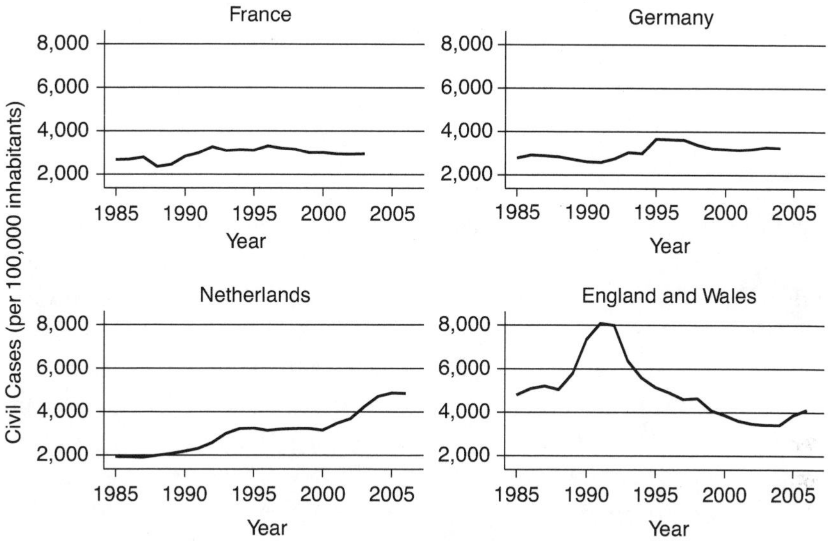

Figure 3.12. Civil litigation cases, 1985–2005. (Data on file with author. *Source:* for England and Wales—UK Ministry of Justice; for France—Annuaire Statistique de la Justice; for Germany—Statistisches Bundesamt, Ausgewählte Zahlen für die Rechtspflege; for the Netherlands—Centraal Bureau voor de Statistiek, Rechtspraak in Nederland.)

and the cancellation of public events due to local governments' fear of litigation. Moreover, aggregate data on litigation may reflect patterns and trends that have little or nothing to do with adversarial legalism. For instance, in countries where a substantial amount of litigation is employment related, economic downturns and layoffs will lead to a spike in litigation rates (and economic booms have the opposite effect). More generally, the best cross-national data on litigation rates compiled in the 1990s showed that Germany, Sweden, and Austria, all three of them corporatist countries, all had higher aggregate civil litigation rates than did the United States, the very archetype of adversarial legalism (Wollschläger 1998; Kritzer 2001, 2002a). Finally, in assessing shifts in litigation rates longitudinally, one runs into the difficulty that, precisely because litigation rates were spiraling out of control or were at least perceived to be (Zuckerman 1999), governments introduced reforms aimed at promoting alternative dispute resolution or otherwise channeling potential cases away from overloaded courts.

This was clearly the case in England and Wales, where a series of reforms were introduced during the 1990s in an effort to channel disputes out of the courts and to reduce eligibility for legal aid.[69]

Conclusion

Without question, well-established institutions and norms at the national level across EU member states work to counter the spread of adversarial legalism. Moreover, many EU policy makers are well aware that the EU's approach to regulation in many policy areas may spark a considerable amount of litigation and are keen to prevent EU member states from experiencing the worst excesses of American legal style. In recent years, EU Competition Commissioner Neelie Kroes and Consumer Affairs Commissioner Meglena Kuneva have emphasized that they are determined to encourage more private enforcement of EU competition and consumer law, while avoiding the excesses of the American system (Parker, Buck, and Tait 2007).[70] However, the developments discussed above suggest that many of the institutional impediments to adversarial legalism in Europe are eroding and that despite the intention of policy makers to avoid the cost, uncertainty, and adversarialism of the American model, the EU is taking significant steps toward it. Remaining institutional and cultural impediments and the desire of policy makers to avoid the pitfalls of the American system ensure that the EU will never converge completely on the American model. And yet the EU is developing its own brand of adversarial legalism—Eurolegalism.

CHAPTER 4

Securities Regulation

Europeans invented securities trading. Shortly thereafter, they invented securities fraud, frenzied market bubbles, and the related pathologies that have periodically afflicted stock markets ever since. In the early seventeenth century, the Dutch East India Company became the first company in history to issue stocks and bonds, and the Amsterdam Stock Exchange emerged as the world's first stock exchange. By 1688, Joseph de la Vega had published the first book ever on stock trading, *Confusión de Confusiones,* advising investors of the excesses and dangers of trading on the Amsterdam exchange.

Times have changed, but that old brew of malice and avarice still threatens securities markets, and investors today remain vulnerable to many of the risks they faced more than three centuries ago. To guard against such risks, advanced economies around the world have put in place extensive systems of securities regulation. Securities regulation addresses a wide range of issues, including the listing of new securities on a stock exchange, ongoing disclosure and transparency requirements for listed companies, insider trading and other forms of market abuse, the practices of investment services providers, and the "infrastructure" (closing and settlement) of the securities market. In principle, securities regulation has two fundamental aims. First, regulation aims to protect investors who suffer an information asymmetry vis-à-vis the companies who list securities and the financial intermediaries who help clients invest. Second, regulation guards against the systemic risk to the financial system that fraud and malfeasance on the securities markets could provoke. In the European Union (EU) context, securities regulation has a third aim: to support the EU's underlying goal of establishing a single European market in which "the free movement of goods, persons, services and capital is ensured" (EC Treaty, Article 14[2]). From the outset, the EU's efforts to harmonize national securities regulations were seen as a way to eliminate barriers to the free movement of capital and investment services and to encourage the construction of an integrated, pan-European financial market. Many proponents of EU securities regulation hoped that this market integration would eventually encourage a transformation in European capitalism by drawing more retail investors into the market and encouraging firms to rely increasingly on market (rather than bank) finance. The creation of deep, pan-European securities markets, it was thought, would give investors more choices and make it cheaper for firms to raise capital and thereby promote growth (Moloney 2008, p. 6).

Over the past two decades, the regulatory regimes governing securities markets across Europe have experienced a dramatic transformation. Before the mid-1980s, securities exchanges across Europe generally relied on flexible, informal self-regulation based on trust between closed networks of repeat market players (Karmel 1999, p. 30; S. Vogel 1996, pp. 94–98). While the scope of government regulation of securities markets varied across EU member states, generally governments imposed few disclosure requirements for securities transactions and did little to restrict insider trading (Warren, 1994, p. 185). This was true both in the internationally oriented London Stock Exchange (LSE) and in the more insular exchanges spread across the Continent. In the mid-1980s, seven of the then twelve member states did not require firms to publish a prospectus when issuing a security and did not impose criminal penalties for insider trading. None of the member states had an independent securities regulatory agency at the national level, and enforcement of existing securities regulations by public authorities was extremely lax (ibid; Jackson and Pan 2001). Private enforcement—in the form of the sorts of shareholder derivative suits that play such a central role in US securities regulation—was almost unheard of.

This informal, self-regulatory approach was underpinned by the one form of regulation that was strictly enforced at the time: restrictions on access to the marketplace. The professional self-regulatory organizations that regulated Europe's stock exchanges operated as cartels, strictly controlling access to the markets that they dominated. These systems were clearly protectionist and anticompetitive, but by restricting market access to a limited number of reliable domestic firms, these organizations did facilitate the operation of systems of self-regulation based on informal contacts and peer pressure. As Manning Gilbert Warren (1994, p. 186) explains, "Minimum regulation, whether by government or industry, is certainly more plausible in a closed market than in an open market accessible to the rest of Europe and the world. For socio-cultural reasons alone, it has to be assumed that a nation's control of its own resident players is a far more facile task than controlling an infinite variety of alien players." In other words, lax formal regulation of behavior within markets was acceptable and even effective—or so it was thought at the time—because of the strict controls on access to those markets.

Over the past twenty years, European securities markets have experienced both radical deregulation and radical reregulation. The drive to complete the European single market—along with broader financial globalization pressures—has pried open sheltered national securities markets across Europe. Meanwhile, the EU has issued "a veritable juggernaut" (Moloney 2008, p. 4) of securities regulation and has emerged as the primary regulator of securities markets across the EU (ibid.). National regulatory regimes have been supplanted by a new, increasingly harmonized EU regulatory regime based on detailed disclosure requirements and the threat of public and private enforcement (Enriques and Volpin 2007). The EU has played a central role in pressing member states to replace their traditional, informal national approaches with a harmonized EU regulatory regime that bears the hallmarks of Eurolegalism. As in the other policy areas examined in this book, the economic liberalization and political fragmentation associated with European integration have driven forward these changes.

The liberalization of European financial markets simultaneously undermined existing national systems of securities regulation and created pressures for new forms of reregulation at the EU level. As cross-border investment activity increased and involved an ever larger and more diverse set of players (including investors, firms listing securities, and financial intermediaries active in securities markets), who interacted on a wider variety of new trading platforms, this shift steadily undermined the operation of the opaque systems of self-regulation that had prevailed at the national level. As it sought to promote an integrated, pan-European securities market, the European Commission recognized that divergence between national standards and regulatory approaches would continue to fragment the market (Warren 1994, p. 186). But equally, the Commission recognized that unmitigated deregulation would expose investors to heightened risk and would be politically unacceptable. Thus, from the outset the Commission backed its efforts to promote deregulation of protectionist measures at the national level with a program of financial market reregulation at the EU level.

The EU's approach to regulating securities markets differs greatly from the opaque, informal approaches that had long prevailed at the national level across Europe. The contours of the EU's approach to securities regulation are similar in many crucial respects to those found in the US system of securities regulation. The hallmarks of US securities regulation reflect the broader pattern of adversarial legalism discussed in Chapter 1. Since its foundations were laid in the early 1930s, US securities regulation has relied on a combination of disclosure and strict, legalistic enforcement—some by public authorities and most by private parties—to achieve its regulatory objectives (Karmel 1982; Coffee 2007). The US Securities and Exchange Commission (SEC) imposes strict disclosure and transparency requirements on issuers and on its own regulatory activities (Jennings et al., pp. 111–118, 174–186). Liability provisions of the Securities Act of 1933 and the Securities Exchange Act of 1934, together with procedural devices such as class actions, spawned a shareholder litigation industry in which an active shareholder plaintiff's bar brings claims concerning disclosure failings and various forms of malfeasance and fraud (Coffee 2006). Subsequent reforms, such as the 2002 Sarbanes-Oxley reforms instituted in the wake of corporate scandals at Enron, WorldCom, and other major companies, only reinforced this model of regulation.

As in the United States, the EU securities regime imposes detailed regulation, focusing on disclosure, transparent regulatory processes, and an adversarial, judicialized approach to enforcement with an increasing—though still limited in the EU's case—emphasis on private enforcement. This approach has persisted despite criticisms of the excessive detail, slow pace, and rigidity of early EU initiatives in securities regulation and despite policy makers' promises that reforms would render the EU regulatory regime simpler and more supple. The Lamfalussy approach, a regulatory reform initiative based on the recommendations of the 2001 Lamfalussy Report, promised to simplify and accelerate the process of EU securities regulation. However, as I discuss below, the fragmented institutional structure of EU policymaking has frustrated these goals, leaving the EU with a tortuous regulatory regime based on highly detailed regulations, which increasingly form the basis for legal action.

Certainly, European integration alone was not responsible for the transformation of securities regulation across Europe. Crucial developments at the domestic level within member states (Cioffi 2002, 2009) and international regulatory competition driven by the globalization of financial markets (Coffee 1999; Romano 2001; Stulz 2009; H. Laurence 2001) and the globalization of class actions (Hensler, Hodges, and Tulibacka 2009) also played a role. But in this chapter I will demonstrate that the EU has played a central and indispensable part in establishing a new regulatory regime based largely on a model of adversarial legalism.

This regime is still in its infancy or, at most, its early adolescence. New rules are in place, but vigorous enforcement—in particular, private enforcement via shareholder litigation—has only begun to surface in recent years. But already, initial developments in this regard are causing shock waves. Unprecedented, massive shareholder lawsuits—such as the thousands of shareholder actions brought against Railtrack in the United Kingdom and Deutsche Telekom in Germany—have attracted the attention of shareholders, CEOs, and their respective lawyers across the EU (Ewing et al. 2001; Budras 2004). Minority shareholder associations have mobilized, policy makers in a number of member states have put into place reforms designed to facilitate collective legal action by minority shareholders, and firms have gone on the defensive against this new legal threat. No European jurisdiction has anything approaching the scale of the shareholder plaintiff's bar in the United States, nor should we expect a securities litigation industry on that scale to develop. However, in Europe a network of law firms and financiers that constitutes a nascent shareholder litigation "support structure" (Epp 1998) has emerged, and professional networks focused on defense against such lawsuits have emerged to counter them.

At conferences, such as the European Securities Litigation Conference held at the Radisson Edwardian Mayfair Hotel in London in March 2009, partners of prominent law firms, hedge fund managers, in-house counsel from major financial institutions, and representatives of specialized litigation-financing firms meet to discuss topics such as "What challenges do securities litigation professionals face? Are we set for a wave of action in 2009?," "How are hedge funds and other alternative asset managers getting involved in securities litigation?," "Is Europe on the cusp of a boom in litigation funding?," "The information battle: Doing securities cases without a pre-trial discovery mechanism," and "Does it make sense to go forum shopping in multi-jurisdictional cases?"[1] The collapse of the dot-com bubble in 2000 and 2001 and the massive shareholder losses it caused sparked the first wave of shareholder litigation in Europe. Likewise, the collapse of many securities firms and the massive shareholder losses caused by the 2008 financial crisis are likely to prompt a marked increase in private securities litigation across Europe in coming years.

This chapter traces the transformation of securities regulation in Europe. I begin by discussing the traditional national approaches to securities regulation that predominated in the early 1980s. I then examine the EU's entry into this policy field in the 1980s and the acceleration of EU involvement in the early 1990s and again after 2001. Finally, I explore the impact the EU has had on regulatory regimes at the national level. The discussion will not do justice to all the intricacies and nuances of the extremely complex securities regulation regimes at the member state or EU level. By stepping back to consider the general trends and directions in EU securities regulation, the analysis sacrifices some level of detail. However, this broader perspective helps us recognize the parallels between developments in this policy field and the others analyzed in this book.

Traditional Securities Regulations in Europe

As of the early 1980s, securities exchanges in Europe relied on flexible, informal self-regulation within closed, clubby groups of established market players. This was true both in the United Kingdom, home to Europe's only well-developed, internationally oriented securities market, and across the Continent, where securities markets remained sheltered and insular and played only a minor role in corporate finance (Zysman 1983; Hall and Soskice 2001, p. 19). Most member states imposed few disclosure requirements for the issuance or trading of securities. In the mid-1980s, seven of the then twelve member states did not require firms to publish a prospectus when making a public offering of a security, nine of the member states did not impose criminal penalties for insider trading, and none of them had an autonomous national securities regulatory agency (Warren 1994, p. 185). While the degree of government regulation of securities markets varied across member states, in all cases exchanges were granted considerable autonomy (Karmel 1999, p. 30; S. Vogel 1996, p. 94–98). Public authorities did little to enforce the few securities regulations that did exist, instead leaving it to self-regulatory bodies of financial firms and traders to police the conduct of their members. European securities markets were also shielded from shareholder lawsuits. The informal, self-regulatory approaches to regulation established very few enforceable shareholder rights. And even when there were private causes of action, procedural hurdles discouraged any shareholder litigation. Limits on discovery, loser-pays rules, and prohibitions on contingency fees made it unappealing if not impossible for private parties to sue investment firms or listed companies for malfeasance and fraud.

Manifestations of this approach were evident across European jurisdictions, including in the United Kingdom, France, Germany, and the Netherlands. The UK, or more specifically the City of London, was home to by far the most significant securities market in Europe. And though the City had long been a major global financial center, it was regulated in a manner that—at least in retrospect—appears rather provincial. Describing the regulatory regime that prevailed in the early 1980s, Steven Vogel explains, "Within the City, the ideology of self-regulation reigned. The system thrived precisely because of the cultural homogeneity of the practitioners and the geographical proximity of their offices. Self-regulation was based on frequent contact between regulators and practitioners" (1996, p. 97; see also Moran 1991). In principle, the Department of Trade and Industry (DTI) oversaw the Stock Exchange and Lloyd's (the insurance market), but in practice the DTI allowed these bodies to self-regulate. Even when formal legal rules were adopted, these were rarely enforced. For instance, though insider trading was legally prohibited from 1980, between 1980 and

1986 the DTI prosecuted only five cases of insider trading (Fishman 1991, p. 185).

Similarly, the French approach to securities regulation in the mid-1980s relied on self-regulation within a framework of rules established by a public authority, the Commission des Opérations de Bourse (COB). Established in 1967, the COB was charged with protecting investors and safeguarding the functioning of financial markets. The COB had the authority to conduct investigations, sanction brokers who did not comply with its regulations, and refer cases to the public prosecutor (procureur de la République) for criminal investigations—for instance, of insider trading. On paper, the COB had been modeled along the lines of the SEC in the United States; that is, the COB was designed to be a powerful and independent watchdog. In practice, the COB was influenced by government, especially the Ministry of Finance, and remained a weak regulator. The main mode of regulation was to restrict access to the market and the types of trading activity permitted on the Bourse. Perhaps the best symbol of these restrictions was the fact that trading activity was permitted for only two hours a day. Tight restrictions on membership and trading on the Bourse—some restrictions targeted specifically at foreign issuers and investors—discouraged international participation (Goldman 1992, p. 245). The public regulatory framework was supplemented by a self-regulatory regime in which professional organizations—or cartels—of stock brokers (the Compagnie des agents de change and the Chambre syndicale des agents de change) controlled the daily operation of the market (Goldman 1992; *Economist* 1988).

In the mid-1980s, Germany's eight regional stock exchanges were governed through a cozy, informal style of self-regulation that had prevailed for decades. As Susanne Lütz (1998, p. 156) puts it, "The German model of sectoral governance [in securities regulation] resembled self-regulated cartels, embedded in the system of German Federalism." Federal law provided only a very loose framework, in the form of the 1965 Securities Law (Aktiengesetz, or AktG). There was no federal-level securities regulator (Enriques and Volpin 2007, p. 136). State *(Land)* governments were the lead public actors, but they too provided only loose supervisory controls—setting some of the terms according to which self-regulatory bodies of the regional stock exchanges could be elected and structured (Lütz 2002, p. 238). Though Frankfurt was the dominant exchange in terms of trading volume, all eight stock exchanges cooperated—or, one might say, colluded—to restrict competition with one another (Lütz 1998, p. 156). Each regional stock exchange was governed by a number of self-regulatory bodies composed of the credit institutions and financial intermediaries that were themselves the subjects of the regulations promulgated by these bodies. Each stock exchange was supervised by a stock exchange board *(Börsenvorstand)* and a number of specialized committees dealing with issues such as listings, business practices, and violations of professional codes of conduct (Siebel, Löwenstein, and Finney 1995). These self-regulatory bodies did not establish formal, legally enforceable rules. Rather, they established voluntary codes of conduct, the violation of which resulted in, at most, very modest "punishments" (Peltzer and Scesniak 1995, p. 1). Market participants had to voluntarily consent to be subject to these rules, and many of them did not. Thus, for instance, someone accused of insider trading had to agree to be bound by the proceedings of a self-regulatory ethics committee before the proceedings could commence. As of 1987, however, 100 of the 480 companies quoted on German bourses had not accepted voluntary codes of conduct on insider trading (McGuiness 1988, p. 443). Moreover, disclosure played a minimal role in this regulatory regime. The self-regulatory bodies did not impose rules concerning the disclosure of price-sensitive information to shareholders or market authorities. Prior to 1990, there was no requirement to publish a prospectus for securities listed on German exchanges (Ferran 2004, pp. 35–36). In principle, there was some legal basis for minority shareholders to bring legal action in the event of management misconduct (for instance, under Article 243 of the Aktiengesetz), but in practice a variety of impediments, discussed below, stood in the way of such litigation.

Most of the insiders who participated in and regulated these markets were satisfied with their governance arrangements. The Secretary General of the Frankfurt Stock Exchange lauded the prevailing cozy, informal system of self-regulation, emphasizing that self-regulatory bodies could learn from experience and flexibly adapt their rules without having to resort to cumbersome legislative processes and stating, "Although it is very important that there be confidence in the functioning of an unbiased securities market, nothing is to be gained by criminalizing participation in securities trading"(H. J. Schwarze 1991,

p. 154). Small shareholders—those holding less than 5 percent of the shares in a company—had no voice in these governance arrangements, and any dissatisfaction on their part carried little weight. Small, individual investors played an extremely marginal role in German markets, where shareholding tended to be highly concentrated and small shareholders lacked any strong domestic lobby (Lütz 1998, pp. 156–157).[2] In essence, the German regulatory regime served the interests of the German universal banks, which were the largest market players, and the interests of the regional stock exchanges, which were propped up by the absence of competition.

These and similar national regulatory regimes could only function effectively—to the extent they did—in the context of segmented, sheltered securities markets. In national markets with a limited numbers of participants who shared common norms and who valued their long term reputations, flexible self-regulation was feasible. But, as we shall see below, these types of regimes could not be sustained as European capital markets integrated and as the EU stepped in to reregulate.

EU Securities Regulation

Though the European Union did not become heavily involved in securities regulation until the mid-1980s, the basis for the EU's involvement in securities regulation dates back to the 1958 Treaty of Rome. The Treaty of Rome did not specifically mention securities regulation, but it famously called for the establishment of a common market based on "four freedoms"—the free movement of goods, persons, services, and capital. EU efforts to regulate securities markets have always been linked to this fundamental, underlying goal of creating a common market. An integrated, pan-European securities market in which issuers and investors can raise capital and invest freely across borders would clearly encourage the free movement of capital and the free movement of financial services. Or, to put it another way, it eventually became clear to policy makers that to achieve the goal of an integrated capital market, they would have to harmonize—to some degree at least—the regulation of securities markets and investment services more generally (Mügge 2006).

Deregulation alone could not provide the basis for market integration. Reregulation at the EU level was also necessary. Eliminating controls on the movement of capital that existed when the European

Economic Community (EEC) was founded was of course a necessary first step, but it would be insufficient. Without harmonization at the EU level, divergences between national regulatory regimes governing securities and investment services would create "nontariff" barriers, which would continue to fragment the market. This was true both where national regulations were actively designed to shield domestic players from foreign competition and where national regulations had more benign, consumer protection motives. These regulatory barriers could not simply be deregulated out of existence. Moreover, to the extent that financial market liberalization succeeded, regulatory failures in one member state were more likely to generate cross-border repercussions that posed systemic risks. To meet political demands for investor protection and protection against systemic risks, reregulation would be needed: a new harmonized regulatory regime at the EU level would have to be erected (Moloney 2008, pp. 6–8; Warren, 1994, p. 186; Ferran 2004, p. 29).

EU policy makers began exploring the role the EU might play in promoting an integrated securities market in the mid-1960s. In 1966, an expert committee appointed by the European Commission (Commission 1966) produced a report (the Segré Report) suggesting that integration of securities markets would reduce capital costs for firms, thereby promoting growth and employment, and would also produce greater choice for investors. In 1977, the Commission issued the nonbinding "Recommendation for a European Code of Conduct Relating to Transactions in Transferable Securities" (Commission 1977). Thereafter, the first generation of directives on official listings of securities and disclosure-related issues were adopted between 1979 and 1982—including the Directive on Admission to Official Listing (79/279/EEC) and the Listing Particulars Directive (80/390/EEC). These directives aimed at constructing an integrated securities market that firms from across Europe could access in order to raise capital. The directives established the major outlines of the EU's approach to securities regulation, a model that has persisted to this day, in that they focused on detailed harmonization of mandatory disclosure rules for issuers of securities.

In April 1983, the Commission sought to build on these initial steps and issued a communication to the Council outlining proposals to create a single market in financial services (Commission 1983). However, efforts to harmonize national regulations and reduce barriers to trade in this period were largely unsuccessful, as the combination of the unanimity decision-making rules in the Council and limited support for harmonization blocked progress (Lannoo and Levin 2004, p. 2).

The second phase of EU securities regulation began with the publication of the Commission's 1985 *White Paper on the Completion of the Internal Market* (Commission 1985) and the launch of the so-called 1992 Program.[3] As part of its historic drive to "complete" the single market by 1992, the white paper took up a number of the proposals from the Commission's 1983 proposal and called for the development of a truly pan-European securities market (Commission 1985, para. 197; Story and Walter 1997; Posner 2009). Liberalization of capital markets was already accelerating in the mid-1980s, as national governments started lifting restrictions on cross-border capital movements. While the Euromarkets in London provided one important arena for transnational equities investment, more generally national securities markets remained disconnected from one another, and retail investment in securities was limited across continental Europe (Mügge 2006).[4]

The Commission recognized that existing securities regulations at the national level, which were based on informal, opaque, and sometimes blatantly protectionist practices, would block the establishment of a fully integrated European securities market and a single market for financial services (Karmel 1999). Even if member states adopted more transparent, codified regulatory requirements, divergence between these national requirements would inevitably continue to fragment the market (Warren 1994, p. 186). Divergent national regimes had to be supplanted with a harmonized pan-European regime that could create an open and level playing field. To achieve this, the Commission's white paper called for a linked strategy of deregulation and reregulation. As part of its Single Market Program, the EU adopted a series of financial-market liberalization of directives, a series that culminated in a 1988 directive (88/361/EEC) calling for the complete liberalization of capital movements by 1990. But the white paper also called for the introduction of new regulatory measures that would focus on transparency and disclosure by listing firms and financial service providers.

Following the publication of the white paper, the EU adopted a series of directives establishing minimum EU standards for public offerings and listings, trading activities, and financial intermediaries

(Lannoo 2001; Karmel 1999).[5] These directives introduced stringent disclosure requirements and demands for transparency in regulatory processes, which were broadly similar to those found in American securities law and which were at odds with the regulatory practices that had prevailed in many member states (Ferran 2004, pp. 36–40).

Securities directives adopted in this period sought to apply the "new approach" to regulation that the Commission had made the centerpiece of its 1992 Single Market Program. Across fields of regulation, the Commission sought to move away from an approach based on exhaustive harmonization of detailed regulatory requirements and to instead combine minimum harmonization of essential mandatory requirements with a system of mutual recognition, in which states would agree to recognize and accept each other's regulatory requirements (Sun and Pelkmans 1995;[6] Alter and Meunier-Aitsahalia 1994). Likewise, in the field of securities regulation critics argued that earlier efforts to agree on "detailed, equivalence promoting directives" (Moloney 2002, p. 21) had slowed progress and that the new system should rely on minimum harmonization and mutual recognition. In the securities arena, mutual recognition relied on the concept of the "passport." As the preamble to the Investment Services Directive (93/22/EEC) put it, the goal was to introduce "harmonization necessary and sufficient to secure the mutual recognition of authorization and of prudential supervision systems, making possible the grant of a single authorization valid throughout the Community and the application of the principle of home Member State supervision."[7] The idea was that issuers of securities, managers of collective investment schemes (i.e., mutual funds), and other financial service providers would secure regulatory approval in their home state and then be issued a "regulatory passport" authorizing them to operate across the EU.

However, as in so many other areas of EU regulation, this new approach largely failed. The mutual recognition requirement was subject to exceptions. To address public interest concerns such as consumer protection, member states could still impose additional requirements that went beyond common EU rules and that effectively rendered the passport a dead letter. For instance, an issuer holding a passport for a securities offering from one member state and attempting to offer that security in another member state could be required to translate the prospectus into the local language and to provide additional information for local investors (Ferran 2004, p. 5). Likewise, an investment services firm with a regulatory passport might be subject to divergent conduct of business rules when attempting to operate in another member state (ibid.; Mügge 2006, p. 1007; Story and Walter 1997, p. 266). Member states had adopted so many exceptions and additional requirements that the passport approach did not operate effectively, national securities regulators did not cooperate effectively on cross-border matters, and many member states resisted implementation of securities directives. In addition, the EU had yet to address major areas of financial services regulation, such as rules on market manipulation and conduct of business rules. While the regulatory drive associated with the 1992 initiative had produced a substantial body of EU securities regulation, by the late 1990s it had become clear that this regulatory structure was inadequate in crucial respects (Moloney 2002, p. 24; Ferran 2004, pp. 4–5). Policy makers saw that this feeble regulatory regime could not cope with the upsurge of cross-border activity they were witnessing.

By the late 1990s, a confluence of factors was accelerating the process of financial market integration across Europe (Posner 2009). The first was the impending launch of the euro, which investors, issuers of securities, and financial service providers anticipated would dramatically increase cross-border investment. Second, technological development innovation in financial services and the development of alternative trading platforms was facilitating cross-border trade in traditional securities and in new derivative and securitized products and undermining dominance of traditional exchanges. Third, corporations across continental Europe, which had traditionally relied on bank-based financing, were increasingly turning to securities markets as sources of financing (Gros and Lannoo 2000). The number of listed companies, the number of initial public offerings (IPOs), and overall stock market capitalization across Europe increased dramatically in the 1990s (Ferran 2004, p. 15). Investment funds and large private investors began to take a more pan-European perspective, engaging in more cross-border transactions (Quaglia 2007, p. 279). Fourth, a variety of factors, beginning with the series of large-scale privatizations occurring across the EU (Mügge 2006, p. 1008), were luring more retail investors in equities markets. Above all, the dot-com frenzy and associated stock market boom in the late 1990s were drawing more retail investors into the market, and declining state support for public pensions was encouraging more individuals to invest for their retirement.

With more interest from issuers and investors, the investment fund industry grew rapidly and developed a host of new investment vehicles. Investors, firms, and financial service providers sought opportunities outside their home markets, and cross-border activity increased dramatically. New and more diverse players were trading an increasing number and range of securitized products on a wider range of trading platforms (Commission 2000). However, despite this upsurge of activity in European securities markets, one could still not speak of a truly integrated pan-European securities market. Securities markets continued to be fragmented along national lines, with entrenched national securities regulatory regimes presenting significant obstacles to market integration (Karmel 1999; Warren 1994, 2003). Investors, particularly retail investors, maintained a significant bias toward investing in their home markets, financial service providers could not operate seamlessly across national borders, and pan-European equity offerings remained rare.

The third phase of EU securities regulation was launched against this background. Policy makers sought to seize on the burgeoning retail investment markets and to put in place a regulatory architecture that could enable a truly integrated pan-European securities market to emerge and flourish. In 1998, at the European Council meeting in Cardiff, the Council called on the Commission to prepare a framework for action for financial services regulation reform that could ensure both that the full benefit of the euro would be realized and that the stability and competitiveness of EU financial markets would be ensured. Later in 1998 the Commission published a communication on financial services (Commission 1998) that identified specific issues that should be addressed. Representatives of the Ecofin Council, the European Central Bank (ECB), and the Commission then crafted an action plan, which was published by the Commission in 1999 as the landmark Financial Services Action Plan, or FSAP (Commission 1999b).

The FSAP called for the introduction of forty-two measures that would radically reform the EU's regulatory regime for securities, measures that would both restructure existing rules to enhance their effectiveness and extend EU action to a host of new fields. The FSAP called for measures addressing wholesale markets, retail markets, prudential supervision, and financial market integration more generally. While the principal focus of the FSAP was on wholesale markets and institutional investors, the plan clearly signaled a heightened emphasis on promoting the development of retail investment markets. In the midst of the dot-com bubble of the late 1990s, there was great enthusiasm and confidence in the potential for developing an "equity culture" in Europe and increasing the liquidity of capital markets by attracting millions of new individual investors. This boom in retail investing and deepening of capital markets would in turn—it was hoped—make it easier for firms to raise finance through issuing securities, thereby encouraging economic growth and employment. At the same time, policy makers recognized that existing regulatory structures discouraged small private investors from entering the markets and particularly discouraged cross-border investment. The opaque patchwork of national regulations and poor implementation of existing EU directives undermined investor confidence. To realize the goal of a deep, pan-European retail investment market, a strong, harmonized investor protection regime would have to be put in place. To that end, the FSAP placed great emphasis on investor protection, calling for even tighter disclosure rules, stricter control of market abuse (such as insider trading), and wide-ranging regulation of investment services firms and of trading activities.

Following the publication of the FSAP, a Council convened a "Committee of Wise Men," which was headed by Baron Alexandre Lamfalussy, to assess the state of EU securities and investment services regulation. The Committee issued its Lamfalussy Report in February 2001 (Lamfalussy 2001). The Lamfalussy Report presented a harsh indictment of existing EU securities regulation and heightened the sense of urgency surrounding the EU's drive for regulatory reform. The report found that the EU's legislative process had proven incapable of delivering regulation that could keep up with market developments and encourage further integration of EU securities markets. The report critiqued the EU regulatory process for being too slow and rigid and critiqued directives produced by the EU lawmakers as being in some ways too ambiguous and in many respects far too detailed and inflexible. In particular, the report (Lamfalussy 2001, p. 14) noted that Council tended to add unnecessary complexity to directives in order to accommodate divergent national approaches. The Lamfalussy Report also found that implementation of Community directives was inconsistent and that enforcement by the Commission was weak (Hertig and Lee 2003).

The Lamfalussy Report called for a wholesale reform of the EU's approach to producing and implementing securities regulations. The report called for a new four-level approach. The report suggested that the EU's primary legislative actors (the Commission, the Parliament, and the Council of Ministers) restrict themselves to adopting broad "framework directives" that would establish basic principles at Level 1. They would leave the task of developing detailed implementing measures to expert committees working with the European Commission in a complex "comitology" procedure at Level 2 (Lannoo 2001, pp. 11–12). The hope was that these committees could act quickly to update regulations in light of technological and market developments and could avoid the pathologies of the Community legislative process. Next, the report called for enhanced coordination between national authorities with regard to implementation and enforcement at Level 3, and far stricter enforcement of EU directives by the Commission at Level 4. The aim here was to promote what was labeled "supervisory convergence," to ensure consistent and effective implementation and enforcement of securities directives across the Community (Ferran 2004, pp. 47–48).

At its 2001 Stockholm meeting, the European Council endorsed the Lamfalussy Report's conclusions and endorsed its call for a new regulatory procedure. Following the report's suggestions, the EU established a new pair of regulatory committees. The European Securities Committee (ESC), which some observers viewed as an embryonic EU version of the US Securities and Exchange Commission, was given the power to issue implementing measures on the basis of Community legislation (Lannoo 2002, p. 13). The Committee of European Securities Regulators (CESR), which brings together representatives of national securities regulators, was charged with advising the ESC and with improving coordination among national securities regulators with regard to implementation and enforcement.[8]

On the basis of the FSAP and the Lamfalussy Report and with the new regulatory committees in place, EU lawmakers set about adopting a third generation of EU securities regulations. The main thrust of these directives was to strengthen investor protection through a combination of mandatory disclosure and strict enforcement. Issuers of securities were subject to a new, stricter disclosure regime in the 2003 Prospectus Directive (2003/71/EC), which introduced extensive and strict standards for disclosure in initial public offerings of securities. Likewise, the 2004 Transparency Directive (2004/109/EC) set harmonized standards concerning the information that issuers of listed securities must disclose to investors on an ongoing basis (i.e., in periodic financial reports). Market abuse and insider trading were targeted with the 2003 Market Abuse Directive (2003/6/EC), which set for issuers disclosure rules concerning inside information, in order to prevent insider trading and market manipulation. New investor protection rules were put in place regulating the activities of investment service providers. The 2002 Distance Marketing Directive (2002/65/EC) was designed to protect retail investors through disclosure rules and other contractual protections; and the landmark 2004 MiFID, or the Markets in Financial Instruments Directive (2004/39/EC), regulates relations between investors and investment firms, including issues related to precontractual disclosure and protections for investors who have entered into contracts with investment firms. The "Conduct of Business Rules" mandated in Article 19 of MiFID require that all information that investment firms provide to clients or potential clients (even in any brochures or mailings) must be fair, clear, and not misleading and be written in a "comprehensible form."[9] The general requirements set out in all of these directives (at Level 1) are backed by even more-detailed mandatory disclosure requirements established by CESR in its implementing regulations (at Level 2).

Despite the Lamfalussy Report's call for greater flexibility and despite the supposed commitment of policy makers to follow this advice,[10] disclosure rules and other regulatory requirements introduced in Level 1 directives and Level 2 implementing measures have been drafted with such rigid and detailed requirements that they harmonize at a "maximum level" and leave member states very little discretion in implementation (Moloney 2005, p. 347, 387; see also Lanoo 2001, p. 11–12). Many of these detailed requirements were framed and justified as being necessary to protect investors' rights (Moloney 2007, p. 412).

Having briefly considered the development of EU securities regulation culminating in the third generation of EU securities regulations adopted in the past decade, we can step back to better comprehend the nature of the regulatory regime for securities that the EU has established and the role that political fragmentation and economic liberalization have played in shaping it. The most notable features of the EU's regulatory regime are (1) its reliance on disclosure as a tool to achieve regulatory objectives, (2) the highly prescriptive and detailed nature of regulations (despite promises to promote flexibility), and (3) the emphasis it places on protecting the *rights* of investors. Each of these central features of EU securities regulation can be traced back to the impact of economic liberalization and political fragmentation in the EU.

The emphasis on detailed, mandatory disclosure rules and the protection of investor rights was linked closely to the project of liberalizing the European securities market. As discussed above, in the 1990s the volume of cross-border investment and the diversity of firms, investors, financial service providers, and trading platforms involved were increasing rapidly. The introduction of the euro then further accelerated financial market integration. EU policy makers hoped to build on this momentum and to draw millions of retail investors into integrated pan-European securities markets, which would provide a deep pool of capital that firms could rely on as a source of finance. However, policy makers recognized that opaque securities regimes entrenched at the national level continued to impede free movement of investment and financial services and particularly to discourage retail investors. Variations in the strength of investor protection rules across countries and confusion over the rapidly increasing number of investment firms (of varying national origins) marketing their services and products to investors discouraged many potential investors from putting their savings at risk in equity markets (Moloney 2005, p. 372).

Thus, EU policy makers recognized that deregulation alone could not create a single market. As Internal Market Commissioner Frits Bolkestein put it, "Realising single market freedoms requires some pooling of regulatory sovereignty. Borderless finance in Europe is not synonymous with regulation-free Europe" (Bolkestein 2004 p. 2). To draw in retail investors policy makers had to establish at the EU level a new regulatory regime that would ensure market stability, protect consumers against abusive practices, and—most importantly—strengthen investor confidence. Measures, such as MiFID, that were designed to boost investor confidence in the retail investment advice industry were particularly important. Investment advice firms serve as the gateway into the market for most retail investors. To be lured into the markets, retail investors must be confident that regulations are in place to protect them against the risks associated with improper conduct by financial advisors, in particular those associated with multinationals based in other member states (Commission 2002b, pp. 24–33; FIN-USE 2004, p. 4). In the EU's increasingly heterogenous, liberalized financial markets, traditional and informal approaches to financial regulation based on "reputational disciplines," self-regulation, and trust in reliable, established market players would not be adequate. Law would need to replace trust, and a new regulatory regime with strict, enforceable rules must be put in place (Moloney 2005, p. 364–366; Stout 2002).

The fragmentation of political power at the EU level has further encouraged the EU's tendency to focus on detailed disclosure backed by strict enforcement. Political fragmentation helps explain why EU securities directives have grown steadily more detailed and prescriptive—excessively so, according to critics—despite repeated commitments of member state governments and the European Commission to make EU securities regulation more flexible and responsive. These dynamics are evident in the fate of the Lamfalussy process. As discussed above, the reforms introduced in response to the Lamfalussy Report were designed both to make EU legislation less complex and more flexible and to ensure that the regulations were implemented consistently. Political fragmentation at the EU level significantly undermined the reforms designed to make the system more flexible, while encouraging those designed to tighten legal enforcement.

After the 2001 Lamfalussy Report issued its stinging criticism of existing EU securities regulation, the Council and Commission both strongly endorsed the report's reform proposals that aimed to make EU securities regulation more flexible and responsive to market developments. However, the European Parliament was concerned that the regulatory process the report called for would subvert Parliament's role—and thereby subvert democracy at the EU level. Parliament feared that the new regulatory process handed too much power to unaccountable committees of national bureaucrats (the ESC and CESR), who crafted substantive regulations at Level 2. The Parliament blocked the new regulatory process called for in the Lamfalussy Report until winning formal assurances from the Commission that the Parliament's role would not be undermined and securing "sunset clauses" that limited the delegation of implementing powers to a four-year period (Quaglia 2007, p. 277; Hertig and Lee 2003; Ferrarini 2002). Parliament demanded that the new regulatory process be transparent and that Parliament be given time to review and comment on measures proposed by the ESC (Ferran 2004, pp. 66–67; European Parliament 2001).

Subsequently, the Parliament asserted its power in ways that undermined key aspects of the Lamfalussy process. As it had throughout the history of EU securities regulation, the European Parliament took a staunchly pro–consumer protection position. The Parliament proposed hundreds of amendments to draft securities directives aimed at forcing regulators to protect consumer interests. In essence, the Parliament demanded that more and more details be spelled out at in Level 1 directives, in which it played a powerful role in the legislative procedure, and not be left to be fleshed out by the ESC and CESR at Level 2, over which it had far less influence (European Parliament 2001). As a result, the recent EU securities directives discussed above—on prospectuses (2003/71/EC), transparency (2004/109/EC), market abuse (2003/6/EC), and investment services (2004/39/EC)—are extremely detailed and action forcing and substantially expand rights for shareholders (Lannoo 2002, pp. 11–12; Moloney 2005). Indeed, when the Inter-institutional Monitoring Group, which was set up by the Commission, Council, and Parliament to evaluate the Lamfalussy Process, published its final report in 2007, it criticized EU lawmakers for including "excessive detail" in securities legislation (Inter-institutional Monitoring Group 2007, pp. 4, 8, 11, 22).

The fragmentation of authority between the EU-level and national-level regulators also influenced the design of securities directives. Because the member states so long resisted the idea of creating a single, pan-European securities and exchange commission (Avgerinos 2003; Langevoort 2005; Pan 2003; Karmel 1999; Hertig and Lee 2003; Moloney 2008, pp. 1097–1101), responsibility for implementing EU securities directives remained in the hands of national securities regulators (Wymeersch 2005, p. 994). As in other areas of EU regulation, the delegation of authority to national regulators made uneven application of the law almost inevitable and created opportunities for regulators to favor domestic players. To ensure that EU securities regulations would be implemented consistently and effectively across the European Union, EU lawmakers sought to promote convergence among national securities regulators (Moloney 2008, p. 1103–1107). The pursuit of this "supervisory convergence" (Ferran 2004, p. 47) led EU lawmakers to set minimum standards that any national authority charged with implementation must meet, in terms of its independence, its supervisory and investigatory powers, and the types of sanctions national regulators must impose on violators (Ferran 2004, pp. 219–220).

EU pressure for supervisory convergence has grown more pronounced over time. As Eilís Ferran explains (2004, p. 47), "Laws adopted under the FSAP . . . , to a significantly greater extent than earlier EU securities law, prescribe the minimum characteristics of the agencies to which member states can entrust certain supervisory responsibilities and also standardize the powers and responsibilities of these agencies." These rules have required profound changes, given that none of the member states had had an independent securities regulatory agency at the national level when the EU first entered the field of securities regulation (Warren 1994, p. 185).

More dramatic convergence in financial supervision is imminent, as EU lawmakers recently agreed to establish an EU-level securities regulator—the European Securities and Markets Authority (ESMA)—with the authority to coordinate financial market regulation among national regulators and to ensure the consistent application of community law (Aboulian 2010; European Parliament 2010). In the wake of the financial crisis, it became evident that national regulators had failed to effectively coordinate supervision of Europe's increasingly integrated financial markets. As the Commission put it in its proposal for ESMA, "The [financial] crisis exposed shortcomings in the area of cooperation, coordination, consistent application of Community law and trust between national supervisors" (Commission 2009c, p. 12). ESMA, which will commence operations in 2011, will have considerable authority to develop a single rule book of technical standards for all financial market participants, to ensure consistent implementation of these standards and to settle disputes among national regulators.

The same political dynamics that undermined one half of the Lamfalussy process—the effort to simplify EU regulation—actually supported the second half of the process—the effort to strengthen enforcement. To ensure consistent application of securities directives, the Commission has taken up the Lamfalussy Report's call to strengthen its enforcement activities. Since 2001, the European Commission has launched dozens of infringement procedures against member states for their failure to comply with EU securities directives.[11] Since 2005, the Commission has published the "Lamfalussy League Table" to track member states' compliance with securities directives under the FSAP.[12] In August 2005, the Commission pursued fifty-seven infringement proceedings against sixteen member states for failure to implement the Market Abuse Directive (2003/6/EC) and regulations relating to it (Commission 2005d). By January 2007, all member states but one had relented and come into compliance (Moloney 2008, p. 1084). Likewise, in the case of MiFID, after a slow start on implementation by the member states, the Commission issued "reasoned opinions"—the stage of the infringement procedure that comes before a case is referred to the ECJ—to twenty-four member states. Twenty-one of those states came into compliance quickly, and the Commission brought infringement cases to the ECJ against the three remaining states, which had failed to transpose the directive into national law before the November 2007 deadline (ibid., p. 1085). In short, we can observe that after many years of lax enforcement, the Commission has tightened the screws on the member states in the securities field—as they have done in so many other areas of EU regulation.

Not only has centralized enforcement by the Commission become more aggressive, but also the focus in many of the post-FSAP directives on strengthening disclosure and shareholders' rights has created new possibilities for private enforcement of securities laws—in other words, regulation through litigation. As noted above, prior to EU involvement in securities regulation, shareholder litigation against listed firms or financial intermediaries was almost unheard of in Europe. One major reason for the dearth of litigation was that the flexible, informal style of regulation then prevailing at the national level had created very few "causes of action" (shareholder rights) to serve as the basis for litigation and did little to unearth the information that shareholders would have needed to support their claims. With few mandatory rules concerning disclosure or prohibitions on insider dealing, shareholders were unlikely to access the information necessary to support claims and were unlikely to find a legal basis for claims. The influence of EU securities regulation has changed this situation. New disclosure rules both make it easier for shareholders to discover malfeasance and make it easier for them to bring legal claims and win compensation when they do discover it. Together with changes in procedural rules, such as new rules on collective actions, and the influence of American institutional investors (Kissane 1997) and law firms, these developments have encouraged the emergence of shareholder litigation across Europe (Woolfe 2007; Peel 2007; Tait and Sherwood 2005; Ewing et al. 2001; Kissane 1997).

Transforming Securities Regulation at the National Level

Through careful examination of developments in France, the United Kingdom, Germany, and the Netherlands, we can observe how the emergence of the EU securities regime has transformed national securities regulation and how shareholders across Europe are invoking their newly won EU rights to enforce securities regulations.

France

France's system of securities regulation has been transformed dramatically since the mid-1980s. The system has been both deregulated and reregulated. The cozy and highly sheltered system in which a cartel of brokers worked with government regulators to limit access to the market has been dismantled. Restrictions on access have been replaced by a regulatory regime structured around transparency, disclosure, and shareholder rights. Shareholder litigation, which had been nonexistent, has become commonplace. Pressures associated with European integration are not solely responsible for this transformation, but they are clearly a key cause.

The traditional French system of securities regulation described above began to break down in the mid-1980s. The increased internationalization of financial markets and the anticipation of pressures and opportunities that would be unleashed by the European Single Market Program prompted a series of reforms (Goldman 1992). Initial reforms dismantled traditional French regulation, and subsequent reforms replaced it with a pan-European regime based on transparency and legalistic enforcement. In the mid-1980s, the French government was eager to attract foreign investors to participate in the wave of privatization it was launching. Also, given the severe restrictions on trading activities on the French Bourse, French equities and government bonds were increasingly being traded on London's Euromarket.[13] To staunch the bleeding and to prepare French financial markets for the competition that would be unleashed with the single European market program, policy makers sought to open up France's highly restrictive, protectionist system of securities regulation.[14] A series of liberalization reforms were introduced, which included allowing foreign companies and individuals to acquire ownership in French financial brokers in 1987. The stock market's hours were extended from the traditional two per day, which was deemed rather too short even by French standards. A new trading platform (the Second Marché) with minimal listings requirements and loose oversight was established to attract medium-sized French and international companies (Goldman 1992, pp. 231–233). All these measures reduced the cozy atmosphere of the French financial marketplace. But the frenzied deregulation was not initially accompanied by the introduction of a new regulatory regime based on transparency and shareholder rights (*Economist* 1988), and the absence of effective regulation left the securities markets vulnerable to abuse.

Unsurprisingly, scandals ensued. In 1988, the Pechiney and Société Générale scandals shook the French securities markets to their core. Both affairs involved a toxic brew of insider trading by politically well-connected individuals and lax supervision by securities regulators (the COB) as a result of political pressure from the Ministry of Finance (which was itself implicated in the scandal). The crises laid bare the weaknesses in the French regulatory regime. In reaction to the public outcry and to pressure from the US Securities and Exchange Commission (which had become involved due to cross-border transactions involved in the scandals), the French government quickly passed major securities regulation reforms designed to guarantee the independence of the COB and to strengthen its enforcement powers.[15]

The pressures for regulatory reform stemming from domestic scandal and American pressure were soon superseded by pressures emanating from Brussels. Indeed, as early as 1989, the *Financial Times* reported on the impact that European banking and financial services directives were having on French regulation and concluded that "the entire structure of France's financial services industry has come to be driven by forces from outside its frontiers," especially "from Brussels" (G. Graham 1989). Pressure from Brussels for a new model of securities regulation intensified in the mid–1990s. France transposed the 1993 Investment Services Directive (93/22/EEC) and other second-generation EU securities regulations into national law with its Law on the Modernization of Financial Activities (Loi du 2 juillet 1996 sur la modernisation des activités financières).[16] This 1996 reform significantly extended the judicial powers of the Commission des opérations de Bourse. To comply with EU requirements, the COB was given legal standing as an administrative body before the highest French administrative court, the Conseil d'État. The law also raised substantially the level of administrative penalties that the COB could impose on any investment service providers that violated securities regulations.

Implementation of the third generation of EU securities laws adopted in the wake of the European Union's FSAP led to a stream of new laws, administrative orders, and adaptations to the General Financial Market Regulations (Règlement général de l'Autorité des marchés financiers, or RGAMF). The most significant new legislation was the 2003 Financial Security Law (Loi de sécurité financière),[17] which introduced major changes to the governance structure and the substantive rules for securities regulation in France. The law established a new, unified financial market authority, the Autorité des marchés financiers (AMF), whose remit included controlling and supervising corporate finance, financial information, investment service providers, collective investment schemes, and financial markets. The move toward a unified authority in France reflected the fact that the call for more unified national regulatory authorities enshrined within major EU securities directives was being taken seriously. The Financial Security Law also introduced substantive changes to existing market rules, changes that largely stemmed from EU directives. Issuers of securities were subject to stronger, more explicit disclosure requirements for corporate governance, internal control, and reporting to shareholders.[18] Most importantly, the Financial Security Law introduced the much stricter and more explicit insider dealing rules that were at the core of the EU's Market Abuse Directive. Beyond the legislation adopted by the National Assembly, the AMF also enacted key provisions of the recent EU directives through its rule-making authority in 2004 (Fried Frank 2006).

Between 2005 and 2007, further steps were taken to implement the post-FSAP European Union securities directives. Most importantly, two new laws transposed into French law the EU Prospectus Directive (2003/71/EEC) and remaining requirements of the Market Abuse Directive (2003/6/EEC).[19] These two laws were accompanied by changes to the general regulations issued by the AMF,[20] and further amendments to the AMF's general regulations in 2006 and 2007 completed implementation of the EU Transparency Directive.[21]

Not only did rules and regulatory institutions change, but patterns of enforcement changed dramatically as well. Public enforcement has grown far more vigorous and coercive. Since its establishment in 2003, the AMF has emerged as a powerful watchdog over the securities markets. The AMF's Enforcement Committee has imposed a steadily increasing number of sanctions against violators of securities laws, including substantial increases in the fines it imposes, from thirty-three fines totaling €8.6 million in 2004, to eighty fines totaling €24.7 million in 2008 (Autorité des marchés financiers 2005, 2009). While public enforcement has certainly become more coercive and judicialized, the most striking development in the enforcement of securities regulation in France has been the emergence of minority shareholder litigation.

Prior to the 1990s, various procedural hurdles restricted collective action by shareholders. Since the late 1980s, shareholder rights have been strengthened substantially. These reforms have created new opportunities for shareholder litigation, which has gone from being nonexistent to commonplace (Canu 2000; Danglehant 1996; Astier 2006). A 1989 law (Loi 89–421 of 23 June 1989) recognized new rights for associations of investors *(associations d'investisseurs)*[22] to bring legal actions on behalf of their members (Girard 2009).[23] Also a 1994 law (Loi 94–679 of 8 August 1994) gave associations of shareholders *(associations d'actionnaires)* who together held at least 5 percent of the voting rights in a company a number of new rights, including the right to bring the French equivalent of shareholder derivative suits (*ut singuli* actions) seeking compensation for damages suffered by shareholders (Canu and De Saint Mars 2000; Merle 2005). Despite such reforms, significant procedural impediments continue to limit the scope for shareholder litigation in France and to encourage aggrieved French shareholders to pursue claims in foreign—and especially American—courts. Above all, the absence of an American-style opt-in class action for shareholder litigation makes collective legal action difficult.[24] Nevertheless, a number of French shareholder associations have been formed and have pursued litigation strategies.

The oldest, best-known, and most successful of these associations is the Association for the Defense of Minority Shareholders, or ADAM (Association de défense des actionnaires minoritaires), founded in 1991 (Girard 2009). Among ADAM's well-known cases was a 1998 action in which ADAM challenged the acquisition of an advertising company (Havas) by the Compagnie Générale des Eaux (which was in the process of transforming itself into the media conglomerate Vivendi), with the case leading to an award of almost 1 billion euros in damages to the shareholders.[25] In a similar case in 2001, ADAM objected to the takeover of Nissan by Renault in 2001 and secured compensation of roughly 150 million euros to minority shareholders.

Since roughly 2005, observers have spoken of a "shareholder's revolt" in France (Astier 2006; *BBC News* 2006). Today, there are over twenty shareholder associations in France, including prominent new groups, such as the Active Small Investors Association (Association des petits porteurs actifs) and the Active Shareholder Association (Association des actionnaires actifs), emerging since 2000 and bringing litigation against corporate giants, including Vivendi, Eurotunnel, and defense firm EADS (European Aeronautic Defence and Space Company) in French and foreign courts (Girard 2001, 2009; Astier 2006; Gow 2006; *BBC News* 2006).

Germany

Throughout the 1980s, Germany resisted fully implementing the first and second generations of European Union securities regulation and sought to preserve its traditional, opaque system of self-regulation (Lütz 2002, p. 239; Weber 1994, p. 2850). But by the mid-1990s, opposition to reform faded, and since then Germany has radically restructured its regime for securities regulation. Long an opponent of disclosure requirements and shareholder rights, Germany has adopted and embraced these and other central planks of the EU securities regime. While shifts in German domestic politics and reactions to domestic securities scandals played an important role in this transformation

(Cioffi 2009, 2002; Deeg and Lütz 2000; Lütz 2002, p. 238), the demands of the EU securities regime were unquestionably central drivers of reform. The EU became a crucial ally for proponents of reform within Germany, helping them to overcome entrenched domestic opposition and impose via Brussels reforms that had been blocked in the domestic arena (Ferran 2004, pp. 35–39). The financial market liberalization unleashed by the EU, coupled with the need to implement increasingly stringent EU securities directives, required a wholesale restructuring of the German system of securities regulation.

In the early 1990s, financial market liberalization across the EU and globally undermined the traditional system of securities regulation in Germany. The traditional German model of corporate finance came unglued, as large German firms that had traditionally relied on domestic banks for their financing needs turned increasingly to foreign investment banks and foreign capital markets for financing (Deeg and Lütz 2000). By 1990, shares in German companies were being traded heavily in London and Paris. With their loan business declining, German commercial banks sought to move into investment banking, but German securities markets remained unappealing to investors—especially foreign ones—because of its opaque system of self-regulation. Likewise, German financial firms were blocked from offering some of their products on foreign exchanges (i.e., in the United States) because the German regulatory regime did not provide for enough transparency to satisfy foreign regulators.

Powerful economic stakeholders began to favor reforms that could encourage the development of equity markets in Germany. They saw that to make German securities markets more attractive to investors, Germany's regime for securities regulation would have to strengthen transparency and disclosure requirements and empower shareholders with more legal rights.[26] The Ministry of Finance too saw that European integration and financial globalization made reform necessary. With the integration of European capital markets as part of the 1992 Single Market Program, German financial markets would be subject to even greater competition from London and Paris, and investors would demand a regulatory system that guaranteed transparency and safeguarded investor rights. Securities regulators across Europe were beginning to collaborate in shaping the emerging EU securities regime, and if Germany was to participate effectively in such networks, it would need to establish a federal-level securities regulator. As a result, key stakeholders began to favor a wholesale reform of German securities regulation.

The first major overhaul of German securities regulation came in 1994 with the passage of the Second Financial Market Development Act (2. Finanzmarktförderungsgesetz, or FmFG).[27] The FmFG was designed to enhance the transparency of German securities markets and to bring Germany in line with EU securities directives, including the 1989 Insider Trading Directive and the 1993 Investment Services Directive (Martin Weber 1994; Deeg and Lütz 2000, p. 390). It was a kind of omnibus law, including revisions of existing laws and introducing new ones. The FmFG also introduced a formal legal prohibition on insider trading and introduced numerous reforms designed to strengthen disclosure. The FmFG included the new Securities Trading Act (Wertpapierhandelsgesetz, or WpHG), which laid the basis for the creation in 1995 of Germany's first federal securities regulator—the Federal Securities Supervisory Office (Bundesaufsichtsamt für den Wertpapierhandel, or BAWe). The EU's Investment Services Directive, Insider Trading Directives, and in a broader sense the EU's entire approach to harmonizing securities regulation required member states to designate a single competent authority that would monitor compliance and cooperate with counterparts in other member states (Deeg and Lütz 2000; Lannoo 2001, p. 26). To conform with this system, the federal government had to wrest regulatory authority away from state governments *(Länder)* and regional stock exchanges and centralize it in the hands of a single federal authority.

Since 1994, most German laws passed in the field of securities regulation have served to implement EU directives. For instance, the 1997 Act on the Implementation of EU Directives Relating to the Harmonization of Regulatory Provisions in the Field of Banking and Securities Supervision (Gesetz zur Umsetzung von EG-Richtlinien zur Harmonisierung bank- und wertpapieraufsichtsrechtlicher Vorschriften), the 1998 Third Financial Market Development Act (3. Finanzmarktförderungsgesetz, or FmFG), and the 1998 Corporate Control and Transparency Act (Gesetz zur Kontrolle und Transparenz in Unternehmensbereich, or KonTraG) all served to transpose EU requirements into German law. The pace of reform in Germany accelerated after the publication of the EU's Financial Services Action Plan and the Lamfalussy Report. The establishment of a unified regulator for the entire financial sector—the Bundesanstalt für Finanzdienstleistungsaufsicht (BAFin) in 2001[28]—was driven in large part by pressure from the EU to connect regulation of securities, banking, and finance under a single authority (Lütz 2002, p. 246). The Fourth Financial Market Development Act (4. Finanzmarktförderungsgesetz, or FmFG), passed in 2002, introduces a number of reforms designed to empower investors, including providing shareholders with a right to compensation for losses resulting from market abuse and false, late or omitted disclosure by listed companies.

But have all these new disclosure requirements and investor rights actually led to any litigation? Skeptics insist that a variety of institutional impediments to litigation and political resistance to moving toward American-style adversarial legalism will stifle the development of shareholder litigation (Cioffi 2002, 2009). Contingency fees are still not permitted. Given the absence of punitive damages or jury trials, awards will remain low. Also, the absence of American-style discovery provisions makes it far more difficult for plaintiffs to prove their claims. And while shareholder rights groups press for reforms that would facilitate litigation, business interests remain adamantly opposed, warning of the dangers of the American model.

While these impediments are indeed significant, securities litigation, which was almost nonexistent in Germany before 2001, has unquestionably emerged onto the German legal landscape in the past decade. In part, this was made possible by the dramatic increase in the number of Germans investing in stocks or mutual funds in the late 1990s (Ewing et al. 2001). Many of these new investors were shocked by the downturn in the German stock market after 2000 and the sudden collapse in stock prices of both "new economy" dot-com companies listed on the Neuer Markt and several blue chip companies on the Frankfurt Stock Exchange. These sudden declines led to revelations that companies had made false and misleading statements in public offering statements and prospectuses. Many shareholders brought suits, in some cases piggybacking on criminal investigations by public authorities that brought evidence of corporate malfeasance to light.

The most prominent shareholder action brought in this period involved Deutsche Telekom. The privatization and public offering of shares in Deutsche Telekom in the late 1990s drew thousands of individual investors into the market and was crucial to what many saw as the dawn of an "equity culture" in Germany. But share prices collapsed in 2001, and shareholders alleged that Deutsche Telekom had knowingly overstated the value of its assets in the public offering prospectuses it issued in 1999 and 2000. Between 2001 and 2003, roughly fifteen thousand investors represented by more than seven hundred attorneys filed over twenty-five hundred suits against Deutsche Telekom, seeking compensation for their losses.

A single judge presiding over the Seventh Commercial Panel of the Frankfurt District Court had exclusive jurisdiction over the cases. Given the absence of class actions or other procedures that could bundle together the flood of claims, all the cases had to be heard separately, and the judge was overwhelmed. The litigation dragged on, and eventually some of the plaintiffs appealed to the Federal Constitutional Court, claiming a denial of justice. While the court rejected their appeal, it did encourage experimentation with some form of collective litigation.

The government responded in 2005 by passing the Capital Markets Model Case Act (Kapitalanleger-Musterverfahrensgesetz, or KapMuG), a landmark law that introduced a novel mechanism for collective litigation through a "model case" procedure. The procedure applies only in the field of securities regulation, in cases where plaintiffs seek compensation for violation of securities laws. It is designed both to expedite judicial process by bundling cases and to facilitate shareholder litigation by reducing litigation costs for individual claimants. If ten or more cases on the same subject matter are filed with a district court, the court can ask an appeals court to designate one of those cases as the "model case." The appeals court appoints a "model claimant," suspends all other cases relating to the same subject matter, and publicizes the name and legal representative of the model claimant (in order to attract additional plaintiffs). The court's rulings on the model case will be binding on all plaintiffs, unless they have withdrawn their claim before the model trial commenced.

The new procedures were put to use for the first time in April 2008, as the first-ever model case was launched, against Deutsche Telekom (Sorge 2008; Kuhr 2008). The case, which is expected to last for several years, is widely viewed as a landmark in German law. Behind the model plaintiff and his attorney, sixteen thousand plaintiffs and roughly nine hundred lawyers wait in the wings to make damage claims based on the outcome of the case (Sorge 2008; Milne 2008). While the advent of the Model Case Act in Germany hardly heralds the advent of American-style securities class actions, it is certainly increasing the interest of shareholders and lawyers in securities litigation. Joachim von Falkenhausen, one of the attorneys at Latham and Watkins, the US-based global law firm representing Deutsche Telekom in the litigation, commented in the *Financial Times,* "We are getting a new type of lawyer in this country that will pursue cases akin to class actions" (Wiesmann 2008). As a result, he explained, companies may choose to settle out of court to avoid the length, expense, and uncertainty of going to trial (ibid.).

Another landmark legal battle involved one of the more spectacular failures of "new economy" companies listed on the Neuer Markt. The flamboyant Haffa brothers founded a media company, EM.TV, which generated great investor enthusiasm and emerged as one of the stars of the Neuer Markt. As the firm grew, it went on an acquisition spree, buying controlling interests in the Muppets and Formula One (Ryan 2003, pp. 441–442). As the markets crashed, it was revealed that the Haffas had published grossly inflated revenue statements in EM.TV prospectuses. They were convicted of criminal offenses and fined heavily (ibid., p. 465; Eckert and Zschäpitz 2004). Subsequently, the new management of the successor company to EM.TV (Constantin Media) brought legal action on behalf of shareholders against two insurance companies—Chubb and Ace Europe—which had carried directors and officers (D&O) liability insurance policies, covering the company against damages resulting from wrongdoing by management. Between August and October 2009, the insurers settled with Constantin Media, agreeing to pay a total of over €48 million (Reuters Deutschland 2009).

More generally, it is clear that shareholder litigation, which had until recently been nearly unheard of, has become a regular feature of the securities regulation landscape. Shareholder associations such as the Association for the Protection of Small Shareholders (Schutzgemeinschaft der Kleinaktionäre) and hundreds of individual shareholders frequently file suits against companies whom they accuse of issuing misleading information (Benoit 2001a, 2001b).[29] Given the absence of effective securities class action mechanisms in Germany, German investors have been extremely active in seeking to lead securities class actions in the United States, often in collaboration with US multinational law firms. Between 1996 and 2007, German investors working with US and large European law firms sought to lead fifty securities class actions in the United States (Woolfe 2007)

There is evidence that market participants believe they will experience an upswing in securities litigation. As high-profile securities cases have attracted attention, they have helped spur the emergence of "a dedicated plaintiffs' securities bar" that will seek to support and encourage securities litigation in the future (Freshfields Bruckhaus Deringer 2005, p. 4). Insurers are certainly concerned with increased litigation risks, or at least are able to convince their clients that they should be. Premiums for D&O insurance in Germany nearly doubled in the months following the global financial crisis of 2008–2009, reflecting heightened concerns that company directors could be sued by irate shareholders as stock values tumbled (Guy Carpenter 2009, p. 9; Darcourt 2009).

The Netherlands

Home to the world's oldest stock exchange, the Netherlands had a deeply entrenched system of securities regulation in place before the European Union became involved in the sector. The Dutch system of securities has been transformed since the early 1980s under the heavy influence of EU securities regulation. Prior to the 1980s, the regulatory regime for securities trading in the Netherlands relied primarily on self-regulation originating from the Amsterdam Stock Exchange (AEX) (Wymeersch 1998, pp. 21–23). For example, before the adoption of the 1985 Securities Trading Act (Wet effectenhandel 1985 S.570), there was no legislation concerning public offerings of new securities (see La Porta, Lopez-de-Silanes, and Shleifer 2006, p. 4). The only rules concerning the publication of a prospectus for a new public offering were to be found in the internal regulations of the Amsterdam Stock Exchange (Van de Vijver 2000, p. 13).[30] Likewise, regulation of other aspects of securities trading was entrusted to self-regulatory bodies associated with the Amsterdam exchange. But beginning in the mid-1980s and accelerating in the 1990s, the combination of economic liberalization and the need to comply with EU securities directives led the Netherlands to both deregulate and reregulate. The traditional system of self-regulation was largely dismantled and replaced with a stricter, more formal and judicialized system of regulation that complied with EU obligations.

Dutch securities markets became increasingly internationalized in the 1980s, as more foreign firms listed shares on the AEX, as more foreigners invested there, and as more Dutch firms also listed securities on London's Euromarkets. Also, trading activity significantly increased on off-exchange, over-the-counter markets, which fell outside the scope of the AEX's self-regulatory regime. With more and more instances of fraudulent activities by brokers and issuers coming to light, it became apparent that the established system of self-regulation was inadequate for the increasingly liberalized markets (Van de Vijver 2000, pp. 1, 13). Meanwhile, EU securities directives began requiring extensive reforms of disclosure rules and of the system of the structure of public authorities tasked with securities market supervision.[31] A series of reforms—including the 1985 Securities Trading Act (Wet effectenhandel S.570), the 1991 Securities Transactions Supervision Act (WTE—Wet toezicht effectenverkeer 1991 S. 141), the 1990 Investment Undertakings Supervision Act (WTB—Wet toezicht beleggingsinstellingen 1990 S.380), the 1995 Securities Transactions Supervision Act (WTE—Wet toezicht effectenverkeer 1995 S.574)—were introduced in order to implement EU securities directives such as the Undertakings for the Collective Investment in Transferable Securities (UCITS) Directive, the 1989 Insider Trading Directive, and the 1993 Investment Services Directive.

The institutional structure of securities supervision was also reformed in order to comply with EU directives. A public regulator for the securities markets—the Securities Board of the Netherlands (Stichting Toezicht Effectenverkeer, or STE)—was established in 1988, and its authority was strengthened substantially in the 1991 and 1995 Securities Transactions Supervision Acts (WTE) and the 1998 Insider Trading Act (Wet gebruik van voorwetenschap). The STE was given the status of an autonomous administrative authority, and supervisory powers were extended substantially.

The internationalization of the Amsterdam exchange accelerated after 2000, when it merged with the Brussels Stock Exchange and the Paris Bourse to form the pan-European exchange Euronext. Meanwhile, the raft of EU securities directives launched in the wake of the FSAP and the Lamfalussy Report required further reforms of the Dutch regulatory regime. In 2002, the STE was replaced by the Authority for Financial Markets (Autoriteit Financiële Markten, or AFM), a unified financial market regulator that was given even more wide-ranging regulatory and enforcement powers. For instance, to comply with the 2003 Prospectus Directive, the authority to approve a prospectus was transferred from the stock exchange (Euronext Amsterdam) to the AFM, and to comply with the 2003 Market Abuse Directive, supervision of disclosure of price sensitive information was shifted from the exchange to the AFM.[32]

But the strengthening of public authorities charged with securities regulation at the expense of self-regulatory bodies has not been the most striking aspect of the change in the Dutch regulatory regime. Even more dramatic have been changes in the realm of private enforcement. Many comparative studies in the 1980s and 1990s emphasized that the Netherlands had a legal culture that discouraged litigation and encouraged pragmatic, consensual resolution of conflicts on various policy issues (Blankenburg 1997, 1998; Bruinsma 2005; Van Waarden 2003). And indeed, until recently, shareholder litigation was rare in the Netherlands. However, in the past decade shareholder groups such as the Vereniging Effectenbezitters (Stockholders Association) have mobilized, taking advantage of new legal opportunities to bring securities litigation against listed companies for various forms of malfeasance and fraud (Van Waarden and Hildebrand 2009, p. 270; Velthuyse and Schlingmann 1995). In light of recent legal developments, amazingly, the land of the polder model and consensual dispute resolution seems poised to emerge as a sort of hub for securities class actions in Europe.

A key to that opening was the introduction of the 2005 Dutch Act on Collective Settlement of Mass Damages (WCAM—Wet collectieve afwikkeling massaschade, Staatsblad 2005, 340). While group litigation in the form of "representative actions" brought by associations (such as consumer groups and shareholder groups) had been available previously under provisions of the Dutch Civil Code (Tzankova and Schleurleer 2009; Van Boom 2009, p. 6), the 2005 WCAM for the first time allowed courts to enforce settlement agreements between representative groups and defendants concerning damage awards. These settlement agreements can be made binding on members of the representative organization unless they opt out of the settlement. The WCAM had been created largely at the suggestion of the pharmaceutical lobby, which wanted a mechanism to bundle individual suits so as to avoid being overwhelmed by a flood of suits being brought by consumers injured by the synthetic hormone DES (Goldhaber 2009; Van

Boom 2009). The WCAM put the Netherlands at the forefront of the development of class action mechanisms in Europe, in that it became the first country to offer a procedure giving courts the power to certify a mass damages settlement agreement and to make that agreement binding on members of the "class" unless they actively opt out.

The WCAM was first put to use in the June 2006 product liability settlement (of €38 million) concerning the hormone DES, and next in a January 2007 securities litigation settlement (of €400 million) involving Dexia Bank. But the potential reach and significance of the WCAM became fully apparent in a third case—a securities class action brought by Dutch and other European shareholders against the energy giant Royal Dutch Shell.

In some sense, the case can be dated back to an extremely forthright e-mail, one that was likely sent in haste and repented at leisure. In 2003, Walter de Vijver, the head of Royal Dutch Shell's oil and gas exploration group, sent to the company's chairman an e-mail in which De Vijver wrote, "I am becoming sick and tired about lying about the extent of our oil reserves" (Macalister 2004). The next year, Shell issued a restatement of its oil reserves, downgrading its "proven" reserves by billions of barrels and sending its stock price tumbling. The leaking of De Vijver's e-mail, along with a series of other revelations, indicated that Shell had been knowingly overstating its reserves, and shareholders headed for court (ibid.).

But which court? Bringing the litigation in the Netherlands had a serious disadvantage: none of the existing procedures for collective actions allowed lawyers or representative associations to bring damage claims on behalf of members of the affected class. The WCAM allows courts to enforce damages settlements agreed between plaintiffs and defendants, but it does not actually allow shareholders to bring damage claims before the courts in the first place. The obvious flaw here from the perspective of plaintiffs is that because they cannot make a claim for damages, the defendants have little incentive to settle—at least not to settle for a large amount. And indeed, this was precisely the point: the WCAM was established to help firms settle mass claims efficiently and was quite intentionally designed so as not to create incentives for American-style class action litigation.

So instead of going directly to the Dutch courts, the plaintiffs' lawyers devised an unprecedented legal strategy that revealed and thus opened up new avenues for securities litigation in Europe. The elegant solution devised by the lawyers representing the shareholders was to join a securities class action before a US court (the US District Court of New Jersey) but to attempt to settle it in the Netherlands under the terms of the new class action settlement provisions available there. As Michael D. Goldhaber explains (2009), "The beauty of the Shell model for European plaintiffs is that it allows them to settle litigation on their home turf while enjoying all the advantages of U.S. actions at the front end of the litigation." To put it another way, the European shareholders put the fear of God into Shell by joining a class action in the United States, where the damage awards can be extremely high, and then offered the firm the option of settling the case in the Netherlands—an option which was attractive for the company and far more convenient for shareholders making claims. In May 2009, the Amsterdam Court of Appeal approved a settlement between Royal Dutch Shell and non-US (mostly European) shareholders, under which Royal Dutch Shell will pay $381 million to a foundation representing institutional investors and other shareholders from nineteen countries (Reding, Han, and Sonoda 2009; Stichting Shell Reserves Compensation Foundation 2009).

With all the transnational legal gymnastics involved in the case, one might assume that it is simply a striking anomaly. However, many observers conclude that the case has set a powerful precedent that may signal a new pathway for European securities litigation. Over the last decade, European shareholders who seek to bring securities class actions against European companies have increasingly turned to US courts.[33] The attractions of joining class actions filed in the United States are obvious, given the potential for large damage awards there. At the same time, European plaintiffs must deal with great inconvenience and expense to litigate and settle cases in the United States. Moreover, for European policy makers and judges, there is something more than mildly distasteful about a state of affairs in which European investors have to rely on US courts to solve what are essentially European problems.

The Shell case was the first instance in which a securities class action brought before a US court was settled in Europe (Taub 2007). The ruling constitutes a watershed because it gives European defendants a way to settle claims brought by groups of European shareholders in Europe and have those settlements enforced across the EU. Essentially, this case opened up what we might call the United States–Amsterdam–

Europe litigation pathway. The case demonstrates that European shareholders can bring securities class action litigation in the United States (in this case in the District Court of New Jersey) and can then settle the case in Amsterdam before a Dutch court. Because of EU rules on mutual recognition of judgments in civil and commercial cases (Regulation EC 44/2001, or the "Brussels I Regulation"), claimants can then enforce damages settlements approved by Dutch courts in courts across Europe. As Goldhaber explains (2008), "If the Dutch courts broadly welcome non-Dutch parties [this procedure] may sire a new line of cases. . . . Perhaps predictably, the Dutch lawyers on both sides of the deal can foresee the Netherlands becoming a Mecca for European class action settlements, in the way that Delaware has become a destination for bankruptcy law. But they are joined in this view by many independent European lawyers and academics." Many lawyers and academics share this view, anticipating that the Dutch courts may emerge as a center for the settlement of securities class actions. By 2006 a group of French investors, the Association of Active Shareholders (Association des actionnaires actifs), turned to the Dutch courts to avail themselves of the Netherlands' opportunities for class actions (which were not available in France). The association filed before a Dutch court a class action against EADS, the parent company of Airbus, after production delays caused share prices to drop by over 25 percent (Gow 2006; *BBC News* 2006).

The more general lesson provided by developments in the Netherlands since the adoption of the 2005 WCAM is that legal entrepreneurs can rapidly transform the legal field when a new opportunity arises. Few could have predicted how a law on the settlement of mass claims that was introduced largely at the behest of pharmaceutical companies would be transformed by entrepreneurial lawyers using a combination of transatlantic litigation and EU rules on the recognition of judgments. A small set of Dutch law firms, such as NautaDutilh, has emerged as specialists in class actions and works to encourage both domestic and foreign clients to bring mass claims before Dutch courts (Goldhaber 2009).

United Kingdom

The City of London is the world's premier financial center and home to by far the largest and most internationalized equities markets in Europe. To assess the impact that European integration and EU securities regulation have had on the British regulatory regime for securities, we must first recognize that British securities regulation was moving, to some degree at least, in the direction of American-style adversarial legalism before the EU took major steps in this direction. British securities markets went through a cycle of economic liberalization and reregulation in the 1980s that presaged what was to happen later at the pan-European level. Thus, EU securities regulation initially had a less marked impact in the United Kingdom than in the member states discussed above, because the UK was already moving in direction the EU would later encourage.

Scholars such as Steven Vogel (1996) and Michael Moran (1991) have detailed the story of the shift in the UK in the mid-1980s from the traditional model of securities regulation based largely on informal, self-regulation among a restricted clique of insiders to a more strictly enforced, rule-based model. In the autumn of 1986, the UK government dramatically deregulated and reregulated British financial markets. First, with the so-called Big Bang the London Stock Exchange deregulated commissions on stock transactions, opened membership to banks and foreign financial institutions, and eliminated other restrictive practices in the operation of financial service firms. Two weeks later Parliament adopted the Financial Services Act, which established new structures for regulatory supervision, including the quasi-governmental Securities and Investments Board (SIB), and introduced a host of detailed new rules.[34] In matters of regulation, the Financial Services Act "replaced the informal with the formal, the flexible with the rigid and the personal with the legalistic" (S. Vogel 1996, p. 93).

Compared to the cozy system of self-regulation based on moral suasion that had prevailed previously, the new system—with its proliferation of detailed rules and new investor rights to sue (Financial Services Act, Article 62)—involved a marked shift toward American-style adversarial legalism. As Vogel puts it so eloquently (1996, p. 108), after the Big Bang and the Financial Services Act "the gentlemen's luncheon was replaced by the power breakfast, civilized rivalry was replaced by cutthroat competition, and discrete self-regulation was replaced by a nightmare from America: the proliferation of regulatory bodies, the endless creation of rules, and an invasion of lawyers."

But for all the change wrought by the Big Bang and the Financial Services Act, much more change, moving far further in the direction of adversarial legalism, was yet to come. And much of that change was to be animated by pressures from the EU. Though the Financial Services Act did create a statutory framework for securities regulation, within that framework the system continued to rely heavily on traditional patterns of self-regulation (Andenas and Kenyon-Slade 1993, p. 150). The Securities and Investments Board relied on self-regulating organizations (SROs)—such as the Securities and Futures Authority (SFA) and the Financial Intermediaries, Managers, and Brokers Regulatory Association (FIMBRA)—as the primary regulators in their respective issue areas. Policy makers and market players continued to see self-regulatory approaches as the most effective form of regulation, and enforcement remained lax (Fishman 1991, pp. 184–186).

Coming into compliance with EU securities regulations in the late 1980s and early 1990s required less reform in the UK than in other member states. As a major formalization and juridification of securities regulation had been pushed through already with the Big Bang reforms, complying with the EU directives usually required only minor alterations. As Ferran (2004) explains, the UK already had a "mature legal framework to support its equity market culture prior to significant EU regulatory activity in the field, and so changes required during the 1980s and 1990s in order to conform national law to EU requirements were usually more by way of adjustment to the detail than fundamental reform" (p. 40). But even in this period, it became apparent that the EU was pushing regulation in an even more legalistic direction than the UK's Financial Services Act had. For instance, throughout the late 1980s the British government continued to resist key elements of the Commission's proposal for a prospectus directive. The UK favored greater reliance on self-regulation and opposed the strict, uniform disclosure regime that the Commission advocated (Warren 2003, pp. 93–94), and the UK worked to water down the directive before it was finally adopted in 1989 (Council Directive 89/298). Likewise, the UK resisted for years the Commission's 1989 proposal for a thirteenth directive on takeover bids (COM[90] 416 final),[35] which was designed to promote transparency and protect the interests of minority holders in case of takeover bids on listed companies. British critics argued that the Commission's approach would encourage a more legalistic, US-style approach to regulation, a style "plagued by excessive bureaucracy, inflexibility, and constant tactical litigation that would imperil the entire [British] regulatory agenda" (Mace 1991) and emphasized that up to that point "the self-regulatory basis of the City Code [had] shielded British take-over regulation from such infirmities" (ibid.).

The UK did introduce some reforms in this period to come into compliance with EU securities directives. The Criminal Justice Act 1993 reformed British insider-dealing rules to comply with the EU's Insider Trading Directive (89/592/EEC), extending the prohibition on insider trading beyond shares to other securities, such as futures and derivatives, and extending disclosure requirements (Fisher and Bewsey 1997, p. 289; Alexander 2001). The 1995 Investment Services Regulations implemented the EU Investment Services Directive (93/22/EEC) and the Capital Adequacy Directive (93/6/EEC). These reforms introduced the "passporting" process into the UK and imposed new reporting requirements on investment firms. But despite such changes and minor reforms of governance structures, such as the creation of a new SRO (the Personal Investment Authority), the approach to governance continued to be based on self-regulation within a statutory framework.

This fragmented self-regulatory structure proved confusing, ineffective, and prone to regulatory capture. When the Labour government took office in 1997, Chancellor of the Exchequer Gordon Brown announced a dramatic reorganization of financial market regulation. Key to this reform was an effort to centralize regulation, leading to the establishment of the Financial Services Authority (FSA) in 1997. It became fully operational in December 2001, after the Financial Services and Markets Act (FSMA) of 2000 came into force. The FSMA introduced a comprehensive reregulation of UK securities markets, replacing the patchwork of self-regulating organizations with a centralized system under single, powerful financial regulator—the FSA (Toube 2001, pp. 1–8).[36] A division of the Financial Services Authority, the UK Listings Authority (UKLA), took over from the London Stock Exchange as the listing authority for the United Kingdom. The FSMA introduced new legislation on disclosure and market abuse and gave the UKLA far wider powers to enforce market abuse and insider dealing rules (Fearnley and Hines 2003; Toube 2001; Sabalot and Everett 2004; Blair 2005 p. 12).

Much of the Financial Services Authority's work over the past decade has concentrated on implementing directives and regulations associated with the EU's Financial Services Action Plan (FSAP) and the Lamfalussy process. The Financial Services Authority reports that 70 percent of its policymaking effort is driven by EU initiatives.[37] Implementing the FSAP in the UK required extensive reforms of existing regulations (HM Treasury, Financial Services Authority and Bank of England 2004), and these reforms have substantially expanded the legal bases for shareholder litigation (Adams, Tait, and Jopson 2005). For instance, implementing the EU's Market Abuse Directive (2003/6/EC) required broadening the definition of "insider dealing" in the UK, imposing stricter disclosure and reporting requirements on financial sector professionals (HM Treasury and Financial Services Authority 2004, p. 3; Hansen 2004, p. 191), and strengthening of the FSA's enforcement powers.[38] Likewise, the Transparency Directive required substantial changes to the FSA's listing rules that concerned continuing reporting obligations and forced issuers on regulated markets to disclose new information on semiannual reports and interim financial statements.[39] The Markets in Financial Instruments Directive required substantial changes to the FSA's *Conduct of Business Sourcebook* for regulated firms, in terms of their organizational structure and conduct of business rules (FSA 2005, 2008, 2009).

EU securities regulation continues to press the UK's regulatory regime to adopt stricter, more legalistic approaches to governance. In recent years, the UK's Financial Services Authority has consistently advocated a "principles-based" or "outcomes-based" approach focused on adhering to underlying principles rather than rigid compliance with rules (FSA 2007). The FSA has implicitly—and sometimes explicitly—criticized the EU for its more rigid, less pragmatic approach and blamed the persistence of highly detailed rules in the UK on requirements imposed by EU directives (FSA 2007, pp. 10, 20). The Law Society of England and Wales has argued that the implementation of the MiFID and transparency directives through the Lamfalussy regulatory process has produced "over-prescriptive" rules (Law Society of England and Wales 2005, p. 6).

The proliferation of detailed regulatory requirements and investor rights has changed not only the "law on the books" in the UK but the "law in action" as well. The Financial Services Authority has emerged as a robust enforcer of UK and EU securities regulation. Between 2002 and 2009, the FSA imposed fines totaling over 127 million pounds on violators of securities laws. In 2008, it imposed its greatest number of fines in one year, and it has imposed five of its ten highest fines since the 2008 financial crisis.[40] In its 2008 report on securities litigation, PriceWaterhouseCoopers concluded (2008, p. 54), "The UK's Financial Services Authority (FSA) is arguably becoming more aggressive and adopting more SEC-type tactics in its battle against insider trading and financial crimes."

But these good deeds have not gone unpunished. The FSA has found itself increasingly dragged into litigation before the Financial Services and Market Tribunal by firms who wish to appeal the fines issued by the FSA. In 2004, Callum McCarthy, chairman of the FSA, bemoaned the increase of business litigation brought against regulators, warning that it was threatening to turn the United Kingdom into a "litigious society" like the United States. He emphasized that increasing business litigation against the FSA would result in greater costs and delays in the regulatory process, concluding, "The UK has traditionally enjoyed over North America the advantage of being a less litigious society. There is much to be lost if that advantage is eroded." (Orr 2004).

Private shareholder litigation too has become commonplace in Britain. As the *Daily Telegraph* reported in 2002, "No financial scandal is complete these days without a host of action groups, law firms and consumer champions offering to fight the good fight on behalf of angry investors or policyholders" (Farrow 2002). In the past decade, financial scandals involving Equitable Life, Independent Insurance, split-capital investment trusts, Railtrack, Northern Rock, and Royal Bank of Scotland, among many others, were followed by litigation brought on behalf of investors. Such litigation was facilitated by the dramatic reforms of the UK's Civil Procedure Rules in 1999, which were designed to facilitate multiparty litigation (Hodges 2009a). The UK Shareholders Association (UKSA), the leading national association of small shareholders, has played a central role in promoting shareholder activism and in supporting "action groups" that launch civil suits against particular firms. Also, with the growth of the securities litigation bar, a number of lawyers and firms have specialized in representing shareholders.

However, the rise of private securities litigation certainly has not been smooth. The Railtrack litigation, the largest class action–style group litigation in British history, ended in failure in 2005. Over fifty thousand disgruntled shareholders in Railtrack, a rail infrastructure company that was privatized in 1996 and that later became insolvent, banded together to pursue litigation through the Railtrack Private Shareholders Action Group (Robins 2005). Ultimately, however, a High Court judge rejected the shareholders' claim, finding that they could not establish malice on the part of the government. When Class Law, one of the law firms that had pioneered collective litigation in the UK and had been involved in high-profile investor actions, folded in 2006, the firm's founder explained that it could not attract enough clients for its group actions (Goldhaber 2008; Dyson 2006).

Despite the travails experienced by the early movers in the field of class actions, many market players expect private securities litigation to remain a potent force in the UK. A recent survey of European executives and lawyers conducted by the Economist Intelligence Unit found that Britain offered "the most fertile ground in Europe" for the emergence of collective litigation, with 59 percent of respondents expecting collective litigation to take root in the UK in the near future (Economist Intelligence Unit 2007, pp. 4, 12; Peel 2007; Werdigier 2007). Respondents indicated that financial services sector was one of the industries most likely to be affected by group litigation (Economist Intelligence Unit 2007, p. 13).

The English securities litigation bar continues to grow and to develop linkages with American securities plaintiffs' lawyers. In 2007, the prominent American plaintiffs class action firm Cohen, Milstein, Hausfeld, and Toll established an office in London, citing securities as one of the fields in which it expected to take on plaintiffs (Garamfalvi 2007; Goldhaber 2008).[41] British financial services firms clearly perceive a heightened litigation risks and are purchasing far more D&O insurance as they become more frequent targets of collective actions. A 2009 survey of British companies conducted by the Association of Insurance and Risk Managers (AIRMIC) and consulting firm Advisen Ltd. found that purchases of D&O coverage by UK firms were at unprecedented levels and that the financial services sector was nearly the biggest purchaser, with financial firms' annual D&O premiums at an average of £12.4 million (AIRMIC and Advisen 2009, Hays 2009; Bradford 2009).

Conclusion

Across Europe, securities regulation has undergone a fundamental transformation over the past two decades. Before the mid-1980s, securities markets were subject to national regulatory regimes that restricted market entry and relied on informal self-regulation by sheltered cliques of established market players. Of course, national regulatory regimes varied in many ways, but these were variations on a common theme of self-regulation, lax supervision by public authorities (where regulators even existed), minimal disclosure requirements, and a paucity of rules on insider trading. Shareholders had few rights, and shareholder litigation was extraordinarily rare.

Today, securities regulation in the European Union has been substantially harmonized around a model based on Eurolegalism. National regulators collaborate in implementing a voluminous and detailed body of EU securities regulation that has largely supplanted national regulation. Nearly all aspects of securities regulation—including rules concerning admission to listing on a stock exchange, disclosure and transparency for listed companies, insider trading, market manipulation and other forms of market abuse, and the activities of investment advisors and other financial intermediaries—are subject in some way to EU directives and regulations. Informal self-regulation has been replaced by strict legal requirements enforced by significantly strengthened national securities regulators and increasingly by private shareholder litigation (Enriques and Volpin 2007). Once unheard of, shareholder lawsuits are now commonplace.

A "litigation support structure" (Epp 1998) for securities litigation has emerged in Europe, a structure involving American and European law firms, small shareholders associations, and institutional investors. More recently, new players have emerged on the scene, including third-party investors who finance large-scale litigation (Hodges 2009c) and international, full-service investor consultancies, such as the Brussels-based Deminor Group, which specialize in grouping together investors from across Europe to launch "damage recovery" actions.[42] Entrepreneurial securities lawyers and associations representing shareholders have pioneered a variety of channels and techniques to seek compensation for disgruntled shareholders and have brought civil litigation in both American and European courts against firms, for disclosure and transparency failings and other violations of securities rules. In response, listed companies have gone on the defensive, buying more directors and officers insurance and otherwise working to defend themselves against litigation. The trends in EU securities regulation described above show no signs of abating. In the wake of the 2008 financial crisis, the EU has again asserted itself with the Commission by proposing a directive (COM[2009] 207 final) that would impose new registration and disclosure rules on hedge funds, private equity firms, and other "alternative investment fund managers," whose activities are now largely unregulated by either national or European law.

The transformation of securities regulation in Europe cannot be attributed entirely to the process of European integration, but it is unimaginable without it (Moloney 2002, pp. 4–5; Ferran 2004, p. 40). The European Union's drive to integrate European financial markets, coupled with the EU regulatory process, has led EU policy makers to engage in a cycle of deregulation and reregulation, which has dismantled traditional national patterns of securities regulation and replaced them with a new, highly legalistic regime backed by public enforcement and increased opportunities for private enforcement. Certainly, developments in domestic politics within European states and international forces—developments emanating primarily from the United States—played important roles. But even these factors were intertwined with the influence of the European Union, as EU pressure helped domestic reformers overcome entrenched opposition at home and as EU liberalization measures made it possible for American law firms and investors to emerge as significant players in European securities markets.

American law, American law firms, and American institutional investors have all played an important role in the development of the EU's regulatory regime for securities. American securities regulation was clearly salient in the minds of reformers. But the American model, with its heavy reliance on shareholder class actions, repelled as many market players and policy makers as it attracted (Peel 2007; Goldhaber 2009). In recent years, American law firms, American investors, and American courts have come to play a greater direct role in European securities regulation. Large-scale American investors, from pension funds such as CalPERS (California Public Employees' Retirement System) to investment banks such as Goldman Sachs, have played a key role in spreading shareholder activism to Europe (Kissane 1997; Astier 2006). American law firms play prominent roles in European securities markets, advising clients in many of Europe's largest initial public offerings and mergers and acquisitions. These firms bring with them legal practices honed on US markets, practices that lean more in the direction of adversarial legalism than might strictly be required by EU directives (Kelemen and Sibbitt 2004). Securities enforcement too has become a transatlantic affair. As restrictions on securities class actions in the United States increased, American plaintiffs law firms—such as New York's Milberg, Weiss, Bershad, and Schulman; Schiffrin and Barroway; Murray, Frank, and Sailer; Bryan Cave; and Cohen, Milstein, Hausfeld, and Toll—saw growth opportunities in Europe, where lawmakers were working to facilitate more collective litigation (Jacoby 2005; Peel 2007). American courts have also become directly involved in European securities enforcement as more European investors, working through networks of European and American law firms, seek redress before American courts.

Cornerstone Research, in conjunction with the Stanford Law School Securities Class Action Clearinghouse, tracks securities class action filings against foreign corporations (i.e., those with non-US headquarters) and has developed an index that tracks the number of filings against foreign corporations relative to the total number of filings in the United States. Cornerstone notes a near doubling of filings against foreign corporations, most of which are European, over the past decade. Between 1997 and 2003 there were, on average, 6.8 filings against foreign corporations annually. Between 2004 and 2008, there were 13.3 per year. The year 2008 witnessed the greatest number of filings against foreign corporations on record, with 31 filings against foreign corporations, representing 13.8 percent of the total filings in the United States (Cornerstone Research 2009, p. 7).[43]

Increasing use of American courts by European investors in turn generates pressure on European lawmakers and judges to find ways to facilitate collective litigation by shareholders in Europe—a phenomena we saw at work in the Royal Dutch Shell litigation described above. It is unseemly to air Europe's dirty laundry in America, and litigation conducted in the United States represents lost business for the European legal services industry. Above all, European business leaders prefer to see such cases resolved "at home," to avoid the massive awards sometimes handed out by American juries. Ultimately, class actions may come to Europe, not because Europeans want to emulate American law, but because they want to avoid American courts. Policy makers and legal practitioners are seeking to develop their own approach to collective litigation that addresses the issues which US class actions address, but in a distinctly European fashion.

Though European integration and EU securities regulation have had a deep impact on regulation in all member states, this impact has not been uniform (Ferran 2004, pp. 35–46). The EU has forced the greatest changes in those states that previously had in place the weakest, most informal and insular regimes—such as Germany and the Netherlands. In states such as France and in particular the United Kingdom, where moves were already under way to open market access, strengthen public regulators, and increase transparency and shareholder rights, EU regulation did not require as profound changes as in Germany and the Netherlands—at least not initially. Nevertheless, it is clear that even in the UK—the clear national leader in terms of reform of securities regulation—the EU has forced significant changes. In 1986, the Big Bang and the Financial Services Act heralded a new age in UK securities regulation, an age in which regulation was to be more formal and transparent and to better protect shareholder rights. As noted above, Steven Vogel (1996) captured the critical view of these changes, explaining that "discrete self-regulation was replaced by a nightmare from America: the proliferation of regulatory bodies, the endless creation of rules, and an invasion of lawyers" (p. 108). In the years since then, under the weight of EU requirements, the UK's regime for securities regulation has become far more rigid and juridified. In retrospect, critics would view the supposed "nightmare from America" described by Vogel in the mid-1980s as merely an innocent prelude to the nightmare from Brussels that was to come.

The irony of EU securities regulation is that this nightmare of rules and lawyers was necessary to achieve the dream of a vibrant, pan-European securities market. Defenders of the EU approach could point out that extensive disclosure requirements and measures designed to facilitate private enforcement—key elements of the supposed nightmare—are in fact closely associated with the development of strong, well-capitalized stock markets (La Porta, Lopez-de-Silanes, and Shleifer 2006; La Porta et al. 1997).

Looking to the future, we are almost certain to see a greater emphasis on enforcement (Langevoort 2005, p. 25), which in turn will encourage further strengthening of national regulators and increasing opportunities for private enforcement via the courts. In response to the financial crisis, securities regulation is experiencing dynamic familiar to scholars of EU regulatory politics. A large body of European law had been put into place, with implementation left largely in national hands. This inevitably lead to differences in implementation and widely publicized (and in this case catastrophic) national-level implementation failures, leading in turn to calls for strengthening enforcement across the European Union.

These failures in turn lead to calls for strengthening enforcement across the European Union. EU leaders finally responded to these calls in September 2010 by establishing a new pan-European securities regulator, the European Securities and Markets Authority, with unprecedented rule-making and enforcement powers.

CHAPTER 5

Competition Policy

In the staid world of European Union (EU) regulation, competition policy has long held a kind of rock star status. Over the years, EU competition officials have gone head to head with corporate giants the likes of IBM, Nestlé, Boeing, General Electric, Vodafone, Pfizer, and Microsoft. With its "dawn raids," epic legal battles, and multimillion euro fines, competition policy has long been one of the few sources of drama in EU regulation, demonstrating to those who doubted the EU's strength that at least in the field of competition policy there were indeed muscles in Brussels. The Treaty of Rome, subsequent legislation, and judicial decisions have empowered the European Commission to break up cartels, prohibit anticompetitive behavior, regulate mergers, and control state aid (subsidies) to industry.[1] Beginning in the early 1960s and accelerating from the mid-1980s onward, competition officials in the European Commission exercised powers that their colleagues in other policy domains could only dream of. While officials in other European Commission directorates struggled to coax and cajole member states to implement EU law, officials in the Commission's Directorate General for Competition (known earlier as DG IV and now as DG Comp or DG Competition) could implement and enforce EU competition law directly against offending firms. Commission competition officials could conduct so-called dawn raids, entering the premises of suspect companies and seizing documents and records; officials could penalize offending companies with massive fines, up to 10 percent of their annual turnover. And by the 1990s, officials could grant or withhold approval for mergers between some of the world's largest companies.

The US system of antitrust regulation has always served as an important reference point for policy makers in Europe, and EU competition policy has always reflected some aspects of American antitrust regulation. However, in designing the EU competition regime, policy makers initially rejected central aspects of the American system, such as its heavy reliance on private enforcement and its narrow focus on using a consumer welfare test to assess anticompetitive conduct. Instead, EU policy makers built a system based largely on a distinctly European "administrative control model" of competition policy developed by European legal scholars and economists in the 1920s and 1930s. In this model, regulators were granted the discretion to balance the promotion of competition against other government priorities, such as unemployment, technological innovation, support for small- and medium-sized enterprises, and regional or sectoral crises (Gerber 1998, p. 422). The European Commission stood at the core of this system. While its decisions were subject to judicial review, the Commission's regulatory process was opaque and politicized, and in practice the Commission enjoyed considerable discretion in implementing competition policy.

The EU's approach to competition policy has evolved significantly since the mid-1980s, and its development presents a clear case of the rise of Eurolegalism as a mode of governance. First, the EU competition regime has been heavily juridified. Since the 1990s, the European Court of Justice (ECJ) and the Court of First Instance (CFI) have pressed the Commission to increase the transparency of its regulatory process and to provide more robust, legally defensible justifications for its decisions. As a result, today the behavior of regulators, market participants, and their legal advisors is all conditioned by the prospect of rigorous judicial review. In other words, EU and national competition policies now operate in the shadow of potential litigation. Second, changes with regard to private enforcement have been even more dramatic. Traditionally, private enforcement of competition policy was almost unheard of in Europe.[2] However, when the EU introduced a package of reforms in 2004 to "modernize" competition policy, a central goal was to move the EU away from a centralized administrative control model and toward a decentralized private enforcement model, in which private litigation before national courts would play a central role (Wigger 2007, p. 99). As Competition Commissioner Mario Monti explained when proposing the reforms, "It is our aim that companies and individuals should increasingly feel encouraged to make use of private action before national courts in order to defend the subjective rights conferred on them by the EC competition rules" (Monti 2001). The modernization package and the Commission's more recent efforts to remove remaining impediments to private enforcement reflect a determined effort to harness private litigation as the means of enforcing EU policy (Woods, Sinclair and Ashton 2004). This shift in the EU's approach is having profound implications for member state competition regimes, as they too have been pressured to shift to a regulatory regime based on adversarial legalism.[3]

On the surface, there is something highly puzzling about these developments. Competition policy has long been the jewel in the crown of EU regulation, the apotheosis of Commission regulatory power. Why then would the European Commission willingly surrender its prized possession, devolving power on national competition authorities, courts, and private litigants?

Some might argue that these changes were introduced in response to political or competitive pressure from the United States. Certainly, the US model of antitrust has played a powerful role in shaping European competition policy, particularly in the immediate post–World War II years (Dumez and Jeunemaître 1996; Quack and Djelic 2005). The US experience continues to inform debates on EU competition policy but is invoked as often as an example of what to avoid as of what to emulate (Van Gerven 2005, p. 3). Moreover, EU competition policy experienced its biggest shifts toward American-style adversarial legalism only in the last few years, at a time when American political influence in Europe was weakest and when the United States itself was moving away from private enforcement of antitrust.[4] Had regulatory competition been driving changes in competition policy, we might have expected to see countries across the EU relax competition regulations in order to attract firms and employment. Instead, member state regulations have converged on an ever-stricter approach to antitrust enforcement, following the EU model (Van Waarden and Drahos 2002, p. 915; Wigger and Nölke 2007, p. 506).

Some have argued that the 2004 competition policy modernization reforms reflect the broader shift toward "new modes of governance" in

EU regulation (Lehmkuhl 2008). However, an approach to regulation based on strict judicial oversight of detailed legal norms backed by private enforcement is hardly what policy makers have in mind when they speak of flexible new modes of governance. More commonly, observers have accepted the Commission's own rhetoric and interpreted the 2004 modernization reforms as a radical decentralization of authority, initiated in response to national governments' demands to repatriate regulatory power from Brussels (in EU parlance such claims are framed as demands for greater "subsidiarity"). This explanation does not stand up to close scrutiny. The perspective presented in this book suggests another interpretation entirely. The modernization of competition policy actually aims to strengthen EU control over competition policy across Europe. The new system is dressed up in the rhetoric of decentralization, but it actually allows the EU to co-opt and harness national competition authorities, national courts, and regulated firms and their lawyers all as the agents of EU law (Wilks 2005a, p. 438, 2007; Riley 2003; Wigger and Nölke 2007, p. 502).

Viewing recent developments in EU competition policy through the broader framework provided in this book suggests that we are observing a wholesale shift away from a traditional, European administrative model centered around the Commission and toward a model of governance based on Eurolegalism, in which private enforcement before national courts will proliferate. As in the other cases we examine in this book, the shift toward adversarial legalism in competition policy has emerged in response to changing political and economic conditions in the European Union. Economic liberalization associated with the 1992 single market initiative, along with the expansion of the European market that came with EU enlargement, presented serious challenges to the traditional administrative approach to competition policy. The fragmented political structure of the EU and the combination of a powerful judiciary and an inadequately resourced EU executive made it attractive for EU policy makers to turn to an approach to regulation that relied heavily on decentralized enforcement by private actors.

The move toward adversarial legalism in competition policy is likely to have broader repercussions for the structure of the European economy. An extensive academic literature on varieties of capitalism shows that many continental European countries have structured their economies around a distinctive "Rhenish" variety of capitalism. Various forms of cross- shareholding and interfirm collaboration play a central role in this model. Many of these practices violate understandings of fair competition that prevail in the Anglo-Saxon variety of capitalism. However, European competition regulators have permitted them, viewing them as crucial to enabling firms to focus on long-term strategies that ultimately benefit innovation, efficiency, employment, and broader conceptions of the public interest.

The rise of Eurolegalism in competition policy, particularly the new emphasis on private enforcement, threatens to undermine key aspects of this model. In enforcing EU competition law, private actors will not conduct the same sort of balancing of competition norms with the broader public interest considerations that national regulators or the European Commission did. Instead, private actors will bring litigation when it serves their private interests to do so, basing their claims—as new EU regulations require—on a much narrower microeconomic analysis of the alleged anticompetitive practice. The threat of private litigation and the inability of public authorities to shield firms from being sued creates a far more unpredictable regulatory environment. As Angela Wigger and Andreas Nölke note (2007, pp. 489, 500), this volatility makes it far more risky for firms to engage in the sort of strategic long-term investments and interfirm collaborations that have long been staples of the Rhenish variety of capitalism. The threat of private litigation will cast a long shadow over this variety of capitalism—and some plants do not grow well in the shade.

The chapter begins by reviewing the traditional European model of competition policy as it developed in the early twentieth century. We then discuss the development of EU competition policy from the late 1950s through the impact of the modernization reforms of 2004, emphasizing how the European Union has embraced an approach to competition policy based on Eurolegalism. The next section examines the impact of EU competition policy on national competition policy in the Netherlands, the United Kingdom, France, and Germany. The conclusion assesses the significant normative implications of the spread of an approach to competition policy rooted in Eurolegalism.

The Traditional European Model of Competition Policy

To appreciate the impact the European Union has had on the development of competition policy in Europe, we must begin by considering the traditional model of competition law in Europe. Many observers and scholars have treated competition policy in Europe as a postwar American import (Dumez and Jeunemaître 1996; Djelic 2002). According to this view, competition policy—or antitrust—was largely foreign to the European tradition, in which cartels and other forms of interfirm collaboration were tolerated or actively promoted by governments.[5] The United States, as postwar hegemon and funder of the Marshall Plan, thrust its antitrust model on European governments, who reluctantly accepted a mild version of it.

While it is true that the United States played a vital role in the development of competition policy at the national and EU level in postwar Europe, this is only part of the story. EU competition policy and the competition policies that emerged at the national level in Germany, France, the UK, the Netherlands, and other west European states were also influenced by a distinctly European tradition of competition policy. While European governments had little practical experience with operating competition policy regimes,[6] there was an extensive academic debate and an intellectual framework setting out a European model of competition policy, with means and aims distinct from the American model. US pressure was vital in pushing European policy makers to introduce new competition laws, but the laws and policy regimes they introduced reflected the distinctive European model of competition policy (Gerber 2001, p. 1–10).

The European competition policy tradition has its roots in debates among academics and policy makers, debates that spread across Europe between the 1890s and the 1920s. Academic debate emerged first in Austria and was then developed by German legal scholars and economists. By the 1920s, the need for competition law was being debated in several European countries, and the first national competition law in Europe was adopted in Germany in 1923, followed quickly by Sweden and Norway in 1925 and 1926 (Gerber 2001, pp. 155–159). By the close of the decade, international organizations such as the International Parliamentary Union were fostering a pan-European debate on the importance of strengthening competition policy (Gerber 2001, pp. 160–161).

However, with the Great Depression, the rise of fascism, and the outbreak of war, nascent competition law regimes in Germany and elsewhere crumbled. The Great Depression sparked greater suspicion of unregulated markets. Governments tolerated and in many cases actively supported the formation of cartels. Support for cartels and trusts strengthened during World War II, as national planning replaced competition and governments turned to cartels and other corporatist arrangements to increase their control over production (Dumez and Jeunemaître 1996). However, even during this period, a group of liberal critics of the Nazi regime who were associated with the Freiburg School met secretly and developed an "ordoliberal" vision of society, a vision in which competition policy played a central role (Quack and Djelic 2005, p. 258).

In the ordoliberal view, unregulated capitalism had been in part responsible for the rise of fascism. In the absence of government regulation, powerful cartels could abuse their economic power, ultimately threatening the economy and democracy itself. The ordoliberals advocated an active form of competition policy in which government regulators intervened to manage competition, in accordance with strict legal norms. While the American Chicago School approach to antitrust called on regulators to focus on consumer prices as the single yardstick in assessing anticompetitive conduct, the ordoliberals emphasized a range of long-term economic and social goals. The impact of commercial practices on consumer prices was important, but regulators also had to take into account broader public goals, such as limiting the concentration of economic power and promoting employment and innovation (Gerber 1998; Dumez and Jeunemaître 1996; Wigger and Nölke 2007; Budzinski 2003).

While advocates of the Freiburg School had kept the alive the embers of the European competition law tradition, their ideas remained on the fringe of European politics in the immediate aftermath of the war. As west European governments set about rebuilding their economies after the war, the mainstream view was that cartels, interfirm networks, and monopolies were useful partners. Many anticompetitive practices were viewed as perfectly legitimate and were even encouraged by governments (McGowan 2000, p. 118).

This approach did not sit well with the United States. Domestically, the United States had pioneered aggressive antitrust policies beginning in the 1880s. After World War II, as part of its broader free trade agenda, the United States sought to promote the spread of antitrust policy internationally. Leading US officials saw antitrust as vital to breaking up European cartels that would otherwise stand in the way of free trade and, not coincidentally, in the way of US exporters. The United States placed direct pressure on occupied Germany and on the Allied powers to introduce antitrust policies (Gerber 2003, p. 172).

In the late 1940s and 1950s, the combination of US pressure and changing domestic political conditions triggered a wave of new antitrust legislation in Europe. By the end of the 1950s, Austria, Belgium, Denmark, Finland, France, Germany, the Netherlands, Norway, Sweden, and the UK had all adopted national competition policies (Dumez and Jeunemaître 1996, p. 221; Gerber 2003, p. 172; Martin 1998). US pressure was crucial in stimulating the rapid introduction of new competition laws in Europe but did not lead to a wholesale adoption of the American model. European policy makers flatly rejected the American emphasis on judicial control and enforcement by private parties (Gerber 1998, p. 429). Instead, when faced with US demands to introduce antitrust legislation, European governments created regulatory regimes rooted in the European competition law tradition developed in the 1920s and 1930s, a tradition which differed in fundamental ways from the American model. Each national system was of course distinctive, and the German competition law regime was a clear outlier. Nevertheless, all the European systems shared enough basic similarities that we can identify a coherent "European model" of competition law in the early postwar decades.

The European model of competition policy was an administrative control model in which competition legislation granted regulators wide discretion to regulate competition in the public interest. This model differed from the American antitrust model in a number of respects. First, postwar European competition laws were based on a so-called abuse model rather than an American-style prohibition model. Particular categories of activities or arrangements (such as cartels) were not prohibited as a general matter. Business conduct would be restricted only if regulators deemed it to be abusive and harmful to the public interest. This approach provided considerable latitude to government regulators, because it was they who had the power to determine whether business conduct was abusive and warranted punishment.[7]

The combination of vague legal norms, discretionary enforcement, and politicization gave political elites leverage in negotiating with industry. Policy makers generally worked cooperatively with business, trying to steer businesses' conduct while holding in the background the threat that policy makers could use their discretion to bring an enforcement action if need be. For administrators to maintain this flexibility and leverage in dealing with industry, it was crucial that they maintain exclusive control over enforcement and limit the role of judicial review. To this end, private enforcement actions by competitors or consumer groups were permitted very rarely and only under extremely restricted conditions. While private enforcement of antitrust had played a central role in the American model, private enforcement of competition law in Europe was almost nonexistent. Also, in practice, judicial review of regulatory decisions was infrequent, as regulators and regulated industries settled disputes through negotiation.

The major exception to the prevailing European model of competition was found in Germany. The German system was similar to other European systems in that it concentrated authority in the hands of a public regulator the Federal Cartel Office (Bundeskartellamt, or BKA). However, the German system differed with regard to the principles and procedures that guided regulators, and the rigor of enforcement. The BKA was not granted broad discretion to regulate competition in the "public interest" as competition regulators in other European systems did. Instead, the BKA was called on to apply the letter of the law as established in the 1958 Law against Restraints on Competition (Gesetz gegen Wettbewerbsbeschränkungen, or GWB). The BKA was required to state clear reasons for its decisions, and these decisions could then be appealed in court. The BKA was granted far more independence than were competition regulators in other European countries. The BKA was also given the authority and the resources necessary to apply competition law vigorously, and did so. In short, the BKA was far more powerful, independent, and rigorous than its counterparts in other states and German competition policy was by far the strictest in Europe.

Clearly, there were many differences between the various national competition regimes that emerged in Europe in the 1940s and 1950s, and the German regime was a particular outlier. Nevertheless, all the regimes, including the German, bore hallmarks of the general European model of competition policy, with its roots in economic and legal thought of the 1920s and 1930s. While US demands that European countries introduce competition policies certainly played a role, it is striking that no European country opted for the US model of antitrust law, which was based on a strict prohibition regime and extensive private enforcement. These early developments will appear all the more striking when we observe what has happened in the last decade. West European governments resisted the Americanization of their competition policies in the 1950s, when the United States dominated much of the Continent. Yet today the EU is succeeding where the United States failed and promoting the spread of American-style competition policy, with an emphasis on rigorous microeconomic analysis, strict judicial control, and widespread private enforcement.

The Development of EU Competition Policy

In the years after World War II, just as competition policies were being introduced at the national level, a parallel set of developments was occurring at the European Union level. Since the very launch of the European Communities, competition policy has always enjoyed a special status (McGowan and Wilks 1995). The founders of European integration recognized that a robust, supranational competition policy was necessary to break down barriers between national economies. Without a supranational competition policy, dominant players in national markets might abuse their market power to quash would-be competitors from neighboring states, and cartels could carve up the European market.

EU-level competition policy—first in the European Coal and Steel Community (ECSC) and later in the European Economic Community (EEC)—initially combined aspects German ordoliberalism and the general European model of competition with elements of the American model (Quack and Djelic 2005; Büthe and Swank 2007). While the imprint of European traditions clearly remains to this day, over the years the economic and institutional environment of EU competition policy has led EU policy makers to shift their approach closer to American practice. As EU competition policy has moved in this direction, it has pulled the member states along with it slowly but unmistakably in the direction of adversarial legalism.

From the outset, EU and national competition laws were supposed to exist in separate, parallel universes (Gerber 1998, p. 392). The EU would exercise exclusive competence over matters that affected interstate trade, and member states would retain control over purely national matters.[8] In practice, this separation did not hold up. Over time, as the EU developed a distinctive model of competition policy and grew increasingly assertive, it pressured member states to adapt their norms and practices to those of EU policy (Dumez and Jeunemaître 1996; Van Waarden and Drahos 2002, p. 923–925; Laudati 1998, p. 384; Drahos 2001, p. 210–211). To trace this process, we must first turn back to the origins of EU competition policy.

Foundations of EU Competition Policy

In 1957, the drafters of the Treaty of Rome built on the experience of the European Coal and Steel Community's competition regime and established the legal basis for a supranational competition regime for the new European Economic Community (Milward 1992, p. 217; Büthe 2007).[9] Advocates of a robust competition policy for the EEC saw it as necessary for the creation of a common market. The elimination of tariffs and trade barriers (deregulation) would not create a common market unless an aggressive supranational competition policy (reregulation) prevented cartels and monopolies from discriminating against foreign firms and dividing up the European market. The framework for EU competition policy was established in Articles 85 to 94 of the Treaty of Rome, which were later renumbered as Articles 81 to 89.[10] Articles 81 and 82 formed the bedrock of the competition rules. Article 81 prohibits formal cartels and other forms of informal interfirm collusion that distort competition in the common market. Article 82 targets monopolies and oligopolies. It prohibits firms that enjoy a "dominant position" in the common market from abusing their position in ways that affect trade between member states. Both articles listed a number of actions and practices that would specifically be prohibited, such as price-fixing, market-sharing, or limiting production so as to harm consumers.

While the Treaty of Rome borrowed aspects of the American-style prohibition model, the treaty situated these within what remained fundamentally a European-style administrative control model. The general prohibitions on collusive practices contained in Article 81 are not absolute. Rather, Article 81(3) gives the Commission the authority to grant exemptions and thereby to permit firms to engage in business practices that would otherwise be prohibited, if the Commission determines these practices would promote broader economic objectives.

Just how much power and discretion the Commission would enjoy in implementing competition policy, and how it would relate to national competition regulators, remained unclear. The Treaty of Rome did not establish a detailed institutional and procedural framework for implementing competition policy; instead, Article 83 called on EU lawmakers to agree on a more detailed implementing regulation within four years. While some involved in the drafting of the Treaty of Rome, in particular German officials, clearly hoped that EU competition policy would be enforced strictly, this was not the consensus view. Rather, most observers expected that EU competition policy, like the few feeble national competition policies that existed at that time, would be applied rarely and loosely (Büthe 2007, p. 182; Gerber 1998, p. 346).

In 1962, EU lawmakers finally adopted the necessary implementing regulation—Regulation 17 (Council Regulation 17/62). The regulation formed the basis of a regime that would structure EU competition policy for the next forty years. It gave the Commission unprecedented powers. In other policy areas, the Commission could enforce EU law only vis-à-vis national governments. In competition policy, the Commission could deal with firms directly. While officials in other policy areas had to rely on member states or private complainants to provide them with information on noncompliance with EU law, Commission competition officials could conduct dawn raids on company premises and impose substantial fines on violators (Articles 14 and 15). The regulation guaranteed firms a right of defense and called for the ECJ adjudicate in cases when Commission decisions were challenged (Articles 17 and 19).

Regulation 17 also established the framework for relations between EU competition authorities and their counterparts at the national level. The Commission was placed in a clearly superior position, with the power to preempt investigations by national authorities (Article 9[3]). Also, Regulation 17 (Articles 4–8) granted the Commission a monopoly on the power to grant exemptions under Treaty Article 81(3).

In essence, Regulation 17 set up the institutional framework for a European-style—in particular, a German ordoliberal–style—*ex ante* administrative control system of competition policy with the European Commission's Competition Directorate General at its center (Wigger and Nölke 2007, p. 494–495; McLachlan and Swan 1963, p. 57;

Trebilcock and Iacobucci 2002). The regulation established a notification system (Article 4) through which firms could notify the Commission in advance of proposed agreements and practices that might run afoul of EU competition rules. The Commission would then review the notification and either prohibit the proposed deal or grant an exemption.[11] Firms had a strong incentive to seek Commission approval, because securing it gave them immunity from prosecution by national authorities, private parties, or the Commission itself. It became normal business practice for firms to seek Commission clearance for deals that might fall under Article 81. The system did allow for judicial review at this ex ante stage, in that firms could appeal Commission decisions, but the Commission maintained considerable discretion. This predominantly ex ante control system was backed up by occasional ex post enforcement, in which the Commission conducted investigations to uncover secret cartels and abusive practices and imposed heavy fines on violators.[12]

The norms guiding EU competition law were also in keeping with German ordoliberal thinking in that competition was not pursued as an end in itself or simply as a method to reduce consumer prices but rather as a means to promote broader policy objectives. Above all, the distinctive aim of EU competition policy would be to promote the creation of a single European market (McLachlan and Swan 1963, p. 55). In addition, EU competition policy promised to promote objectives such as reducing unemployment in distressed sectors and promoting collaboration between firms in research and development (Wigger and Nölke 2007, pp. 491–495; E. Fox 1997, p. 342).

With the basic framework of competition policy in place, the Commission and the ECJ set about implementing and enforcing it. They worked in concert throughout the 1960s and 1970s, with a degree of success that surprised supporters and opponents alike. In the early years of EU competition policy, with most member state governments at best ambivalent about competition policy, the Commission tried to avoid sparking any backlash and refrained from levying fines on violators (Gerber 1998, p. 354; Büthe and Swank 2007, p. 19). Initially, the Commission did little to target monopolistic "abuse of dominant position" or horizontal cartels.[13] Instead, the Commission's early enforcement activities focused on "vertical restraints on trade" that posed a serious threat to the creation of a single European market, such as those restraints between manufacturers and retailers (Büthe 2007).[14]

The court began receiving competition law cases in the mid-1960s, just as the EU was entering a period of "Eurosclerosis," when progress in many areas of integration stalled. As legal scholars have demonstrated, in this period of political gridlock, the ECJ played an indispensable role in sustaining the process of European integration (Weiler 1991; Stein 1981). This was certainly true also in the field of competition, where the Court seized on competition law as a tool to open up the common market.

The ECJ went far beyond the traditional role of courts in European models of competition law. The Commission had little political support from the member states for pursuing a vigorous competition policy and thus had to rely on the ECJ to frame the development of EU competition policy as a legal necessity following from the requirements of the Treaty of Rome. The ECJ played a proactive role in shaping the legal principles and the scope of EU competition policy. For instance, in *Grundig* (Cases 56 and 58/84) and related cases,[15] the ECJ interpreted the concept of "effect on trade" between member states expansively, such that an ever-wider range of economic activities fell under EU jurisdiction (Gerber 1998, pp. 352–353; D. Goyder 1998, p. 52).

In the 1970s, the European Union's fledgling competition policy came under great pressure. The economic crises unleashed by the oil shocks led many governments to grow increasingly hostile to EU competition policy and simultaneously made it more tempting for firms to engage in anticompetitive practices. But even in this hostile environment, the Commission and ECJ strongly defended the competition law norms established in the 1960s and in fact expanded the scope of EU policy. The Commission began to impose fines on companies that violated competition law.[16] By the end of the 1970s, the Commission had significantly intensified its enforcement efforts, starting to go after cartels (horizontal restraints) and firms engaged in abuse of dominant position.

The Commission's efforts to expand the scope of EU competition policy were regularly backed up by rulings from the European Court of Justice.[17] The most striking developments concerned the regulation of mergers. In its 1972 *Continental Can* ruling,[18] the ECJ endorsed the Commission's argument that although the Treaty of Rome did not specifically empower the Commission to regulate mergers, they implicitly fell within the Commission's competition policy authority (McGowan and Cini 1999, p. 179). Finally, the ECJ also addressed the troubling issue of the relationship between national and European competition law. EU and national competition policies were intended to operate in parallel, with the EU addressing competition issues with cross-border dimensions and national authorities addressing issues that affected only the national economy. However, increasing intra-EU trade blurred the boundaries of national markets, leaving it unclear when anticompetitive practices should be regarded as purely national matters. This raised the potential for conflict between EU and national rules. In its 1969 *Wilhelm* judgment,[19] the ECJ ruled that in cases of conflict between EU and national competition rules, EU law had supremacy (J. Goyder 2003, p. 440). In its 1974 *Belgische Radio en Televisie* ruling,[20] the ECJ established the "direct effect" of Articles 81 and 82, meaning that, at least in principle, private plaintiffs could enforce these EU competition rules in national courts. However, as we will see below, in practice a variety of impediments strongly discouraged private actors from doing so for the next three decades.

Competition Policy and the Single Market

Between the mid-1960s and mid-1980s, the European Commission and the European Court of Justice had worked in tandem to lay the foundations for an expansive EU competition policy. However, in practice the Commission had remained "noticeably reluctant" (McGowan and Wilks 1995, p. 150) to exercise its powers vigorously, and the practical effects of EU competition policy remained limited. This changed from the mid-1980s as the launch of the Single Market Program led to a dramatic transformation of EU competition policy.

In 1985, the new Commission president, Jacques Delors, initiated a drive to "relaunch" European integration and to complete the single market by 1992 (Sandholtz and Zysman 1989; Jabko 2006). The Commission's famous 1985 *White Paper on Completing the Internal Market* (Commission 1985) specifically framed competition policy as a form of "reregulation" necessary to complement the "deregulation" associated with the single market project (Wilks and McGowan 1995, p. 151). The report stated, "As the Community moves to complete the Internal Market, it will be necessary to ensure that anti-competitive practices do not engender new forms of local protectionism which would only lead to a re-partitioning of the market" (Commission 1985, p. 39). The single market project would remove barriers to trade, and a vigorous competition policy would ensure that this market opening did not lead to unfair competition. Officials in the Commission's Competition Directorate General quickly took up this charge. Under the leadership of Competition Commissioner Peter Sutherland and his successor, Leon Brittan, the directorate intensified its enforcement of EU competition law, launching high-profile investigations, imposing heavy fines on violators, and forcing dramatic changes in corporate practices and structures (McGowan 2000, p. 121; Büthe 2007, p. 183; McGowan and Wilks 1995, p. 150; Wilks 2005b).

The launch of the Single Market Program also unleashed economic forces that raised the profile of competition policy. As firms prepared to adjust to and take advantage of the single market, there was a surge in merger activity (Tsoukalis 1993, p. 103). This generated pressure for the EU to take on a greater role in merger regulation, as businesses faced with a patchwork of national competition regimes began to favor a "one-stop shop" for merger regulation (McGowan and Cini 1999, p. 180).

Though the ECJ had ruled as early as 1973 that the Commission could play a role in merger regulation,[21] the scope of EU merger review remained unclear, and member states steadfastly refused to adopt a merger control regulation that might provide clarity (Büthe 2007, p. 187). This created great uncertainty for business. This uncertainty was dramatically heightened in 1987 with the ECJ's *Philip Morris* judgment,[22] when the court boldly affirmed and extended the scope of the Commission's merger review powers. More and more large firms recognized that they might be subject to EU merger control review and began to seek advanced clearance from the Commission for proposed mergers. Likewise, more and more firms complained to the Commission regarding the anticompetitive effects of proposed mergers among their competitors. Many multinationals sought greater legal certainty and pressed the member state governments to adopt a merger regulation with clear guidelines as to which mergers fell within the Commission's authority and what the criteria were for evaluating them.

The combination of legal pressure from the ECJ, industry pressure, and the desire of national governments to establish some bounds on the Commission's discretion finally led member states to adopt the Merger Control Regulation in December 1989.[23] The regulation mainly reaffirmed powers the Commission had already staked out for itself, but it was significant in that it enhanced legal certainty for regulated entities by establishing clear quantitative thresholds for mergers. The regulation also enhanced Commission powers in certain respects and affirmed that the Commission would be the dominant player in the EU's merger control regime (Quack and Djelic 2005, pp. 270–271; Gerber 1998, p. 381).

The launch of the Single Market Program and the adoption of the Merger Control Regulation did not, however, usher in an unbridled expansion of Commission power. In the very period when the European Commission was gaining new powers, it was also being confronted with a steadily tightening set of legal constraints imposed by the ECJ and by a newly created European court—the Court of First Instance. In a sense, the Commission began to get a taste of its own medicine: it had grown accustomed to using EU competition law to force the hand of private actors. Increasingly in the 1980s and 1990s, the Commission found that EU law could bite back, as private actors could successfully challenge its decisions before the ECJ and, from 1989, before the CFI.

The ECJ began to demand that the Commission provide better reasoned, empirically defensible justifications for its decisions and to adhere to strict administrative procedures (Harding and Joshua 2003, p. 179; Büthe 2007, p. 184). Likewise, the CFI asserted a strong, independent role in competition policy, turning a very critical eye on the Commission's regulatory practices.[24] The CFI began to demand that the Commission adhere to strict administrative procedures and began to review the Commission's substantive fact finding and economic analysis (McGowan and Wilks 1995, p. 150; Wilks 2005b, p. 130; Bailey 2004, p. 1358; Lehmkuhl 2008).[25] The CFI developed a reputation as a "litigants' court" that took private challenges to Commission decision making seriously and that would not hesitate to overturn unlawful Commission decisions.[26] Together, the CFI and ECJ forced the Commission to better justify its decisions and to adhere strictly to administrative procedures (Harding and Joshua 2003, p. 179; Büthe 2007, p. 184).

Competition Policy, 1992–2003: Power and Criticism

The European Commission's power and assertiveness in competition policy grew dramatically in the 1990s and the first decade of the new millennium. The Commission enforced European Union competition law vigorously, increasing the use of fines after adopting a new, stricter set of guidelines regarding fines in 1998 (Guersent 2004).[27] In 2001 the Commission launched what insiders referred to as the "crackdown" on cartels and increased the intensity of its monitoring activities, including its famous dawn raids (Guersent 2004). The total fines imposed in 2001, €1.87 billion, exceeded the total of all fines imposed in the history of EU cartel enforcement (Wilks 2005a, p. 434). Between 2001 and 2003, the Commission issued an average of 8 cartel decisions per year, compared with an average of 1.5 decisions per year over the previous thirty years (Commission 2004a, pp. 23–24). And yet, even in this period of confidence and assertiveness, the EU's system of competition policy based on centralized enforcement by the Commission was revealing its limits.

In the 1990s, Commission competition officials faced a dramatically heightened regulatory burden as a result of the combined effects of the Merger Control Regulation, the Single Market Program, and EU enlargement. The resources and regulatory capacity of the Commission's Competition Directorate General did not keep pace with its new regulatory burdens, as national governments flatly refused to expand the staff of the Commission (McGowan and Wilks 1995, p. 154). The Commission reacted to its administrative overload by relying on a variety of soft law mechanisms, through which it could dispatch with cases quickly and informally. Rather than deal with competition cases on a strictly case-by-case basis, the Commission resorted to block exemptions, whereby it could issue a notice exempting an entire sector or set of practices from EU competition rules. The Commission also favored communicating with firms informally, responding to their queries with nonbinding "comfort letters" and reaching agreements with them through informal "settlements" (McGowan 2000, pp. 123, 144; McGowan and Wilks 1995, p. 155; Hofmann 2006, p. 170; Neven, Papandropolous, and Seabright 1998).

Critics attacked these practices. They charged that in its effort to expedite the regulatory process through negotiation and compromise, the Commission had resorted to opaque decision-making procedures and reached decisions that lacked rigorous justifications. The decision-making process was prone to political interference by national governments, particularly in areas such as merger review, where decisions were made by the Commission as a whole. For the most part, Commission decision making was opaque, politicized, inconsistent, and unpredictable. Leaders of industry, legal experts, and the German and UK governments decried these inconsistencies and called for reform (Wilks and McGowan 1995, p. 267; Laudati 1998, p. 404; Morgan and McGuire 2004, pp. 52–53).

European courts responded to such criticisms, demanding greater transparency, rigor, and legal certainty in the regulatory process. In short, the Commission's effort to rely on a highly discretionary administrative model collided with the intensification of judicial review by the European Court of Justice and Court of First Instance. The ECJ and CFI tightened the limits on Commission discretion in the 1990s and even more so in the first years of the new millennium. Under pressure from the courts, many of the Commission's supposedly soft instruments of regulation became very hard indeed, producing enforceable "legal effects."[28] The ECJ and CFI allowed the Commission to enunciate norms through soft law mechanisms, such as guidelines, but then held the Commission to those norms strictly, saying that it could not deviate from them in individual cases and would have to justify decisions in terms of those norms (Hofmann 2006 pp. 159–177).[29] Moreover, the courts ruled that the Commission must establish any soft-law competition rules through transparent procedures.[30] Judicial restrictions on Commission decision making reached a kind of climax in 2002, when the Court of First Instance overturned three Commission merger decisions,[31] blasting the Commission's decisions as being based on inadequate economic analysis and legal reasoning and as failing to adhere to procedural rules.

The second set of major tensions confronting competition policy in the 1990s concerned the relationship between national and EU competition law. With increasing cross-border trade and the internationalization of European firms after the launch of the single market project, long-standing tensions between national and EU competition law intensified (Drahos 2000, p. 387; Laudati 1998, p. 384; J. Goyder 2003, p. 440). As the dividing lines between national and European markets blurred, national regulators faced an ongoing threat of being overruled by an increasingly assertive European Commission. Recognizing this, firms bypassed national authorities and went directly to the Commission when seeking exemptions (Drahos 2000, p. 403; Van Waarden and Drahos 2002, p. 925). National competition authorities grew increasingly frustrated with what they perceived as an overcentralization of power in Brussels. Many national competition authorities harmonized their norms and practices with the EU's, hoping this would make it less likely that the Commission would intervene (Drahos 2001, p. 400).

Growing frustration with overcentralization in competition policy coincided with the broader emphasis member states were placing at the time on the principle of subsidiarity. Governments pressed the EU to respect the principle of subsidiarity—which suggests that the EU should act only when an issue cannot be adequately addressed at a lower (i.e., national) level of government—in the competition field. The Commission promoted greater decentralization through a two-pronged strategy: the Commission focused first on increasing the involvement of national competition authorities (NCAs) in EU competition law and second on increasing enforcement of competition law by private parties before national courts.

The first prong of the Commission's decentralization strategy focused on national competition authorities. The European Commission had long encouraged involvement of national competition authorities in the application of EU competition law (Büthe and Swank 2007, pp. 30–32). In 1997, the Commission took a further step to promote decentralization, issuing a notice that called for national competition agencies to play a greater role in applying EU competition policy (McGowan 2000, p. 139; Commission 1997b). However, these efforts were hampered by significant differences among national competition laws, many of which did not adhere to EU competition law principles (S. Martin 1998; Riley 2003).

The second prong of the Commission's strategy focused on promoting decentralized enforcement by private parties before national courts. While private complaints to the Commission had long played an important role in helping the Commission to uncover competition law violations (Guersent 2004; Paulis and De Smijter 2005, p. 12), actual private enforcement—in the form of private parties bringing claims for damages they suffered as a result of violations of antitrust law—was almost nonexistent (Whish 2001, p. 281; Wils 2003, p. 475; Wigger and Nölke 2007, p. 495; Waelbroeck, Slater, and Even-Shoshan 2004). The idea that private damage claims might play a role in EU competition law enforcement was certainly not new. The European

Parliament had been an early advocate,[32] and the Commission had long supported the idea.[33] In February 1993, the Commission intensified its effort to encourage private enforcement actions, issuing a notice outlining procedures for national courts to follow in applying community law (Ehlermann 1992; Commission 1993b). The notice also announced a program of legal advice and support for national courts to address their lack of expertise on EU competition law. From the perspective of the Commission, decentralized enforcement was attractive in offering a cheap way to reduce its overwhelming caseload. With decentralized enforcement, the Commission hoped to enlist the resources of private parties and national courts to enforce EU competition law, without ever relinquishing its superior position in the system.

However, a number of major impediments stood in the way of private enforcement, and very few cases were brought before national courts (Riley 2003, p. 665). Reliance on private enforcement was totally alien to competition law systems in the member states. As discussed above, the administrative control model on which these systems were premised required that enforcement power remain concentrated in the hands of public authorities. Thus, it was no coincidence that the sorts of legal norms and procedural mechanisms that facilitated private enforcement in the American antitrust system—such as liberal discovery rules, contingency fees, class actions, and the awarding of treble damages to successful litigants—were absent in the legal systems of EU member states. Instead, significant procedural hurdles in national civil justice systems discouraged private litigation. The weakness of rules on discovery, the absence of significant damage awards, the lack of contingency fee arrangements and class actions, and the high costs and delays involved in judicial procedures made private antitrust litigation an unattractive proposition. Costs were high, while the prospects for success and the potential financial rewards of litigation were low (Ehlermann 1996; Riley 2003, pp. 668–669; Wigger and Nölke 2007, p. 495). Also, the Commission's notification regime reduced the scope and incentive for private enforcement. If the Commission cleared a case or granted an exemption, the firms involved enjoyed immunity from prosecution by private parties. Litigants faced the risk that their enforcement action before a national court might be torpedoed if the defendant made a notification to the Commission and won a clearance for its action (Wigger 2007, p. 104). Together, all of these factors made European legal systems a "hostile environment for private antitrust action" (ibid.).

However, even in this period when the institutional landscape and legal traditions discouraged private antitrust damage claims, other forms of private litigation concerning EU competition law did develop. As Wouter Wils explains (2003, p. 473), although private parties very rarely used EU competition law "proactively (as a 'sword') to claim damages or injunctive relief," they did regularly invoke Articles 81 and 82 "as a defence (or a 'shield'), mainly in contractual disputes."[34]

The significance of this defensive litigation is that it helped to build up an infrastructure of lawyers specializing in EU competition law. The wave of cross-border mergers and strategic alliances that accompanied the Single Market Program increased demand for legal advice on EU competition law, encouraging the growth of "Euro law firms" (Gerber 1998, p. 370). Lee McGowan and Stephen Wilks (1995, p. 151) highlight the spike in recruitment of competition law specialists by law firms in Brussels and conclude, "The legal profession certainly proved to be one of the major beneficiaries of the advance of competition policy." Once put in place for defensive purposes, this body of competition lawyers could also be mobilized for offensive forms of litigation, including private enforcement actions seeking damages for competition law violations. And, as we will see below, these lawyers did not wait passively for such opportunities to arise but actively promoted the expansion of private antitrust litigation.

Ultimately, the Commission's efforts to promote both cooperation with national authorities and decentralized enforcement in national courts in the 1990s proved ineffectual. Though national authorities were authorized to enforce the anticartel and antimonopoly provisions of Articles 81 and 82, doing so was not an attractive proposition. Above all, because national competition authorities could not grant exemptions (that power being reserved for the European Commission), national authorities were loath to get involved in enforcing EU competition law, and regulated parties had little interest in dealing with them (Wigger and Nölke 2007, p. 496; Riley 2003, p. 662). By the end of the 1990s, the Commission admitted that its efforts to promote cooperation with national authorities and decentralized enforcement before national courts were not working. The Commission found itself in a seemingly intractable position. The member states steadfastly refused to increase its staffing and resources, and yet the regulatory burden of EU competition policy continued to grow and promised to grow far more should the EU proceed with eastern enlargement. The proposal for an independent European competition office, which the Commission had in any case opposed, had been rejected by the member states.[35] The Commission needed to find a way to increase the EU's regulatory capacity in competition policy, but hoped to do so without relinquishing control of the crown jewel of EU regulation.

In 1999, the Commission came forward with a white paper on the "modernization" of competition policy (Commission 1999c). The white paper suggested a series of fundamental reforms, which were justified—at least rhetorically—on the basis that they would significantly decentralize power while also reducing the compliance burden on firms and the regulatory oversight burden on the Commission. The white paper called for the abolition of the centralized notification procedure run by the Commission and called for national courts and competition authorities to take on a frontline role in implementing and enforcing competition policy, including the power to grant exemptions from EU antitrust rules (under Article 81[3]). The Commission would safeguard the consistency of the competition regime by overseeing the activities of the national authorities and reserving the authority to preempt them when necessary.

Many of these proposals seemed rather untenable at the time. However, over the next four years, as negotiations over the modernization of competition policy continued, the ECJ and CFI made a number of rulings that increased the feasibility of the Commission's proposed model. Two landmark decisions stand out. First, in its 2000 *Masterfoods* decision,[36] the ECJ tightened the leash on national courts, emphasizing that they must not to take decisions "running counter to" a Commission decision (Komninos 2007, p. 1388–1395; O'Keeffe 2001, pp. 301–304). By affirming the hierarchical relationship between the Commission and national courts, *Masterfoods* enabled the Commission to delegate adjudication to national courts while maintaining the clear primacy of its competition decisions (Komninos 2007, pp. 1391–1392, 2002, pp. 447–449).

The second European Court of Justice ruling was even more significant. One of the long-standing impediments to private enforcement of

EU competition law was the lack of a private right to damages for victims of illegal conduct. The ECJ addressed this issue in its 2001 judgment in *Courage v. Crehan.*[37] In *Courage,* the ECJ ruled that any individual injured by anticompetitive conduct that violated Article 81(1) must be able to claim damages for losses the individual suffers as a result (Van Gerven 2005; Reich 2005; Komninos 2002; Eilmansberger 2007). The ECJ's broad language establishing that any individual victim has a right to claim damages meant that even indirect purchasers and consumers might bring claims. The ECJ explained that it saw increasing private damage actions as essential to the effectiveness of the EU competition regime (*Courage v. Crehan,* paras. 26–27). Also, the ECJ emphasized that while domestic rules would govern the procedures for making claims, such rules must not render it "excessively difficult to exercise [Community] rights" (ibid., para. 29).

With its decisions in *Masterfoods* and *Courage,* the ECJ helped to set the stage for the modernization reforms. By affirming the primacy of the Commission in its relations with national courts and by encouraging private damage claims, the ECJ made it more feasible for the Commission to pursue a new model of competition policy, which would rely heavily on national courts and private litigation.

The Modernization Program

Among students of European politics, 1 May 2004 will forever be remembered as the day of eastern enlargement—when the EU added ten new member states and reunited a divided continent. On that day of flag waving and speech making, a less awe-inspiring but nevertheless profound transformation occurred in EU competition policy. Council Regulation 1/2003 came into effect,[38] inaugurating the so-called modernization of EU Competition policy.[39] The new regulation replaced Regulation 17, which had governed the competition regime since 1962, and it was without question the most significant reform in the history of EU competition policy (Wilks 2007; Ehlermann 2000).

The Commission pitched the modernization reforms to member states as an exercise in decentralization and subsidiarity—principles that had great rhetorical appeal for national politicians across Europe at that time. Most observers have accepted the notion that modernization involved a reassertion of national control over EU competition policy. This view is misguided. Instead, with the 2004 modernization reforms, the Commission invoked the rhetorical appeal of decentralization and subsidiarity in order to harness national agencies, courts, and private litigants in the Commission's efforts to extend the reach of EU competition policy. As Stephen Wilks explains (2005a, p. 438), "The evidence suggests that the Commission has engineered an audacious coup that has extended its powers, marginalized national competition laws and corralled the national authorities." Likewise, Alan Riley concludes (2003, p. 657), "The Commission has orchestrated a political masterstroke. It has given the impression of radical reform to the Member States by abolishing the notification procedure and offered decentralization provisions . . . which in no way undermine its central role in the development of EC competition policy or the enforcement of EC competition law. DG Competition has in fact managed to centralize European competition law even more than under Regulation 17."[40]

Placing these developments in the wider perspective presented in this book, we can see that the modernization of competition policy is a manifestation of the more general shift toward Eurolegalism as a mode of governance. As in other policy areas, a combination of economic liberalization and political fragmentation has encouraged European Union policy makers to rely on an approach to regulation that relies heavily on decentralized enforcement by private actors before national (and European) courts. EU competition policy had long been heavily judicialized and had frequently involved adversarial relationships between regulators and regulated firms. However, before 2004, EU competition policy had relied overwhelmingly on centralized enforcement by the Commission and had emphasized legal norms that preserved considerable discretion for the Commission. As Angela Wigger (2007, p. 99) argues in her trenchant analysis, the 2004 modernization reforms fundamentally reoriented the system, transforming it into one in which decentralized enforcement by private actors would play a central role (see also Reich 2005). Firms and consumer groups would enforce competition law by suing each other—much as they do in the United States (Chapman 2003).

The modernization reforms contained three main elements, which were closely intertwined. First, Regulation 1/2003 abolished the notification system under which companies sought advance clearance from the European Commission for commercial agreements that might violate competition law (Article 1). Instead, companies have to rely on their own judgment—or more likely that of the legal counsel they hire—to assess the legality of their commercial practices and agreements. Firms make these judgments subject to the threat that they could be sued after the fact by competitors, consumers, or regulatory authorities should they get it wrong (Wigger and Nölke 2007, pp. 488, 499).

Thus, the first element of the reform, the abolition of the notification system, was linked to the second, the decentralization of enforcement to national authorities and courts (Wilks 2007, p. 2). Importantly, Article 3 requires national competition authorities and courts to apply EU competition law, rather than national law, in cases that may affect interstate trade, and the article empowers national competition authorities and national courts to grant exemptions from EU competition rules. Articles 11–16 establish a framework for cooperation between the Commission and national competition authorities and courts. Though Regulation 1/2003 did not detail the role envisaged for private parties, it did state (Recital 7) that national courts would have a vital role to play in deciding suits for damages brought by private parties. As we will see below, the Commission soon returned to the issue, calling for more reforms to stimulate private enforcement.

The third element of the modernization reform involved a shift in the criteria used to assess anticompetitive conduct (Wilks 2005). Wigger and Nölke (2007) explain that, with the 2004 competition reforms, "much more importance is now given to short-term consumer welfare considerations" and that, "increasingly, rigorous economic analysis underpins antitrust assessments" (pp. 498–499). Ostensibly, a shift toward more rigorous economic analysis might appear to have little to do with decentralization and private enforcement of competition law. In fact, Wigger (2007) demonstrates that the two are closely connected. Previously, in assessing anticompetitive conduct, the Commission had relied largely on a German-inspired ordoliberal approach, in which the Commission balanced the promotion of competition against a variety of public interest considerations, such as the impact of commercial practices on innovation and employment. This approach was possible only in a system in which enforcement was dominated by a public agency that could engage in such balancing of objectives. Private litigants, who will bring damage claims when it serves their self-interest, cannot be expected to engage in such balancing. Likewise, national judges applying the law on a case-by-case basis will not tend to take into account the broader macroeconomic issues (Wigger 2007, p. 110). Therefore, if private enforcement before national courts were to play a greater role, then more straightforward, objective microeconomic criteria must be used to assess anticompetitive conduct. By turning toward a Chicago School, short-term consumer welfare test of anticompetitive conduct, the Commission established criteria "that can been trusted to courts and private litigants" (Wigger and Nölke 2007, p. 498). Though this shift was not specifically mentioned in Regulation 1/2003, it emerged through changes in Commission practice after 2002 and was clearly linked to the modernization program.

Political scientists typically associate decentralization of tasks with devolution of power. Paradoxically, the modernization of competition policy involved decentralization without a real devolution of power. Quite to the contrary, the Commission actually increased its control over national competition authorities (Riley 2003, p. 672). By dressing up the modernization reforms in the fashionable garb of subsidiarity and decentralization, the Commission convinced national governments to have their national competition authorities and courts do most of the work of applying EU competition law, while the Commission preserved for itself a dominant role in the system and in many important ways actually extended its powers (Wilks 2007; Riley 2003). First, because the Modernization Regulation (Article 3) requires national competition authorities and courts to apply EU law in cases that may affect interstate trade, it will significantly extend the reach of Community law and restrict the application of national law.[41] Also, under Regulation 2003/1 (Articles 11–13), NCAs are required to inform the Commission in writing before commencing investigations of competition policy violations and before taking any regulatory action. The Commission reserves the right to intervene in any case that falls under its jurisdiction, and if the Commission chooses to intervene, it completely preempts any ongoing case brought by an NCA.[42] For an NCA, the Commission's preempting one of its cases would seriously damage its credibility with regulated firms. Though the Commission has not yet resorted to such outright preemption, the threat of it serves as an important check on the behavior of NCAs. Finally, Regulation 2003/1 also extends the Commission's powers of investigation, empowering inspectors to seal business premises, interview staff, enter private homes in search of business records, and impose far greater fines on those who provide incorrect information than on those who do not.

Regulation 1/2003 had envisioned that the Commission and national authorities would together form a network to coordinate their activities. The structure of the European Competition Network (ECN) was elaborated in a 2004 Commission notice (Commission 2004b; see also Wilks 2007; Paulis and De Smijter 2005). The notice establishes a framework for information sharing and case allocation and requires NCAs to notify the ECN when they initiate cases. The idea that competition policy would be regulated through a horizontal network of national regulators was very much in keeping with the Commission's decentralization rhetoric and with the "new modes of governance" fashionable at the time (Wilks 2007, p. 2). In practice, however, the ECN is not structured as a network to promote information sharing and cooperation among equals. Rather, it is designed to operate as a hierarchical network through which the Commission can corral and harness national authorities. As this became clear, national competition authorities, in particular the German Bundeskartellamt, have expressed concern that they may become mere servants of the Commission (D. Lehmkuhl 2009).

The one significant respect in which the Commission did surrender power in the modernization reforms was through the promotion of private enforcement. During the forty years when Regulation 17 and its notification system structured the EU competition regime, the Commission essentially maintained a monopoly on the application and enforcement of EU competition law. With modernization, the Commission privatized much of the regulatory process, relying on the tools of Eurolegalism to pursue its policy objectives. As Wigger (2007, p. 103) explains, the new regime is privatized in two senses. First, firms can no longer seek advance clearance from the Commission for their commercial agreements but must instead conduct their own analysis to determine if the agreement is legal. Second, though the Commission will continue to bring enforcement actions of its own, the new regime will rely heavily on competing firms, consumers, distributors, or suppliers to bring private enforcement actions before national courts against firms that violate EU competition law. In competition policy, as in the other policy areas examined in this book, the Commission hopes to rely on private parties acting in their own self-interest to serve as the enforcement agents of EU law. While a number of significant impediments to private enforcement of competition law remain in place, the Commission is working to address these, as we will see in the next section.

Encouraging Private Enforcement

In 2004, the Commission contracted Ashurst, a prominent British law firm, to conduct an extensive comparative study of the current use of private damage claims to enforce EU competition law, and existing impediments to private enforcement. The first sentence of the nearly eight-hundred-page Ashurst Study put the thrust of its findings in striking terms: "The picture that emerges from the present study on damage actions for breach of competition in the enlarged EU is one of astonishing diversity and total underdevelopment" (Waelbroeck, Slater, and Even-Shoshan 2004, p. 1). The report found evidence of only sixty national court rulings on competition damages actions in the history of the EU, with only twelve cases in which damages had been awarded at least partially on the basis of EU law (ibid.).[43] The report also identified a series of obstacles to private enforcement that were found repeatedly across member states, including limits on standing to sue, limits on aggregate claims (i.e., group or class actions), the absence of contingency fees, an excessively high burden of proof, inadequate discovery rules, absence of punitive damages and uncertainty regarding calculation of damages, high costs, the loser-pays rule, length of proceedings, and the absence of a clear statutory basis for bringing EC competition law-based damage actions (Waelbroeck, Slater, and Even-Shoshan 2004; Van Gerven 2005; Riley and Peysner 2006, pp. 749–750). None of this came as a surprise to competition law experts, who recognized that to foster an active system of private enforcement, the EU would have to adopt legislation to remove procedural impediments that were rooted in national legal systems (Eilmansberger 2007, pp. 433–434; Van Gerven 2005, p. 5).

The Commission quickly signaled its intention to address these impediments. In a 2004 speech, Competition Commissioner Monti (2004b) emphasized that increasing private enforcement was crucial to the success of the new merger regime. In 2005, Neelie Kroes, Monti's successor, was even more vocal, stating quite plainly that "not enough use [was] made of courts" in competition enforcement (Kroes 2005b). The Commission took the first formal step in addressing these impediments in 2005, publishing a green paper that explored the question of how private enforcement might be increased (Commission 2005c; Eilmansberger 2007). In April 2008, after receiving extensive input on the green paper from stakeholders, the Commission took the next step in developing a legislative proposal by publishing a white paper arguing that private antitrust damage actions must be strengthened both to protect victims' rights and to deter lawbreakers (Commission 2008d, p. 3). The white paper identified a series of "legal and procedural hurdles" (ibid., p. 2) that discouraged private parties from bringing damage claims and suggested measures to address them. First, the Commission noted that rules concerning collective actions were inadequate and indicated that it might propose common EU rules on collective redress, allowing for representative actions and opt-in collective actions (ibid., p. 4).[44] Second, the Commission called for improving disclosure such that claimants could access the information needed to prove their claims (ibid., p. 5). Third, the Commission called for the adoption of legislation to codify and clarify ECJ jurisprudence on damages and to ensure that claimants could obtain full compensation. Finally, in addressing litigation costs, the Commission suggested that national courts should be empowered to deviate from normal cost rules (i.e., "loser pays") in order to protect legitimate claimants against the risk of paying unreasonable defendants costs.

The Commission's green and white papers on antitrust damage actions sparked a heated debate in the competition law community (Wils 2003; Van Gerven 2005; Hodges 2006; Waelbroeck and Slater 2006). The outcome of the Commission's various legislative initiatives to promote private enforcement remains uncertain. Most recently, the Commission's Competition Directorate General drafted and leaked the "Proposal for a Directive on Rules Governing Damages Actions for Infringements of Article 81 and 82 of the Treaty" (Alfaro and Reher 2010). The leaked draft elicited withering criticism from business groups and in the period running up to his confirmation process for a second term as European Commission president, José Manuel Barroso shelved the proposal. Nevertheless, both the new commissioner for competition and the new commissioner for consumer affair in the second Barroso Commission have expressed a commitment to resurrecting the proposal in some form.[45] What is abundantly clear is that in order to encourage private litigation, both the Commission and the European Parliament are committed to removing procedural impediments, reducing the cost to claimants, and increasing potential rewards. Rhetorically, the Commission repeatedly emphasizes the importance of avoiding "the excesses that we have seen in other legal systems" (Monti 2004b) and of relying on measures "that are rooted in *European legal culture* and *traditions*." (Commission 2008d, p. 3, emphasis in original; see also Tait 2008a).[46] In truth, the thrust of the white paper and most of the measures it contains are certainly not rooted in European legal culture and traditions. Rather, the EU is introducing a series of exotic plants to European soil.

While many impediments to decentralized enforcement remain in place, one clear source of strength with regard to private enforcement is the existence of a large community of lawyers specializing in EU competition law. As noted above, lawyers specializing in EU competition law, many of whom are associated with large multinational (primarily American and English) law firms, proliferated in the 1980s and 1990s. Though most of their legal work has involved representing clients in their interactions with the Commission or in private contractual disputes affected by EU competition policy, these specialists could certainly put their expertise to use in private damage claims. Indeed, law firms specializing in EU competition law played an active role in advising the Commission on the modernization reforms, and these specialists were strong supporters of increasing opportunities for private enforcement litigation (Wigger and Nölke 2007, p. 504; Wigger 2007; Wilks 2007).[47] The competition law bar constitutes a vital part—and indeed the greater part—of the epistemic community that has pressed for this reform of EU competition law. We should hardly be surprised that competition law practitioners advocate a juridified system in which they will play a central role (Wilks 2005a, p. 447).

Not only do these legal practitioners have the expertise necessary to advise clients on EU competition law and to bring enforcement actions; they also have a clear financial self-interest in doing so. Legal services related to EU competition law already constitute one of the largest and most lucrative areas of legal practice for large, multinational law firms in Europe. The modernization reforms will increase demand for legal counsel and litigation services related to EU competition policy. The abolition of the Commission's administrative notification system means that the Commission will no longer assess the legality of commercial practices for firms. Firms will have to perform such assessments themselves with the aid of their legal counsel and then defend themselves in the event of private civil suits challenging their actions (Wigger 2007, p. 117). The prospects for growth in private antitrust litigation have attracted attention from across the Atlantic, particularly given the growing restrictions on class action litigation in the United States, as one scholar notes: "Leading US class action firms such as Bryan Cave and Cohen, Milstein, Hausfeld & Toll have expanded their European operations, encouraged by efforts by both European and British authorities to make collective litigation more attractive and accessible to both consumers and claimant lawyers. The increased interest is driven in part by tougher regulatory action in areas such as cartels" (Peel 2007).

Scholars of EU law and politics such as Lisa Conant (2002) have argued, quite rightly, that in some areas of EU law, the inadequacy of legal support structures discourages plaintiffs from enforcing their EU rights. In the area of EU competition law; however, legal support structures are far from inadequate. It remains the case that a number of procedural impediments—rules regarding collective actions, disclosure, damage awards, and litigation costs—discourage private antitrust enforcement. Nevertheless, already a large group of legal practitioners exist who are eager to profit from helping clients enforce their EU rights, and these practitioners are active in supporting policy makers who seek to remove the procedural impediments that stand in the practitioners' way.

It remains far too early to assess the long-term impact of the 2004 modernization reforms. Already, though, it is clear that centralized enforcement by the Commission continues to grow more coercive, punitive, and juridical. The Commission has begun to exercise the new powers it won in the Modernization Directive, including sealing parts of business premises and questioning the staffs of firms under investigation, and it plans to increase the frequency of dawn raids in coming years (Paulis and De Smijter 2005, p. 13). In 2006, the Commission set a new record for cartel fines, imposing a total of nearly €2 billion on forty-one companies (Demetriou and Gray 2007, p. 1429). It easily broke this record in 2007, imposing over €3.3 billion in fines. Also in 2006, the Commission adopted a new set of guidelines for setting fines.[48] The new rules will allow the Commission to impose far steeper fines in the future, in particular for long-lasting violations and for repeat offenders (Völcker 2007; Tait 2008c). Figure 5.1 illustrates just how dramatic the escalation of fines by the Commission has been.

The new fining regime also promises to encourage further juridification, as regulated firms fight back in the courts. Already, today firms routinely challenge Commission cartel fines before the Court of First Instance, hoping for an annulment or a reduction in the penalties imposed. Oliver Guersent, a high-ranking DG Competition official, estimates that since the crackdown on cartels in 2001, every cartel decision generates an average of four to five appeals (2004, p. 51). The 2006 fining guidelines increase the transparency of the Commission's fining policy, imposing new constraints on how the Commission calculates fines and strengthening the procedural rights and guarantees of regulated firms (Völcker 2007; Wils 2007). With more and stronger grounds on which to base their legal challenges, firms will be more likely than ever to go to court to challenge Commission penalties.

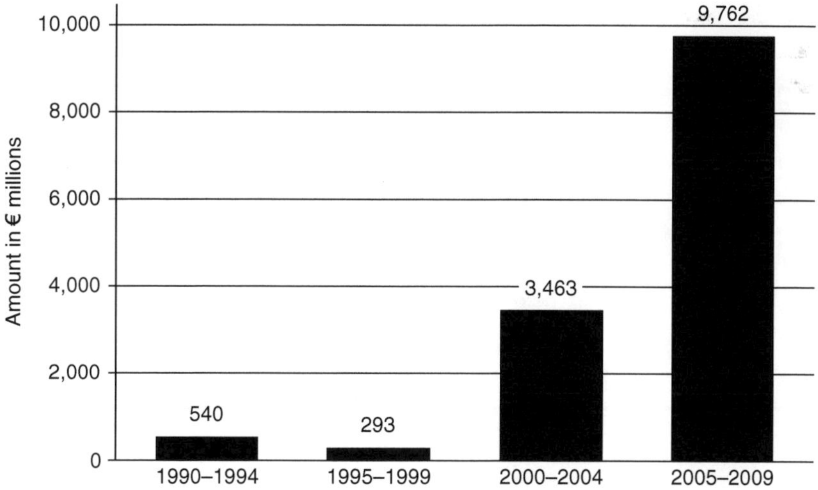

Figure 5.1. Commission fines imposed in cartel cases, 1990–2009. (*Source:* Cartel Statistics, http://ec.europa.eu/competition/cartels/statistics/statistics.pdf.)

This juridification is illustrated in striking terms by the Commission's nearly decade long legal battle with Microsoft, a battle that has involved a series of competition decisions, fines of nearly a billion Euros, and legal appeals by Microsoft (Tait 2008b; Castle 2008). While such epic legal battles provide vivid illustrations, the full impact of the juridification of competition law can be observed in more mundane, quotidian changes in corporate behavior. As Wilks (2005b) explains, "Today, the 'competition rules' are a dominant regulatory constraint when companies formulate their corporate strategy or consider their competitive behaviour. They employ legal expertise to advise on the impact of the rules and most big firms will have an in-house 'compliance programme' to train their staff to avoid breaching the competition provisions" (p. 116). As Frank Dobbin and John Sutton (1998) argued in the US context, the strength of a weak administrative state relies precisely on stimulating organizations to internalize legal norms—to create departments and compliance programs that make consideration of legal requirements a part of an organization's standard operating procedures. In other words, the EU's competition regime has "gotten inside" corporate Europe, reshaping the very way it does business.

With regard to the decentralized enforcement by private parties that was called for in the modernization reforms, there are indications of rapid growth. These changes are best illustrated by the developments at the national level, which I discuss below. But generally, we can observe that in the first two years of the modernized competition regime, more than 50 percent of national court judgments on matters of EU competition law were in cases initiated by private plaintiffs, whereas previously only approximately 5 percent of cases had been initiated by private plaintiffs (Wigger and Nölke 2007, p. 497; also see Van Gerven 2005, p. 20).

While the future is notoriously hard to predict, we can clearly see, looking back, that incremental changes beginning in the late 1980s and the 2004 modernization reforms already have led to a significant juridification of the EU competition regime. A system that initially concentrated power and discretion in the hands of the Commission has been transformed into a system that increasingly relies on private parties and their lawyers to enforce the law before national courts. This juridification at the EU level has encouraged similar juridification of competition regimes at the national level. Ultimately, the impact of the new decentralized and privatized EU regime will depend on the outcome of ongoing efforts to reduce impediments to private enforcement and on the mobilization of legal entrepreneurs at the national level, as I discuss below.

The Move to Eurolegalism at the National Level

Delineating the impact of European Union competition policy on changes in national competition policies is challenging, because EU and national policies developed in tandem (McGowan 2000, p. 118). Before the 2004 modernization reforms, the EU had never acted to formally harmonize national competition laws. Nevertheless, the EU had generated substantial pressure on member state governments to "voluntarily" harmonize their national competition laws with the EU model (Van Waarden and Drahos 2002). As discussed above, the national competition law models that developed in the 1960s and 1970s were characterized by wide administrative discretion, limited judicial review, a paucity of private enforcement, and a focus on controlling abuse rather than prohibiting certain activities outright (Riley 2003, p. 659). By the early 1990s, several member states had introduced new national competition law systems or altered existing systems such that they were clearly converging on the EU competition law model (Van Waarden and Drahos 2002; Drahos 2001; Gerber 1998, p. 414; Quack and Djelic 2005, p. 272).

Pressure from the EU took many forms. First, Commission decisions and European Court of Justice rulings in competition cases frequently put indirect pressure on national competition laws. The Commission and ECJ occasionally overruled decisions of national competition authorities, for instance, by prohibiting cartels that national authorities had authorized. As Frans van Waarden and M. Drahos explain (2002, p. 925), national authorities sought to harmonize their rules with European norms to reduce the likelihood that the European Commission and European courts would meddle in national affairs. The Commission encouraged this reaction by signaling that it would grant greater autonomy to authorities that converged on EU norms (ibid). Also, the legal uncertainty generated by divergences between national and EU competition laws increased compliance costs for business and hence increased support in the business community for convergence on a common model of competition law. Business demands for legal certainty mounted at the start of the 1990s, as the deadline for the "completion" of the single European market approached and businesses anticipated a spike in merger activity. Finally, for the growing epistemic community of practicing lawyers and academics specializing in the EU competition model more generally, EU law served as a focal point and "a source of norms in the development of national competition policies" (Van Waarden and Drahos 2002, p. 933). Since the mid-1990s, the EU has worked to cultivate one vital section of this community, national judges, by sponsoring competition law–training programs for national judges from across Europe (Wigger and Nölke 2007, p. 503). By 2010, the Commission had sponsored approximately 30 projects involving three thousand five hundred judges.[49]

The thrust of these national reforms was unmistakable. The harmonization of national competition regimes on an EU model involved a shift from the traditional administrative model toward a juridical model of competition law. As David Gerber (1998) puts it, "The general pattern of these changes has been to move toward systems that have more 'juridical' characteristics and institutions that perform more 'juridical' roles" (p. 403). With this juridification, national competition laws became far more strict and robust, and they were often applied by newly created independent competition regulators modeled on the European Commission's Competition Directorate General (Van Waarden and Drahos 2002, p. 915). Though the pace and character of these developments varies across member states, we can observe broadly similar developments across the European Union, including in the Netherlands, the UK, Germany, and France.

The Netherlands

In the Netherlands, convergence pressure from the European Union has led to a dramatic reorientation of the competition regime. The Netherlands has had a national competition law in place since 1958 (the 1956 Wet Economische Mededinging, or WEM). However, it was enforced so rarely and ineffectually that in 1990 a leading Dutch academic labeled the Netherlands as Europe's cartel paradise, and as late as 1994, the national Social-Economic Council (Sociaal-Economische Raad) conceded that Dutch competition policy had had little impact

(De Jong 1990). The WEM's requirements were vague. It empowered the minister of economic affairs (and his subordinate, the state secretary of economic affairs) to regulate competition in the public interest. Essentially, officials operated an abuse system in which they reserved the right to ban abusive cartels. But the law was interpreted and enforced leniently such that, in the first few years it was in force, hundreds of cartels were registered and accepted by regulators (Drahos 2001, pp. 347–354). The Ministry of Economic Affairs viewed cartels as partners and negotiated with them informally regarding price levels and other practices. Even when firms failed to notify a cartel to the authorities, they were not punished in practice (ibid, p. 355; Asbeek Brusse and Griffiths 1998). The Dutch competition regime reflected the long-held Dutch view that strict competition policy would lead to destructive competition and undermine the Dutch tradition of informal, cooperative negotiation between business and government (Van Waarden and Drahos 2002, p. 932). The role of courts was minimal, as regulators and firms resolved disputes informally and private litigation was uncommon.

As the EU competition regime grew stricter in the 1980s, it increasingly came into conflict with the lax, opaque Dutch competition regime. Dutch cartels became frequent targets of Commission investigations, prompting a long-running domestic debate about the need to reform the Dutch competition system (Drahos 2001, p. 356–372). Reform advocates argued that by converging on EU competition law norms, national regulators could shield themselves against EU intervention and could win a greater role in applying EU competition law within the Netherlands. Finally, in 1998 the new Dutch Competition Act (Mededingingswet) came into force and brought Dutch antitrust regulation into conformity with EU competition law, rendering Dutch regulation considerably more rigorous (Van Waarden and Drahos 2002, pp. 923–925). The new Competition Act adopted the main elements of the EU competition regime: the act introduced a prohibition (rather than an abuse) regime for cartels (Article 6), prohibited abuse of dominant position (Article 24), and established a merger control procedure (Article 26) (Wesseling 2008). It also established a new, independent enforcement body, the Dutch Competition Authority (Nederlandse Mededingingsautoriteit) and a specialized court to hear appeals of the authority's decisions, the administrative chamber the Rotterdam Civil

Court (Rechtbank Rotterdam). The Competition Authority was granted extensive powers to terminate infringements and penalize violators. Private parties are also able to bring actions for damages against antitrust violators under the general provisions of the Dutch Civil Code (Burgerlijk Wetboek) (Verloren van Themaat and Hettema 2004, p. 2).

Though the number of private actions for damages in antitrust cases in the Netherlands remains very low, it has been increasing rapidly in recent years. For instance, a number of municipalities recently joined forces, forming a representative foundation for the express purpose of pursuing damage claims against construction companies that violated competition law and inflated prices through a bid-rigging cartel (Verloren van Themaat and Hettema 2004, pp. 4, 16).

United Kingdom

The competition policy regime that prevailed in the United Kingdom until the 1980s reflected the traditional European administrative control model. Legislation dating back to the late 1940s was revised and consolidated in the 1973 Fair Trading Act (FTA).[50] The FTA created an opaque system that vested discretionary power in the hands of administrators (and ultimately elected officials) and restricted the involvement of courts and private parties in enforcement. The Office of Fair Trading (OFT) and Monopolies and Mergers Commission (MMC) provided the secretary of state for trade and industry with advice on whether mergers or the activities of cartels or dominant players harmed the public interest. Ultimately, the secretary had discretion to determine whether mergers or other commercial practices were in the public interest and what, if any, regulatory action was warranted. The entire regulatory process was opaque, and there was no obligation for the Secretary to give reasons for his decisions. Regulators did not involve the courts when imposing remedies on firms, and courts did not intervene to challenge decisions of the public authorities. Competition regulators had only weak investigative and sanctioning powers. Private actors were locked out of the system, generally unable to bring damage claims when they were injured by anticompetitive conduct (C. Graham 2004; Yeung 1998). Throughout the 1970s and 1980s, British competition regime remained far more informal, politicized, and lax than the EU regime (Wilks 1999, pp. 296–297; Cini 2004).

By the 1990s, as the EU competition regime developed, the UK competition regime looked increasingly anachronistic and ineffective. UK competition policy was subject to intense criticism from a range of domestic actors (Cini 2004; Eyre and Lodge 2000). As increasing trade blurred the distinction between the national and European markets, the two competition regimes often overlapped, and "quite simply, in the eyes of both industry and consumer groups, the national law had not been able to compete with Community law. Faced with the option of bringing an action on the basis of Community law, or national law, whether through the courts or the administrative agencies, professional advisers in the UK would advocate the Community route every time" (Furse 2000, p. 277). Thus, the gradual encroachment of the EU regime created incentives to harmonize the UK approach with the European.

Finally, the British system was thoroughly overhauled with the Competition Act of 1998 and the Enterprise Act of 2002. The Competition Act of 1998 was modeled closely on EU competition law and lead to "a fundamental shift in the core characteristics of the traditional UK policy" (Eyre and Lodge 2000, p. 69). The act replaced the British abuse model with a prohibition model and incorporated other central principles of EU competition law. The Competition Act reduced political interference in the enforcement process and gave UK regulators the kinds of investigative powers that Commission officials enjoyed, such as the power to conduct dawn raids and to impose massive civil penalties (C. Graham 2004; Wilks 1999, p. 323). Similarly, the 2002 Enterprise Act brought merger regulation more in line with EU norms, removing ministerial influence, introducing an EU-style substantial lessening of competition test and even introducing criminal penalties for participants in hardcore cartels (Cini 2004).

The Office of Fair Trading has put these powers to use, emerging as an aggressive enforcer of UK and EU competition law. As Julian Joshua (2002) concludes, the UK competition regime quickly went from being one of the "feeblest" in the world to one of the most "ferocious" (p. 231). A central aspect of these changes has been the juridification of what had been a flexible administrative system (Morris 2005), or what Wilks (2005a) calls a "Europe-inspired legalization of the UK regime" (p. 448). The OFT established a new "litigation unit" to spearhead enforcement efforts and navigate the increasingly litigious environment in which OFT operates. Describing that environment, the OFT's general counsel explained that as the OFT gained new enforcement powers, companies instructed their lawyers to fight back against any adverse OFT decisions. As a result, he notes, "We anticipated a lot of litigation, and we have seen a lot. Indeed, we persuaded the [OFT] board to establish a dedicated Litigation Unit . . . Once you get large cases, large corporations with big city [law] firms, the OFT has to try to match that" (General Council, OFT 2007). The head of the OFT Litigation Unit underscored the impact of the litigious environment on their working methods, explaining that "almost any time the OFT does anything, litigation could result, so staff are very careful to use proper processes" (Head of Litigation Unit, OFT 2007).

The Competition Act of 1998 and the Enterprise Act of 2002 also ushered in dramatic changes designed to encourage private enforcement of competition law. The 1998 act began extending the rights of private parties to bring damage claims against violators. The 2002 Enterprise Act established the Competition Appeal Tribunal (CAT), a specialist judicial body that hears actions for damages and other claims under the 1998 Competition Act.[51] The 2002 Act also requires courts to apply findings from OFT investigations, which makes it far easier for private parties to bring follow-on damage claims after an OFT finding. Finally, the 2002 Enterprise Act empowered approved bodies (so far, only the national Consumer Protection Association) to bring damage claims on behalf of consumers.

The number of antitrust claims filed in English courts has increased significantly in recent years, and the UK is seen as an attractive jurisdiction in which to pursue private antitrust damage claims (Davis and Farrell 2010; Alfaro and Reher 2010). It was in answer to a reference from an English court in *Courage v. Crehan* that the ECJ established the principle that injured parties must be able to claim damages before national courts in competition cases.[52] In a 2004 ruling related to the *Courage v. Crehan* litigation, the English Court of Appeal issued the first judgment from an English court awarding private damages for a breach of EU competition law.[53] Subsequently, firms have started to file standalone actions before English civil courts, and follow-on actions before the Competition Appeal Tribunal, in pursuit of civil damage claims against competitors whom the OFT has found to be in violation of competition law.[54] In a January 2010 decision, the English High Court opened an important new pathway for private enforcement, by ruling that companies can pursue private damage actions against former directors or employees who were involved in competition law violations.[55]

Without question, a number of entrenched institutions continue to present significant obstacles to the growth of private antitrust litigation. The potential costs of litigation continue to deter many potential litigants. While plaintiffs can rely on conditional fee arrangements ("no win, no fee") and legal expenses insurance, they continue to face the prospect that they may be forced to pay some portion of the defendants' legal costs if plaintiffs lose their case (Davis and Farrell 2010). Also, while forms of "representative" actions (brought by consumer groups) and "collective" actions on behalf of groups of persons sharing a common grievance are permissible under English law, these are not equivalent to American-style class actions, and in practice it can be difficult to bring litigation on behalf of a class of claimants (ibid.). However, despite such ongoing impediments, it is clear that the EU has encouraged a juridification of the UK competition regime and that public and private enforcement litigation is on the rise.

Germany

As discussed above, Germany developed a highly distinctive and widely admired approach to competition policy in the post–World War II decades, a policy grounded in the ordoliberal tradition. After the 1958 adoption of the Law against Restraints on Competition, or GWB (Gesetz gegen Wettbewerbsbeschränkungen), and the establishment of the powerful Federal Cartel Office, or BKA (Bundeskartellamt), Germany established the strictest and most rigorously enforced national competition policy in Europe. Nevertheless, this distinctive German model did share some important features with other European models: like other administrative control systems, it concentrated implementation and enforcement authority in a powerful public regulator. The BKA controlled against abusive behavior by firms in dominant market positions, and firms that planned to engage in potentially restrictive agreements had to notify and seek advance clearance from the BKA. As in other European systems, private enforcement played very little role (Hoffman and Schaub 1983).

The first serious attempt to harmonize German competition law with Community competition law came in 1998 with the Sixth Amendment to the GWB. These reforms aligned some aspects of German rules on cartels and on abuse of dominant position with the standard set in EC Treaty, Articles 81 and 82, but many important differences between European and German competition law remained (Jung 2004). Far more dramatic changes were introduced in 2005 with the Seventh Amendment to the GWB. After more than two years of heated debate, the Seventh Amendment was adopted specifically to bring German competition law in line with requirements of the EU's Modernization Regulation. The Seventh Amendment effectively "Europeanized" German competition law, ushering in a near-complete harmonization of German rules with the EU competition regime and introducing a series of reforms designed to encourage private enforcement of competition policy, as called for in the EU's new approach (Klees 2006; Dietrich, Gruber, and Hartmann-Rüppel 2010, p. 89; Buxbaum 2006).

With the Seventh Amendment, German competition policy shifted from the traditional administrative-control model toward the ex post judicial control–model called for in the EU's modernization program. Rather than seeking advanced clearance from competition authorities, firms are to self-assess their compliance with competition rules and, if they violate the law, are subject to the possibility that they can be sued by competition authorities, competitors, or consumers. Effective deterrence is crucial to the operation of this new system, and lawmakers sought to strengthen deterrence by increasing the level of fines that competition authorities could levy on violators of competition law and by introducing a number of major reforms designed to facilitate private enforcement of competition law.

With regard to public enforcement, the BKA has been given a range of new powers, including authority to conduct investigations of suspect sectors or agreements (and to impose injunctive measures on companies (GWB, section 32) (Jung 2004; Wurmnest 2005). The amount of the fines that the BKA can impose has been increased drastically (GWB, section 81) (ibid.). These reforms aimed to empower the BKA to impose "every remedy which is necessary" to bring violations of EU or German competition law to an end (Klees 2006, p. 408). The BKA has been quick to put these new powers to use, increasing the average annual total of the fines it issues by two and a half times since 2005.[56]

With regard to the role of private enforcement, changes have been even more dramatic. Before the Seventh Amendment to the GWB, it was extremely difficult for victims of cartels to make successful compensation claims before German courts (Quack and Djelic 2005; Wach et al. 2004; Buxbaum 2006; Hempel 2002). A number of procedural changes were introduced in the Seventh Amendment, with the aim of facilitating private enforcement of competition law in the form of civil damage claims. The burden of proof for plaintiffs was alleviated, and the use of the "passing on defence" (section 33[3]) was limited; requirements for establishing standing to sue for damages were loosened to include any affected parties, including indirect purchasers and individual consumers (section 33[1] and [3]); private follow-on actions were facilitated;[57] the amount of damages that could be claimed was extended to include any of the infringing party's profits that resulted from the competition law violation, though these profits must be paid to the government (section 34a) (Wach et al. 2004; see Wurmnest 2005; Mühlbach and Rinne 2010; Böge and Ost 2006; Hempel 2004). Though no "class action" along American lines was introduced, individual consumers can now "assign" their claim to a third party, who can thereby assemble what amount to collective claims on behalf of a group of similarly affected consumers (Wach et al. 2004). To be sure, despite these reforms, numerous obstacles to private antitrust litigation remain—particularly for consumers. German law still does not provide for the sort of pretrial discovery rules, the level of damage awards, or a class action mechanism such as those found in the United States, all of which would clearly facilitate private damage claims.

Despite these remaining impediments, the changes have had a marked impact on the practice of competition policy in Germany since 2005. Private enforcement of competition policy, in both cartel cases and abuse of dominant position cases, has clearly increased in recent years (Dietrich, Gruber, and Hartmann-Rüppel 2010). Bernhard Heitzer, president of the BKA, reports that the number of private competition damage actions in Germany has tripled since the introduction of the Seventh Amendment, to one hundred filings per year or more since 2006 (Scott 2009). Indeed, Germany has quickly emerged, alongside the UK, as an attractive jurisdiction for forum shopping by the nascent competition damages claims industry (Alfaro and Reher 2010).

A pathbreaking case brought by the Belgian company Cartel Damage Claims (CDC) illustrates how transnational legal entrepreneurs can use new provisions of the GWB to bring private competition damage claims in Germany. CDC's private enforcement action follows on a 2003 public enforcement action in which Germany's BKA fined six leading German cement manufacturers a total of €660 million for participating in a cartel. In 2005, CDC sought to take advantage of the new provisions of the Seventh Amendment to the GWB, provisions that permitted injured parties to "assign" their claims to a third party. In effect, CDC went into the business of "claims bundling" for antitrust litigation, bringing together the claims of twenty-nine companies that had suffered due to the cartel and organizing a legal action on their behalf. Working with a German law firm, CDC brought an action for damages, seeking over €150 million before the Regional Court of Düsseldorf in 2005 (Ref. 34 O [Kart] 147/05) (Mühlbach and Rinne 2010; Dietrich, Gruber, and Hartmann-Rüppel 2010; Alfaro and Reher 2010). The Düsseldorf court deemed this unprecedented group filing admissible, and the admissibility of the claim was upheld on appeal (Federal Court of Justice [Bundesgerichtshof], 7 April 2009, Case KZR 42/08). As of this writing, the claim is being adjudicated before the Regional Court of Düsseldorf.

Meanwhile, wasting no time, just a week after the Federal Court of Justice announced its ruling upholding the admissibility of CDC's bundled damage claim, CDC filed another such action in Germany. This time the company lodged a claim with the Regional Court of Dortmund against members of a pan-European cartel of hydrogen peroxide manufacturers; CDC seeks up to potentially €430 million in damages (Case 13 O 23/09 [Kart]) (see Cartel Damage Claims 2009). Notably, CDC could have filed the claim in any number of EU member states, given that the members of the cartel and their victims were spread across the Continent. The fact that it chose to sue in Germany reflects the company's determination that Germany is now an attractive forum for private antitrust litigation (Dietrich, Gruber, and Hartmann-Rüppel 2010, p. 74).

CDC has identified, or rather invented, a creative new model for private competition enforcement in Europe. It uses the bundling of claims to get around the absence of class actions. It skirts the prohibition on lawyers' contingency fee arrangements by "purchasing" claims from aggrieved parties for nominal fees, in exchange for a promise that CDC will receive 20 to 25 percent of any damage award collected. This approach also relieves clients of the financial risks of litigation. In effect, CDC assumes the financial risks of litigation and hires and pays the lawyers in exchange for 20 to 25 percent of any damage award they win. The initial success of the CDC model has prompted law firms in Germany and elsewhere to begin exploring rival models through which they could capture a share of this emerging litigation market (Scott 2009).

France

Since the mid-1980s, the process of European economic integration and the development of EU competition law have pressured France to fundamentally reorient its competition policy and transformed it from a weak and highly politicized regime to a vigorous and highly juridified one. Prior to 1986, enforcement of competition policy in France rested in the hands of the minister of economic affairs and was highly politicized (Souam 1998). Quasi-independent competition regulators existed (from 1953 to 1977 the Commission technique des ententes, and after 1977 the Commission de la concurrence), but the minister retained the authority to conduct actual investigations and discretion over enforcement of any recommendations made by competition officials (Jenny 1990). Active promotion of competition was out of step with the prevailing dirigiste economic policies of governments throughout this period, and ultimately competition rules were enforced only very rarely (Jenny 1990).[58]

France adopted a fundamentally new competition law in 1986,[59] making the country the first EU member state to revamp its competition law in the midst of the European Single Market Program (Jenny 1997). The new system was influenced heavily by both the German and the European Community models (Gerber 2001, p. 404). As Marie-Laure Djelic says of these reforms (2002, p. 247), "Undeniably, a key pressure there for France has been the process of European construction and its associated policies on competition. The principles associated with the French 1986 Decree have been in a very direct manner inspired from the articles in the European Treaties dealing with restrictions to competition and monopolies." The 1986 reforms introduced legal norms that paralleled the central norms of EU competition law (at the time, Article 85 and 86) and called for these rules to be enforced by a strong, politically independent competition regulator.

To that end, the weak Competition Commission (Commission de la concurrence) was restructured and renamed the Competition Council (Conseil de la concurrence) and given new decision-making and enforcement powers (Gerber 2001, p. 407; Djelic 2002). These reforms marked a watershed. As Djelic puts it (2002, p. 247), until 1986 competition policies in France "had all but no impact. . . . But then they came to that country with force and speed." But as with EU competition policy at the time—and unlike the US model—private enforcement of competition policy played almost no role in France.

The drive to reshape French competition law in line with EU norms continued in the 1990s and accelerated after 2004 when the EU's competition policy Modernization Regulation came into effect. Reforms made in 2004 further enhanced the Competition Council's decision-making and enforcement powers.[60] After 2004, the Competition Council stepped up its enforcement activity against cartels and against individual firms for abuse of dominant position, with landmark cases such as *Mobile Phones* and *Air Fuel* for cartels and *France Telecom* and *Corsican Cement* in 2007 for unilateral conduct (Lasserre 2009).[61] The average annual total of fines imposed by the Conseil de la concurrence rose nearly sevenfold between the first and second halves of the decade, from an average of €63.3 million per year between 2001 and 2004 to an average of €433.7 per year between 2005 and 2008 (Lasserre 2009; Lévy and Assadi-Tardif 2009). The threat of such fines, coupled with the use of leniency programs introduced in 2006 and 2007 for cooperating companies, has encouraged many companies to settle cases with regulators prior to formal findings of infringement (Lassere 2009).

Even more dramatic changes occurred in 2008 and 2009, further juridifying France's competition regime and setting the stage for increased private enforcement. The August 2008 Law for the Modernization of the Economy created a new, powerful and independent Competition Authority (Autorité de la concurrence),[62] which began operations in March 2009 (Lasserre 2009). The new Authority consolidates powers that were previously split between the Competition Council (Conseil de la concurrence) and the Ministry of Economy. For instance, jurisdiction over merger control was transferred from the Ministry to the new Competition Authority. The Authority was given a series of new enforcement powers, including the power to grant interim relief, issue injunctions, craft structural remedies, and impose fines of up to 10 percent of a firm's annual turnover. The Authority also has far greater regulatory capacity than its predecessor: while the Competition Council had to rely on the Ministry of Economy to conduct inspections, the Competition Authority has its own inspectors, who can carry out dawn raids. The consolidated, independent Authority was designed in part to adhere to the model expected of regulators participating in the European Competition Network and to enable French regulators to cooperate more effectively with the Commission.

Recent reforms set the stage for protracted legal battles between regulators and the regulated. The increased enforcement powers of the French Competition Authority have been coupled with stronger due process rights for defendants in competition cases (Cleary Gottlieb 2009). Firms under investigation now have the right to be assisted by an attorney during visits and seizures by investigators, and firms have new rights of appeal against regulators actions (Article L. 450-4 of the Commercial Code—Code de commerce). Also, a series of detailed new time limits stipulate the schedule that investigations must follow (see Article L 430-5 of the Commercial Code). French civil and commercial courts engage in increasingly strict scrutiny of competition regulators' decisions, regularly overturning them on appeal (Petit and Rabeux 2008).

While private enforcement of competition law remains rare in France, it has become more common in recent years (Momège and Bessot 2005, p. 1; Thill-Tayara and Giner Asins 2008; Luke 2004). Any party that suffers damages as a result of competition law violations can in principle bring civil damage claims, but in practice there are many serious barriers to doing so.[63] The lack of American-style discovery procedures makes it difficult for plaintiffs to gather the evidence necessary to prove and quantify the impact of breaches of competition law. Also, legal proceedings in competition cases are long and costly, and attorneys cannot offer services on a contingency fee basis (Momège and Bessot 2005; Lévy and Assadi-Tardif 2010; Baker and McKenzie 2006; Petit and Rabeux 2008). Despite such obstacles, a number of civil damage claims have been brought in recent years, and a handful have been successful (Assadi-Tardiff and Cohen 2009, p. 86). Looking forward, more aggressive public enforcement will facilitate private enforcement, because the information brought to light in public enforcement actions can be used by private parties in so-called follow-on claims (ibid.; Lévy and Assadi-Tardiff 2009, p. 84).

Consumers who suffer as a result of competition law violations, and the consumer associations who represent them, face particularly high barriers to recovering damages. Legal proceedings are lengthy, and costs are typically orders of magnitude higher than the damages any individual may hope to recover in a competition case. Despite years of debate on the subject—there is still no equivalent of American class actions under French law, and existing mechanisms for collective actions are problematic (Magnier 2009; Legal Director FCU 2006; ORGECO 2006; Gatinois 2010). Consumer associations can bring collective litigation on behalf of consumers via two routes. Either associations can bring an action in the general interest of consumers (under Article L. 421-1 of the Consumer Code—Code de la consommation)—a procedure which can be used primarily to obtain injunctions—or they can bring damage actions on behalf of a group of consumers at the consumers' explicit request. However, these so-called joint representative actions (*action en représentation conjointe,* under Article L.422-1 of the Consumer Code) face serious hurdles.

The experience of UFC–Que Choisir, the leading French consumer association, in its recent action against the mobile-phone operators' cartel illustrates the challenges to collective consumer litigation in France. After the French Competition Council found three mobile-phone companies guilty of cartel abuses in 2005 and fined them over €500 million, the French consumer association UFC–Que Choisir sought to bring a follow-on action, to claim damages on behalf of injured consumers. However, the association managed to attract only just over 12,000 consumers of the more than 20 million victims of the cartel to join their action (Que Choisir 2006). In January 2010, some four years after UFC–Que Choisir had initiated legal proceedings, its damage claim was rejected by the Paris Court of Appeal, which argued that the plaintiffs had relied on an improper legal basis for their claim, and that the Web site that the organization had set up to notify consumers of the cartel abuse (www.cartelmobile.org) constituted "solicitation of clients" *(démarchage juridique),* which is forbidden under French law (Thill-Tayara and Giner Asins 2008, p. 181; Magnier 2009; Agence France Press 2010). There was a certain irony in this outcome, in that French consumer groups, including UFC–Que Choisir, had themselves used the charge of illegal solicitation in a 2005 suit to shut down a group of entrepreneurial lawyers who had started a Web site—http://classaction.fr—to attract consumers to join collective legal actions.[64]

Conclusion

The Gospel according to Matthew (26:52) relates an incident in which Jesus said unto the Apostle Peter, "All they that take the sword shall perish with the sword." That biblical dictum may have had a certain resonance for European Union competition officials in July 2007, when they felt the sting of the judicial forces they themselves had unsheathed. In a landmark judgment that month, the Court of First Instance ordered the European Commission to pay compensation to a French electrical equipment company, Schneider Electric, for having wrongly blocked its 2001 merger with rival Legrand. The CFI found that the Commission had committed a variety of grave and manifest errors. It rejected the Commission's economic analysis of the merger as inadequate and admonished the Commission for violating Schneider's rights of defense by basing its decision on objections that the Commission had not raised in the preliminary Statement of Objections it had presented to Schneider.[65] The ruling established the precedent that when Commission merger or antitrust decisions are later overturned by European courts, the Commission may have to compensate firms for losses caused by those decisions (Bailey 2007). In the *Schneider* case, that would include compensation for a substantial proportion of the €1.66 billion in losses associated with Schneider's divestiture of Legrand. Seizing on the *Schneider* precedent, the travel operator company Thomas Cook sought over €630 million in compensation for losses associated with a flawed Commission merger decision.[66] The CFI annulled nine Commission Merger decisions between 2003 and 2007 (Bailey 2007, p. 104). When these or future decisions are judged to have been based on "grave" errors, the Commission may again face claims for compensation from firms who suffered as a result of its merger decisions. To describe this as an illustration of "Live by the courts, die by the courts" may be slightly melodramatic, but it is certainly a case of "Live by the courts, occasionally face compensation claims to the tune of hundreds of millions of euros."

Despite feeling the sting of judicial oversight, the EU shows no signs of heeding Jesus's advice to Peter to "put up again thy sword into its place." There will be no legal armistice between the Commission and the firms it regulates. Rather, with the 2004 modernization reforms, the EU continues to promote a juridified model of competition policy with a central role for lawyers, courts, and litigation. And with its ongoing effort to promote private enforcement, the EU is inviting others to join it on the legal battlefield.

The combined effects of economic liberalization and political fragmentation have provided the impetus for these shifts. The economic liberalization associated with the completion of the single market generated enormous regulatory burdens and strained the capacity of the EU's centralized competition regime. For liberalization to succeed, cartels and former national monopolies had to be prevented from partitioning and otherwise distorting the market. However, this reregulation could not follow the highly discretionary, administrative model of competition law found in most member states. Member states were increasingly distrustful and critical of the Commission, and the European courts placed ever-tighter constraints on its decision making. As for political fragmentation, the EU's character as a "weak state" and the fragmentation of power between the Commission, EU courts, and national administrations encouraged the emergence of a model based on Eurolegalism.[67]

That the Commission would encourage these developments is striking in some senses. Competition policy has long stood out as the policy area in which the Commission commanded the greatest powers—and therefore had potentially the most to lose by delegating these powers. National competition authorities had little if any experience enforcing the strict, prohibition-style regime favored by the Commission, and private enforcement of competition law at the national level was almost unheard of (Riley 2003, p. 659). And yet, even in these inauspicious conditions, the Commission relinquished its monopoly on enforcement, inviting private parties, national courts, and national competition authorities to take on a central role.

A competition regime based on adversarial legalism was not the Commission's ideal but emerged as an attractive option, given the constraints the Commission faced. Throughout the late 1980s and early 1990s, powerful member states regularly criticized the Commission's Directorate General for Competition and refused to allow the Commission to build up the regulatory capacity necessary to sustain a centralized administrative apparatus that could cope with the regulatory burden. In the late 1990s, the Commission was even confronted with failed a proposal, discussed above, to strip away its powers and transfer them to an independent European competition office. The Commission then sought to remold and to harness national administrative capacity by helping to establish a network of national competition authorities and assigning them a role—though a subordinate role—in the enforcement of EU competition law. The Commission is also seeking to harness the capacity and the energies of private litigants, by opening the door for them to enforce EU competition law before national courts in litigants' own self-interest.

The advent of a model of regulation based on Eurolegalism is significant for a number of reasons. Proponents of increased private enforcement argue that it will both provide greater justice for victims and enhance the effectiveness of EU regulation by exerting a powerful deterrent effect on would-be law breakers (Brodley 1995, p. 36; Wils 2003, p. 478; Roach and Trebilcock 1996). In this view, public and private enforcement can complement one another: given the limited resources of public authorities, additional monitoring and enforcement by private parties can play a key role in ensuring compliance (Komninos 2006, 2007; Van Gerven 2005).

Critics of private enforcement paint a starkly different picture. Pointing to the American antitrust experience, they emphasize that whatever the benefits of private enforcement, these are easily outweighed by the massive costs of the litigation it unleashes and other undesirable side effects. Rather than trying outcompete their rivals, firms may bring bogus antitrust claims against them (Snyder and Kauper 1991; Hodges 2006; Eilmansberger 2007, pp. 455, 477). Also, in litigation between competitors there will often be incentives to settle cases quietly. Unpublicized private settlements do nothing to clarify the law, and more worryingly, they may even result in illegal backroom agreements between competitors (Wils 2003, p. 483). Consumers represented in class actions constitute another key category of private enforcers, but class actions suffer from numerous drawbacks (Coffee 1983; Hodges 2006). Class actions are extremely costly and difficult to administer, and often in practice the lawyers drive the agenda, frequently with their profits rather than clients' interests in mind.[68] The US Chamber of Commerce and other US business interests have warned their European counterparts of the risks associated with excessive antitrust litigation, and management boards across Europe have expressed concern over new litigation risks (Wigger and Nölke 2007, p. 500).

Finally, as we saw above, a shift toward a model of competition policy in which private actors play a lead role in enforcement entails a shift in the substance of regulation as well. In the traditional European model, a public regulatory body wielded its discretion to balance a variety of goals and to pursue a broad understanding of healthy competition and economic efficiency. Private actors simply cannot be entrusted with enforcing a policy that balances these multiple goals. The shift to private enforcement and judicial empowerment necessarily involves a shift to competition law norms focused on short-term consumer welfare considerations (Wigger 2007, p. 110).

This shift in norms and increase in enforcement by private actors may have profound implications far beyond the realm of competition policy. This shift is likely to place great strains on the Rhenish variety of capitalism, with its focus on long-term firm strategies, interfirm collaboration, cross-shareholding, and policies to support small- and medium-sized enterprises (Wigger and Nölke 2007, p. 489; Wilks 2005a; Wilks 2007, p. 18; Gerber 1998, p. 420). The frequency of private enforcement in Europe will not need to approach that in the United States for it to have a major impact. As Wigger and Nölke (2007, p. 500) explain, "The volatility induced by private enforcement makes strategic long-term investments or commercial collaborations more risky." Wilks (2007) even suggests that the emerging model of competition policy in the EU could contribute to the dismantling of "the managed economy and the state economy models which predominate in continental Europe" (p. 18). As in other areas of business regulation, the specter of private enforcement reduces businesses' incentives to work cooperatively with regulators. Regulators can no longer offer a calibrated mixture of carrots and sticks, because regulators no longer wield the only sticks. Leniency schemes, whereby regulators shield from further prosecution firms that disclose cartels, can play a helpful role in this regard, but firms facing heightened risks of damage claims from competitors or consumers will still be more reluctant to collaborate with regulators (Guersent 2004, p. 53). While the heightened risks of lawsuits will discourage violations of competition law, these risks will also impose costs of their own, eroding the foundations of European models of capitalism.

CHAPTER 6

Disability Rights

Roughly one in six Europeans of working age has some form of disability (Eurostat 2003, 2001). Disability affects all segments of society in all European Union member states, and disabled people are highly diverse in terms of the nature and severity of impairments they face. From the perspective of employment policy, addressing questions surrounding disability has long presented a major challenge. Across Europe, labor force participation rates are far lower among disabled persons than among those without disabilities (ibid.). At the end of the 1990s, public expenditures on disability-related programs in EU member states amounted to on average 2.7 percent of the GDP, roughly twice the spending on unemployment programs (OECD 2003, p. 17).

Modern national disability policies in Europe date back to the period after World War I. As millions returned from the war with severe injuries, many national governments introduced policies to aid disabled veterans and promote their reentry into the workforce. In subsequent decades, national governments extended such policies, to cover more and more disabled civilians. Given this long history, it is unsurprising that traditional national approaches to disability policy became deeply engrained. To be sure, many aspects of national policies differed (Hvinden 2003), yet the approach that underlay these policies and the tools they employed to achieve their objectives were similar in important ways.

National policies were based on what we can refer to as a medical/welfare model of disability.[1] This model views disabled persons as victims of physical or mental impairments and holds that society is morally obliged to assist them in securing gainful employment when possible and to provide them with income support and social services if they are unable to work. Accordingly, national disability policies were designed around a variety of rehabilitation programs, employment quota schemes, sheltered work programs that aimed to create employment opportunities for disabled people, and social assistance and income support programs. These policies produced "positive feedbacks" (Pierson 1993) in that they encouraged the proliferation of institutions and constituencies (including various care providers and professionals), which in turn provided political support for the policies.

While many EU member state governments have maintained disability policies for nearly a century, the European Union itself is a newcomer to the disability field. The EU took its first, tentative steps in the area of disability policy in the 1970s and took more decisive action only beginning in the late 1990s. The first firm legal requirement imposed by the EU in the disability field, the Framework Equal Treatment Directive, or Employment Equality Directive,[2] was adopted in 2000 and fully came into force in 2006. Despite its brief history of engagement in disability issues, the EU is already having a profound impact on disability policy.

The involvement of the EU has emerged as a crucial factor in reorienting disability policy across Europe, away from the paternalistic, medical/welfare model and toward a civil rights, antidiscrimination model that emphasizes the right of every disabled individual to protection against discrimination. EU involvement is by no means the only factor behind this transformation. Pressure for such a reorientation of disability policy was generated by disability rights activists within a number of member states. Further pressure has come from external forces—such as the example set by the United States with its Americans with Disabilities Act, new international norms promoted through United Nations (UN) conventions, and the activities of networks of international disability rights activists. The reorientation of disability policy from a medical/welfare model to a rights-based model is a global trend (Degener and Quinn 2000), and some movement in this direction certainly would have occurred in some member states regardless of EU involvement. That being said, the EU has clearly had a profound impact. The EU has spread the rights model of disability across the European Union to states that were not contemplating it and has pressed stricter legal standards on even those states that had adopted some aspects of a rights model.

As in the other cases examined in this book, the confluence of economic liberalization and political fragmentation worked both to undermine traditional national disability policies and to encourage a turn to a new approach at the EU level, an approach based on Eurolegalism. Economic liberalization associated with the single market project posed a challenge to traditional national policies that were both highly costly and dependent on informal cooperation between national regulators and large domestic employers. The fragmented political structure of the EU stymied efforts to enact policies based on the traditional medical/welfare model at the EU level and instead created political incentives to rely on a rights-based approach.

The rights model of disability was a perfect fit for the EU. While the medical/welfare model of disability that prevailed at the national level relied on a combination of social assistance programs, income transfers, and economic regulations (in the form of employment quotas), the rights model focuses on empowering individuals with legal rights that they can enforce before national or European courts. It requires little expenditure and little centralized enforcement. Thus, the medical/welfare model requires structures and resources, namely, large bureaucracies and budgets, that the EU did not possess, while the rights model relies on litigants and courts—both of which the EU can access in abundance. Finally, the legitimating power of rights played a crucial role. While EU policy makers invoked rights rhetoric for its legitimating power in other fields examined in this book—take, for instance, the emphasis on shareholder rights in the securities field—the field of disability policy illustrates most clearly how the desire to enhance the legitimacy of EU governance led EU policy makers to champion rights-based policies (Burke 2004).

The success of disability advocates in enshrining the notion of disability rights in the 1999 Treaty of Amsterdam and in a binding directive a year later cannot be understood in isolation. Advocates of disability rights benefited from linking their cause to the EU's broader rights agenda. The disability rights movement essentially rode the EU rights wave, which was surging in the late 1990s (Burke 2004; Mabbett 2005). As we explore below, the 1990s witnessed a dramatic increase in the salience of "rights talk" at the EU level and the proliferation of campaigns and policy proposals designed to embed social rights and fundamental civil rights at the EU level. The disability rights movement benefited by linking its demands to those of other campaigns for antidiscrimination rights—such as those concerning discrimination based on race, ethnicity, sexual orientation, and religion.

Given the close linkage between disability and other EU rights policies, examining the development of EU disability rights sheds light on the development of other EU social rights, particularly other antidiscrimination rights. Focusing on disability is also useful because, in comparison with other forms of antidiscrimination rights, disability rights would seem to constitute an unlikely (if not "least likely") case (Eckstein 1975). By the time the EU began to promote its rights-based model of disability, the medical/welfare model of disability was deeply entrenched in most member states and backed by a host of policies, programs, and associated interest groups. Arguments that emphasize the impact of policy legacies, legal cultures, and path dependence would expect that the deep entrenchment of institutions and practices associated with the medical/welfare model of disability would have obstructed the spread of a new, rights-based approach in the field of disability (Kagan 2006). In comparison, action to combat racial discrimination fit better with existing national frameworks, in that all member states except for Greece and Austria already had laws in place prohibiting racial discrimination in employment (Bell and Waddington 2003, p. 366).

To trace the EU's role in transforming disability policy this chapter begins by reviewing the traditional medical/welfare model of disability policy at the national level that prevailed across Europe before the EU became involved in the field. The next section examines the development of disability policy at the EU level and the EU's embrace of the rights model. We then explore the impact of the EU rules on disability discrimination on national policies in Germany, France, the Netherlands, and the United Kingdom. The concluding section considers some of the benefits and potential costs of the rise of the rights model of disability in Europe.

Traditional Disability Policies in Europe

The medical/welfare model that formed the basis of the national disability policies that developed across Europe beginning in the early twentieth century holds that the difficulties a disabled person faces in terms of housing, employment, transport, and other facets of daily life result from the individual's medical impairment. Disabled persons are expected to adapt, insofar as possible, to the conditions of the predominant, "able" society. The role, indeed the moral obligation, of government is to assist disabled persons in making such adaptations and to support them with various forms of social assistance.

Specifically in the sphere of employment, national disability policies across Europe had two main elements—one on the supply side and one on the demand side. On the supply side, governments set up vocational training and rehabilitation programs to help prepare disabled persons to take up employment. On the demand side, governments established quotas obliging employers to hire a set minimum percentage of disabled workers and in some cases to establish subsidized sheltered employment programs for disabled workers.

Such employment quota systems date back to the period after World War I. After nearly 8 million soldiers across Europe returned from the war with disabilities (Cohen 2001), a number of national governments responded by adopting legislation encouraging, and in some cases requiring, employers to employ set quotas of disabled veterans. By 1923, Germany, Austria, Italy, Poland, and France had mandatory quotas in place, and the United Kingdom had adopted a voluntary quota system (Waddington 1996, pp. 62–64). Voluntary approaches proved largely unsuccessful in the interwar years, and more governments, including the UK, the Netherlands, Greece, Luxembourg, Spain, Ireland, and Belgium, adopted mandatory quotas after World War II. Also, governments gradually extended quotas beyond disabled veterans to included disabled civilians. As of the 1980s, national variants of this medical/welfare, quota model were well established across most European countries, including Germany, the UK, the Netherlands, and France.

Germany had been a pioneer in the use of quota systems after World War I. The Weimar Republic tried to build its legitimacy by establishing innovative welfare and rehabilitation programs, including quota schemes, for disabled war veterans (Cohen 2001, p. 57). In the aftermath of World War II, West Germany returned to the practice of mandating employment quotas. The 1953 Schwerbeschädigtengesetz required firms in various sectors to reserve between 6 and 10 percent of the positions in their workforce for people with severe disabilities. A levy system was also established, in which employers paid an "employers redemption" if they were unable to meet their quota (Thornton 1998). To address various shortcomings of this system, the federal government introduced a new quota scheme in the 1974 Severely Handicapped Persons Act (Schwerbehindertengesetz). The law required all public and private employers with more than sixteen employees to maintain a quota of 6 percent disabled employees and required those businesses that did not fulfill their quota requirements to pay a monthly levy for every unfilled quota position (Waddington 1996, p. 69).[3]

The Dutch Employment of the Disabled Act of 1947 established a quota system requiring employers with more than twenty employees to employ a fixed percentage of workers who had registered with the government as disabled workers.[4] In 1986, the Dutch government reformed the quota system, introducing the new Handicapped Workers Employment Act,[5] eliminating the registration requirement and expanding the range of disabled people covered by the scheme. The new quota system began on a voluntary basis but was backed by government promises to introduce a more rigid system should the voluntary approach fail. After the three-year trial period, the government itself concluded that the voluntary quota scheme was failing to achieve employment targets for disabled workers. Nevertheless, the government backed away from its promise to introduce binding quotas and left the voluntary scheme in place (Waddington 1996, p. 65). As I discuss below, the disability quota scheme has been linked to government efforts to reduce the large number of people claiming disability benefits. Persons eligible for disability benefits are also categorized as disabled for the purposes of the employment quota. This encourages employers to hire persons who might otherwise be on the government's disability benefits rolls.

The quota-based approach in the UK dated back to 1919, when a royal proclamation announced the launch of the King's National Roll Scheme, a program that encouraged employers to take on veterans disabled during the Great War as 5 percent of the workforce. The scheme was entirely voluntary, and it attempted to induce firms to participate by offering them some preference in the allocation of government contracts and permitting them to use a special King's Roll emblem on their stationery. The voluntary scheme met with, at best, limited success (Malisoff 1952; Waddington 1996, p. 62), and to prepare for the expected influx of disabled veterans into the workforce after World War II, the government introduced an obligatory quota scheme in 1944.[6] The new legislation both made employment quotas mandatory and extended them beyond veterans to cover all disabled persons. Employers falling below the quota would be barred from hiring new nondisabled employees, under threat of fine or imprisonment. Ultimately, however, quota scheme was all bark and no bite, as governments consistently proved unwilling to enforce the quotas and to penalize noncompliant firms (Fredman 2002). With governments refusing to enforce the quota, there was little benefit for eligible disabled persons to register with the scheme, and over time fewer and fewer did so (Waddington 1996, p. 67).

France too had long relied on a quota system as the principal means through which to encourage the employment of disabled persons (Besner 1995). A 1924 law (Law of 26 April 1924) obliged employers to reserve 10 percent of their workplaces for workers wounded in war (and for related categories of disabled workers). In 1957, a more comprehensive quota system was established that extended the quota system to include all persons whose employment prospects were affected by mental or physical disabilities (Thornton 1998, p. 10). A far wider range of social welfare supports and programs designed to aid entry into the workforce for the disabled was put into place in the 1970s, and finally a far stricter quota system was introduced in 1987 (Law 87-517 of 10 July 1987), which obliged all employers with over twenty employees to meet a 6 percent quota (Thornton and Lunt 1997, p. 118; Thornton 1998; Besner 1995). The law also clarified the standards by which workers would qualify as disabled, and it allowed companies that could not meet the quota to instead pay into a vocational training fund.[7]

* * *

In principle, governments across Europe might have simply enforced quotas strictly, forcing employers to take the steps necessary to meet them. In practice, governments proved reluctant to strictly enforce quota systems. Instead, governments developed a variety of complementary policies designed to support the employment of disabled persons and to entice firms to hire them. These measures included vocational rehabilitation and training programs, job placement services, direct wage subsidies to employers, grants to employers for workplace adaptations necessary to accommodate disabled workers, and support of sheltered employment programs, which reserved workplaces specifically for disabled persons. Employment quotas, backed by such supporting measures, clearly had an impact, securing employment for tens of thousands of disabled persons in some countries (Waddington 1996, p. 62; Thornton 1998; Cohen 2001). More generally, through a combination of sheltered employment programs and quotas, income support, and other social assistance programs, national social welfare systems frequently did succeed in providing a basic income and essential forms of care and social support for disabled citizens.

Critique of the Medical/Welfare Model

In the 1970s, the employment quota approach and the medical/welfare model of disability that underlies it became the target of mounting criticism from a new generation of disability advocacy groups. Where long-established disability groups had been led by medical professionals, experts, family members, and others who cared for the disabled, the new generation of groups were composed of and led by disabled people themselves. The new disability rights movement attacked the assumptions that underlie the employment quota approach and the entire medical/welfare model of disability. Rights advocates proposed nothing less than a paradigm shift. The medical/welfare model, they explained, is based on the assumption that disability is the result of a defect or ailment in an individual that makes him or her unable to function in society or to compete in the labor market. Disability activists proposed a fundamentally different understanding of disability—which they referred to as the social model of disability (Oliver 1983, 1990). They argued that the difficulties that disabled persons faced in society and in the workplace stemmed primarily not from a medical ailment residing within the individual but rather from prejudice, discrimination, and various impediments put in place by mainstream society and institutions. Disablement was as much a social construct as a medical fact. A British activist group, the Union of Physically Impaired against Segregation, captured this perspective in a statement of principles it issued in 1976, explaining, "It is society which disables. . . . Disability is something imposed on top of our impairments, by the way we are unnecessarily isolated and excluded from full participation in society. Disabled people are therefore an oppressed group in society" (UPIAS/Disability Alliance 1976, p. 3).

Disability activists argued that though the medical/welfare model of disability and the quota systems and sheltered employment programs associated with it might be well intentioned, they actually encouraged the social exclusion and disempowerment of people with disabilities. Such policies were highly paternalistic: they treated disabled people as objects of charity rather than as equal citizens and decision makers in their own right. The entire quota approach was based on and perpetuated the notion that persons with disabilities were inferior and unable to compete in an open market. According to this notion, they could rightly be segregated into "special" training and employment programs. By perpetuating these assumptions, such policies masked the role of prejudice and institutional discrimination in disadvantaging persons with disabilities.

From the perspective of the social model, when a workplace is not wheelchair accessible, it is not the ailment of the wheelchair user that is the impediment but the failure of the employer to provide a facility accessible to wheelchair users. Thus, rather than tracking disabled workers into special (often low-status) jobs reserved for people with disabilities, public policies and employer practices should focus on eliminating discrimination and barriers that prevent the disabled person from participating in mainstream employment.

Advocates for this new rights-based model of disability demanded that mainstreaming replace segregation. Above all, they demanded that disability policy be approached as a matter of fundamental civil rights, not as a matter of charity. While the European medical/welfare model of disability provided important benefits to many disabled people, one thing it did not provide was rights. Disabled people themselves did not have enforceable rights under the traditional model of disability (Hendriks 2005, p. 187–190). In the employment sphere, neither individuals nor associations representing them could enforce employment quotas against firms that failed to meet them.

More generally, before the 1990s, governments across Europe did not rely on an antidiscrimination approach to promoting the employment of persons with disabilities. This approach was not unknown in the employment field, as it had been applied to promote equal treatment of women in the workplace since the 1970s. However, governments did not extend this approach to disabled people. Indeed, there was considerable suspicion of the antidiscrimination, rights-based approach among many observers. As Aart Hendriks (2005), former head of the Dutch Equal Treatment Commission, explains, "Many Europeans were proud of their generous social welfare laws and policies on disability and considered this type of approach superior to the civil rights model of disability adopted in the United States" (p. 187).

While the new wave of disability activists demanded continued support for social welfare programs benefiting people with disabilities, they also questioned the efficacy of many existing policies. Critics pointed out that quota systems regularly failed to deliver promised employment opportunities for disabled persons. Governments generally were loath to enforce quota requirements on private employers or indeed to adhere to them themselves. In systems that imposed automatic levies on employers that failed to meet their quota obligations, many employers opted to pay levies rather than to employ disabled workers. In such cases, the schemes operated effectively as a tax. While the revenue generated by such levies for vocational training and rehabilitation programs was welcome, the fact that employers continued over many years to fall short of quotas suggests that such schemes failed to achieve their overarching objective of increasing the integration of disabled people into the workforce. Even when there was pressure to comply, employers were able—and in many cases actively encouraged—to satisfy quota requirements by segregating disabled people into special sheltered jobs reserved for them. These were typically low-status, poorly paid positions, which encouraged the ongoing social exclusion of persons with disabilities rather than opening up opportunities for rewarding work and career development.

Finally, the efficacy of the medical/welfare model of disability was also attacked from an entirely different perspective—not by disability activists but by critics of uncontrolled welfare state spending. By the end of the 1990s, EU member states were spending, on average, nearly twice as much on disability benefits as on unemployment benefits (OECD 2003, p. 17). Some EU member states, such as the Netherlands, experienced significant upsurges in the number of workers filing for disability benefits. Labor force participation among people with disabilities was relatively low, and across EU member states the percentage of "outflow" from disability benefit programs—that is to say, the percentage of benefit recipients who leave the rolls in any given year—was extremely low, approximately 1 percent (OECD 2003, p. 58). Policy makers feared that generous long-term disability benefits programs were diminishing incentives to work and were being used as a substitute for unemployment benefits and other social assistance benefits as criteria for such benefits were tightened.

Global Shift toward a Rights Model of Disability

Disability activists around the world mobilized around this new understanding of disability, with many viewing the disability movement as the latest manifestation of the civil rights movement. Disability activists won their first major policy victories in the United States and Canada. American disability activists took up the rhetoric and strategy of the civil rights movement, demanding equality and legal protection for the rights of disabled people. Activists won an early victory with the enactment of Section 504 of the Rehabilitation Act of 1973,[8] which prohibited employment discrimination against disabled persons by the federal government and federal contractors. Section 504 was grounded in the social model of disability. As the Supreme Court later noted in a ruling concerning Section 504, in enacting the provision, "Congress acknowledged that the society's accumulated fears about disability and disease are as handicapping as are the physical limitations that flow from actual impairment."[9]

The disability rights movement then struggled for years to secure the passage of federal legislation that would extend antidiscrimination requirements to private sector employers (Switzer 2003). Activists finally achieved their legislative breakthrough with the 1990 Americans with Disabilities Act (ADA).[10] With regard to employment, the ADA prohibits employers from discriminating against individuals on the basis of disability. Crucially, the ADA also requires employers to make a "reasonable accommodation" for disabled workers to allow the individual with a disability to perform "essential functions" of a job, unless making such accommodations would cause "undue hardship" on the employer.[11] Such accommodations could include physical modification of the workplace, changes in scheduling, or other adjustments that enable the worker to perform the essential functions of the job in question. Employers can escape this obligation only if making adjustments would in any way endanger their business or the health and safety of other workers. Otherwise, an employer's refusal to make "reasonable accommodations" itself constitutes discrimination. With regard to enforcement, the ADA was designed as a litigious policy (Burke 2004). Though the Department of Justice was expected to play some role, the ADA was to be enforced primarily through private civil law suits brought by victims of discrimination (Mezey 2005).

The growth of the disability rights movement across a number of countries and the dramatic policy developments in the United States stimulated action at the international level. The UN and related organizations such as the International Labour Organization (ILO) had long addressed disability issues through the traditional medical/welfare model of disability. This began to change in the early 1970s, when the UN issued two nonbinding declarations recognizing the human rights of persons with disabilities. The UN declared 1981 the International Year of Disabled Persons, and in 1982 it launched the UN Decade of Disabled Persons (1982–1993). Throughout this decade, under pressure from the disability rights movement, the UN shifted toward the rights model of disability. After proposals for a binding treaty on the human rights of disabled persons failed to win support, the UN concluded the Decade of Disabled Persons with the adoption of a nonbinding instrument designed to provide a model for reform of national disability policies—the 1993 *UN Standard Rules on the Equalization of Opportunities for Persons with Disabilities.*[12] The UN's *Standard Rules* called on governments to promote an equal opportunities approach, emphasizing nondiscrimination rights and the integration of disabled persons into mainstream employment and social institutions.

Meanwhile, in Europe the 1980s witnessed a gradual shift away from the most segregationist aspects of the medical/welfare model. Many countries began to emphasize mainstreaming as an aim of disability policy, working to deinstitutionalize the disabled people and integrate them into mainstream schools, housing, and jobs (Degener and Quinn 2000, p. 20; Thornton and Lunt 1997). While the growing emphasis on social integration did signal the beginning of a paradigm shift, it was not tantamount to prohibiting discrimination and creating enforceable rights for people with disabilities. Demands for a rights-based approach intensified after the passage of the Americans with Disabilities Act.

The ADA, and to a lesser extent the UN *Standard Rules,* set a model for rights-based disability legislation that disability activists in Europe sought to emulate. As discussed in more detail below, the UK followed suit in 1995, with the passage of the Disability Discrimination Act (DDA), which was modeled closely on the American ADA. Germany took the symbolic step of adding a reference to disability to the equality clause of its Basic Law (Grundgesetz),[13] but this move alone did not provide disabled persons with clear, legally enforceable nondiscrimination rights (Heyer 2002; Waddington and Diller 2002; Degener and Quinn 2000, p. 25).

These early steps toward the rights model of disability in a handful of EU member states certainly marked a significant break with past practice. However, it would be wrong to conclude from these examples that the medical/welfare model of disability was crumbling across Europe. Quite to the contrary, the medical/welfare model of disability clearly remained the predominant model across Europe throughout the 1990s. Writing in the mid-1990s, Lisa Waddington (1996) noted, "The quota system has emerged as the main legislative tool in Europe to promote the employment of disabled people" (p. 64). In the late 1990s, ten of the then fifteen member states had in place some form of obligatory employment quotas for disabled persons (Waddington and Bell, 2001, p. 603). As Patricia Thornton (1993) put it, "Quota systems represent a deeply embedded policy approach . . . based on long-standing acceptance of a social obligation to employ individuals with disabilities" (p. 3). Likewise, A. Hendriks (2005) emphasizes that the medical/welfare model of disability is "firmly rooted in the European legal traditions" (p. 192), and Björn Hvinden (2003) emphasizes that policies based on this model are supported by long-established "power balances and vested interests" (p. 611). Thus, when the EU approached questions of disability policy, it could not write on a blank slate. National disability policies had deep historical roots and were supported by a range of entrenched institutions and vested interests. At the same time, disability activists across the world had mounted a sustained attack on the assumptions underlying the traditional medical/welfare model that underpinned these national policies, and the international climate was turning against the traditional model of disability. It was against this background that the EU stepped into the fray.

As I detail below, in its initial forays into the disability field in the 1970s and 1980s, the EU adhered closely to the traditional medical/welfare model, simply encouraging national governments to "harmonize" certain aspects of their policies. This approach foundered. In the 1990s, the EU turned decisively to the rights model of disability, which was spreading internationally at that time. The EU was able to seize the initiative here and emerge as a powerful champion of the rights model. While its earlier harmonization efforts had produced precious few results, with the rights model the EU achieved major legislative breakthroughs that reshaped disability policy across Europe in fundamental ways.

EU Disability Policy

The European Union entered the field of disability policy in 1974 with the adoption of its first multiannual "Action Program" on disability.[14] At that time, the EU treaties made no mention of disability issues. Despite the absence of a clear legal basis for disability policy, the EU adopted three more multiannual disability action programs and established a unit dealing with disability issues in the Employment and Social Affairs Directorate.[15] As in other areas where the European Community (EC) lacked a clear treaty basis to enact binding directives, the Commission focused first on stimulating a policy debate and on laying the groundwork for a more substantial EU disability policy in the future.

To this end, the disability action programs focused on establishing pan-European networks of nongovernmental organizations (NGOs), experts, and policy makers. The Commission brought together these networks and funded regular meetings, conferences, and newsletters. Through these networks, the action programs promoted information sharing and the exchange of experience and best practices. In a more general sense, the Commission sought to stimulate a European-level dialogue among stakeholders—a dialogue that the Commission hoped might lead to demands from stakeholders for a greater EU role in disability policy and eventually to greater harmonization of policies. Where important stakeholders had trouble mobilizing or simply did not exist, the EU helped to support or create them. As we will see below, EU action programs in the 1990s played an indispensable role in building connections between disability NGOs across Europe and stimulating the pan-European disability rights movement (Degener and Quinn 2000, p. 82).

In substantive terms, the EU's early initiatives were based on the traditional medical/welfare model of disability. This approach was reflected at a conceptual level, in the way EU policy makers defined and understood disability (Waddington 2006a, p. 13). It was also reflected in the membership of networks sponsored by the Commission. In keeping with the medical/welfare model, these networks drew together medical and care professionals and other experts who worked for people with disabilities, rather than seeking input and leadership from disabled people themselves. Finally, the EU's focus on the traditional model was evident in the policies and programs the EU supported, namely, rehabilitation programs and quota systems to promote the employment of disabled people (Lawson 2006, p. 5; Mabbett 2005, p. 107). For instance, in 1986, the Commission recommended that all member states adopt quotas for the employment of disabled people and that a European directive mandating such quotas should be introduced if the member states failed to act (Commission 1986). The European Parliament strongly backed this proposal. The proposal later stalled, as member states in the Council rejected any firm demands for quotas. Though the Commission's focus on quotas was clearly in line with the approach that prevailed across the member states, they were unwilling to accept any mandatory harmonization of their national quota systems (Mabbett 2005, p. 107). Instead, the Council adopted a nonbinding recommendation that outlined a number of measures that member states should consider to promote the employment of disabled people.[16]

There was little evidence that such nonbinding recommendations were having any effect at the national level (Waddington 2006, p. 7), and in 1991 the Commission sought to introduce binding disability legislation. As the treaties provided no specific basis for disability policy, the Commission needed to be creative and to find an existing section of the treaties that it could plausibly link to—and use as a justification for—action on disability issues. The Commission had great experience, and considerable success, in playing similar treaty basis games (Jupille 2004) in other areas. In this case, the Commission turned to Treaty Article 118a, which empowered the Commission to take measures concerning the health and safety of workers. The Commission proposed a directive concerning transportation to work for disabled workers, arguing that improvements in transportation for disabled workers were necessary on health and safety grounds (Commission 1991a). Focusing on transportation for workers promised to yield indirect benefits for all disabled persons: if the EU could press member states to increase the accessibility of public transport in the name of disabled workers, such transport would then be available for all disabled persons (Waddington 2006, p. 8). Though the Commission has succeeded in the creative use of legal bases to launch initiatives in many policy areas, in the field of disability policy the member states resisted this maneuver, and the Commission proposal was never adopted.

The EU's early initiatives in the field of disability policy adhered closely to the medical/welfare model of disability that prevailed among all EU member state governments. While the EU had long prohibited employment discrimination on the basis of sex and national origin, it did not attempt to extend this rights-based, antidiscrimination approach to disability. The Commission did not attempt to foist new policies or programs on member state governments but simply encouraged some harmonization of national policies. Nevertheless, national governments refused to support even a modest harmonization of their policies. Early EU efforts to develop policies on disability produced very few tangible results. Summarizing the impact of EU initiatives taken prior to the mid-1990s, Waddington soberly concludes (2006, p. 11), "It is difficult to identify improvements originating in the European Community legal order during this period, which have benefited disabled people." While EU initiatives in the 1970s and 1980s achieved little of substance, they did lay the groundwork for dramatic developments in EU disability policy in the 1990s. With the failure of its initiatives in the late 1980s and early 1990s, the EU reconsidered its approach, in what proved to be a dramatic case of *reculer pour mieux sauter*. As we will see in the next section, the EU achieved a constitutional and legislative breakthrough when it turned away from the prevailing medical/welfare model of disability and embraced the disability rights movement.

Toward a Rights-Based Model of Disability in the EU

In the 1990s, the EU shifted away from the traditional medical/welfare model of disability and toward an antidiscrimination, rights-based approach. At the start of the 1990s, the European Commission faced increasing demands from disability NGOs and their allies in the European Parliament to move in this direction. The European Parliament emerged as an early champion of the disability rights movement. In 1991, when the Commission proposed a new action program on disability, a program that continued the approach the Commission had pursued in earlier programs (Commission 1991b), the Parliament demanded significant changes. The Parliament demanded greater involvement of disabled persons and disability NGOs in the planning and implementation of EU activities (Waddington 1995, p. 125). In response, the Commission proposed the establishment of a new consultative body, the European Disability Forum, which would be made of up twenty-four disability NGOs and included commitments that the Commission would strengthen its cooperation with disability NGOs.

After the Helios II Action Program to Assist Disabled People (1993–1996) was adopted in February 1993,[17] the Commission funded the establishment of the European Disability Forum (EDF). The EDF brought together disability rights NGOs from across Europe and quickly emerged as a major force lobbying for the establishment of disability rights in EU treaties and legislation. As part of its new action program, the Commission, together with the European Parliament, sponsored the first European Day of Disabled Persons in December 1993, during which a gathering of 518 disabled people from across the EU held the European Disabled Person's Parliament in the European Parliament building in Brussels. The gathering focused on the theme of disability as a human right and concluded with the European Parliament adopting a resolution inviting the Commission and member states to adopt binding legislation on disability discrimination (Waddington 1995, p. 126–129).

The Commission quickly reacted to these demands. In its November 1993 *Green Paper on Social Policy* (Commission 1993c), the Commission framed its approach to disability policy in the language of the disability rights movement. While recognizing the need for special facilities to aid disabled people, the Commission emphasized that the main aim of policy should be mainstreaming—the integration of disabled persons into all aspects of society, including education, training, and employment. Any policy, however well intentioned, that encouraged segregation of disabled people was unacceptable: "Social segregation, even with adequate income maintenance and special provision, is contrary to human dignity and corrosive of social solidarity and community morale. Special facilities, institutions and legal rights are obviously necessary, but they should not be an obstacle or an alternative to the principle of 'mainstreaming'" (Commission 1993b, p. 48).

The European Parliament and disability NGOs welcomed the green paper's call for social integration of people with disabilities and particularly called on the Commission to propose "concrete measures" to combat discrimination based on disability—along with discrimination based on race, religion, and age. In its 1994 white paper on social policy, the Commission argued forcefully for Community-level action to fight discrimination but noted that the treaties failed to provide a legal basis for antidiscrimination legislation. The Commission threw down the gauntlet and challenged the member states to amend the treaties so that the EU could act in this field (Commission 1994a, p. 40). The Commission cited the new international norms on disability established by the UN's 1992 *Standard Rules on Equalization of Opportunities for Persons with Disabilities* and promised to act to promote this approach in the EU.

Finally, in 1996, the Commission announced a dramatic overhaul in its approach to disabilities, in its *Communication on Equality of Opportunities for People with Disabilities* (Commission 1996b). The new strategy departed significantly from the EU's previous approach and from the approach that still predominated in most member states. With its 1996 communication, the Commission stated clearly its intention to move toward an equal opportunities, rights-based approach to disability policy. The stated aim of the communication was to give "a renewed impetus toward the right-based equal opportunities approach to disability"(ibid., para. 7). Five months later, the member states largely endorsed the Commission's approach, when the Council of Ministers issued a nonbinding resolution supporting an equal opportunities approach.[18]

The Broader EU Rights Agenda

That the European Union would shift somewhat toward the disability rights approach is unsurprising. With a growing disability rights movement in the European NGO community and with the UN providing strong international backing for the rights model, some movement in this direction was, in a sense, overdetermined. Nevertheless, the scale and scope of the transformation wrought by the EU during the 1990s was startling. At the start of the decade, it was by no means clear that the EU would undertake a fundamental reorientation of its approach to disability, much less that it would establish a legally enforceable right to nondiscrimination in employment.

The EU's embrace of the rights-based approach to disability in the 1990s and constitutional and legislative breakthroughs the EU achieved after turning to that approach, must be understood in the context of the much broader drive to promote EU rights. The Commission's adoption of the rights model of disability between 1993 and 1996 coincided with a much broader drive to expand the protection of rights at the European level. The 1990s witnessed the proliferation of demands for EU rights of various sorts: economic and social rights; fundamental human rights; and antidiscrimination rights for particular groups, such as racial and ethnic minorities, homosexuals, elderly people, and individuals with disabilities. These rights movements converged powerfully in the time leading up to the negotiation of the 1997 Treaty of Amsterdam.

The disability rights movement rode the rights wave that was sweeping over EU politics at the end of the 1990s, gaining strength by linking its fortunes to those of other human rights and antidiscrimination causes. The broader EU rights agenda affected disability policy in two important ways. First, the European Union's inclination to expand EU rights in this period meant that EU policy makers were very receptive to rights claims advanced by civil society groups. Second, disability activists and their allies in the European Parliament and Commission benefited by linking their rights demands to those being advanced by other groups, as a broad coalition joined in calling on the EU to adopt general antidiscrimination measures.

Why then did the language of rights attain such prominence in so many areas of Community law during the 1990s? To some extent, the growing demands for EU rights can be understood simply as part of growing awareness and political salience of human rights across Europe and the rest of the Western world in the post–World War II era (Henkin 1990; Cappelletti 1989). However, the fact that many groups across postwar Europe were framing their demands in terms of rights does not explain why in the 1990s they looked to the EU as the forum in which to pursue their rights claims. Nor does it explain why the European Parliament and other advocates of deeper European integration proved so eager to supply EU rights. The EU had long been seen as an institution with only a marginal interest in or impact on fundamental rights. Questions of fundamental human rights had long been viewed as the province of national governments and courts or, at the supranational level, of the Council of Europe and its European Court of Human Rights (ECHR)—institutions wholly separate from the European Union. Why did the EU itself take on a rights agenda in the 1990s?

With the resurgence of European integration in the mid-1980s, EU policy makers in the Commission and European Parliament and other advocates of deeper European integration saw EU rights as a means to enhance the EU's legitimacy and to expand its authority to new policy areas (De Búrca 1995). With regard to legitimacy, strengthening the protection of fundamental human rights and social rights promised to redress a grave legitimacy deficit that had developed in the EU (Mabbett 2005, p. 103). From its inception in the late 1950s, the European Economic Community, or EEC (forerunner to today's EU), was viewed largely as a technical exercise in economic policy coordination. The technical work of the EEC had little to do with questions of fundamental rights, which were instead the concern of Europe's human rights watchdog—the Council of Europe. This view ran into trouble as early as the mid-1970s, in a series legal confrontations between the ECJ and national constitutional courts (Craig and De Búrca 2008, p. 344–377; Weiler 1986; Stone Sweet 2000, pp. 170–178; Weiler and Lockhart 1995). These conflicts boiled down to the following tension: national constitutional courts—above all, the German Bundesverfassungsgericht—would not accept the supremacy of European law if the European Community did not guarantee the protection of fundamental human rights. As the Treaty of Rome made no mention of fundamental rights, this seemed highly problematic. However, the ECJ found a creative way out of the fundamental rights conundrum. In a series of decisions, the ECJ affirmed that it would uphold fundamental rights as general principles of Community law. Though such rights were not explicitly cataloged in EC treaties, they could be divined from the common constitutional traditions of the member states and from international human rights treaties—such as the ECHR—to which these countries were signatories.

With the adoption of the Single European Act in 1987 and the Treaty on European Union in 1993, the range and sensitivity of policy areas in which the EU exercised power expanded dramatically. National governments and EU policy makers realized that the integration project could no longer be legitimated on a narrow technocratic basis and that they could not rely solely on ECJ case law as the basis for fundamental rights protections. Greater democratic inputs and greater protection of fundamental civil and social rights would be necessary.

When the member states amended the Treaty of Rome, first in the 1987 Single European Act and later in the 1993 Maastricht Treaty, they took modest steps to bolster the EU's fundamental rights credentials. The preamble to the Single European Act mentioned the member states' commitment to uphold fundamental rights, and the Maastricht Treaty committed that the European Union would protect the fundamental rights of European citizens (Article 6 and Article 2). However, these provisions fell far short of constituting a European "bill of rights" and failed to satisfy critics who argued that in light of the dramatic expansion of its powers, the EU needed to greatly strengthen its commitment to protecting fundamental rights.

Another stream of criticism focused on the EU's failure to protect social and economic rights. When the Commission launched its Single Market Program in the mid-1980s, critics on the Left argued that it served the interests of big business and threatened the economic and social rights that were so central to the European Social Model. Commission President Delors was highly sensitive to these critiques and saw that in order to shore up the EC's legitimacy, the single market project must be accompanied by a social dimension. However, his ambitions for a Social Europe were constrained by the fact that the EU simply lacked the capacity and policy tools necessary to deliver redistributive schemes or social programs normally associated with social policy. The Commission therefore relied on the one tool it did have at its disposal—lawmaking—and proposed a variety of social regulations and social rights. Central to this social rights agenda was a Commission proposal, launched in 1988, for a Community charter of fundamental social rights for workers (Bercusson 1990). The charter received strong backing from the European Parliament, which called for the adoption of legally enforceable social rights at the Community level. The member states, however, had the last word, and the Council of Ministers favored a weaker approach that would set out workers' rights as aspirations but would not make them legally enforceable. Even this modest approach proved too controversial for the Thatcher government. Finally, in December 1989, eleven member states adopted the watered-down charter (Commission 1990), while the UK refused to sign on. The charter then formed the basis for the Social protocol that was appended to the Maastricht Treaty, with the UK again opting out.

Breakthrough at Amsterdam

The Maastricht Treaty had strengthened EU rights by establishing the notion of EU citizenship and affirming that the protection of fundamental human rights and social rights were central aims of the European Union. This was symbolically significant and certainly did much to encourage "rights talk" at the EU level. In practical terms, however, the treaty did little to advance EU rights protection, because it failed to specify what rights EU citizens would enjoy and failed to empower the EU to act in defense of fundamental rights. Rights advocates, however, did not have to wait long to demand more action at the EU level. One of the final provisions of the Maastricht Treaty (Title VII, Article N) had called on the member states to convene an intergovernmental conference in 1996, with a view to revising the treaties once more. The promise of an upcoming treaty revision provided a window of opportunity, which was seized on by disability rights advocates and groups fighting other forms of discrimination, such as racism, xenophobia, ageism, and homophobia.

European disability advocates campaigned intensely for disability rights to be formally incorporated into the Amsterdam Treaty. From the outset, disability rights advocates linked their cause to other antidiscrimination campaigns, demanding that the revised treaty include a general antidiscrimination provision (European Disabled People's Parliament 1993). Disability rights advocates set out their demands emphatically in 1995, on the occasion of the 1995 European Day of Disabled People, when the EDF issued a report titled *Disabled Persons' Status in the European Treaties: Invisible Citizens* (Degener et al. 1995). The report set out legal arguments for the incorporation of a disability rights provision into the European treaties.

Disability advocates and other civil rights campaigners found a powerful and enthusiastic set of allies in the European Parliament. Disability rights campaigners were among the most organized and effective of these groups and maintained close ties with the European Parliament (Mabbett 2005, p. 108). Championing the cause of antidiscrimination rights was attractive to the European Parliament for several reasons. First, for reasons of institutional self-interest, the Parliament favored a deepening of European integration and recognized that this required the sort of legitimation that EU citizens' rights could bring. Also, as an institution whose legitimacy rested on its role as the "voice of the people" in the EU, the Parliament was eager to be seen as advancing causes that resonated with European publics—such as human rights and equal treatment. Finally, returning to the notion of political fragmentation, the European Parliament recognized that as a weak legislative actor, championing rights presented it with an effective way to deliver results for its interest group allies. If the Parliament could succeed in establishing EU rights that were enforceable in national and EU courts, then its allies in the NGO community could enforce those rights themselves.

The European Parliament had long called for the strengthening of human rights in the European Community (for instance, by repeatedly calling for the Community to accede to the ECHR) and for the establishment of legally enforceable nondiscrimination rights for disabled persons and other victims of discrimination, and Parliament intensified its demands after the Treaty of Maastricht (De Búrca 1995). In 1995, the Parliament called on the member states to extend Article 6 of the treaty to prohibit all forms of discrimination (European Parliament 1995). In 1996, in the period before the Amsterdam Intergovernmental Conference, the Parliament highlighted as the first of its "Key Priorities for the Future of Europe" the "extension of specific rights for European citizens within the Treaty," the "strengthening of fundamental human rights and the principles of equal treatment and non-discrimination" and the "full guarantee of legal protection" of those rights by the ECJ (European Parliament 1996).

Rights campaigners also lobbied the Reflection Group, which was set up by the European Council to prepare for the Amsterdam Intergovernmental Conference. They won a significant victory in 1995 when the Reflection Group issued its report, which argued that extending and detailing citizens' fundamental rights, including protections against discrimination, were an essential part of making the EU acceptable to public opinion (Westendorp 1995; Flynn 1999, p. 1130). Similarly, in 1996 the Wise Men's Committee (Comité des Sages 1996), established by the Commission to explore the future of the Community Social Charter, called for strengthening EU rights protections by moving from a limited focus on workers' rights to a broader notion of citizens' rights, which would encompass both civil and social rights.

Importantly, disability rights groups and others who supported the adoption of a broad antidiscrimination provision in the Amsterdam Treaty advocated a "unified" approach to rights. That is, they did not attempt to distinguish between social rights and civil rights or between positive and negative rights, but instead insisted that these rights were "indivisible" (Mabbett 2005, p. 100). This unified approach to rights proved to be powerful because it facilitated coalition building between those actors concerned primarily with the protection of fundamental human rights and those focused on the protection of social rights.

Ultimately, the member states agreed to add a new, general antidiscrimination provision to the Amsterdam Treaty, a provision that includes a reference to disability. Article 13 states:

> Without prejudice to the other provisions of this Treaty and within the limits of the power conferred by it upon the Community, the Council acting unanimously on a proposal from the Commission and after consulting the European Parliament, may take appropriate action to combat discrimination based on sex, racial or ethnic origin, religion or belief, disability, age or sexual orientation.

The unified approach to rights proved decisive in the intergovernmental negotiations. The package of antidiscrimination rights proposed in Article 13 was more compelling collectively than many of the particular rights would have been individually. As Mark Bell (2000) explains, "One of the lessons of Article 13 was the ability of more controversial grounds of discrimination to make unexpected progress through seeking inclusion in a broad anti-discrimination instrument" (pp. 168–169). Indeed, some member state negotiators, particularly the Dutch, originally objected to including disability in Article 13 (Flynn 1999,

p. 1132). Finally, ambiguity surrounding the language of rights facilitated agreement between the member states (Mabbett 2005, p. 100). The uncertainty concerning just how legally binding rights provisions in the treaty would be allowed those who viewed statements of rights as only declarations of policy aims to come together with those who hoped to establish legally enforceable rights (ibid., p. 105).

Article 13 was expansive in some ways and weak in others. It provided a treaty basis for the EU to adopt binding legislation to combat various forms of discrimination.[19] However, it was designed not to have direct effect. Unlike the long-standing treaty provision on equal treatment of the sexes, Article 13 did not provide victims of discrimination with legally enforceable rights that they could rely on in their national courts. Article 13 empowered the EU to combat discrimination, but it did not directly empower individuals to do so.

The Employment Equality Directive

With a firm treaty basis in place, the European Union acted quickly to adopt antidiscrimination legislation, adopting two landmark measures in 2000—the Racial Equality Directive and the Employment Equality Directive.[20] The legislative process for the two directives moved unusually quickly. The European Commission presented its first proposals in November 1999, and the European Council adopted both directives by November 2000. The speed with which the EU acted must be understood against the backdrop of the political crisis instigated by the rise of Jörg Haider and his Freedom Party in Austria and concerns over racism and xenophobia in east European applicant states. Though extreme right parties were a staple of European politics, they had long been relegated to the margins. The 1999 electoral success of Austria's extreme right-wing, xenophobic Freedom Party and its entry into a coalition government sent shockwaves across the EU. Leaders of the other EU member states initially reacted by imposing an informal diplomatic isolation on Austria. Though EU leaders eventually abandoned this diplomatic isolation, the Haider crisis catalyzed action to combat discrimination at the EU level. The Commission presented its proposals for a racial equality directive and an employment equality directive just a month after the Austrian election. Member state leaders were eager to make a strong statement about the EU's opposition to racism and xenophobia and pressed for speedy adoption of the Racial Equality Directive. In addition to the Haider phenomenon, the prospect of eastern European enlargement and concerns over racism and xenophobia in applicant states—particularly against the Roma minority—generated greater pressure to adopt antidiscrimination legislation before the EU proceeded with enlargement (Ellis 2002, p. 291).

While the Employment Equality Directive had its own set of supporters, it clearly gained momentum by riding the coattails of the Racial Equality Directive. In June 2000, the EU adopted the Racial Equality Directive, which prohibited racial discrimination in a wide range of fields, including employment, education, housing, social security, health care, and access to goods and services. In November 2000, the EU followed up on this by adopting the Employment Equality Directive, which was designed to address the other forms of discrimination listed in Article 13 of the Amsterdam Treaty—discrimination on the basis of "religion or belief, disability, age or sexual orientation."[21] The Employment Equality Directive prohibited only discrimination in employment and occupation; unlike the Racial Equality Directive, it did not address issues of discrimination in other areas, such as education, housing, health care, or social security.

With regard to disability discrimination, the Employment Equality Directive does not simply mandate that employers treat disabled persons exactly the same as they treat nondisabled persons. Rather, drawing particularly on the experience of the United States, the directive sets a more demanding standard of equal treatment. Beyond prohibiting direct discrimination (treating a person "less favorably" on the basis of their disability) the directive also restricts indirect discrimination (discrimination that occurs when employers apply rules equally to all employees in a fashion that seems neutral but that actually puts disabled persons at a "particular disadvantage").[22] Finally, Article 5 provides what is arguably the directive's most significant disability rights provision: the reasonable accommodation requirement.[23] Reasonable accommodation obliges employers to make adjustments to workplace facilities or to work arrangements, policies, or practices, in order to accommodate a disabled individual, unless doing so imposes a disproportionate burden on the employer. Failure to make such reasonable accommodations itself constitutes discrimination.

The Employment Equality Directive was not designed merely to call for equal treatment rights in some symbolic sense but to encourage enforcement of those rights in practice. Drawing on lessons from shortcomings in the enforcement of EU rules on equal treatment of the sexes, the new equality legislation aimed specifically to facilitate enforcement and to reduce the discretion accorded to member states (Bell 2005, p. 273; Waddington and Bell 2001, pp. 588, 607). The directive requires member states to provide victims of discrimination with procedures to enforce their rights, before either courts or administrative bodies (Article 9[1]). The directive also requires member states to give associations, such as disability NGOs or trade unions, standing to bring cases on behalf of or in support of disabled individuals (Article 9[2]). The insistence on ensuring standing for associations was based on the recognition that individuals will often lack the resources, information, and skills necessary to enforce their rights. Finally, the directive also requires member states to impose a "reversal of burden of proof" in discrimination cases. In other words, once a plaintiff has established facts "from which it may be presumed that there has been direct or indirect discrimination," it is then for the defendant to prove that there has been no violation of the principle of equal treatment (Article 10). However, advocates of strict enforcement did not get all they wanted in the Employment Equality Directive. Most importantly, the Council of Ministers rejected amendments favored by the European Parliament and Commission that would have required member states to establish public bodies to support enforcement of antidiscrimination rights.

Member states were required to transpose most aspects of the Employment Equality Directive by 2 December 2003. Upon request, they were granted an additional three years to transpose the provisions relating to disability and age discrimination into national law. As I discuss below, for many member states the directive required significant legislative changes, as they had no domestic laws in place prohibiting forms of discrimination listed in the directive. Since the directive took force, the European Commission has worked to promote implementation by bringing infringement actions against laggard member states and by actively promoting decentralized enforcement by actors in civil society.

With regard to centralized enforcement, in 2005 the European Commission brought four member states before the ECJ for failures to transpose the directive into national law on time and won judgments against each of them.[24] After all member states had at least formally transposed the directive into national laws, the Commission honed in on persistent inadequacies in their implementation. In January 2008, the Commission moved ahead with infringement procedures against eleven member states, issuing "reasoned opinion letters" highlighting their continuing implementation failures (Commission 2008a). The Commission followed this with another infringement action against the UK in November 2009 and another against Poland in January 2010 (Commission 2009b, 2010).

The ECJ has also started to receive preliminary ruling references from national courts asking it to issue judgments on the directive's disability provisions. In the first such case, *Chacón Navas,*[25] the court was asked to clarify the definition of disability. As the directive had neglected to define disability, a Spanish court asked ECJ to clarify whether "sickness" fell within the scope of "disability" under the directive. The ECJ ruling offered a definition of disability and explained that sickness was distinct from disability and that an employee dismissed because they were sick would not be protected under the directive. The ECJ's rather limited definition of disability disappointed many rights campaigners; however, they were pleased that the court strongly reaffirmed employers' obligation to make reasonable accommodations for disabled employees (Cantor 2009). The ECJ's next disability ruling, in the 2008 *Coleman v Attridge* case,[26] was far more favorable to disability rights campaigners. In its judgment, the ECJ expanded the potential coverage of the directive by ruling that it not only prohibits discrimination against persons who are disabled but also prohibits "discrimination by association" with a disabled person. In other words, it forbids discrimination against an employee based on their association with a disabled person (e.g., against a parent who is the primary caregiver for a disabled child). The ECJ ruling extended discrimination protection to roughly two and a half million Britons who try to combine employment with their role as caregivers for disabled family members (Hirsch 2008).

While the Commission is clearly working to pressure member governments to implement the directive and while the ECJ will inevitably hear cases concerning the implementation of the directive, the most striking aspect of the Employment Equality Directive's approach to enforcement is the directive's almost exclusive reliance on private enforcement by private parties before national courts and tribunals. Unlike the Racial Equality Directive, the Employment Equality Directive does not require member states to set up disability rights commissions or other public enforcement bodies. Instead, the Employment Equality Directive relies on legal action by individuals and associations.

The European Commission has not taken a "build it and they will come" approach, waiting idly for litigants to seek out courthouses across Europe. Rather, the Commission has worked to cultivate litigants by sponsoring a series of seminars and summer schools designed to encourage private enforcement of disability rights. For instance, in July 2005, the Commission sponsored a two-week summer school on disability discrimination, for academics, lawyers, and disability activists. The aims of the program were stated clearly in its title, "Toward Effective Test Case Strategies: Using the European Union Employment Equality Directive (2000/78/EC) in a Disability Context."[27] In other words, the Commission is working to train activists on how to bring test cases to enforce EU antidiscrimination rights for disabled individuals across EU member states. The Commission's efforts to encourage organizations to initiate disability rights litigation based on the Employment Equality Directive go beyond convening seminars; in at least some cases the Commission proactively contacts disability rights organizations to encourage them to bring cases (DG Employment and Social Affairs 2006; Interrights Legal Director 2007). Also, the Commission has supported the development of a scholarly community and a literature on EU antidiscrimination law, helping to fund the European Network of Legal Experts in the Non-Discrimination Field and to fund projects leading to the publication of a casebook on EU antidiscrimination law (Schiek, Waddington, and Bell 2007) and the *European Anti-Discrimination Law Review.*[28]

While many legal experts predict that over time the Employment Equality Directive is likely to spark a considerable amount of litigation (Skidmore 2001, p. 132; Whittle 2002), to date, the volume of case law remains low (Commission 2007d, p. 53). A variety of significant impediments to disability rights litigation remain in place across the member states. Victims of disability discrimination often find themselves in a vulnerable position vis-à-vis their employer. Highly skilled legal assistance for victims of disability discrimination remains scarce, publicly funded legal aid for antidiscrimination claims remains inadequate in many member states, time limits for filing claims are too tight, and legal procedures are too lengthy and complex (ibid.). Also, awareness of disability rights, such as the right to reasonable accommodations in employment, remains relatively low (Interrights Legal Director 2007; European Disability Forum 2006).

Despite the persistence of such hurdles, it is clear that the EU's approach to disability is based on a rights model grounded in adversarial legalism. Ultimately, the success of the Employment Equality Directive in discouraging disability discrimination will hinge on disabled persons, and associations representing them, to mobilize to enforce their rights.[29] Most of this legal mobilization will of course take place before courts, employment tribunals, and specialized equality bodies at the national level. I discuss initial developments in Germany, France, the United Kingdom, and the Netherlands below.

Toward the Rights Model of Disability at the National Level

Germany

As noted above, Germany was a pioneer of the medical/welfare model of disability in Europe. By the 1980s, Germany had in place not only a quota-levy scheme requiring employers to reserve 6 percent of their workplaces for disabled employees or to pay a levy *(Ausgleichsabgabe),* but also a range of rehabilitation and training schemes, sheltered work programs *(Werkstätten für Behinderte),* and generous social supports. While German policy clearly provided many supports and benefits to people with disabilities, one thing it did not provide was rights. German law did not establish legally enforceable rights against employment discrimination for persons with disabilities. Quite to the contrary, German policies and the rulings of German courts supported segregation of disabled people rather than their integration into mainstream institutions (Degener and Quinn 2000, p. 18).

Gradually during the 1980s, a disability rights movement led by disabled persons emerged in Germany, inspired largely by the disability rights and independent living movement in the United States. From 1990s onward, people with disabilities began to mobilize on a national scale, demanding legal protection against discrimination (Heyer

2002). These activists scored a major victory in 1994, when they succeeded in convincing German lawmakers to insert into the German Basic Law an amendment prohibiting discrimination on the basis of disability.[30] While the amendment certainly provided a powerful statement of the norm of nondiscrimination, it failed to provide an adequate legal basis for combating disability discrimination in the workplace. The constitutional amendment did not clarify what constituted discrimination or disability, and without more specific legislation, the courts tended to adhere to the prevailing segregationist, medical model of disability.[31] The vague constitutional norm against disability discrimination clearly needed to be backed up with more specific legislation, but German lawmakers did not adopt such legislation until they were forced to implement the EU's Employment Equality Directive.

Implementation of the EU's 2000 Employment Equality Directive proved extremely controversial in Germany. Disputes over how to implement the directive dragged on over several years, involving two successive German governments, a series of failed legislative proposals, and a 2005 ECJ ruling against Germany for failure to transpose the directive into national law on time. Eventually, the disability discrimination provisions of the directive were implemented, primarily through three major pieces of legislation. First, in 2001 revisions to the German Social Code IX, or Sozialgesetzbuch (SGB) IX, addressed some aspects of discrimination against severely disabled persons in the employment sphere.[32] The 2002 Disability Equalization Act (Behindertengleichstellungsgesetz, or BGG) called on public providers of goods and services to remove barriers that prevented disabled people from participating in all aspects of social life.[33] However, neither of these laws fully implemented the EU directive's prohibition on discrimination in employment, and Germany was condemned by the ECJ in 2005 for failure to transpose the directive into national law.[34] Finally in 2006, German lawmakers implemented the directive and its prohibition on employment discrimination on the basis of disability, with the introduction of the landmark General Equal Treatment Act (Allgemeine Gleichbehandlungsgesetz, or AGG).[35]

Under the General Equal Treatment Act and the revised Social Code IX, disabled workers have a variety of new rights, including a right to "reasonable accommodations" from employers (SGB IX, section 81.4) and a right to compensation for material and nonmaterial (i.e., pain and suffering) damages they suffer as a result of violation of their rights (AGG, section 15). Associations representing people with disabilities enjoy the legal standing to represent victims of disability discrimination under SGB IX, section 63 (Mahlmann 2009, p. 27). The General Equal Treatment Act also established the new Federal Antidiscrimination Agency (Antidiskriminierungsstelle des Bundes), which is charged with raising public awareness of the new equal treatment law and to provide advice to victims of discrimination and to employers.

Implementing the EU's Employment Equality Directive has forced profound changes in German law on disability discrimination—creating enforceable rights where there had been none. Actual enforcement of these new rights and changes in employers' practices, however, have been far slower to materialize. In the debate that preceded the adoption of the General Equal Treatment Act, business groups warned that German employers would be flooded with discrimination suits, with harmful consequences for the economy. In particular, critics warned that serial litigants—so-called AGG-Hoppers—would abuse the system, applying for multiple jobs with the intention of filing discrimination claims and receiving settlement payments when they were turned down for the positions (Siedenbiedel 2007; Amann 2008; Kruthaup 2009). In 2007, critics of the AGG phenomena specifically warned that disability discrimination claims were emerging as the leading form of abusive AGG-hopping (Diller 2007). A German law firm, Gleiss Lutz, even established a Web site (www.agg-hopping.de) in 2006, to help employers track abusive litigants, though German data privacy regulators soon forced the site to shut down.

Despite the ominous warnings from business groups of an impending flood of lawsuits and despite any isolated abuses of the new General Equal Treatment Act, there has been very little disability discrimination litigation in Germany since 2006. Certainly, a handful of disability discrimination claims have been filed before German labor courts, and some of these have resulted in legal victories for individual victims of disability discrimination.[36] However, overall, there were only 251 decisions by German labor courts concerning the General Equal Treatment Act during its first two years in force, and only a fraction of these concerned disability discrimination. Considering that German labor courts heard a total of over 1.2 million complaints during this period, the volume of disability discrimination litigation is very modest indeed (Bundesministerium für Arbeit und Soziales 2009, p. 25).

The support structure for disability discrimination litigation remains extremely weak, and most claims have been brought by individual victims of discrimination. The public bodies established to support antidiscrimination policy, such as the Federal Antidiscrimination Agency, the Federal Commission for Matters Relating to Disabled Persons (Beauftragter der Bundesregierung für die Belange behinderter Menschen), and various local antidiscrimination offices *(Antidiskriminierungsbüros),* are not authorized to directly support litigation by victims of discrimination. While nonprofit associations representing people with disabilities are authorized to represent individual victims of discrimination under certain conditions, many of these associations lack the expertise, or even the inclination, to pursue such litigation. To address the weakness of litigation support structures, in 2009 the Federal Ministry of Labor and Social Affairs launched a program to train disability NGOs on how to use their rights to bring litigation *(Verbandsklagerecht)* under the General Equal Treatment Act and Social Code IX (Bundesministerium für Arbeit und Soziales 2009, p. 24). In the meantime, support for individual litigants is provided by private attorneys, including those working in firms that specialize in antidiscrimination litigation, which have emerged in recent years (Tolmein 2010). Likewise, employers' legal advisors now offer advice on how to handle recruitment procedures so as to avoid liability for potential disability discrimination claims (Ohlendorf and Schreier 2008; Diller 2007). Over time, private enforcement of disability rights is likely to increase, as awareness of disability rights spreads. However, given the high hurdles and disincentives to litigate that many disabled individuals face, private enforcement will come to play a significant role in addressing disability discrimination only if and when a stronger legal support structure for victims of discrimination comes into place.

France

As in Germany, disability policy in France was rooted squarely in the medical/welfare model of disability. As mentioned above, by the time the European Union entered the field of disability policy, France had long relied on a quota-levy system as the principal means to encourage the employment of disabled persons, and the quota levies had supported a variety of job training and sheltered work programs and generous social assistance programs for disabled people (Doyle 1995, pp. 66–75). As of the mid-1980s, French law did not, however, prohibit employment discrimination against disabled persons. Though the quota-levy system certainly helped many disabled people find employment, critics pointed out that unemployment among disabled people remained as much as three times higher than among the general population and that many firms simply chose to pay the levy rather than meet their quota (Thornton 1998, p. 21; Jolivet 2004).

Like the United Kingdom, France was an early mover in adopting some aspects of the rights model of disability (Cooper 2000, pp. 45–48, 90–91; Waddington 1996, pp. 96–97). France's initial steps in this direction stemmed not from EU pressure but from protests over revelations of discrimination against persons living with HIV. In response, in 1990 French lawmakers introduced amendments to the French Penal Code, to outlaw discrimination on the basis of health status or disability. With the adoption of Law 90-602, dismissing or refusing to hire an individual due to their state of health or disability became a criminal offense punishable by up to two years' imprisonment.[37] On the surface, making disability discrimination a criminal offense punishable by fines and imprisonment might appear a very strict approach. In practice, however, the French criminalization approach proved ineffectual. First, the French law set a very high bar for what would constitute employment discrimination. The antidiscrimination rules adopted in 1990 did not require employers to make "reasonable accommodations" to enable disabled workers to perform a job and did not prohibit indirect discrimination. Also, the criminal approach took enforcement entirely out of the hands of the actual victim of discrimination. Only public prosecutors could decide to pursue criminal prosecutions, and they did so very rarely.

Against this background, the strict antidiscrimination rules and the private enforcement model in the EU's 2000 Employment Equality Directive required major changes in French law. France notified the Commission that the country would take advantage of the three-year extension and not complete transposition of the directive into national law until as late as 2006. French lawmakers transposed the disability provisions EU Directive into French law with a series of reforms between 2001 and 2005, the most important of which was the 2005 Law for Equal Rights and Opportunity of Persons with Disabilities (Law on Disability).[38] These reforms introduced all the major elements of the EU directive, including the "reasonable accommodation" requirement,[39] the ban on indirect discrimination, and the standing for disability NGOs to bring cases on behalf of victims of discrimination (Latraverse 2007, 2008). The 2005 Law on Disability extends antidiscrimination protection far beyond the scope of the EU directive, prohibiting discrimination in a range of spheres beyond employment (such as education and transportation). Also, to promote awareness and enforcement of the new antidiscrimination rules, France established in 2004 a new public antidiscrimination authority—HALDE (Haute Autorité de Lutte contre les Discriminations et pour l'Égalité).[40] Unlike the UK, which abolished its quota system when it moved to a rights-based model of disability, France retained its quota-levy scheme and other elements of its medical/medical welfare model, layering the new EU requirements on top of them.[41]

Although the recent reforms to disability law have clearly expanded opportunities for individuals and associations to bring legal action enforcing nondiscrimination rights in employment, such litigation has not emerged. Generally, disability NGOs lack the specialist legal personnel needed to pursue strategic litigation campaigns. Moreover, most disability NGOs in France are generally averse to relying on litigation as a means of pursuing their policy aims (Disabled People's International Europe 2006). Moreover, employers have not experienced an increase in individual disability discrimination suits before French courts (MEDEF 2008). Rather, as awareness of new disability discrimination rights has spread, individual complaints against employers have been channeled to the new antidiscrimination authority—HALDE (ibid.). HALDE operates a system through which victims of disability discrimination can file complaints and seek support from HALDE. Since its establishment in 2005, HALDE has experienced a steady upsurge in complaints from victims of disability discrimination. Disability claims make up over 20 percent of HALDE's total case load, with HALDE having received 1,349 disability discrimination claims in 2007 and 1,623 in 2008 (HALDE 2009, p. 13). HALDE conducts investigations of these claims and can then issue recommendations, act as a mediator in an effort to resolve disputes, refer cases to public prosecutors, or support individual litigants in bringing claims before civil or administrative courts. Most disputes are settled with the issuance of recommendations or through some form of mediation; only approximately 1 percent of claims received by HALDE actually result in a case being brought before a court (HALDE 2009, pp. 16–20).[42]

In short, the EU has ushered in the advent of the rights model of disability in France, but this has not resulted in widespread litigation. While there has been a marked increase in disability discrimination claims, these have been channeled through a government body that has handled the overwhelming majority of them without recourse to the courts.

The Netherlands

The Netherlands presents a clear case of a member state that followed a well-established medical/welfare model of disability and that was pressured by the European Union to introduce central elements of a rights-based model. The Dutch voluntary quota scheme had been reformed in 1986, and prior to EU involvement in disability policy, Dutch legislators had repeatedly resisted addressing disability issues through an equal-treatment approach. For instance, in the early 1990s, when the Dutch Parliament was amending the Dutch General Equal Treatment Law (Algemene Wet Gelijke Behandeling), it specifically refused to add disabled persons to the list of groups protected against discrimination under the law (Waddington 1996, p. 72). There was some debate among parliamentarians and academics in the Netherlands at the end of the 1990s over the question of whether to introduce disability rights, but this discussion was quickly overtaken by the passage of the EU's Employment Equality Directive. Only when the Dutch government implemented the disability provisions of the EU's Employment Equality Directive in 2003 and 2004 did Dutch law forbid discrimination on the grounds of disability or chronic disease in the field of employment and occupation (Waddington and Gijzen 2004, p. 4). The 2003 Act on Equal Treatment on Grounds of Disability and Chronic Disease (Wet Gelijke Behandeling op grond van Handicap en Chronische Ziekte, or WGB h/cz) explicitly forbade direct and indirect "differentiation" in the field of employment and occupation on the grounds of disability or chronic disease, and further reforms were introduced through the 2004 EC-Implementation Act on the General Equal Treatment Act (EG-Implementatiewet AWGB) (Waddington and Gijzen 2004, p. 4).[43] As a result of these reforms, discrimination on the basis of disability or chronic disease was forbidden on issues including recruitment, commencement or termination of the employment relationship, employment and dismissal of civil servants, employment mediation, employment conditions, education or training prior to employment, and promotion" (Holtmaat 2009; Waddington and Gijzen 2004, p. 9–10). Articles 9–13 of the WGB h/cz provide for new legal remedies to back up the new rights of disabled persons, empowering them to pursue discrimination claims before the Commissie Gelijke Behandeling, or Equal Treatment Commission—a semijudicial body—or ordinary civil or administrative courts (Holtmaat 2009). Moreover, the WGB h/cz (Article 10) makes it easier for plaintiffs to prevail by introducing a partial reversal of the burden of proof in disability discrimination cases (ibid.). Following the EU Employment Equality Directive, the WGB h/cz also requires employers to provide an "effective accommodation" to enable disabled employees to perform their jobs (Waddington 2000, p. 18). The establishment of a legal basis for antidiscrimination claims has led to a modest number of claims being brought by individuals to the Dutch Equal Treatment Commission, which, as a quasi-judicial body, can investigate complaints, issue nonbinding opinions, and facilitate mediation. However, the existence of disability rights generated very little litigation before civil or administrative courts, and disability NGOs have not waged strategic litigation campaigns. Prior to 2004 the Equal Treatment Commission never received disability discrimination complaints, as there was no legal basis for such complaints. Between 2004 and 2008, the Equal Treatment Commission received 329 requests for opinions on matters relating to disability discrimination, amounting to 12.2 percent of the total requests it received in this period (Commissie Gelijke Behandeling 2006, 2008).[44] In contrast, only a handful of cases invoking the prohibition on disability discrimination have been brought before Dutch courts.

Individuals' preference for pursuing cases through the Equal Treatment Commission is understood easily enough: taking claims to the Equal Treatment Commission is free, while bringing litigation before

Dutch courts can be extremely expensive (Judicial Advisor, Equal Treatment Commission 2006). Disability NGOs in the Netherlands have generally shown little enthusiasm for directly supporting disability discrimination litigation before Dutch courts or claims brought before the Equal Treatment Commission (ibid.). The umbrella organization of Dutch disability groups, the Dutch Council of the Chronically Ill and the Disabled (Chronisch zieken en Gehandicapten Raad Nederland, or CG-Raad) did launch a legal support program in 2001 to provide mediation services and legal assistance for disabled persons, and the CG-Raad occasionally supports clients bringing discrimination complaints to the Equal Treatment Commission. More generally, however, the high cost of litigation and lack of adequate human resources prevent the CG-Raad and other disability groups from bringing more cases before Dutch courts (Senior Legal Policy Officer, CG-Raad 2009).

The EU Employment Equality Directive has forced dramatic changes in Dutch law, establishing a legal basis for disability discrimination claims. To date, however, these changes have yet to produce much tangible impact. Public awareness of antidiscrimination rights for people with disabilities remains low. Most complaints have been channeled to the Equal Treatment Commission, and neither individuals nor NGOs have turned to the courts. Given this situation, employers are not concerned about the threat of disability discrimination claims (Judicial Advisor, Equal Treatment Commission 2006; Senior Judicial Advisor, General Employers Organization of the Netherlands 2006). Unsurprisingly, disability groups have observed "hardly any change" in employers' policies or practices with regard to disability discrimination (Senior Legal Policy Officer, CG-Raad 2009).

United Kingdom

UK disability policy has shaped EU disability policy more than it has been shaped by it. The United Kingdom pioneered the rights-based approach to disability within Europe, and the British example, together with active lobbying by British disability activists (Burke 2004), helped carry that model to the EU level. In the wake of the passage of the Americans with Disabilities Act across the Atlantic in 1990, British disability activists and a number of backbench members of Parliament argued that the UK should follow the American example and adopt legislation prohibiting disability discrimination in employment. Finally, after a series of failed private members bills (Doyle 1993, p. 90), the government put forward its own measure, which was readily adopted as the Disability Discrimination Act 1995 (DDA).[45] The DDA prohibits employers from discriminating against disabled persons in recruitment, employment terms and conditions, opportunities for promotion, transfer and training, and dismissal and requires employers to make reasonable adjustments to enable disabled workers to perform their jobs. The DDA also extends beyond the employment sphere, prohibiting discrimination in education and the provision of goods and services.

The Disability Discrimination Act marked a watershed in the United Kingdom's approach to disability. With the adoption of the DDA, the long moribund quota scheme under the 1944 Disabled Persons Employment Act was finally abolished. Rights would replace quotas. But these nondiscrimination rights would not be enforced by the government or a quasi-governmental authority. Where the earlier antidiscrimination statutes dealing with racial and sex discrimination had established quasi-governmental monitoring and enforcement bodies, no such body was established for disability by the DDA. Instead, the DDA simply created enforceable nondiscrimination rights and left it to victims of discrimination to vindicate these rights before industrial tribunals and courts (Doyle 1999; Vanhala 2006). The DDA was strengthened significantly after Disability Rights Commission Act 1999 established the Disability Rights Commission (DRC), an equality enforcement body equivalent to those that existed for racial and gender discrimination.

Complying with the disability rights provision of the EU Employment Equality Directive required only modest modifications of the DDA. Most importantly, exemptions from the nondiscrimination requirement that the DDA had permitted for small employers and for particular occupational categories (such as police and prison officers) were removed as required by the EU directive (through the Disability Discrimination Act 1995 [Amendment] Regulations 2003).[46] More generally, though, compliance with the EU directive required very little modification of UK laws or practices, as the DDA already went further than the directive.[47]

Litigation to enforce disability rights in the UK was well established before the EU Directive took force. Thousands of disability discrimination claims were brought annually in the late 1990s, and the volume of disability discrimination litigation brought by private parties increased steadily from the late 1990s through 2010—far exceeding rates of litigation in other EU member states. The vast majority of claims in the UK are brought before employment tribunals, where the costs of litigation are far lower and the procedures simpler than those available for claims brought before county courts (Human Rights Barrister, Matrix Chambers 2007).[48] Between 1999 and 2009, individuals brought over fifty thousand disability discrimination claims before employment tribunals in England and Wales, and the number of claims brought annually has climbed steadily, from 3,765 in 1999–2000 to 6,578 in 2008–2009 (Employment Tribunals Service 2000–2006; Tribunals Service 2007–2009). Damage awards have generally been modest, but some decisions involving public authorities have imposed very large awards. For instance, in 2008–2009 the median disability discrimination award was £7,226, while the highest award reached £388,612 (Employment Tribunal Service 2000, 2009).

The Disability Rights Commission legal service pursued an active strategic litigation strategy from the outset and helped victims of discrimination pursue employment discrimination cases before employment tribunals and the Court of Appeal (Vanhala 2006; Disability Rights Commission 2002, 2003). Indeed, the DRC took on such a leading role and pooled so much of the legal expertise in the disability field on its legal team that in some ways it diverted the focus and energies of disability NGOs away from litigation (Vanhala 2009b). In essence, disability NGOs left it to the DRC to use the courts to extend disability rights. Likewise, trade unions showed little interest in pursuing disability discrimination claims on behalf of their members, given the potentially high costs involved if a case goes before a court and the unpredictability of the results (Disability Policy Officer, Trade Union Congress 2007).

In 2007, the DRC, along with the Commission on Race Equality and the Equal Opportunities Commission, was replaced by the new Equality and Human Rights Commission (EHRC), which had powers cutting across all areas of equality law, including discrimination based on race, sex, disability, religion and belief, sexual orientation, and age. The EHRC professes a commitment to provide legal assistance for individual victims of discrimination and to pursue strategic litigation to ensure the enforcement of European and domestic antidiscrimination laws (EHRC 2008). In practice, however, the EHRC has proven reluctant to emphasize strategic litigation, instead pursuing less adversarial approaches.

The EU Employment Equality Directive has had far less impact on the UK than on other member states. The DDA had introduced the rights model of disability to the UK years before the EU directive went into affect, and the DDA was in many ways more far-reaching than the EU directive (Human Rights Barrister, Matrix Chambers 2007; Head of Policy and Campaigns, Mencap 2007; Disability Policy Officer, Trade Union Congress 2007). However, the ECJ's 2008 ruling in *Coleman v. Attridge* (Case C-303/06), discussed above, demonstrated that even in the United Kingdom the EU directive can in fact have a significant impact. Prior to the Employment Appeal Tribunal's reference to the European Court of Justice in *Coleman*, British courts had not interpreted the DDA or the EU directive as extending discrimination protection to the caregivers of disabled persons. Applying the ECJ judgment, the Employment Appeal Tribunal extended antidiscrimination protection to their caregivers, opening the door to claims by caregivers (estimated to number over 2.5 million) if they experience discrimination due to their role in caring for a disabled person (Hirsch 2008).

More generally, legal practitioners in the UK emphasize that lack of awareness of disability rights continues to prevent victims of discrimination from pursuing claims. As awareness of those rights continues to spread, we are likely to observe an increase in claims in years to come, particularly as English courts' more liberal approach to standing for public interest groups in recent years facilitates litigation by disability NGOs (Discrimination Law Association 2007; Human Rights Barrister, Matrix Chambers 2007). With the EHRC turning away from the courts, there are signs that disability NGOs are considering taking the lead on strategic litigation campaigns; for instance, in 2009 a prominent British disability group, Scope, began coordinating a working group of disability organizations to explore litigation strategies.[49]

Conclusion

In Max Weber's terms, European integration and rights-based approaches to social policy (including the rights model of disability) enjoyed an "elective affinity" (Gerth and Mills 1946, pp. 62-63). The two phenomena, when brought into contact, were drawn to one another and reinforced one another. Pursuing social policies through a rights model was very attractive to EU policy makers and other advocates of deeper European integration for two sets of reasons. The first set of reasons concern the institutional factors explored in Chapter 1. The European Union is a weak state and lacks the administrative capacity to effectively enforce EU policies from the center. Most implementation and enforcement is conducted by member state administrations, and EU lawmakers (the principals) face considerable agency problems in that they cannot rely on national administrations (their agents) to reliably enforce EU mandates. Rights-based policies present an attractive way to mitigate these capacity and principal-agent problems. By pursuing policy objectives through a rights model, the EU empowers citizens to enforce EU law themselves before national courts. For EU policy makers, rights-based policies are very cost effective: individuals bear the cost of enforcement, and when they succeed, national governments or private actors bear the compliance costs.

Secondly, rights-based approaches to social policy are attractive to EU policy makers because they promise to enhance the EU's legitimacy in the eyes of European citizens. For over two decades, proponents of deeper European integration have sought to strengthen the EU's social dimension in order to enhance the EU's legitimacy with European publics. EU policy makers saw the social dimension as desirable for its own sake (simply in that it extended EU power into new areas), but more importantly policy makers saw it as necessary to make the EU's market-making project acceptable to European voters. However, the EU's efforts to build a Social Europe have been frustrated by the fact that the European Union lacks the fiscal resources necessary to support distributive and redistributive social programs. As a result, the EU has focused on social regulation (Majone 1994, 1996). And for the purposes of enhancing EU legitimacy, the most powerful forms of social regulation are those rooted in a "rights" paradigm. EU laws that confer legally enforceable rights on individuals provide substance to the notion of "EU citizenship" and show that the EU is doing something concrete for citizens.

Likewise, for advocates of various social rights, such as the activists in the disability rights movement, the EU constitutes an attractive partner. Rather than fighting fifteen (or, later, twenty-seven) battles to institute disability rights protections at the national level, the EU provided activists with a forum within which they could wage a single campaign that promised to institute disability rights across the Continent.[50] Also, where traditional social policies based on approaches other than a rights model are entrenched at the national level, national governments may be reluctant to accede to the demands of rights campaigners. In contrast, for the reasons mentioned above, EU lawmakers and officials may be eager to join forces with rights campaigners and to champion the cause of EU social rights. Of course, rights campaigners can and do target other supranational and international organizations (such as the Council of Europe), but the EU is particularly attractive because the strength of its legal system holds the promise of meaningful rights enforcement. While the EU is neither a primary stimulus of campaigns for social rights nor their only target, movements advocating new social rights will often find enthusiastic partners among EU policy makers.

Critics are right to point out the shortcomings, and often the false promise, of individual rights-based approaches to social policy (Conant 2002; De Búrca 1995; Alston and Weiler 1999, p. 13). The EU's effort to rely on a rights-based, Eurolegalism mode of governance in the disability field has run up against a variety of impediments to access to justice facing victims of disability discrimination. Compared with the other policy areas examined in this book, EU disability policy to date has had less success in mobilizing victims of disability discrimination or associations representing them to enforce their rights. And in the absence of significant mobilization, changes in employers' practices concerning disabled workers—such as making reasonable accommodations—have been slow to emerge.[51] Despite these evident shortcomings, rights-based approaches to social policy seem irresistible to EU policy makers, and to the extent the EU extends its reach into more matters of social policy, it is likely to encourage the spread of an approach to governance based on private enforcement of individual rights. We observed this clearly in the EU's approach to disability, and similar trends can be observed in the EU's approach to other forms of discrimination and inequity.[52]

While EU law sometimes merely formalizes rules and practices that are already common across the member states, this was certainly not the case with regard to the EU's new disability discrimination rules. The Employment Equality Directive imposed significant new requirements on all member states. At the time the directive was adopted, only the United Kingdom, Ireland, and Sweden had disability nondiscrimination legislation in place, and the directive has even imposed new requirements on these three states. For the other twelve member states, and for the ten accession states, the EU directive led to a far-reaching transformation in the protection of disabled workers.

The intervention of the European Union in the disability field and the adoption of the Equal Treatment Directive has not led rights-based policies to totally displace policies based on the medical model. Rather, there has been a layering of policies (Waddington and Diller 2002; Schickler 2001; Thelen 2003). In pressing for an antidiscrimination, individual rights–based approach to disability, advocates simultaneously have sought to preserve the beneficial aspects of the medical/welfare model of disability. While pushing policy makers to move away from a paternalistic approach that views people with disabilities as helpless objects of charity, disability advocates demand that generous social-welfare and redistributive programs remain in place (Waddington 2006a, p. 17). While advocates may be entirely justified in demanding both strong individual rights and generous social programs, some fear that strengthening the former may imperil the latter (Degener 2006; Waddington and Diller 2002). One fear is that if people with disabilities are guaranteed "equal treatment" in the workplace, this may erode political support for programs that provide more generous forms of social welfare and "special treatment" for disabled individuals.[53] As Aart Hendriks (2005), former head of the Dutch Equal Treatment Commission, puts it, skeptics have been "genuinely concerned that the adoption of disability non-discrimination laws would undermine the benefits of the European social welfare model and deter the development of positive equality duties" (p. 190). To date, there is little evidence that extending antidiscrimination rights to disabled people has undermined support for social welfare policies benefiting people with disabilities, but disability advocates must maintain a delicate balance in attempting to layer these two approaches.

CHAPTER 7

Conclusion

Public discourse concerning the supposed litigation crisis in America is distorted by sensationalist media coverage and apocryphal litigation horror stories (Haltom and McCann 2004). Some of the discussion about increasing litigation in Europe is taking on a similarly alarmist tone. This is particularly true in the United Kingdom, where business leaders, academics, and even Prince Charles have warned of the dire threats to the British economy posed by the mounting "compensation culture" in British society (Bates and Maguire 2002; Bates and White 2002; Sherwood 2003; Willett 2005; Furedi 1999). In Germany too, as we saw in Chapter 6, many employers have voiced fear of vexatious litigants abusing the new Equal Treatment Law.

In arguing that European integration is encouraging the advent of Eurolegalism, I certainly do not wish to encourage such distortion or to provide fodder for Eurosceptics. As I emphasized in Chapter 1, we should not expect European legal and regulatory systems to experience the most notorious excesses—real or imagined—of the US legal system. And to the extent that Eurolegalism is taking root, the normative consequences of this development are by no means one-sided. As Robert A. Kagan (2001, pp. 18–33) notes in the US case, adversarial legalism has virtues along with its vices. Likewise, in the European Union (EU), the spread of a European variant of adversarial legalism would bring clear benefits as well as clear costs, with the precise balance of these varying across particular policy areas and countries.

While the normative implications of the changes in legal and regulatory style described in this book may remain ambiguous, they clearly warrant close scrutiny and sober assessment. I explore these normative questions at the end of this chapter, but first let us begin by reviewing briefly the major findings of this study.

Findings

The central argument of this book is that the process of European integration is encouraging the spread of a European variant of adversarial legalism—Eurolegalism. The European Union's fragmented institutional structure and its efforts to promote economic liberalization generate political incentives and functional pressures that regularly lead policy makers to rely on adversarial legalism as a mode of governance. Time and time again, across a wide range of policy areas, EU lawmakers enact detailed, transparent, judicially enforceable rules—often framed as "rights"—and back these with a combination of public enforcement and enhanced opportunities for private enforcement litigation by individuals, interest groups, and firms.

Chapter 3 highlighted crosscutting reforms and trends that are both products of the spread of Eurolegalism and catalysts for its further growth. The discussion focused first on the growing catalog of EU rights and other detailed, judicially enforceable legal norms produced by EU lawmakers and courts. I then examined a wide range of procedural reforms, some sponsored directly by the EU and others encouraged more indirectly by the process of European integration—reforms that were designed to improve "access to justice" for private parties. Third, I looked at indicators of legal activity: not merely litigation but also broader trends in the legal services industry. I argued that a wide range of seemingly disparate phenomena—including the EU's penchant to frame legal norms as rights, the impact of EU administrative law on national legal systems, the EU's drive to create a European area of justice, the spread of class actions and conditional fee arrangements, the growth of legal insurance markets, the dramatic increases in the number of attorneys, the growing size of law firms and the overall market value of the legal services industry, Britain's protective cost orders and "Italian torpedoes"—should all be understood as part of a broad transformation of the "legal field" (Vauchez 2008), a transformation linked inextricably to the process of European integration.

Chapters 4 through 6 provided case studies of developments in securities regulation, competition law, and disability rights. This chapter traced the impact of European integration in each of these very different fields. Though the particularities varied, in each case we saw that the institutional context of EU policymaking and economic pressures associated with European integration encouraged a shift from traditional national modes of governance toward new approaches that manifested central attributes of adversarial legalism.

In the field of competition policy, we observed a marked shift toward adversarial legalism. Prior to the 1980s, the prevailing model of competition policy at the EU and national level had been an administrative control model, in which competition legislation granted regulators wide discretion to regulate competition in the public interest and to punish abusive business conduct—if they chose to do so. Private enforcement of competition law in Europe was almost nonexistent. There was little opportunity for consumers or other interested parties to assess whether competition authorities were actually enforcing the law; and outside of Germany, most national authorities took a lax approach to enforcement. Competition law played a prominent role at the supranational level since the launch of the European Communities in 1958. Since the 1980s, the EU competition law regime has shifted decidedly in the direction of adversarial legalism, pressuring member states to adapt their norms and practices in the process. Reforms have shifted the EU competition regime toward a "decentralized, ex post private enforcement model" (Wigger 2007, p. 99) in which private parties, national competition authorities, and national courts play a greater role (ibid.). These shifts at the EU level have had a powerful impact on member state competition regimes, which have been pressured to conform with a regulatory regime that emphasizes greater transparency, juridification, and increased opportunities for private enforcement. The transformation of competition policy across Europe did not result from emulation of or pressure from the United States but was instead clearly a product of European integration and policymaking initiatives launched at the EU level.

In the field of securities regulation, we observed a dramatic cycle of deregulation and reregulation over the past twenty years. The liberalization of European financial markets introduced a host of new players (including investors, listing firms, and financial service providers) to previously sheltered markets and undermined national regulatory regimes that had been based largely on informal self-regulation by trusted domestic market players. Meanwhile the EU emerged as the Continent's leading securities regulator, supplanting national regulatory regimes with a new, harmonized EU regulatory regime based on detailed disclosure requirements and the threat of public and private enforcement. In other words, European integration has pressed member states to replace their traditional, informal approaches to securities regulation with a harmonized EU regulatory regime that bears the hallmarks of adversarial legalism.

With regard to policies concerning the employment of persons with disabilities, the European Union played a central role in reorienting disability policy across Europe, away from the paternalistic, welfare model and toward an antidiscrimination model that emphasizes the rights of disabled persons to protection against discrimination in the workplace—including the right to reasonable accommodations. The EU's fragmented political structure impeded early efforts to introduce EU-level disability employment policies based on the traditional welfare model, and economic liberalization associated with the Single Market threatened national policies that relied on informal cooperation between national regulators and domestic employers. In contrast, the rights model of disability that was gaining support internationally in the 1990s was well suited to the EU's repertoire of governance. While the welfare model of disability demanded large bureaucracies and budgets and employment quotas, which the EU did not possess and could not impose, the rights model relied on the empowerment of private litigants to bring discrimination suits before national courts—a technique well suited to the EU's weak, fragmented regulatory state. Moreover, a rights-based approach held the allure of legitimacy: the EU's support for disability rights was intimately linked to its broader drive to promote antidiscrimination rights as a way of strengthening the democratic legitimacy of the EU and appealing to skeptical citizens.

The causal path through which the European Union encouraged adversarial legalism differed somewhat in each case. For instance, economic liberalization played a far greater role in securities regulation than it did in disability policy, and the legitimating power of rights rhetoric played a powerful role in the disability field and a limited role in the field of competition policy. But in each case, we could observe how both economic liberalization and the political fragmentation at the EU level influenced the direction of policy reform.

The mobilization of law has taken on a different character and proceeded at a different pace in each of these policy areas. In keeping with decades of research on the United States and Europe in the "mobilization of law" tradition (Galanter 1974; McCann 2006; Harlow and Rawlings 1992; Conant 2002), we saw that well-resourced corporate actors in the competition and securities fields have responded more quickly and had greater success in exploiting legal opportunities created by the EU than have victims of disability discrimination in the workplace. The fact that the haves and "repeat players" enjoy more success in mobilizing the law than do the have-nots and "one-shotters" is deeply important and forces us to question the efficacy of rights-based policies in some fields. However, this observation in no way challenges the central claim that the EU is encouraging a shift to modes of governance based on Eurolegalism. We also observed in each case that developments at the EU level had a differential impact across member states. These findings comport with those of a rich body of research on the "Europeanization" of domestic policy (Radaelli 2000; Börzel 1999; Featherstone and Radaelli 2003; Green Cowles, Caporaso, and Risse 2001; Knill and Lehmkuhl 2002; Börzel and Risse 2003), in that we saw that resistance to pressures for regulatory reform emanating from Brussels was generally greatest in states where national policymaking traditions differed most from the approach pursued by the EU and where domestic institutions were most ill suited to regulation based on adversarial legalism.[1]

Future studies of adversarial legalism in European governance should explore variations across policy areas and member states more systematically than did this study, explaining the conditions under which and the extent to which this mode of governance takes root. The central aim of this study, however, was not to explain such variations but to demonstrate the breadth of the phenomena and to offer a synthesis. I have offered a theoretical framework that can explain how European integration is encouraging the spread of Eurolegalism and that can thus link together developments in seemingly disparate areas of law and public policy. The study has also sought to provide a healthy corrective to the current academic fashion and the flurry of studies that trumpet the EU's role in promoting flexible, informal "new modes of governance." Of course, adversarial legalism does not constitute the only mode of governance in the EU's repertoire, and it does not completely displace other modes of governance in the fields where it is deployed. As we noted in Chapter 1, the EU's experiments with informal "new modes of governance" are interesting and noteworthy, but these are outweighed by the EU's persistent tendency to promote the spread of adversarial legalism across a wide range of policy areas.

How generalizable are the trends described in this book? Beyond the crosscutting reforms to civil procedure and administrative law described in Chapter 3 and the policy area case studies in Chapters 4 through 6, can we observe the spread of Eurolegalism in other policy domains affected by the European Union? The trends described in the case studies are readily observable in other areas of regulation affected by the EU, and a series of recent studies supports the claim that modes of governance based on variants of adversarial legalism are indeed taking root across a wide range of policy areas.[2]

Recent developments in EU health law are particularly striking. In a series of decisions that link aspects of national health-care policies to the construction of the EU's internal market, the European Court of Justice (ECJ) has established a body of law with significant impacts on national healthcare systems (Hervey and McHale 2004; Kaczorowska 2006; Greer 2006, 2009a, 2009b). In one line of cases beginning with the 1998 *Kohll* and *Decker* decisions,[3] the ECJ has established a variety of patients' rights—including the right, under some circumstances, to seek nonemergency medical care in other EU member states and to be reimbursed for it by your home country insurer or national health system. In its famous *Watts* ruling,[4] a case involving an elderly British woman who traveled to France for hip replacement surgery and sought reimbursement from the British National Health Service (NHS), the European Court of Justice ruled that the NHS must reimburse patients for treatments in other member states if the waiting time for treatment in the UK exceeds "the period which is acceptable in the light of an objective medical assessment of the clinical needs of the person concerned" (paras. 68 and 149[4]). The NHS cannot, as it did in Watts's case, base its refusal to authorize and reimburse treatment abroad on the fact that the waiting time for the patient met the standard NHS target. It must instead allow clinical experts to assess the acceptable waiting time for the individual in question—depending on that person's particular case and level of pain. Also, in *Watts,* as in previous cases on patient mobility, the ECJ held that patients must be able to challenge refusals to grant authorization for treatment abroad in "judicial or quasi-judicial proceedings" that involve "independent experts" (*Watts,* paras. 116–117). This is essentially an invitation to substitute litigation for administrative discretion. Gareth Davies (2007) anticipates that the NHS will face numerous legal disputes over what constitutes an acceptable delay and what rate of reimbursement will be permitted and that these legal disputes will generate pressure for restructuring in the NHS.

The European Union is juridifying not only the issue of patient mobility but also other aspects of national health systems as well. In applying the Working Time Directive, the ECJ has issued rulings on acceptable working hours for doctors.[5] And though health services were long treated as exempt from the EU's internal market rules, recently EU competition law, state aid, and public procurement laws have started to impact the health services and health insurance industries, as private providers bring legal challenges concerning state aids.[6] Scott L. Greer (2010) describes how the European Union is disturbing the "secret gardens" of national health-care policy, in which national health policy was based on "a few privileged groups influencing policy in close contact with the Health Ministry" (p. 10). In contrast, Greer suggests that the development of EU health-care policy has been based on adversarial legalism and argues that "under present trends, EU law will shape health care systems when and insofar as there are market entrants who are willing to sue" (ibid., p. 4). Greer highlights the role of the European Commission and even more so that of private litigants in extending EU law concerning patient mobility and competition in health-care markets and concludes, "The exact nature of the challenges that will be made [under EU law] to health care systems will vary with the litigants, the country, and the case, but they will reverberate through each health care system as they establish practices, principles and new grounds for litigation" (ibid., p. 5).

In the field of industrial relations, Britta Rehder's (2009) careful study of recent developments in Germany concludes that a variant of adversarial legalism has taken hold in Germany. As she puts it, "Processes of decisionmaking, interest intermediation, and conflict resolution have to some extent shifted away from the corporatist tradition. In the case of *Deutsche Bahn AG,* they have become more 'adversarial' as the collective bargaining parties have turned to the courts as a forum for conflict resolution. Moreover, the political process has become more 'legalistic' because it is constantly interrupted by interventions from the courts." (Rehder 2009, p. 230) As for the causes of this trend, Rehder concludes, "The causal chain suggested by Kelemen can explain my German case study very well" (ibid., p. 221). Though Rehder's study is limited to Germany, the ECJ's rulings on the right to strike and the freedom to provide services in *Viking* and *Laval* demonstrated how EU litigation strategies could impact Scandinavian systems of industrial relations.[7] The rulings provoked a furor across Europe among trade unionists, who were concerned that EU law might undermine systems of industrial relations based on collective agreements and open the door to widespread "social dumping."

My own earlier work (Kelemen and Sibbitt 2004; Kelemen 2006) and the work of others (see Hodges 2008, 2009c; Cafaggi and Micklitz 2009) demonstrates that the European Union has promoted adversarial legalism in the field of consumer policy.[8] Though legal mobilization by consumer groups has remained weak, the EU's approach to consumer policy has clearly relied on the establishment of substantive rights and procedural tools to empower consumers to litigate EU consumer rights. The establishment of the single market has undermined regimes of consumer protection based on strict control of market entry and has opened consumers to a host of new risks. The EU has responded by putting in place a series of measures designed to strengthen rights and access to justice for consumers, measures ranging from a strict product liability regime (Directive 85/374/EEC) introduced more than two decades ago, to rules on unfair consumer contracts (Directive 93/13/EEC), injunctions for consumer protection (Directive 98/27/EC), access to justice in cross-border consumer disputes (Directive 2003/8/EC), and unfair commercial practices (Directive 2005/29/EC).[9]

In the field of employment discrimination, this study focused on developments in the disability discrimination field, but the European Union has clearly sought to rely on a similar private enforcement model to combat other forms of discrimination. Building on the model pioneered in the field of EU sex discrimination law (Alter and Vargas 2000; Cichowski 2007), the EU has empowered victims of discrimination on the basis of race, religion, age, or sexual orientation to enforce their EU rights. The upsurge in age discrimination claims before national tribunals and recent age discrimination referrals to ECJ suggest that older workers are mobilizing in an effort to enforce their newfound antidiscrimination rights.[10] With regard to fundamental rights more generally, the Charter of Fundamental Rights linked to the Lisbon Treaty proved to be such a focal point of controversy precisely because critics in some member states worried that this charter would establish new grounds for fundamental rights litigation and encourage a flood of claims that would promote an expansion of EU power vis-à-vis the member states.

We began this study in an airport lobby, and we can end it in a train station. As we discussed in Chapter 1, the establishment of EU air passenger rights in 2004 and the European Union's active effort to notify passengers of these rights have had a significant impact. Air passengers have brought thousands of compensation claims against airlines, airlines have brought failed legal challenges against the EU air passenger–rights regulation, the ECJ has extended the scope of air passenger rights, and a nascent industry of claims facilitators has emerged. On 3 December 2009, the EU moved from planes to trains. A regulation (Regulation 1371/2007/EC) went into force, establishing a new set of rights for railway passengers, including rights to compensation for delayed trains, and requiring railway companies to notify passengers of their rights and to establish complaint boards. As in other areas examined in this study, rail passenger rights were introduced as part of a cycle of deregulation and reregulation. The new regulations on rail passenger rights and a number of EU rail safety regulations were coupled with a much broader drive to liberalize passenger rail transport across Europe, as part of the "third railway package." As part of this package, international rail passenger service was liberalized from 1 January 2010, such that all European rail operators had the opportunity to access rail networks across the EU and offer international passenger services between any EU member states. The European Commission underlined the connection between deregulation and reregulation in this sector, explaining, "In such a context, where a single market is emerging, measures to promote users' [i.e., rail passengers'] rights are essential to grant the consumer adequate protection on opening markets and the rail industry a level playing field and thus take full advantage of the benefits of the integrated market for rail transport services" (Commission 2009d, p. 2). Having covered trains and planes, the Commission has moved on to automobiles and boats, proposing regulations to establish bus passenger and maritime passenger rights (see Commission 2008e and Commission 2008f).

Normative Implications

For critics, the advent of Eurolegalism can be viewed as the regrettable spread of an American disease, leading to increased legal expenses, slower regulatory processes, increasingly adversarial relations between stakeholders in the policy process and to forms of judicial activism that ultimately erode democracy. Indeed, this is how some critics, particularly from the American business community, have greeted recent legal developments in Europe (Willett 2005; Wallace 2007). In contrast, those who focus on adversarial legalism's virtues may look forward to the increased legal certainty, access to justice for previously marginalized groups, transparency, and accountability of government that adversarial legalism's spread might encourage in Europe. In this view, by strengthening transparency and accountability, establishing enforceable individual rights, and creating new opportunities for participation in policymaking through the courts, adversarial legalism could ultimately strengthen democracy in Europe (Cichowski 2006, 2007).

With regard to economic implications, much of the comparative literature cited in Chapter 1 praised traditional consensual European regulatory styles—with their greater speed and flexibility and lower expenses—for their advantages over the American model. Indeed, during the US recession of the early 1990s, critics suggested that the inflexibility, stringency, and litigiousness of US regulatory politics was a significant cause of the United States' poor economic performance (Epp 1992; Galanter 1996; Kagan 1997). Claims concerning the damaging macroeconomic implications of adversarial legalism are surely overwrought;[11] nevertheless, it is clear that costs associated with adversarial legalism can be significant in some regulated sectors. Fear concerning such costs has led business groups in Europe to warn of the rise of a "litigious society" in Europe and to strenuously oppose the import into Europe of some legal reforms associated with American-style adversarial legalism, such as class actions (Thornhill 2005; Parker, Buck, and Tait 2007; Willett 2005; Peel 2007; Lloyd's 2008a, 2008b; Fleming 2004).

Beyond the specific legal and regulatory costs that it would entail, the rise of a European variant of adversarial legalism would have, more generally, a major impact on European approaches to economic management—or what scholars term "varieties of capitalism" (Hall and Soskice 2001). In Europe's coordinated market economies (CMEs), economic regulation in many sectors relies on cooperation between government officials and stakeholders such as employers, unions, and other interest groups who seek compromises that balance various private and public interests. The rise of Eurolegalism threatens to undermine key aspects of this model. As Angela Wigger and Andreas Nölke explain (2007, p. 489), an approach to regulation that relies on enforcement by private actors is incompatible with the Rhenish variety of capitalism. In competition policy, financial market regulation, and various areas of sectoral regulation, greater reliance on adversarial legalism is certain to undermine traditional relationships between regulators and regulated entities. When private actors can go to court to pursue their claims, they have less reason to remain at the negotiating table, seeking consensual solutions; indeed, the credibility of bargains reached at such tables is undermined if those involved anticipate that subsequent litigation could upend such bargains. Thus, juridification and associated changes in regulatory style may ultimately encourage much broader changes in European varieties of capitalism.

Eurolegalism also has important normative implications for democracy in Europe—some desirable and some undesirable (Kelemen 2006). On the positive side of the ledger, a shift toward adversarial legalism in the European Union may strengthen democracy in vital respects. EU law pressures member states to enhance the transparency, legal certainty, and access to justice in their national regulatory processes—and these pressures are greatest in the member states where transparency, legal certainty, and access to justice are weakest. EU lawmakers and the ECJ have together established a host of new substantive and procedural rights for individuals, rights guaranteed under EU law. Eurolegalism's emphasis on transparency, accountability, and judicial enforcement of individual rights may enhance opportunities for broader, more active public participation in governance and thus improve the quality of democracy across Europe (Schepel and Blankenburg 2001; Shapiro 2001; Stone Sweet 2000; Cichowski and Stone Sweet 2003; Kelemen 2006; Cichowski 2006, 2007). For some citizens and social groups who were long excluded from insider policymaking networks, EU law litigation may provide enhanced opportunities to participate in the political process and hold their governments to account (Cichowski 2007; Hartnell 2002).[12] Indeed, many democratic theorists see the strengthening of a rights-based model of citizenship as crucial to the future of the European Union. In this view, despite the absence of a unifying ethnic or national identity, the EU may strengthen its legitimacy and public support by promoting a form of transnational constitutional patriotism based on a commitment to a common set of European rights (Frowein 1986; Habermas 1992; Weiler 1996, 1999; Bellamy 2005, 2006). In this view, the European Charter of Fundamental Rights, and the existing *acquis* of fundamental human rights, can form the basis for a legitimate EU democracy.

However, critics of such a European rights model suggest how the rise of Eurolegalism may in fact undermine democracy. Rightly or wrongly, the EU is often criticized for its "democratic deficit." Critics argue that the European Union undermines democracy because it shifts decision making further from the citizen and because it eliminates many national social rights and policies in the name of the free market (Follesdal and Koslowski 1997; Scharpf 2003; Moravcsik 2002). Eurolegalism strengthens the role of countermajoritarian institutions—such as courts and independent regulatory authorities—at the expense of elected representatives. As Kip Viscusi (2002) argues, "Policies that result from litigation almost invariably involve less public input and accountability than government regulation" (p. 1). The juridification of the EU policy process may provide fodder for critics of judicial activism or "government by judges" *(gouvernement des juges),* critics who can invoke the trope that unelected judges are substituting their will for that of elected representatives (Dehousse 2000, p. 27.)[13]

The rights discourse that inevitably accompanies a rights-based model of citizenship also places pressure on traditional European models of democracy. As Arend Lijphart (1999) has demonstrated, the prevailing model of democracy across EU member states, and within the EU itself, is the consensus model of democracy. In part, consensus democracy must be understood in institutional terms: consensus democracies have multiple veto players and require political actors to collaborate in broad supermajority coalitions. In part, however, consensus democracy also requires the development of a political culture oriented to compromise and consensus building. Critics of the excessive focus on "rights discourse," or the "politics of rights," in American politics argue that a focus on rights can inhibit just such compromise. For instance, Mary Ann Glendon (1991) explains that "rights talk, in its absoluteness, . . . inhibits dialogue that might lead toward consensus, accommodation, or at least to the discovery of common ground" (p. 14).[14] The focus on rights and legal enforcement of rights may undermine the culture of compromise that is vital in many European democracies. Likewise, the focus on individual rights can conflict with the pursuit of broader public interests. As the chairman of a US lobbying group critical of tort litigation put it, "Europe will find, as America has, that it's difficult to take sensible public judgments if litigants can use the threat of court action to get their own way at the expense of the broader public interest" (quoted in Fleming 2004). This concern underlies critics' objections to the advent of adversarial legalism in EU health policy, in which the legal claims of individual patients or of private medical service providers threaten to undermine policy decisions and financing models established by health ministries in the collective, public interest (Greer 2009b, 2010).

There is certainly much scope to debate as to whether the rise of Eurolegalism will have, on balance, a positive or negative impact on European democracy. What seems indisputable is that recourse to the strict, judicialized approaches to regulation associated with Eurolegalism is placing tremendous pressures on the rule of law in the European Union. Many scholars have noted the crucial role that the European Court of Justice, and its interlocking system of jurisdiction (Lenaerts 2007) involving thousands of national courts, has played in sustaining the process of European integration (see especially Stein 1981; Weiler 1991; Burley and Mattli 1993; Alter 2001; Stone Sweet 2004). The EU legal system has served as the linchpin of the integration process, but today the courts are being asked to bear a very heavy load.

With an ever-growing body of European law and an increasingly diverse network of thousands of national courts—including inexperienced (and, in cases such as Bulgaria and Romania, politically compromised) courts in new, post-Communist democracies—the ECJ faces greater challenges than ever before in simply maintaining the coherence of the Community legal order (Lenaerts 2007; H. Rasmussen 2007). Yet the courts are being asked to bear added burdens. Many advocates of deeper European integration hope that citizen support for a "Europe of rights" will bolster otherwise anemic levels of common identity and public support for European integration. Essentially, these advocates hope to rely on the EU legal system to make up for the political system's failure to secure a stronger base of legitimacy for the integration project. Policy makers who are focused on the implementation of EU law increasingly seek to rely on decentralized enforcement before national courts, to make up for the EU's lack of a strong, centralized administrative apparatus. It remains to be seen whether the EU legal system can sustain the load being placed upon it.

We must hope so. For, as we stated at the outset of this study, the European Union is a community built on the rule of law. Formal law, courts, lawyers, and private litigation have all played central roles in European governance over the past half century (Stone Sweet 2004; Alter 2001; Weiler 1991; Stone Sweet and Brunell 1998; Vauchez 2008). Critics might rightly argue that the EU has relied on an excessively juridical and litigious approach in addressing some policy issues. However, given the EU's fragmented political structure, its limited administrative capacity, and the nature of the single market it seeks to regulate, a heavy reliance on adversarial legalism as a mode of governance is likely unavoidable. We may lament the European Union's intrusion on flexible and informal national policy styles and the erosion of more flexible national policy styles based on insider networks and trust, but too much litigation and too many lawyers may simply be a price to be paid for the uniting of Europe. And a Europe united with an excess of strict laws, lawyers, and litigation is better than a Europe divided without them.

NOTES

REFERENCES

ACKNOWLEDGMENTS

INDEX

Notes

1. The Juris Touch

1. Regulation 261/2004/EC, OJ L 46 (2004), p. 1.
2. C-344/04, *IATA and ELFAA v. Department for Transport,* [2006] ECR I-403
3. C-333/06, *Commission v. Sweden,* OJ C 183 (4 Aug. 2007), p. 14; C-264/06, *Commission v. Luxembourg,* OJ C 96, (28 Apr. 2007), p. 17; C-235/06, *Commission v. Austria Transport,* OJ C 1651 (5 Jul. 2006), p. 22.
4. The firms' Web sites can be found at www.euclaim.co.uk, www.euclaim.co.uk, and www.ticketclaim.nl/pages/home.php, last accessed on 10 Feb. 2010.
5. C-396/06, *Kramme v. SAS Scandinavian Airlines Danmark A/S,* OJ C294 of 2 Dec. 2006, p. 29; C-173/07, *Emirates Airlines Direktion für Deutschland v. Diether Schenkel,* OJ C223 of 30 Aug. 2008, p. 14; C-549/07, *Friederike Wallentin-Hermann v. Alitalia,* OJ C64 of 8 March 2008, p. 18; C-402/07, *Sturgeon and Others v. Condor Flugdienst GmbH,* OJ C283 of 24 Nov. 2007, p. 12; C-432/07, *Böck and Lepuschitz v. Air France SA,* OJ C283 of 24 Nov. 2007, p. 21; C-529/08, *Schulze and Others v. Deutsche Lufthansa AG,* OJ C 44 of 21 Feb. 2009, p. 32; C-525/08, *Bienek v. Condor Flugdienst GmbH,* OJ C 55 of 7 March 2009, p. 8.
6. C-549/07, *Wallentin-Hermann v. Alitalia* (22 December 2008).
7. Joined Cases C-402/07, *Sturgeon,* and C-432/07, *Böck and Lepuschitz,* 19 November 2009.
8. One should not conflate Kagan's specific concept of "adversarial legalism" with the general concept of an "adversarial" or "adversary" system of justice typical of common law countries (as opposed to the inquisito-

rial system typical of civil law jurisdictions). The generic concept of an adversarial system of justice refers primarily to the process through which trials are conducted (Damaska 1986), whereas Kagan's concept of adversarial legalism refers to broad patterns of regulation.

9. See, for instance, Badarraco (1985); Braithwaite (1985); Brickman, Jasanoff, and Ilgen (1985); Church and Nakamura (1993); Jasanoff (1986); Kagan and Axelrad (2000); Kelman (1981); Schwartz (1991); Sellers (1995); D. Vogel (1986); S. Vogel (1996).
10. The term "American disease" and various metaphors relating to pathogens and metastasizing cancers are regularly used in European discussions of American litigation. See, for instance, Fleming (2005).
11. Throughout the rest of the text, I use the terms "adversarial legalism" and "Eurolegalism" interchangeably. Whenever I refer to the spread of adversarial legalism in the European context, I am referring specifically to the spread of the European variant of adversarial legalism, which is also labeled as Eurolegalism. I thank Robert Kagan for suggesting the term Eurolegalism.
12. As discussed in Chapter 2, the EU tends to rely primarily on flexible, new modes of governance only in those policy areas—such as social policy—where it lacks the legal authority to engage in "hard law" governance. In the areas of the EU's core competencies, flexible, new modes of governance have had little impact. For a similar argument see Dehousse (2008).
13. Indeed, as I discuss in Chapter 2, the very prevalence of adversarial legalism can generate pressure for regulators to experiment with more flexible, informal approaches to regulation. However, the existence of such pilot programs does not constitute a change in the prevailing mode of regulation.
14. In this respect, this research fits within the broad tradition of studies of the "Europeanization" of domestic institutions (see Radaelli 2000; Börzel 1999; Featherstone and Radaelli 2003; Green Cowles, Caporaso, and Risse 2001; Knill and Lehmkuhl 2002).
15. The typology of Van Waarden (1995) identifies six dimensions of regulatory styles: (1) liberal-pluralist versus etatist versus corporatist, (2) active versus reactive, (3) comprehensive versus fragmented, (4) adversarial versus consensual, (5) legalistic versus pragmatic, and (6) formal versus informal. Knill (1998) argues that national regulatory styles are distinguished primarily by the mode of state intervention (hierarchical versus self-regulation, substantive versus procedural regulation, and uniform, detailed requirements versus flexible, discretionary ones) and by the pattern of interest intermediation (formal, legalistic relations be-

tween regulators and social actors versus informal, pragmatic relations, and open relationships between regulators and social actors versus closed relations).

16. Social scientific concepts can be arrayed on what social scientists call a "ladder of abstraction" (Sartori 1970) or "ladder of generality" (Collier and Mahon 1993). Atop the ladder sit abstract, universal concepts, which have few defined properties but a wide range of application. Near the bottom of the ladder are concepts defined by many specific properties, and these concepts, as a result, have a limited range of application. The concepts of adversarial legalism and Eurolegalism sit on a middle rung of this sort of ladder of abstraction.
17. Scholars of the varieties of capitalism have described such institutional interdependence with the concept of "institutional complementarities" (Hall and Gingerich 2004). Such complementarities exist whenever the presence of one set of institutions raises the returns available from the other.
18. Blankenburg (1994) makes a similar point in discussing national legal cultures. He argues that a national legal culture comprises substantive laws, public and private legal institutions, and actual patterns of behavior and attitudes, and he emphasizes that an analysis of a nation's legal culture must take into account the interaction between all three of these levels.
19. Rehder (2007) notes that some areas of corporatist policymaking, in particular labour law, "did involve high levels of court activity" (p. 9) and that the legal system may have contributed to the stability of corporatist networks but that the role of courts in corporatism has been ignored by most analysts.
20. In analyzing the emergence of the "European legal field" Vauchez builds on the theory of fields first developed by Bourdieu (1977) (see also Fligstein 2001). A field is a local social order comprising an interrelated system of actors, social positions and institutions.
21. One could of course attempt to isolate the impact of the EU in a variety of ways, but each of these has significant shortcomings. For instance, one might consider comparing trends in legal activity in EU member states with those in comparable (possibly neighboring) states that are not EU members. However, the EU's *acquis communautaire* and its approach to regulation have impacts on regulation in states throughout the region—both those with aspirations to EU membership and those who simply trade heavily with the EU. Likewise, one might attempt to gauge EU influence by focusing on accession states and comparing their regulatory style before EU membership and after accession. How-

ever, most applicant states adjust their regulations and regulatory styles in order to qualify for EU membership, sometimes over the course of many years. Also, most states that have joined the EU since the early 1980s have done so in the wake of regime transitions (from authoritarianism or communism to democracy), which would also have caused significant changes in regulatory style.

22. In most social science research, it is impossible to follow Mill's method strictly and to ensure that cases differ on all potential causal factors save one. In practice, comparative studies using the method of agreement, or most different systems design, simply aim to select cases that differ with regard to the factors deemed most theoretically relevant.
23. A rich tradition in the study of public law and legal mobilization demonstrates that well-resourced, privileged litigants (the haves) and "repeat players" are more likely to successfully mobilize the law to enforce their rights and pursue their policy objectives than have-nots and "one-shotters." Analysis of the varying ability of different types of litigants to mobilize the law was pioneered by Galanter (1974) and has been extended by numerous studies of legal mobilization in the United States (see McCann 2006 for a review). This perspective has also been applied to various categories of litigants in the EU context (see, for instance, Harding 1980, 1992; Rawlings 1993; Harlow and Rawlings 1992; Conant 1998, 2002; Costa 2003).
24. The case studies allow for structured, focused comparison (George 1979; George and McKeown 1985; George and Bennett 2005, pp. 67–72) in that I ask the same set of questions in each case and deal only with those aspects of each case that relate to my research objectives. The case studies are designed not to provide the most comprehensive account possible of the policy areas in question but to assess the extent to which European integration has encouraged adversarial legalism in the policy area.
25. However, EU law has a clear influence even on areas of policy one might assume to be immune from its influence, such as foreign policy (see Cremona and De Witte 2008).

2. The Political Economy of Eurolegalism

1. Paul Pierson has offered a useful typology of the "time horizons" of causal accounts in the social sciences. As Pierson explains (2004, pp. 79–102), causal accounts can involve causes that unfold over the short term or over the long term and can involve outcomes that emerge over the short term or over the long term.

2. Also see Caporaso and Tarrow (2009) on the role of juridical reregulation in adding social content to the process of market building.
3. For more general discussions of the democratic deficit, see Majone (1998); Moravcsik (2002) (2006).
4. See the network's Web site at www.eu-newgov.org, last accessed 18 Jan. 2010.
5. The following section draws heavily on Idema and Kelemen (2006).
6. US experience with efforts to encourage more flexible, informal approaches to regulation provide a useful lesson for the EU. The Clinton administration's efforts to "reinvent government" through new modes of flexible regulation generated a number of pilot programs along these lines, but the broader effort to shift the prevailing mode of governance foundered. The institutional structure of the US political system, like that of the EU, was simply not conducive to informal, nonjudicialized modes of regulation.
7. US law firms, conversely, have been active proponents of adversarial legalism. We return to this in the next chapter.
8. I use the term family resemblance here in Wittgenstein's (1953/1973) sense to emphasize that Eurolegalism and American adversarial legalism are connected not by one essential shared characteristic, but by a series of overlapping sets of features.

3. Europe's Shifting Legal Landscape

1. In contrast, Bignami (2007, 2010) finds that the EU has not encouraged the spread of adversarial legalism in the field of data privacy regulation, which she takes to be a "most-likely case" for Americanization.
2. Fifth Environmental Action Program, OJ C 138 17 (1993), p. 5.
3. On legal mobilization in the field of EU environmental policy more generally, see Cichowski 2007, pp. 207–241.
4. For descriptions of such activities, see the European Commission's "Your Europe" Web site at http://ec.europa.eu/youreurope/, last accessed 4 Oct. 2010.
5. The one significant exception was found in the area of gender equality: Treaty Article 119 established the right to equal treatment in employment regardless of gender.
6. C-1/58, *Stork v. High Authority,* [1959] ECR, 17.
7. For overviews see Craig and De Búrca 2008, p. 379–402; Weiler 1986; Stone Sweet 2000, pp. 170–178; Cassese, Clapham, and Weiler 1992; Weiler and Lockhart 1995; Alston and Weiler 1999; Mancini and Keeling 1994. Early landmark cases include, for instance, C-29/69, *Stauder v.*

City of Ulm, [1969] ECR 419, and C-11/70, *Internationale Handelsgesellschaft v. Einfuhr- und Vorratstelle für Getreide und Futtermittel,* [1970] ECR 1125, and subsequent landmark cases include C-5/88, *Wachauf v. Bundesamt für Ernährung und Forstwirtschaft,* [1989] ECR 2609, and C-260/98, *ERT,* [1991] ECR I-2925.

8. See, for instance, the European Parliament, Council, and Commission's joint declaration concerning the protection of fundamental rights, OJ C 103 (27 Apr. 1977).
9. Notably, this distinction did not prevent the Court of First Instance of the European Communities (CFI) and the European Court of Justice from referring to the charter in subsequent decisions.
10. Keen to convince domestic audiences that the new treaty would not undermine Britain's flexible labor regulations, British Prime Minister Tony Blair, identified a UK opt-out from the Charter as a "red-line" issue. Similarly, the Polish government demanded assurances that the Charter would not affect Polish family law or laws on public morality (i.e., abortion). Meanwhile the German government insisted that the new treaty must make the Charter legally enforceable (Taylor 2007; Beunderman 2007; Traynor 2007).
11. To further reassure the UK and Poland that the charter could not be used to justify intrusions into sensitive policy areas, an "opt-out" protocol was appended to the treaty, a protocol specifically stating that the Charter would not create any new rights in the UK or Poland. Though these provisions would seem to place a severe limit on the ability of litigants to invoke the charter to expand the reach of EU law or to attack national laws or practices, experience suggests this is not the case (Eeckhout 2002; Engel 2001). First, the experience of other federal polities suggests that the establishment of common charters of rights has dramatic centralizing effects in federal-type systems (Cappelletti 1989, p. 395; Sunstein 1990; Epp 1998; Melnick 1996; Katz and Tarr 1996; Baar 1991; Manfredi 2001). Second, the experience of the EU itself suggests that the ECJ and CFI may make expansive interpretations of the Charter. For instance, drafters of the Maastricht Treaty emphasized that Articles 17 and 18 on European citizenship rights were not intended to create any new rights. Nevertheless, subsequent litigation before the ECJ invoking these articles clearly did lead to an expansion of rights (H. Rasmussen 2007, p. 1686).
12. These are also referred to as the Racial Equality Directive and Employment Equality Directive.
13. While detailed, inflexible regulations—aka red tape—are famously unpopular, those same regulations, when reframed as "rights," may have great rhetorical appeal.

14. Likewise, the ECJ and national judiciaries have in some ways deferred to one another's rights agendas (Schimmelfennig 2006; Stone Sweet 2000; Shapiro 2005, 2006).
15. See C-33/76, *Rewe v. Landwirtschaftskammer für das Saarland,* [1976] ECR 1989, esp. para. 5; C-158/80, *Rewe v. Hauptzollamt Kiel,* [1981] ECR 1805, para. 44. More generally, see Harlow (2000, p. 74); Kilpatrick (2000, p. 3); Himsworth (1997, p. 296).
16. The EU has applied this approach to procedural rights with regard to both implementation carried out by EU institutions (direct implementation) and implementation carried out by national authorities on behalf of the EU (indirect implementation). Ultimately, the impact of EU administrative law at the national level extends beyond instances in which national authorities are implementing EU law, because once a procedural right or remedy is granted in EU-related matters, it becomes difficult to withhold that right or remedy in purely national matters.
17. EU lawmakers have addressed procedural issues, though not in a comprehensive fashion. For instance, particular substantive directives sometimes include requirements concerning procedures and remedies.
18. C- 222/84, *Johnston v. Chief Constable of the Royal Ulster Constabulary,* [1986] ECR 1651.
19. C-208/90, *Emmott v. Minister for Social Welfare and Attorney-General,* [1991] ECR I-4629 (but see Flynn 2000 for discussion of subsequent ECJ retrenchment on issue of national time-limits); C-326/96, *Levez v. T. H. Jennings (Harlow Pools) Ltd.,* [1998] ECR I-7835.
20. C-213/89, *Regina v. Secretary of State for Transport, ex parte Factortame Ltd. and others,* [1990] ECR I-2433.
21. Joined Cases C-6/90 and C-9/90, *Francovich and Bonafaci v. Italy,* [1991] ECR I-5357.
22. This requirement in effect establishes a right for parties involved in those proceedings to be given a reason for the administrative decision.
23. National procedural autonomy threatened to undermine the rule of law in the EU and the fundamental legal principle of *ubi jus, ibi remedium* (for every right, there must be a remedy). If the EU was serious about guaranteeing the rights of EU citizens , it had to guarantee them effective access to justice and remedies as well (Kilpatrick 2000, p. 6; Himsworth 1997). It took only a very small doctrinal leap for the ECJ to assert that national courts must ensure full and effective protection of EU rights (Harlow 2000, p. 72).
24. C-6/64, *Costa v. ENEL,* [1964] ECR 583.
25. C-26/62, *Van Gend en Loos v. Nederlandse Administratie der Belastingen,* [1963] ECR 1.

26. See Advocate General Tesauro's Opinion, Joined Cases C-46/93 and C-48/93, *Brasserie du Pecheur SA v. Germany* and *Regina v. Secretary of State for Transport ex parte Factortame Ltd,* [1996] ECR I-1029, para. 39.
27. In the United States, contingency fee arrangements—whereby attorneys charge no fee if the litigant loses but take a percentage (typically 33.3 percent) of any settlement or judgment awarded—have played a crucial role in litigation finance. In a 1990 study, Kritzer (1990, p. 58) found that 87 percent of plaintiffs in tort cases retained their attorneys on a contingent fee basis (see also Kritzer 2002b). Likewise, procedural devices such as class actions have played a vital role in facilitating litigation by diffuse groups, such as consumers.
28. On the theory of fields more generally, see Bourdieu (1977) and Fligstein (2001).
29. Even before the EU embraced enhancing access to justice as a general goal, it had focused on access to justice as a key objective in consumer policy (Hodges 2007, p. 97).
30. The so-called Italian torpedo is a litigation technique used most often in the intellectual property field and involves exploiting the notoriously glacial pace of the Italian civil justice system. Patent infringers who suspect that they may be sued for intellectual property violations launch preemptive litigation (a "declaration of noninfringement") before courts in jurisdictions known to have extremely inefficient legal systems—most often in Italy. Under the EU's "first come, first served" rules on parallel proceedings, the filing of this case then blocks all other proceedings between these parties before any courts in Europe (see Brussels Convention, OJ L27 [1998], p. 1, Art. 21; the "Brussels I" Regulation, EC 44/2001, OJ L12 [2001], p. 10, Art. 27). And since Italian civil cases often take more than seven years to conclude, this Italian torpedo allows the patent infringer to continue engaging in its suspect practices for years, shielded from any legal claims. In a newer form of this practice, there are indications that potential plaintiffs in class actions in Europe are taking advantage of differences in national rules on collective actions to engage in forum shopping (Tait 2008a; Lloyd's 2008a). Likewise, a report from the insurer Lloyd's of London suggests that forum shoppers may be seeking out jurisdictions that offer more attractive remedies (Lloyd's 2008b, p. 24).
31. This omission was not lost on the European Commission's first president, Walter Hallstein, himself a former professor of private law and comparative law. Hallstein was keenly interested in the debate over the search for a *ius commune* (Hallstein 1964).

32. For an early statement of this view, see the European Parliament, OJ C 68 (1983), pp. 32–34.
33. The European Judicial Network in Civil and Commercial matters (EJ-NET) (Council Regulation 743/2002). See http://ec.europa.eu/civiljustice/news/whatsnew_en.htm, last accessed 15 Jun. 2009.
34. For a full list of measures adopted as part of this initiative, see http://ec.europa.eu/justice_home/judicialatlascivil/html/rc_information_en.htm, last accessed 15 Jun. 2009. The EU coupled judicial dispute settlement measures with a number of measures designed to promote forms of "extra-judicial" dispute settlement. However, the fact that the EU has in some instances worked to promote alternative dispute resolution does not undermine the claim that more generally the EU promoted access to justice for judicial dispute settlement.
35. The notion of the "right to counsel" dates even further back, to the codifications of "poor man's law" that occurred in most Continental jurisdictions in the nineteenth century (Blankenburg 1999).
36. In France and Germany per capita funding was two and a half times that in the United States; in the Netherlands, four times as much; in England, seventeen times as much (Johnson 2000).
37. The British legal aid system dates back to the 1940s, decades before the UK's membership in the European Communities. Throughout the 1980s and 1990s the costs of the system continued to escalate dramatically (Blankenburg 1999, p. 123; Flood and Whyte 2006; Regan 1999; Abel 2003). Finally in 1999 the government introduced a system that severely restricted access to publicly funded legal aid and instead relied primarily on private "conditional fee arrangements" as the mechanism for funding civil claims.
38. *Airey v. Ireland,* [1979] 2 Eur. Ct. HR Rep. 305. Also see *Steel and Morris v. United Kingdom,* [2005] Application no. 6841/01.
39. See for instance Resolution 76(5) on legal aid in civil, commercial, and administrative matters and Resolution 78(8) on legal aid and advice.
40. Some insurers argue that by replacing legal aid with CFAs, the government shifted the costs off its books but increased the total social costs in that the increased insurance premiums associated with CFAs will cost many times what government-funded legal aid had cost (Zander 2002, p. 271).
41. Such fee arrangements were first permitted in 1991 with the passage of Act 91-647, 10 Jul. 1991.
42. See, for instance the ruling in Corner House, *Regina [Corner House Research] v. Secretary of State for Trade and Industry,* [2005] EWCA Civ 192.

43. Both of these figures were calculated using reports that were obtained from the Comité Européen des Assurances. Raw data and procedures used for conversion are available from the author.
44. Moreover, the insurance industry has demonstrated the ability to respond to demands for new forms of legal expenses coverage. For instance, with the advent of conditional fee arrangements in England and Wales after 1999, a market quickly emerged for after-the-event legal expenses insurance, which enabled litigants to cover themselves against the risks of paying the defendants' costs should the plaintiffs lose their case (Hodges 2007, p. 101).
45. Traditionally, in civil law systems, punitive damages were considered criminal sanctions and thus not awarded in civil cases (Bergkamp 2003, p. 417).
46. C-14/83, *Von Colson and Kamman v. Land Nordrhein-Westfalen,* [1984] ECR I-1891; C-79/83, *Dorit Harz v. Deutsche Tradax GmbH,* [1984] ECR I-1921; C-222/84, *Johnston v. Chief Constable of the Royal Ulster Constabulary,* [1986] ECR 1651.
47. C-271/91, *Marshall v. Southampton and SW Area Health Authority,* [1993] ECR I-2367.
48. Ibid.
49. C-168/00, *Simone Leitner v. TUI Germany,* [2002] ECR I-2631. The court held that the EU's directive (90/314) on package holiday travel gave consumers a right to compensation for nonmaterial damages (in this case psychological damages resulting from loss of enjoyment of a holiday, or *entgangene Urlaubsfreude*), despite the fact that the directive had not explicitly mentioned nonmaterial damages and that such damages were not recognized in Austrian law.
50. Joined Cases C-6 and C-9/90, *Francovich and Bonafaci v. Italy,* [1991] ECR I-5357.
51. C-453/99, *Courage v. Crehan,* [2001] ECR I-6297. Also see Joined Cases C-295 and C-298/04, *Manfredi v. Lloyd Adriatico Assicurazion SpA,* [2006] ECR I-6619.
52. T-351/03, *Schneider Electric SA v. Commission,* [2007] ECR II-02237.
53. At least in one respect, however, the emerging rules on damages for breach of antitrust violations may surpass those in the United States. Though US antitrust law provides for treble damages, it does not provide the right to recover interest for damages suffered. The Commission's April 2008 *White Paper on Damages Actions for Breach of Anti-trust Rules* (Commission 2008d) recommends the recovery of interest from the date of infringement. Interest payments in major, long-running an-

titrust cases may be massive, leading a member of the US Federal Trade Commission to conclude, "In the end, I would not be surprised to see damage awards in Europe equal or even exceed those seen in the United States" (Rosch 2008 p. 6).

54. Carol Harlow (2000, p. 79) observes a "spillover effect" of ECJ rulings on remedies into national law in the UK.
55. The December 12-14 conference, titled "The Globalization of Class Actions," was cosponsored by Oxford University's Centre for Socio-Legal Studies and Stanford Law School.
56. French supporters of expanding collective actions have consistently emphasized that the French approach must steer away from the excesses of the American model. See for instance Meneval 2004, p. 3; Hollinger 2005.
57. For information on these meetings see http://ec.europa.eu/consumers/redress_cons/collective_redress_en.htm, last accessed 20 Feb. 2010.
58. Indeed, it is striking that the EU and member state governments launched a series of initiatives to expand collective redress mechanisms in a period when the US federal government was attempting to restrict them (Tait and Sherwood 2005).
59. Neither the EU nor individual jurisdictions will introduce mechanisms that mimic US class actions, in particular the American opt-out approach, whereby members of a class are covered by the settlement of the case unless they actively opt out. Across Europe, this approach is viewed as contrary to human rights and basic constitutional principles guaranteeing the individual the right to a trial, and the consensus across Europe is that any form of collective action should be opt-in (or a hybrid opt-in scheme), whereby potential members of the group in question need to opt in in order to be covered by the settlement (Hodges 2009c; Tait 2008).
60. Lawmakers were in fact forced to adopt a reform by the Federal Constitutional Court, which had ruled that delays led to an unconstitutional denial of justice (Baetge 2009, p. 127).
61. Of particular significance were the Lawyer's Services Directive (77/249, OJ L78 [1977], p. 47) and Directive 98/5/EC OJ L77 (1988) of 14 Mar. 1998.
62. In Eastern Europe, American firms of course had been prohibited during the Communist era. Lawyers were in any case largely unnecessary, given the absence of the rule of law. With the fall of Communism, American law firms made a rapid influx into the region, rising from zero in 1985 to thirty-nine firms employing 810 attorneys in 2005 (see Ajani 1995).

63. For instance, German firms Bruckhaus and Deringer merged with the English firm Freshfields; the German firm Oppenhoff and Rädler merged with the English giant Linklaters; and a group of other European firms and German firm Pünder, Volhard, Weber, and Axster merged with the English firm Clifford Chance and the American firm Rogers and Wells.
64. Neither the Organization for Economic Co-operation and Development (OECD) nor most national statistics offices report data on the legal services industry as a distinct category.
65. However, Vanhala (2006, 2009b) finds a shift toward litigation strategies among some EU disability groups. See also the discussion of disability in Chapter 6 of this book.
66. Kelemen (2002), "Survey of European Union Interest Groups," data on file with author and with Princeton University Survey Research Center. The survey was administered to 1,014 EU-level and national interest groups drawn from the Commission's database of EU-level Civil Society Organizations (CONECCS), and 412 responses were received.
67. In comparison, in a similar survey conducted in the United States in the early 1980s, 72 percent of groups reported engaging in litigation (Schlozman and Tierney 1983).
68. For instance, as I discuss in Chapter 6, the European Commission sponsored a Disability Discrimination Law Summer School at the National University of Ireland, Galway in 2005, to train lawyers and activists on "effective test case strategies" to enforce the EU disability discrimination rules.
69. This reform began with the Courts and Legal Services Act 1990 (C.41) and culminated in the landmark Woolf Reforms (Civil Procedure Rules 1998, or CPR), which took effect in 1999 (Gray 1994; Rickman, Fenn, and Gray 1999).
70. See, for instance, speech by Competition Commissioner Neelie Kroes (Kroes 2005a) that advocates more private enforcement of competition policy and in which she explained she wanted to use private enforcement to promote a "competition culture, but not a litigation culture." Likewise, the Commission's *Green Paper on Collective Redress* alluded to the US litigation culture as something that must be avoided (Commission 2008b, p. 12).

4. Securities Regulation

1. See the conference agenda for Euromoney's European Securities Litigation Conference, www.euromoneyseminars.com/EventElement/0/809/

8/0/European-Securities-Litigation-Conference.html, last accessed 25 Feb. 2010.

2. Shareholding in most German companies was and remains highly concentrated, often with a "dominant shareholder" exercising substantial control over management (Enriques and Volpin 2007; Baums and Schmitz 1999).
3. Moloney (2002, p. 21) identifies three main phases in the development of EU securities regulation. The first phase involved the directives introduced after 1979 to harmonize rules on admission to official listing and disclosure requirements, the second phase began with the publication of the Commission *White Paper on the Single Market* in 1985, and the third phase began in 1998 in anticipation of the launch of the euro.
4. The Euromarkets were London-based markets in which trading was done in offshore currencies (typically dollars) and in which trading was not subject to British regulations.
5. Some of the major directives adopted in this period included the 1985 Collective Investment Schemes (UCITS—Undertakings for Collective Investment in Transferable Securities) Directive (Council Directive 85/611/EEC [1985] OJ L375/3), the Public Offerings Directive (Council Directive 89/298/EEC [1989] OJ L124/8), the Insider Trading Directive (Council Directive 89/592/EEC [1989] OJ L334/30), and the landmark 1993 Investment Services Directive (Council Directive 93/22/EEC [1993] OJ L141/27). The Investment Services Directive was the centerpiece of EU investment services regulation in this period. It granted a "regulatory passport" to financial services firms and imposed authorization and operating requirements on them. It was supplemented by measures such as the 1993 Capital Adequacy Directive (93/6/EC, OJ L141 [1993], p. 1) and the Investor Compensation Schemes Directive (97/9/EC, OJ L84 [1997], p. 22), which were designed to protect investors and market stability.
6. The Commission had seized on the concept of the "new approach" in the wake of the ECJ's *Cassis de Dijon* decision, which established the principle of mutual recognition (C-120/78, *Rewe-Zentral AG v. Bundesmonopolverwaltung für Branntwein [Cassis de Dijon]* [1979] ECR 649.) See Alter and Meunier-Aitsahalia (1994).
7. Directive (93/22/EEC [1993] OJ L141/27).
8. The CESR replaced the Forum of European Securities Commissions (FESCO), a weaker cooperative body established by national regulatory authorities in 1997 without any formal EU mandate. In 2011, CESR will be replaced by the new European Securities and Markets authority discussed below.

9. The conduct of business regime applies when investment firms provide services to investors and covers the obligation to act fairly, honestly, and in the best interests of investors (Art. 19[1]); information and marketing disclosure that is fair, clear, and not misleading (Art. 19[2]); the information to be provided prior to contract conclusion (Art. 19[3]); suitability rules (Art. 19[4]–[6]); the customer agreement (Art. 19[7]); reporting requirements (Art. 19[8]); best execution (Art, 21); and order handling (Art. 22). These requirements go far beyond the range of issues that were addressed in the Investment Services Directive.
10. The Commission reemphasized the Lamfalussy Report's call for simplification. In its mandate to CESR for Level 2 regulations, the Commission emphasized that CESR should avoid "overprescriptive, excessively detailed legislation, adding undue burdens and unnecessary costs to the firms and hampering innovation in the field of financial services" (Final CESR MiFID Mandate [n 31] 5; see Moloney 2007, p. 416 for discussion). Also in its 2005 financial services green paper, the Commission (Commission 2005c) warned other EU lawmaking bodies against adding "unnecessary, sapping complexity" to Commission proposals and warned national governments against "gold-plating" EU rules with additional national obligations during the process of implementation.
11. See the European Commission's regularly updated review of infringement actions in the securities sector: http://ec.europa.eu/internal_market/securities/infringements/index_en.htm, last accessed 20 Feb. 2010.
12. For the most recent version of the "Lamfalussy League Table," see http://ec.europa.eu/internal_market/securities/transposition/index_en.htm.
13. By 1988, roughly 20 percent of the daily turnover in French government bonds and 15 percent of the turnover in equities was being done in London. Likewise, until the late 1980s there was no market for commercial paper (short-term loans to French companies) in Paris, so French firms did their short-term borrowing on London's Euromarket (*Economist* 1988, p. 111; also see *Financial Times* "Securities Firms Look across Borders," 7 Jan. 1991, as cited in Mügge 2006, p. 1006).
14. As Leslie Goldman put it (1992, p. 252), "France's deregulation occurred as a controlled, step-by-step process in anticipation of a rapidly approaching single European market. As a result of this process, France realized that liberalization means not only eliminating access restrictions, but also increasing transparency."
15. See Loi NE 88–70, 22 Jan. 1988 [Law on Security and Disclosure in the Financial Markets]; Loi NE 89531, 2 Aug. 1989 [Security and Disclosure Law]. See Goldman (1992, p. 245).

16. See Title IV (Free Establishment and Free Provision of Services in EEC Member States) of Loi 96–597, 2 Jul. 1996, in JORF 154 (4 Jul. 1996), p. 10063, available at www.legifrance.gouv.fr/WAspad/UnTexteDeJorf?numjo=ECOX9500164L, last accessed 20 Feb. 2010.
17. Loi de sécurité financière, 1 Aug. 2003, in JORF (2 Aug. 2003), p. 13220, available at www.legifrance.gouv.fr/WAspad/Visu?cid=14840647&indice=126&table=LEGI&ligneDeb=121, last accessed 20 Feb. 2010.
18. Ibid., Art. 117.
19. Loi du 20 juillet 2005 portant diverses dispositions d'adaptation audroit communautaire dans le domaine des marchés financiers [Law Concerning the Adaptation of Legislative Provisions Relating to the Accountancy of Companies for the Community Provisions in the Field of Financial Markets], 2005–811; and Loi du 26 juillet 2005 pour la confiance et la modernisation de l'économie [Law for the Confidence and Modernization of the Economy], 2005–842, also known as the "loi Breton"). See http://ec.europa.eu/internal_market/finances/actionplan/transposition/france/d16-ml-fr.pdf and http://ec.europa.eu/internal_market/finances/actionplan/transposition/france/d13.1-ml-fr.pdf, last accessed 20 Feb. 2010.
20. Autorité des marchés financiers, "La régulation française dans la future Europe financière—Panorama des directives applicables," available at www.amf-france.org/documents/general/6479_1.pdf, last accessed 20 Feb. 2010.
21. Dechert LLM Law Firm, "Implementation of the Transparency Directive Changes Shareholder Notification Requirements across Europe," available at www.dechert.com/library/FSG_Update3_2–07.pdf, last accessed 20 Feb. 2010.
22. To be recognized as an association of investors by the COB (now the AMF), associations had to be in existence for at least two years and have at least one thousand members.
23. The associations could not bring American-style class actions, as each individual shareholder had to be named in the proceedings, but they could bring "representative action" *(action en représentation conjointe)* under 1992 revisions to the French Consumer Code (Art. L. 422–1). This is a joint compensation claim on behalf of investors, but claimants must actively opt in to the action and be named in the proceedings.
24. Well-established French legal doctrines forbid individuals from being made plaintiffs without their knowledge. Thus participants in "joint representative action for investors" (see Art. L. 452-2 and 452-3 of the Monetary and Financial Code) must actively opt in to any litigation (Magnier 2009). Moreover, conditions on admissibility of shareholder

actions remain stringent, making the rights established in the 1989 and 1994 laws difficult to exercise in practice (Canu 2000).

25. See www.melchior.fr/L-Association-de-Defense-des-A.4827.0.html, last accessed 5 Oct. 20010; Girard 2001, 2009.
26. High-profile insider trading cases in the early 1990s heightened attention to the shortcomings of existing German regulations (Lütz 2002, p. 238; Cioffi 2002).
27. Earlier, piecemeal reforms had been undertaken to comply with particular EU directives. See Roquette (1994).
28. The BAFin was created through the merger of federal insurance and securities regulatory authorities (the Bundesaufsichtsamtern für das Versicherungswesen und das Kreditwesen and the Bundesaufsichtsamt für das Wertpapierwesen).
29. *Financial Times,* 26 Jan. 2001, p. 6; *Financial Times,* 27 November 2001, p. 18.
30. The Dutch Civil Code (Sections 1416a–d) had provided some legal backing for this self-regulatory regime since 1928, with rules addressing the issue of liability for damages resulting from publication of a misleading prospectus (Velthuyse and Schlingmann 1995, p. 229).
31. Initially, the Netherlands sought to implement the first EU securities regulations, such as the 1979 Directive on Admission to Official Listing (79/279 EEC) and the Listing Particulars Directive (80/390 EEC), by working with the Amsterdam exchange to revise its internal regulatory code (Van de Vijver 2000, p. 25).
32. Many existing securities regulations were consolidated in the 2007 Act on Financial Supervision (Wet op het financieel toezicht, or WFT).
33. The Shell case belonged to a particular variety of these cases—so-called *f*oreign-*f*oreign-*f*oreign or F-cubed actions. F-cubed cases are securities cases in which foreign shareholders who bought securities of a foreign company on a foreign exchange sue in a US court. F-cubed litigation has followed a number of major securities frauds perpetrated in Europe, such as those involving Parmalat and Vivendi. American courts will sometimes hear these cases if the courts determine that some aspect of the fraud was perpetrated in the United States (Longstreth 2009). For data on securities litigation against foreign firms in the United States more generally, see Cornerstone Research (2009).
34. The Securities and Investments Board was a private organization but was established with the backing of the government.
35. The directive was not adopted until 2004. See Directive on Takeover Bids, (2004/25 EC), OJ L 142 (2004), pp. 0012–0023.
36. There had already been some consolidation of SROs in 1995, when the

insurance and financial intermediaries SROs were merged into a single SRO, the Personal Investment Authority (PIA).

37. See Financial Services Authority Web page at www.fsa.gov.uk/Pages/About/What/International/index.shtml, last accessed 20 Feb. 2010.
38. The Market Abuse Directive was implemented with the Financial Services and Markets Act 2000 (Market Abuse) Regulations 2005, Statutory Instrument 2005, no. 381.
39. See FSA fact sheet on implementation of the Transparency Directive at www.fsa.gov.uk/pages/About/What/International/pdf/TD.pdf, last accessed 20 Feb. 2010.
40. The Financial Services Authority publishes data on fines that it has issued, at www.fsa.gov.uk/Pages/About/Media/Facts/fines/top/index.shtml, last accessed 20 Dec. 2009. The annual total amount of fines imposed since 2002 are as follows: 2002—£7,444,000; 2003—£10,975,000; 2004—£24,769,000; 2005—£16,905,000; 2006—£13,309,143; 2007—£5,341,500; 2008—£22,706,526; 2009—£35,005,522; 2010 (through Sept.) £84,257,536.
41. In 2009, named partner Michael Hausfeld left Cohen, Milstein, Hausfeld, and Toll (Cotts 2009). Hausfeld had been the firm's leading exponent for developing a European class action litigation practice (Robins 2005), and his new firm, Hausfeld LLP, maintains a London office.
42. For a list of Deminor's services and examples of the damage recovery actions it has sponsored, see www.deminor.com, last accessed 20 Feb. 2010.
43. Strikingly, this increase in litigation against foreign corporations in the US is not a result of the increased presence of such firms on US exchanges. Quite to the contrary, the share of foreign companies listed on major US exchanges such as the NYSE and NASDAQ has been declining in recent years.

5. Competition Policy

1. This chapter will focus on the antitrust aspects of EU competition policy.
2. In the United States, in contrast, private enforcement actions have long played a central role in the enforcement of competition policy (Waelbroeck, Slater, and Even-Shoshan 2004; Wils 2003, p. 477; Wigger 2007, p. 104)
3. As discussed below in greater detail, although national and EU competition policies were supposed to exist as separate parallel universes, in practice there was substantial intermingling, and the EU competition

regime had long generated pressure on member states to conform with EU norms and practices. The official separation of national and EU regimes was abandoned with the introduction of the 2004 modernization reforms, when national competition authorities and courts were explicitly tied to the EU competition regime and required to enforce EU norms.

4. Davidow (2002, p. 496) points out that while the United States has pushed the EC to adopt certain substantive and procedural aspects of American antitrust law, the United States has not advocated that Europe follow the American example in terms of increasing private enforcement of antitrust. Indeed, the United States was trying to rein in this model just as the EU was trying to expand it.
5. Gerber (1998, p. 431) discusses this "widespread assumption."
6. Only three of the original six EU member states (France, the Netherlands, and Germany) introduced national competition laws in the 1950s. Laudati (1998) summarizes the situation in 1950s Europe: "Prior to the formation of the European Community in 1957, regulation of competition essentially did not exist in any of the countries which were to become the Member States" (p. 381).
7. This model of ex post administrative control of abuse fit well with the highly interventionist macroeconomic policies that prevailed in postwar Europe. The discretionary, ex post administrative-control model allowed governments to tolerate or encourage cartels when they were seen to strengthen domestic industry, while reserving the right to intervene if they were abusing their position (Gerber 2003, p. 179).
8. Because of this separation, the EU did not issue directives or regulations designed to harmonize national competition policies.
9. The first European-level competition policy was established with the signing of the Treaty of Paris and the creation of European Coal and Steel Community in 1951. The Treaty of Paris competition provisions reflected a combination of American and European influences, introducing aspects of the American-style prohibition model along with central elements of the European administrative control model. Though US academics and officials were closely involved in crafting the ECSC's competition provisions, from the outset all involved tried to keep the appearance of US influence to a minimum, fearing that some states might reject measures perceived as thrusting American-style capitalism on Europe (Gerber, 1998, pp. 338–341; Djelic 2002, p. 244; Majone 1991; Büthe 2007).
10. The original numbering scheme was revised in the Treaty of Amsterdam. To avoid confusion, I use the revised, post-Amsterdam numbering scheme throughout this book.

11. After the Commission experienced a flood of notifications, the Council responded in 1965 by granting it the power to legislate through issuing block exemptions for particular situations and categories (Regulation 19/65, OJ 533 [1965]). See Goyder (2003, pp. 114–115).
12. Even in the case of ex post enforcement, the Commission played a more central role than was the case for regulators in the United States. In the United States, federal regulators who detected a violation of antitrust law had to litigate before federal courts and win a court order. In the EU, the Commission could issue decisions and impose fines on violators by fiat, and courts entered the picture only if violators appealed.
13. Targeting dominant firms would have run against the Commission's broader industrial policy agenda at that time, which was focused on promoting large, internationally competitive European champions (McLachlan and Swan 1963).
14. See, for instance, C-56/65, *Societé Technique Minière v. Machinenbau Ulm GmbH,* [1966] ECR 235, and joined cases C-56 and 58/64, *Commission v. Consten and Grundig,* [1966] ECR 299.
15. Joined cases C-56 and 58/64, *Commission v. Consten and Grundig,* [1966] ECR 299.
16. The Commission imposed its first fines in 1969 in a case involving a quinine cartel (OJ L 192 [1969], p. 5; see also Joined Cases C-41, C-44 and C-45/69, *ACF Chemiefarma NV v. Commission* [1970] ECR 661). A week later it imposed penalties on members of a dyestuffs cartel (Harding and Joshua 2003, pp. 121–123; see also C-48/69, *Imperial Chemical Industries Ltd. v. Commission,* [1972] ECR 619).
17. See for instance joined cases C-6 and C-7 /73, *Istituto Chemioterapico Italiano S.p.A. and Commercial Solvents Corp. v. Commission,* [1973] ECR 357, and C-27/76, *United Brands v. Commission,* [1978] 1 ECR 207, in which the ECJ supported the Commission in extending the reach of Art. 82.
18. C-6/72, *Europemballage Corporation and Continental Can Co. Inc. v. Commission,* [1973] ECR 215.
19. C-14/68, *Wilhelm v. Bundeskartellamt,* [1969] ECR 1.
20. C-127/73, *Belgische Radio en Televisie v. SV Sabam,* [1974] ECR 51.
21. See discussion of the *Continental Can* (C-6/72), ruling above.
22. C-142 and C-156/84, *Philip Morris v. Commission,* [1987] ECR 4487, holding that mergers could be classified as "restrictive agreements" and therefore be regulated by the Commission under Article 81.
23. Council Regulation 4064/89 EEC of Dec. 1989, on the control of concentrations between undertakings (OJ L 395 [December 1989]).
24. The 1986 Single European Act had called for the creation of the new Court of First Instance, at a jurisdictional level below the European

Court of Justice. The member states agreed to the establishment of this court in an effort to address the backlog of cases before the ECJ, a backlog which resulted largely from the proliferation of competition cases (McGowan and Wilks 1995, p. 150).

25. Beginning with its 1990 decision in the *Italian Flat Glass* case (T-68, 77 & 78/89, [1990] 4 CMLR 535), the CFI asserted the authority to review the facts of competition cases de novo.
26. Interview, Commission Legal Service, 23 Nov. 2005, Brussels.
27. Guidelines on the method of setting fines, OJ C 9 (14 Jan. 1998), p. 3.
28. Dirk Lehmkuhl (2008, 2009) suggests that the Commission's use of guidelines and recommendations demonstrates the importance of flexible "new modes of governance." These were actually very much "old modes of governance," in keeping with the traditional European administrative model of competition policy discussed above. In any case, these policy tools were and are applied in the shadow of coercive, hard law, and ECJ jurisprudence has rendered them far less flexible and soft than the Commission had intended.
29. See C-382/99, *Netherlands v. Commission,* [2002] ECR I-5163, para. 24; Joined Cases C-189, 202, 205, 208, and 213/02, *Dansk R€rindustri and Others v. Commission,* [2005] ECR I-5425, para. 209; C-171/00, *P Libéros v. Commission,* [2002] ECR I-451, para. 35; C-310/99, *Italian Republic v. Commission,* [2002] ECR I-2289, para. 52; T-214/95, *Vlaamse Gewest v. Commission,* [1998] ECR II-717, paras. 79, 89; C-397/03, *Archer Daniels Midland v. Commission* [2006] ECR I-4429. See Wils (2007, p. 203).
30. C-310/99, *Italian Republic v. Commission,* [2002] ECR I-2289, para. 52.
31. T-342/99, *Airtours v. Commission,* [2002] ECR II-2585; T-310/01, *Schneider Electric v. Commission,* [2002] ECR II-4071; T-5/02, *Tetra Laval v. Commission,* [2002] ECR II-4381.
32. OJ 1410 [15 November 1961], p. 61, point 11.
33. From the early 1970s onwards, the Commission repeatedly expressed its support for private enforcement. See list of references in "Opinion of AG van Gerven of 27 October 1993" in C-128/92, *Banks,* [1994] ECR I-1251.
34. Under Regulation 17 and Treaty Article 81, contracts and other commercial agreements that should have been notified to the Commission but were not were rendered void. In the 1990s, it became common for defendants in breach of contract cases to argue that they could not be forced to honor their contract, as the contract was never notified to the Commission and was therefore void.
35. The German government had proposed the creation of an independent European cartel office after 1994, as a way to address the increasing politicization of EU competition policy (Wilks and McGowan 1995,

pp. 262–263). Ultimately, the German proposal found little support among other member states at the 1996 Intergovernmental Conference and was abandoned.

36. C-344/98, *Masterfoods Ltd. V. HB Ice Cream Ltd.*, [2000] ECR I-11369.
37. C-453/99, *Courage v. Crehan*, [2001] ECR I-6297.
38. Council Regulation 1/2003 EC of 16 Dec. 2002, OJ L 1 (4 Jan. 2003), pp. 1–25.
39. Later that year, the modernization reforms were extended to the area of merger control, with Council Regulation 139/2004/EC, OJ L 24 (Dec. 16, 2003), p. 1.
40. See also Wigger and Nölke (2007); Wigger (2007, p. 502). For a skeptical view that questions the centralization thesis, see Kassim (2007).
41. In states with small, open economies, where most cases may affect interstate trade, EU competition law will essentially supplant national law (Riley 2003, p. 664).
42. National courts and competition authorities are bound by decisions adopted by the Commission, and national courts must avoid making decisions that conflict with one contemplated by the Commission in pending cases.
43. Behind the tiny number of cases that reached a final court judgment, however, certainly a far greater number are settled out of court (Woods, Sinclair, and Ashton 2004, p. 32). In any case, it remains clear that private damage claims had played at most a very minor role in European competition law up to that point (Wils 2003).
44. With the opt-in model, victims must expressly decide to opt in to the collective legal action. In contrast, US class actions rely on an opt-out model, whereby all members of the certified class are presumed to be party to the action unless they have expressly opted out.
45. Hearing of Competition Commissioner Designate Joaquin Almunia before the European Parliament, 12 Jan. 2010; Hearing of Health and Consumer Policy Commissioner Designate John Dalli before the European Parliament, 14 Jan. 2010. Summaries available at www.europarl.europa.eu, last accessed 24 Feb. 2010.
46. Similarly, the European Parliament's *Report on the Commission Green Paper* strongly endorses its call for a strengthening of private enforcement, while emphasizing that this should not lead to excessive US-style litigiousness (European Parliament 2007, pp. 11–13).
47. Shareholder rights groups have also pushed this agenda, for instance, by calling for reforms that would facilitate class action antitrust suits (Wigger and Nölke 2007, p. 505; Hollinger 2005; Tait and Sherwood 2005).

48. "Guidelines on the Method of Setting Fines Imposed Pursuant to Article 23(2) (a) of Regulation no. 1/2003," OJ C 210 (2006), p. 2.
49. See descriptions of the programs at http://ec.europa.eu/competition/court/training.html (accessed Oct. 5 2010)
50. For detailed histories of the early origins of British competition policy, see Mercer (1995); Wilks (1999).
51. The Competition Appeal Tribunal (CAT) hears only "follow-on" actions, claims brought by private parties after a decision by the OFT or the European Commission has established that an infringement occurred. "Stand-alone" actions brought by private parties before any ruling by a public regulator must still go through the High Court of England and Wales.
52. C-453/99, *Courage v. Crehan,* [2001] ECR I-6297.
53. Judgment of the Court of Appeal of 21 May 2004 in *Crehan v. Inntrepreneur,* [2004] EWCA 637.
54. See, for instance, Case 1060/5/7/06, *Healthcare at Home v. Genzyme; National Grid Electricity Transmission plc v. ABB Limited and others,* [2009] EWCH 1326; Case 1028/5/7/04, BCL *Old Co & Others v. Aventis SA & others* [2005] CAT2; *Devenish Nutrition Ltd. and Ors v. Sanofi-Aventis SA* (France), and *Ors,* [2008] EWCA Civ 1086, at page 75, para. 161.
55. *Safeway Stores Limited, Safeway Limited and Stores Group Limited v. Twigger and Others,* judgment of 15 Jan. 2010 of Mr. Justice Flaux, Commercial Court 2009 FOLIO 881, [2010] EWHC 11 (Comm).
56. The average annual total of fines issued by the Bundeskartellamt between 1993 and 2004 was €95.3 million. This rose to €238 million between 2005 and 2009. See Bundeskartellamt (2009 p. 19) for 1993–2008 data. Data for 2009 is available through press releases of the Bundeskartellamt, available at www.bundeskartellamt.de, last accessed 24 Feb. 2010.
57. German courts must give binding effect to previous findings made by German or European competition authorities or courts (GWB, section 33, para. 4).
58. France introduced its first competition statutes and created its first competition commission (the Commission technique des ententes) in 1953, under pressure from the United States; however, US pressure clearly did not succeed in changing the actual practice of competition policy at this stage.
59. See Ordonnance 86-1243 du 1 décembre 1986 relative à la liberté des prix et de la concurrence, JORF 9 décembre 1986, p. 14773.
60. See Ordonnance 2004-274 du 25 mars 2004, JORF 74 du 27 mars 2004, p. 5871 and Ordonnance 2004-1173 du 4 Nov. 2004, JORF 258 du 5 Nov. 2004, p. 18689.

61. *Mobile Phones,* Decision 05-D-65 of 30 Nov. 2005; *Air Fuel,* Decision 08-D-30 of 4 Dec. 2008; *France Telecom,* Decision 07-MC-03 of 7 Jun. 2007; and *Corsican Cement,* Decision 07-D-08 of 12 Mar. 2007. See Lasserre (2009).
62. Loi 2008-776 du 4 août 2008 de modernisation de l'économie, art. 96, JORF 181 (5 Aug. 2008), p. 12471. Also see Ordonnance 2008-1161 du 13 nov. 2008 portant modernisation de la régulation de la concurrence, JORF 0265 (14 Nov. 2008), p. 17391.
63. Actions to nullify contracts based on violations of competition law face far lower hurdles and are already commonplace (Baker and McKenzie 2006, p. 4).
64. Lawyers associated with Classaction.fr maintain that the consumer groups were seeking to maintain their potentially lucrative monopoly on legal representation of consumers in collective actions (Le Bris-Munch 2006; see also Magnier 2009; Visseyrias 2006; *New York Times* 2005; Amalou 2005).
65. T-351/03, *Schneider Electric SA v. Commission,* [2007] ECR II-02237.
66. The case follows up on one originally filed by the travel company MyTravel. See T-212/03, *MyTravel v. Commission,* [2008] ECR II-1967. See also Osborne (2008).
67. The European Parliament too has been a longtime advocate of greater harmonization of national laws, strict Commission enforcement of competition policy, and greater reliance on private enforcement, but the legislative procedures in the competition field have severely limited the Parliament's role.
68. These pathologies might not be terribly worrisome if private enforcement served merely as a complement to a strong system of public enforcement. However, when firms face a threat of private damage claims, public authorities may have greater difficulty offering the carrots necessary to elicit cooperative behavior and compliance (Eilmansberger 2007; Hodges 2006).

6. Disability Rights

1. When referring to this approach, some scholars of disability rights use the term "medical model," while others use the term "welfare model." To avoid confusion, and to highlight the link between the two dimensions of this model, I will use the term "medical/welfare model."
2. Council Directive 2000/78/EC of 27 November 2000 Establishing a General Framework for Equal Treatment in Employment and Occupation, OJ L 303 (2 Dec. 2000), p. 16.
3. This money was paid into to a fund promoting the rehabilitation and employment of disabled persons.

4. Wet plaatsing minder-valide arbeidskrachten, Act of 1 Aug. 1947, Stb. 283 (1947).
5. Wet arbeid gehandicapte werknemers (WAGW), Law of 16 May 1986, Stb. 3000 (1986).
6. Disabled Persons [Employment] Act, 7 and 8 Geo. 6, ch. 10 (1944) (Eng.); requiring employers with more than twenty employees to maintain workforces comprised of at least 3 percent registered disabled persons.
7. This fund was managed by the AGEFIPH (Association de gestion du fonds pour l'insertion professionnelle des personnes handicapées, or Association for the Management of Funds for the Vocational Integration of Disabled People). During the 1990s, AGEFIPH developed a series of vocational training programs that prepared thousands of disabled persons for work and negotiated agreements and subsidy schemes with large companies to encourage employment of disabled workers.
8. Pub. L. 93-112, 87 Stat. 390 (codified at 29 USCA section 791 [1995]).
9. *School Board of Nassau County, Florida v. Airline,* 29 CFR section 1630.29(k), 283–284 (1987); quoted in Doyle (1993).
10. Americans with Disabilities Act of 1990 (Pub. L. 101-336) (ADA), as amended (hereafter, ADA).
11. ADA, 42 USCA section 12111(8), 12112(5).
12. GA Res. 48/96, UN GAOR, 48th Sess., Supp. no. 49, app. at 202–11, UN Doc A/Res/48/49 (1994).
13. These were the relevant clauses: Germany, Art. 3(3) Grundgesetz, as amended in 1994; Austria, Art. 7(1), as amended in 1997; Finland, S. II, chap. 2, Basic rights and liberties, section 6, Equality, as adopted in 1999.
14. Initial Community Action Programme for Vocational Rehabilitation of Handicapped Persons 1974–1979, Council Resolution of 27 June 1974, OJ C 80 (9 Jul. 1974), p. 30.
15. First Community Action Programme on the Social Integration of Handicapped People, 1983–1988, OJ C 347 (21 Dec. 1981), p. 1; HELIOS I Community Action Programme for Disabled People, 1988–1991, OJ L 104 (23 Apr. 1988), p. 38; HELIOS II Community Action Programme to Assist Disabled People, 1993–1996, Council Decision 93/136 EEC of 25 February 1993, OJ L56 (9 Mar. 1993), p. 30.
16. Council Recommendation 86/379 EEC of 24 July 1986 on the Employment of Disabled People in the Community, OJ L 225 (12 Aug. 1986), p. 43.
17. Council Decision of 25 February 1993 Establishing a Third Community Action Programme to Assist Disabled People (Helios II, 1993 to 1995), OJ L 56 (9 Mar. 1993), p. 30.

18. Resolution of the Council and of the Representative of the Governments of the Member States Meeting within the Council of 20 December 1996 on Equality of Opportunity for People with Disabilities, OJ C 40, no. 12 (13 Jan. 1997), p. 1.
19. By locating Art. 13 in the section of the treaty covering "general principles," the member states signaled that antidiscrimination measures would not have to be limited to the employment sphere nor have to be viewed solely as aspects of social policy. However, being based in this section of the treaty also meant that legislation in this field would have to be adopted on the basis of unanimity among the member states and with a limited role for the European Parliament.
20. Directive 2000/43/EC of 29 June 2000 Implementing the Principle of Equal Treatment between Persons Irrespective of Racial or Ethnic Origin, OJ L 180 (19 Jul. 2000), p. 22 (the Racial Equality Directive); and Directive 2000/78/EC of 27 November 2000 Establishing a General Framework for Equal Treatment in Employment and Occupation, OJ L 303 (2 Dec. 2000), p. 16 (the Framework Employment Directive).
21. Sex discrimination was not addressed in either directive because the EU had a well-established body of law—treaty requirements, directives, and case law—on sex discrimination.
22. Common examples of indirect discrimination include requirements that employees hold a driving license and prohibitions on bringing dogs to work, both of which would discriminate indirectly against the blind. The directive allows employers to maintain such forms of indirect discrimination only when they can be justified as objectively appropriate and necessary—for instance, when requiring driving licenses for school bus drivers. The definition of indirect discrimination provided in the Employment Equality Directive and in the Racial Equality Directive was intended to reduce the burden of proof for establishing that discrimination had occurred. Earlier definitions of indirect discrimination in Community legislation concerning sex discrimination had sometimes required litigants to produce statistical evidence. The new definition does not require statistical comparisons between groups but simply requires the individual claimant to show that he or she was personally put at a disadvantage (Skidmore 2001, p. 128)
23. Article 5 states, "In order to guarantee compliance with the principle of equal treatment in relation to persons with disabilities, reasonable accommodation shall be provided. This means that employers shall take appropriate measures, where needed in a particular case, to enable a person with a disability to have access to, participate in, or advance in employment, or to undergo training, unless such measures would im-

pose a disproportionate burden on the employer. This burden shall not be disproportionate when it is sufficiently remedied by measures existing within the framework of the disability policy of the Member State concerned."

24. C-70/05, *Commission v. Luxembourg,* OJ C 82 (2005), p. 23); C-43/05, *Commission v. Germany,* OJ C82 (2005), p. 14; C-99/05, *Commission v. Finland,* OJ C 93 (2005), p. 21; C-133/05, *Commission v. Austria* OJ C 143 (2005), p. 20.
25. C-13/05, *Chacón Navas v. Eurest Colectividades SA,* [2006] ECR I-6467.
26. C-303/06, *Coleman v. Attridge Law and Steve Law,* [2008] ECR I-5603.
27. The first conference was held at the National University of Ireland, Galway, 4-15 July 2005. A second summer school on litigation strategies was held in the same location the following summer. It was titled, "Disability Discrimination Law Summer School: Comparative Perspectives on Effective Test Case Strategies under the EU Framework Directive, National University of Ireland, 6-16 Jun. 2006."
28. The nondiscrimination casebook was published as part of an effort to develop the Ius Commune Casebooks for the Common Law of Europe series. See description of project at www.casebooks.eu/nonDiscrimination, last accessed 25 Feb. 2010. The *European Anti-Discrimination Law Review* is available online on a Commission-supported Web site. See www.non-discrimination.net/en/publications, last accessed 25 Feb. 2010.
29. The EU remains committed to a rights model of disability based on private enforcement. In July 2008 the Commission proposed a new directive (COM[2008] 426 final) that would expand antidiscrimination protection (including protection from discrimination on the grounds of disability) beyond the workplace, to include, for instance, protection from discrimination in the provision of goods and services.
30. A sentence was added to Art. 3.3 of the German Basic Law (Grundgesetz), stating, "No one shall be disadvantaged due to their disability" *[Niemand darf wegen seiner Behinderung benachteiligt werden].*
31. For instance, in a 1996 decision concerning disability discrimination in education, the Federal Constitutional Court ruled that school authorities who refused to allow a wheelchair user to attend a regular school did not violate the constitutional antidiscrimination clause. See 1 BvR 1308/96, *Juristen Zeitung* 1073 (1996).
32. *Bundesgesetzblatt* 1 (19 Jun. 2001), p. 1046.
33. *Bundesgesetzblatt* 1 (27 Apr.2002), p. 1467.

34. C-43/05, *Commission v. Germany,* OJ C 82 (2005) p. 14). This case did not put an end to Germany's conflict with the Commission over Directive 2000/78. In October 2009, the Commission again pursued infringement proceedings against Germany by issuing a "reasoned opinion" letter citing, among other remaining problems, the fact that Germany's reasonable accommodation requirement applied only to people with severe disabilities (Commission 2009a). While German legislation (Social Code IX, Art. 81.2) remained out of compliance, in fact Germany's Federal Labor Court had already ruled that the legislation must be interpreted to cover all forms of disability, as required by the EU directive (Bundesarbeitsgericht, 4 Apr. 2007, 9 AZR 823/06).
35. *Bundesgesetzblatt* 1 (14 Aug. 2006), p. 1897. After the adoption of the AGG, Sec. 81.2 of the Social Code IX (Sozialgesetzbuch IX) was amended to explicitly prohibit discrimination against disabled persons in the field of employment and to incorporate various provisions of the AGG.
36. See, for instance, Federal Labor Court (Bundesarbeitsgericht), 3 Mar. 2007, 9 AZR 823/06; Düsseldorf Administrative Court (Verwaltungsgericht Düsseldorf), 2 Oct. 2007, 2 K 2070/07; Frankfurt Administrative Court (Verwaltungsgericht Frankfurt), 3 Dec. 2007, 9 E 5697/06; Berlin-Brandenburg *Land* Labor Court (Landesarbeitsgericht Berlin-Brandenburg), 4 Dec. 2008, 26 Sa 343/08; Munich *Land* Labor Court (Landesarbeitsgericht München), 8 Jul. 2008, 8 Sa 112/08; (Düsseldorf *Land* Labor Court (Landesarbeitsgericht Düsseldorf), 14 May 2008, 12 Sa 256/08; Niedersachsen *Land* Labor Court (Landesarbeitsgericht Niedersachsen), 24 Apr. 2008, 4 Sa 1077/07. For more detailed discussion of case law, see Mahlmann (2009, pp. 23, 81; 2008, p. 5).
37. Law 90-602 of 12 Jul.1990 [Loi 90-602 du 12 juillet 1990 relative à la protection des personnes contre les discriminations en raison de leur état de santé ou de leur handicap], JORF (13 Jul. 1990), p. 8272; D (1990), p. 322. The law amended Art. 225 of the Penal Code (Code Pénal, Art. 225 [Fr.]) In addition to its prohibition on employment discrimination, the law also made it a criminal offense to refuse to provide goods or services to an individual (or legal person) on the grounds of health or disability.
38. The 2005 Disability Law (Loi 2005-102 pour l'égalité des droits et des chances, la participation et la citoyenneté des personnes handicapées) completed transposition of the EU Directive into national law. Important earlier measures taken as part of the transposition process included the 2001 Antidiscrimination Law (Loi 2001-1066) and the 2002 Social Modernization Law (Loi 2002-73).

39. The French law translates reasonable accommodation as "all necessary measures" *(mesures nécessaires).*
40. See Loi 2004-1486. HALDE's work was to be supported at the local (departmental) level by the establishment of a *maison départmentale,* departmental house, which could support the enforcement of the rights of disabled people in each department of France (see Art. 64 of the Loi 2005-102 on Disability).
41. The very 2005 law (Loi 2005-102) that introduced the EU's disability discrimination rights rules into the French legal system also extended aspects of the traditional French model, for instance, by requiring "social partners" (employers, trade unions, and NGOs) to engage in annual negotiations over measures to support integration of disabled workers (Commission 2007d, p. 73).
42. For one of the very few disability discrimination claims that HALDE brought to court on behalf of a complainant, see Cour d'appel de Lyon, Chambre Sociale C, Audience publique, 13 March 2009, no. 08/03450. Available at http://legifrance.gouv.fr, last accessed 25 Feb. 2010. In the rare cases that do go to court and result in a settlement, damage awards for victims of discrimination remain low (Commission 2007d, p. 62).
43. The 2004 reforms added a prohibition on disability discrimination to the AWGB, or Algemene Wet Gelijke Behandeling (General Equal Treatment Act).
44. Though opinions of the Equal Treatment Commission are nonbinding, they are complied with in approximately 70 percent of cases. (Interview, Professor Lisa Waddington, Disability Coordinator of the EC Network of Legal Experts in the Non-Discrimination Field, Maastricht, 14 December 2006).
45. Disability Discrimination Act, ch. 50 (1995) (Eng.). Also see explanatory regulations adopted pursuant to the DDA: Department for Education and Employment, Code of Practice for the Elimination of Discrimination in the Field of Employment against Disabled Persons or Persons Who Have Had a Disability (1996) (Eng.).
46. The DDA was again amended with the Disability Discrimination Act 2005, which established a "public sector equality duty" requiring all public sector organizations to take positive steps to increase employment opportunities for people with disabilities and extending disability discrimination rules to transportation providers. These measures went beyond requirements of the EU directive.
47. Some scholars, such as Katie Wells (2003), hoped that the ECJ would interpret the definition of disability in the directive expansively, forcing the UK to introduce a broader definition of disability. However, in the

Chacon Navas ruling, the ECJ offered a narrow reading of the definition of disability, an interpretation that disappointed rights activists and scholars (Cantor 2009).

48. Other important cost factors that encourage use of employment tribunals rather than courts include the fact that the "English rule" (loser pays) does not apply in cases before employment tribunals and that legal aid is normally not available for employment discrimination claims. Finally, conditional fee arrangements do not offer an effective substitute for legal aid because awards in disability discrimination cases are typically too low to provide an incentive for lawyers (Trade Union Disability Alliance 2007).
49. Personal communication, Lisa Vanhala, University of Oxford, participant in the working group's deliberations, 10 December 2009.
50. This is not to say that activists would not have to continue campaigning (and litigating) at the national level to see that EU rights are actually enforced in practice.
51. And legal mobilization itself is no guarantee of success, as the US experience with the Americans with Disabilities Act suggests. As Susan G. Mezey (2005) explains, restrictive interpretations of the ADA by federal courts have severely limited its impact.
52. The Commission has already proposed extending the equal treatment approach beyond the employment sphere to cover nondiscriminatory access to social protection, social advantages, health care, education, and access to and supply of goods and services. See Commission (2008c).
53. A similar tension can be observed in the area of age discrimination, where there is some concern that efforts to secure for older workers the "right" to continue working past statutory retirement ages may ultimately undermine support for generous pension schemes—which, after all, are premised on the notion that the elderly can no longer work.

7. Conclusion

1. That being said, the ultimate degree of change experienced at the national level tended to be greatest in cases where national policymaking traditions and institutions differed most from the models of adversarial legalism emanating from the EU level. Thus, for example, EU disability policy forced greater changes on a country like the Netherlands, which had no tradition of workplace disability-discrimination rights, than on the UK, which had already introduced such antidiscrimination rights domestically before the EU acted.

2. But see Bignami (2010) for an important study arguing that adversarial legalism is not spreading in Europe in the field of data privacy regulation.
3. C-158/96, *Kohll v. Union des Caisses de Maladie,* [1998] ECR I-1931; C-120/95, *Decker v. Caisse de Maladie des Employés Privés,* [1998] ECR I-1831.
4. C-372/04, *Yvonne Watts v. Bedford Primary Care Trust, Secretary of State for Health,* [2006] ECR I-4325.
5. C-303/98, *Sindicato de Medicos de Asistencia Publica (SiMAP) v. Conselleria de Sanidad y Consumo de la Generalidad Valenciana* [2000] ECR I-7963; C-151/02, *Landeshauptsadt Kiel v. Norbert Jaeger,* Judgment of 9 October 2003.
6. T-167/04, *Asklepios Kliniken GmbH v. Commission,* [2007] ECR II-2379; T-289/03, *BUPA and Others v. Commission,* [2008] ECR II-81. Also see Greer (2009a, 2009b).
7. C-438/05, *International Transport Workers' Federation and Finnish Seamen's Union v. Viking Line ABP and OÜ Viking Line Eesti (Viking)*, [2007] ECR I-10779; C-341/05, *Laval un Partneri Ltd. v. Svenska Byggnadsarbetareförbundet, Svenska Byggnadsarbetareförbundets avdelning 1, Byggettan and Svenska Elektrikerförbundet (Laval)*, [2007] ECR I-11767.
8. For a contrasting argument, holding that adversarial legalism is not spreading in EU consumer law, see Bignami (2010).
9. For a general overview of EU consumer law, see Weatherill (2005).
10. See, for instance, C-411/05, *Palacios de la Villa v. Correfiel Servicios SA,* [2007] ECR I-8531, and C-388/07, *Age Concern England v. Secretary of State for Business, Enterprise, and Regulatory Reform,* OJ C 102 (1 May 2009).
11. Some economists specifically claimed that an increasing number of lawyers (and presumably the lawyering they engaged in) actually impaired economic growth (Magee 1989), but other scholars have convincingly refuted such bald claims (see Epp 1992 and Cross 2001).
12. More generally, on litigation as a form of political participation, see Guarnieri and Pederzoli (2001, pp. 12–13).
13. Similarly, critics may argue that empowering courts can provide an avenue through which groups who do not prevail in the political process to trump decisions made by legislative majorities.
14. See also Scheingold (1974) on the ideology of rights.

References

Aboulian, Baptiste. 2010. 'More power for new EU Supervisor.' Financial Times, 26 September. Available at *http://www.ft.com* (accessed 7 October 2010).

Adams, Christopher, Nikki Tait, and Barney Jopson. 2005. "Investors Win Powers to Sue." *Financial Times,* 2 November.

Adcock, Robert. 2005. "What Is a Concept?" Political Concepts: A Working Paper Series of the Committee on Concepts and Methods, no. 1. Committee on Concepts and Methods, International Political Science Association, Mexico City. Available at http://concepts-methods.org/ (accessed Oct. 7, 2010).

Agence France Presse. 2010. "Entente dans la téléphonie: L'UFC déboutée de son action en réparation," 25 January. Available at www.boursereflex.com (accessed 20 June 2010).

AIRMIC (Association of Insurance and Risk Managers) and Advisen. 2009. *The 2009 AIRMIC D&O Benchmark Survey.* New York: Advisen.

Ajani, Gianmaria. 1995. "By Chance and Prestige: Legal Transplants in Russia and Eastern Europe." *American Journal of Comparative Law* 43(1): 93–117.

Alexander, Kern. 2001. "Insider Dealing and Market Abuse: The Financial Services and Market Act 2000." Working Paper no. 222, Centre for Business Research, Judge Institute of Management, University of Cambridge.

Alfaro, Jesus, and Tim Reher. 2010. "Towards the Directive on Enforcement of EC Competition Law: Is the Time Ripe?" *European Antitrust Review.* London: Law Business Research.

Alston, Phillip, and J. H. H. Weiler. 1999. "An 'Ever Closer Union' in Need of Human Rights Policy: The European Union and Human Rights." In

The EU and Human Rights, pp. 3-66, ed. Philip Alston. Oxford: Oxford University Press.

Alter, Karen. 1998. "Who Are the Masters of the Treaty? European Governments and the European Court of Justice." *International Organization* 52(1): 125–152.

———. 2001. *Establishing the Supremacy of European Law.* Oxford: Oxford University Press.

Alter, Karen, and Sophie Meunier-Aitsahalia. 1994. "Judicial Politics in the European Community: European Integration and the Pathbreaking Cassis de Dijon Decision." *Comparative Political Studies* 26(4): 535–561.

Alter, Karen, and Jeannette Vargas. 2000. "Explaining Variation in the Use of European Litigation Strategies." *Comparative Political Studies* 33(4): 452–482.

Amalou, Florence. 2005. "Un site Internet français propose des actions collectives en justice." *Le Monde,* 27 May. Available at www.lemonde.fr (accessed 10 March 2010).

Amann, Melanie. 2008. "AGG-Hopping: Es gibt klare Anzeichen für Missbrauch." *Frankfurter Allgemeine Zeitung,* 10 September. Available at www.faz.net (accessed 10 March 2010).

Andenas, Mads, and Stephen Kenyon-Slade, eds. 1993. *EC Financial Market Regulation and Company Law.* London: Sweet and Maxwell.

Asbeek Brusse, W., and R. Griffiths. 1997. "Early Cartel Legislation and Cartel Policy in the Netherlands: In Memoriam; The Economic Competition Act (1956–97)." *Acta Politica* 32(4): 375–405.

———. 1998. "Paradise Lost or Paradise Regained? Cartel Policy and Cartel Legislation in the Netherlands." In *Competition Policies in Europe,* pp. 15–39, ed. S. Martin. Amsterdam: Elsevier.

Assadi-Tardif, Natasha, and Delphine Cohen. 2009. "France." In *The International Comparative Legal Guide to Cartels and Leniency 2009,* chapter 17. London: Global Legal Group.

Astier, Henri. 2006. "France's Shareholder Revolt." *BBC News,* June 28. Available at http://news.bbc.co.uk/2/hi/business/5122064.stm (accessed 10 March 2010).

Autorité des marchés financiers. 2005. *Rapport annuel de l'Autorité des marchés financiers—2004.* Paris: Autorité des marchés financiers.

———. 2009. *Rapport annuel de l'Autorité des marchés financiers—2008.* Paris: Autorité des marchés financiers.

Avgerinos, Yannis. 2003. "The Need and the Rationale for a European Securities Regulator." In *Financial Markets in Europe: Towards a Single Regulator?* pp. 145–182, ed. M. Andenas and Y. Avgerinos. The Hague: Kluwer Law International.

Aziz, Miriam. 2004. *The Impact of European Rights on National Legal Cultures.* Oxford: Hart Publishing.

Baar, Carl. 1991. "Judicial Activism in Canada." In *Judicial Activism in Comparative Perspective,* pp. 35–69, ed. Kenneth M. Holland. New York: St. Martin's Press.

Badaracco, Joseph L. 1985. *Loading the Dice: A Five Country Study of Vinyl Chloride Regulation.* Boston: Harvard Business School Press.

Baetge, Dietmar. 2009. "Germany." *Annals of the American Academy of Political and Social Science* 622: 125–137.

Bailey, David. 2004. "Scope of Judicial Review under Article 81 EC." *Common Market Law Review* 41(5): 1327–1360.

———. 2007. "Damages Actions under the EC Merger Regulation." *Common Market Law Review* 44(1): 101–139.

Baker and McKenzie. 2006. *European Competition Law Practice Group—Response to Green Paper on Private Enforcement.* London: Baker and McKenzie.

Bannerman, E. 2002. *The Future of EU Competition Policy.* London: Centre for European Reform.

Barnard, Catherine C. 1995. "A European Litigation Strategy: The Case of the Equal Opportunities Commission." In *New Legal Dynamics of the European Union,* pp. 254–272, ed. G. More and J. Shaw. Oxford: Clarendon Press.

Basedow, Jürgen. 2000. "The Communitarization of the Conflict of Laws under the Treaty of Amsterdam." *Common Market Law Review* 37: 687–708.

Bates, Stephen, and Kevin Maguire. 2002. "Leaks of Prince's Letters to Ministers Spiral." *Guardian,* 27 September. Available at www.guardian.co.uk (accessed 10 March 2010).

Bates, Stephen, and Michael White. 2002. Hunt for Source of Charles' Leaked Letter Puts Both Sides in Firing Line. *Guardian,* 26 September. Available at www.guardian.co.uk (accessed 10 March 2010).

Baums, Theodor, and Rainer Schmitz. 1999. "Shareholder voting in Germany." Working Paper 76, Institut für Handels-und Wirtchaftsrecht, University of Osnabrück. Available at http://www.jura-uni-frankfurt.de/ifawz1/baums/arbeitspapiere.html.

BBC News. 2006. "EADS Shareholders in Legal Action." July 10. Available at http://news.bbc.co.uk/2/hi/business/5164188.stm (accessed 1 March 2010).

Behr, Volker. 2003. "Punitive Damages in American and German Law—Tendencies towards Approximation of Apparently Irreconcilable Concepts." *Chicago Kent Law Review* 78: 105–161.

Bell, David, and Axel Heitmueller. 2009. "The Disability Discrimination Act in the UK: Helping or Hindering Employment among the Disabled?" *Journal of Health Economics* 28(2): 465–480.

Bell, Mark. 2000. "Equality and Diversity: Anti-discrimination Law after Amsterdam." In *Social Law and Policy in an Evolving European Union,* pp.157–170, ed. J. Shaw. Oxford: Hart.

———. 2002. "Beyond European Labour Law? Reflections on the EU Racial Equality Directive." *European Law Journal* 8(3): 384–349.

———. 2005. "Walking in the Same Direction? The Contribution of the European Social Charter and the European Union to Combating Discrimination." In *Social Rights in Europe,* pp. 261–278, ed. Gráinne de Búrca and Bruno de Witte. Oxford: Oxford University Press.

Bell, Mark, and Lisa Waddington. 2003. "Reflecting on Inequalities in European Equality Law." *European Law Review* 28(3): 349–369.

Bellamy, Richard. 2005. "The 'Right to Have Rights': Citizenship Practice and the Political Constitution of the EU." In *Citizenship and Governance in the European Union,* pp. 41–70, ed., R. Bellamy and A. Warleigh Lack. London: Continuum.

———. 2006. "Still in Deficit: Rights, Regulations and Democracy in the EU." *European Law Journal* 12(6): 725–742.

Benoit, Bertrand. 2001a. "Germany's Courts Chase after Its Companies." *Financial Times,* November 27.

———. 2001b. "Tighter Rules for Europe's Nasdaq after a Bad Year." *Financial Times,* January 26.

Bercusson, Brian. 1990. "The European Community's Charter of Fundamental Social Rights of Workers." *Modern Law Review* 53(5): 624–642.

Berger, Suzanne, and Robert Dore, eds. 1996. *National Diversity and Global Capitalism.* Ithaca: Cornell University Press.

Bergkamp, Lucas. 2003. *European Community Law for the New Economy.* Antwerp: Intersentia.

Besner, Eric. 1995. "Employment Legislation for Disabled Individuals: What Can France Learn from the American with Disabilities Act?" *Comparative Labor Law Journal* 16: 399.

Besson, Samantha, and André Utzinger. 2007. "Introduction: Future Challenges of European Citizenship." *European Law Journal* 13(5): 573–590.

Beunderman, Mark. 2007. "Poland to Join UK in EU Rights Charter Opt-out." *EUObserver,* 7 September, available at http://euobserver.com/9/24723 last accessed on 4 October 2010.

Bignami, Francesca. 2003. "Three Generations of Participation Rights in the European Administrative Proceedings." In Jean Monnet Working Paper no. 11/03, Jean Monnet Center, New York University School of Law.

———. 2005. "Creating European Rights: National Values and Supranational Interests." *Columbia Journal of European Law* 11: 241–253.

———. 2007. "Privacy and Law Enforcement in the European Union: The Data Retention Directive." *Chicago Journal of International Law* 8: 233–255.

———. 2010. "The Non-Americanization of European Regulatory Styles: Data Privacy Regulation in France, Germany, Italy and Britain." Working Paper no. 174, Minda de Gunzburg Center for European Studies, Harvard University, Cambridge, Mass.

Bill, James. 1997. *George Ball: Behind the Scenes in U.S. Foreign Policy.* New Haven: Yale University Press.

Black, Donald. 1976. *The Behavior of Law.* New York: Academic Press.

Blair, Michael. 2005. *Annotated Guide to the Financial Services and Markets Act 2000.* London: Butterworths.

Blanck, Peter David. 2005. *Disability Rights.* Surrey: Ashgate.

Blankenburg, Erhard. 1992. "Comparing Legal Aid Schemes in Europe." *Civil Justice Quarterly* 11: 106–114.

———. 1994. "The Infrastructure for Avoiding Civil Litigation: Comparing Cultures of Legal Behavior in The Netherlands and West Germany." *Law and Society Review* 28(4): 789–808.

———. 1996. "Changes in Political Regimes and Continuity in the Rule of Law in Germany." In *Courts, Law and Politics in Comparative Perspective,* pp. 249–314, ed. H. Jacob, E. Blankenburg, H. M. Kritzer, D. M. Provine, and J. Sanders. New Haven: Yale University Press.

———. 1997. "Civil Litigation Rates as Indicators for Legal Cultures." In *Comparing Legal Cultures,* pp. 41–68, ed. D. Nelken. Aldershot: Dartmouth.

———. 1998. "Patterns of Legal Culture: The Netherlands Compared to Neighboring Germany." *American Journal of Comparative Law* 46(1): 1–41.

———. 1999. "The Lawyers' Lobby and the Welfare State: The Political Economy of Legal Aid." In *The Transformation of Legal Aid,* pp. 113–132, ed. F. Regan. Oxford: Oxford University Press

———. 2001. "Indicators of Growth of the Systems of Justice in Western Europe of the 1990s," Working Paper, World Bank. Washington, D.C.: World Bank.

Blankenburg, Erhard, and Freek Bruinsma. 1994. *Dutch Legal Culture.* Deventer: Kluwer Law International.

Böge, Ulf, and Konrad Ost. 2006. "Up and Running, or Is It? Private Enforcement—the Situation in Germany and Policy Perspectives." *European Common Market Law Review* 27(4): 197–205.

Bok, Derek. 1971." Reflections on the Distinctive Character of American Labor Laws." *Harvard Law Review* 84: 1461.

Bolkestein, Fritz. 2004. "Internal Market Commissioner Bolkestein, 'Learning the Lessons of the Financial Services Action Plan." Speech to Finance and Investment Seminar, Edinburgh, UK, January. Speech/04/50 available at http://europa.eu/rapid/ Last accessed 4 Oct. 2010.

Borrás, S., and K. Jacobsson. 2004. "The Open Method of Co-ordination and New Governance Patterns." *Journal of European Public Policy* 11(2): 185–208.

Börzel, Tanja. 1999. "Towards Convergence in Europe? Institutional Adaptation to Europeanization in Germany and Spain." *Journal of Common Market Studies* 39(4): 573–596.

———. 2003. "Guarding the Treaty." In *The State of the European Union*. Vol. 6, pp. 197–220, ed. T. Börzel and R. Cichowski. Oxford: Oxford University Press.

———. 2006. "Participation through Law Enforcement: The Case of the European Union." *Comparative Political Studies* 39(1): 128–152.

Börzel, Tanja, and Thomas Risse. 2003. "Conceptualizing the Domestic Impact of Europe." In *The Politics of Europeanization*, pp. 57–80, ed K. Featherstone and C. Radaelli. Oxford: Oxford University Press.

Bourdieu, Pierre. 1977. *Outline of a Theory of Practice*. Cambridge: Cambridge University Press.

Bradford, Michael. 2009. "Litigation Fears Push D&O Limits Higher: AIRMIC Survey." *Business Insurance*, June 23. Available at www.businessinsurance.com/article/20090623/NEWS/906239993 (accessed 6 October 2010).

Braithwaite, John. 1985. *To Punish or Persuade: Enforcement of Coal Mine Safety*. Albany: SUNY Press.

Brammer, S. 2005. "Concurrent Jurisdiction under Regulation 1/2003 and the Issue of Case Allocation." *Common Market Law Review* 42(5): 1383–1424.

Breslin, M. L., and S. Yee. 2002. *Disability Rights Law and Policy: International and National Perspectives*. Ardsley, N.Y.: Transnational Publishers.

Brickman, Ronald, Sheila Jasanoff, and Thomas Ilgen. 1985. *Controlling Chemicals: The Politics of Regulation in Europe and the United States*. Ithaca: Cornell University Press.

Brodley, Joseph F. 1995. "Antitrust Standing in Private Merger Cases: Reconciling Private Incentives and Public Enforcement Goals." *Michigan Law Review* 94(1): 1–108.

Bruinsma, Fred. 2005. "Judges and Lawyers in the Netherlands—an Overview from 1970 till 2000." In *Reorganisation and Resistance: Legal Professions Confront a Changing World*, pp. 63–87, ed. William Felstiner. Oxford: Hart Publishing.

Brunsden, Jim. 2009. "Business Groups Hit Out at 'Compensation Culture.'" *European Voice*, 23–29 April.

Budras, Corinna. 2004. "Deutsche Telekom's 8-Ton Filing Shows Americanized Lawsuits." *Bloomberg News*, 23 November.

Budzinksi, Oliver. 2003. "Pluralism of Competition Policy Paradigms and the Call for Regulatory Diversity." *Volkswirtschaftliche Beiträge Universität Marburg* 14/2003. Available at http://ssrn.com/ (accessed 8 October 2010).

Bulmer, Simon. 1994. "Institutions and Policy Changes in the European Communities: The Case of Merger Control." *Public Administration* 72(3): 423–444.

Bundeskartellamt. 2009. *Antitrust Enforcement by the Bundeskartellamt: Areas of Focus in 2007/2008.* Bonn: Bundeskartellamt.

Burke, Thomas. 2001. "The Rights Revolution Continues: Why New Rights are Born (and Old Rights Rarely Die)." *Connecticut Law Review* 33:1259–1274.

———. 2004. "The European Union and the Diffusion of Disability Rights." In *Transatlantic Policymaking in an Age of Austerity,* pp. 158–176, ed. Martin Levin and Martin Shapiro. Washington, D.C.: Georgetown University Press.

Burkhard, Eberlein, and Dieter Kerwer. 2004. "New Governance in the EU." *Journal of Common Market Studies* 4: 121–142.

Burley, A. M., and W. Mattli. 1993. "Europe before the Court: A Political Theory of Legal Integration." *International Organization* 47: 41–76.

Büthe, Tim. 2007. "The Politics of Competition and Institutional Change in the European Union: The First Fifty Years." In *Making History. The State of the European Union,* vol. 8, pp. 175–194, ed. S. Meunier and K. McNamara. Oxford: Oxford University Press.

Büthe, Tim, and Gabriel Swank. 2007. "The Politics of Antitrust and Merger Review in the European Union: Institutions and Decisions from Messina to 2004." Working Paper no. 142, Minda de Gunzburg Center for European Studies, Harvard University, Cambridge, Mass.

Buxbaum, Hannah. 2006. "German Legal Culture and the Globalization of Competition Law." *Berkeley Journal of International Law* 23: 474.

Cafaggi, Fabrizio, and Hans-W. Micklitz. 2009. *New Frontiers of Consumer Protection: The Interplay between Private and Public Enforcement.* Antwerp: Intersentia.

Cantor, Jared. 2009. "Defining Disabled: Exporting the ADA to Europe and the Social Model of Disability." *Connecticut Journal of International Law* 24: 399–434.

Canu, Virginie, and Bertand de Saint Mars. 2000. "Les associations d'actionnaires: Élément du gouvernement d'entreprise?" *Revue de Droit Bancaire et Financier,* January/February pp. 46–49.

Capoccia, Giovanni, and R. Daniel Kelemen. 2007. "The Study of Critical Junctures: Theory, Narrative, and Counterfactuals in Historical Institutionalism." *World Politics* 59(3): 341–369.

Caporaso, James A., and Joseph Jupille. 2001. "The Europeanization of Gender Equality Policy and Domestic Structural Change." In *Transforming Europe: Europeanization and Domestic Change,* pp. 21–43, ed. Maria Green Cowles, James A. Caporaso, and Thomas Risse. Ithaca: Cornell University Press.

Caporaso, James A., and Sidney Tarrow, 2009. "Polanyi in Brussels: Supranational Institutions and the Transnational Embedding of Markets." *International Organization* 63(4): 593–620.

Cappelletti, Mauro. 1981. *Access to Justice and the Welfare State.* Fiesole: European University Institute.

———. 1989. *The Judicial Process in Comparative Perspective.* Oxford: Clarendon Press.

Cappelletti, Mauro, and Bryant Garth. 1978. *Access to Justice: The Worldwide Movement to Make Rights Effective.* Milan: Dott A Giuffre.

Cappelletti, Mauro, James Gordley, and Earl Johnson Jr., eds. 1975. *Towards Equal Justice: A Comparative Study of Legal Aid in Modern Societies.* New York: Oceana Publications.

Cartel Damage Claims. 2009. "CDC Cartel Damage Claims Files Action against Member of the Hydrogen Peroxide Cartel." Available at www.carteldamageclaims.com (accessed 1 March 2010).

Cassese, Antonio, Andrew Clapham, and Joseph Weiler, eds. 1991. *Human Rights and the European Community,* 3 vols. Baden-Baden: Nomos.

Castle, Stephen. 2008. "EU Fine Sends Message to Microsoft and Others." *New York Times,* 27 February. Available at www.nyt.com (accessed 21 Feb 2010).

Cavalier, Georges A. J., and Jean-Sébastian Quéguiner. 2007. "Punitive Damages and French Public Policy." Available at http://ssrn.com/abstract=1174363 (accessed 5 October 2010).

CCBE (Conseil des barreaux européens – Council of Bars and Law Societies of Europe). 2006. *Code of Conduct for European Lawyers.* Brussels: CCBE.

CEA (Comité européen des assurances). 1990. Annexe: Le marche de l'assurance de protection juridique en Europe. CEA Document A6 015 (08/90).

———. 1993. Legal Expenses Insurance Committee, Annex to doc. PJ 006 [04/93]. Brussels: CEA.

———. 1994. Legal Expenses Insurance Committee, Annex to doc. PJ 034 [12/94]. Brussels: CEA.

———. 1996. Legal Expenses Insurance Committee, Annex to doc. PJ 001 (01/96]. Brussels: CEA.

———. 1998a. Legal Expenses Insurance Statistics 1990–1997. Annex to doc. PJ 8023 (09/98)

———. 1998b. European Insurance in Figures. Brussels: CEA.

———. 2000. European Insurance in Figures. Brussels: CEA.

———. 2001. European Insurance in Figures 2001. Brussels: CEA.

———. 2002. European Insurance in Figures 2002. Brussels: CEA.

———. 2003. European Insurance in Figures 2003. Brussels: CEA.

———. 2006. European Insurance in Figures 2006. Brussels: CEA.

———. 2008. European Insurance in Figures 2008. Brussels: CEA.

CEPEJ (European Commission for the Efficiency of Justice). 2005. *European Judicial Systems 2002*. Strasbourg: Council of Europe Publishing.

———. 2006. *European Judicial Systems – Edition 2006 (2004 data)*. Strasbourg: Council of Europe.

———. 2008. *European Judicial Systems – Edition 2008 (data 2006)*. Strasbourg: Council of Europe.

Chalmers, Damian. 2000. "The Much Ado about Judicial Politics in the United Kingdom: A Statistical Analysis of Reported Decisions of United Kingdom Courts Invoking EU Law, 1973–1998." Harvard Jean Monnet Working Paper no. 2000/1, Jean Monnet Chair, Harvard Law School.

Chapman, Peter. 2003. "Monti Overhaul of Merger Regime May Not Come Up Smelling Roses." *European Voice,* 20 November. Available at www.europeanvoice.com (accessed 10 October 2010).

Charkham, Jonathan P. 1994. *Keeping Good Company: A Study of Corporate Governance in Five Countries*. Oxford: Clarendon Press.

Chiarloni, Sergio. 1999. "A Comparative Perspective on the Crisis of Civil Justice and on Its Possible Remedies." *Cardozo Electronic Law Bulletin,* 5(10), Cardozo Institute, Unïversità degli Studi di Trento. Available at http://www.jus.unitn.it/cardozo/home.html (accessed Oct. 10, 2010).

Church, Thomas W., and Robert Nakamura. 1993. *Cleaning Up the Mess: Implementation Strategies in Superfund.* Washington D.C.: Brookings Institution Press.

Cichowski, Rachel. 1998. "Integrating the Environment: the European Court and the Construction of Supranational Policy." *Journal of European Public Policy* 5(3):387–405.

———. 2004. "Women's Rights, the European Court, and Supranational Constitutionalism." *Law and Society Review* 38: 489–512.

———. 2006. Courts, Rights and Democratic Participation. *Comparative Political Studies* 39(1):50–75.

———. 2007. *The European Court, Civil Society, and European Integration.* Cambridge: Cambridge University Press.

Cichowski, Rachel, and Alec Stone Sweet. 2003. "Participation, Representative Democracy and the Courts." In *Democracy Transformed? Expanding*

Political Opportunities in Advanced Industrial Democracies, pp.192-220, ed. B. Cain, R. Dalton, & S. Scarrow. Oxford: Oxford University Press.

Cini, Michelle. 2004. "The Europeanisation of British Competition Policy." Paper presented at the Conference on Britain in Europe and Europe in Britain,, Sheffield Town Hall, July 16.

Cioffi, John. 2002. "Restructuring *Germany Inc:* The Politics of Company and Takeover Law Reform in Germany and the European Union." *Law and Policy* 24(4): 355–402.

———. 2007. "Revenge of the Law? Securities Litigation Reform and Sarbanes-Oxley's Structural Regulation of Corporate Governance." In *Creating Competitive Markets: The Politics and Economics of Regulatory Reform,* pp. 60–82, ed. M. Levin and M. Shapiro. Washington, D.C.: Brookings Institution Press.

———. 2009. "Adversarialism versus Legalism: Juridification and Litigation in Corporate Governance Reform. *Regulation and Governance* 3(3): 235–258.

Claes, Monica, and Maartje de Visser. 2008. "European Legal and Judicial Networks." Paper presented at "European Legal Field Conference," European University Institute, Fiesole, 25–26 September.

Cleary, Gottlieb. 2009. "The New French Competition Authority and Competition Law Regime." 30 March. Paris: Cleary Gottlieb Steen and Hamilton.

Coen, David, and Mark Thatcher. 2008. "Network Governance and Multi-Level Delegation: European Networks of Regulatory Agencies." *Journal of European Public Policy* 28(1): 49–71.

Coffee, John C. 1983. "Rescuing the Private Attorney General: Why the Model of the Lawyer as Bounty Hunter Is Not Working." *Maryland Law Review* 42: 215–288.

———. 1999. "The Future as History: The Prospects for Global Convergence in Corporate Governance and Its Implications." *Northwestern University Law Review* 93: 641–708.

———. 2006. "Reforming the Securities Class Action: An Essay on Deterrence and Its Implementation." *Columbia Law Review* 106: 1534–1586.

———. 2007. "Law and the Market: The Impact of Enforcement." Working Paper no. 304, Center for Law and Economic Studies, Columbia University School of Law.

Cohen, Antonin, and Antoine Vauchez. 2007. "Introduction: Law, Lawyers and Transnational Politics in the Production of Europe." *Law and Social Inquiry* 32(1): 75–82.

Cohen, Deborah. 2001. *The War Comes Home: Disabled Veterans in Britain and Germany, 1914–1939.* Berkeley: University of California Press.

Collier, David, and Robert Adcock. 1999. "Democracies and Dichotomies: A Pragmatic Approach to Choices about Concepts." *Annual Review of Political Science* 2: 537–565.

Collier, David, and Steven Levitsky. 1997. "Democracy with Adjectives: Conceptual Innovation in Comparative Research." *World Politics* 49(3): 430–451.

Collier, David, and James E. Mahon Jr. 1993. "Conceptual 'Stretching' Revisited: Adapting Categories in Comparative Analysis." *American Political Science Review* 87(4): 845–855.

Comité des sages. 1996. *For a Europe of Civic and Social Rights—Report by the Comité des Sages.* Luxembourg: Office of Publications of the European Community.

Comité européen des assurances. See CEA.

Commissie Gelijke Behandeling. 2006. *Jaarverslag 2006.* Available at www.cgb.nl (accessed 20 February 2010).

———. 2008. *Jaarverslag 2008.* Available at www.cgb.nl (accessed 20 February 2010).

Commission (Commission of the European Communities/Commission of the European Union). 1966. "Report by a Group of Experts Appointed by the EEC Commission." *The Development of a European Capital Market.* [The Segré Report]. Brussels: Commission.

———. 1977. Commission Recommendation 77/534/EEC of July 25, 1977 Concerning a European Code of Conduct Relating to Transactions in Transferable Securities, OJEC L 212 20.8.1977.

———. 1983. *Financial Integration: Communication from the Commission to the Council.* COM(83) 207 final, 20 April.

———. 1984. "Memorandum from the Commission: 'Consumer Redress.'" COM (629) Final, 12 December.

———. 1985. White Paper on the Completion of the Internal Market. COM(85) 310 final, 14 June.

———. 1986. "Memorandum of the Commission to the Council Concerning the Employment of Disabled People in the European Community." COM (86)9 final. 24 January.

———. 1990. Community Charter of the Fundamental Social Rights of Workers. Luxembourg: Commission.

———. 1991a. "Directive on Minimum Requirements to Improve the Mobility and Safe Transport to Work of Workers with a Reduced Mobility." COM(90) 588 final. 28 February.

———1991b. "Proposal for a Council Decision Establishing a Third Action Programme to Assist Disabled People." COM (91) 350 final.

———. 1993a. *Green Paper: Access of Consumers to Justice and the Settlement of Consumer Disputes in the Single Market.* Brussels: Commission.

———. 1993b. Notice on Cooperation between National Courts and the Commission in Applying Articles 85 and 86 of the EEC Treaty OJ C39, 13 Feb., p. 6.

———.1993c. Green Paper on European Social Policy – Options for the Union. COM (93) 576 final, 16 Nov.

———. 1994a. *European Social Policy—A Way Forward for the Union.* COM(94) 333 final. 27 July.

———.1994b. *XXIIIrd Competition Report from the Commission 1993.* COM(94) 161. 5 May.

———. 1996a. *Commission Communication on Simpler Legislation for the Internal Market,* COM (1996) 204 final. 8 May.

———. 1996b. *Communication of the Commission on Equality of Opportunity for People with Disabilities.* COM(96) 406 final. 30 July.

———. 1997a. *Commission Communication: Towards Greater Efficiency in Obtaining and Enforcing Judgements in the European Union.* COM (97) 609 final. Nov. 26.

———. 1997b. Commission Notice on Cooperation between National Competition Authorities and the Commission in Handling Cases Falling within the Scope of Articles 81 and 82 of the EC Treaty [Commission Notice (97/C 313/03); OJ C 313 of 15 October].

———. 1998. Communication on Financial Services: Building a Framework for Action. COM(98) 625 final, 28 October.

———. 1999a. *Council and Commission Action Plan of December 3, 1998, on How Best to Implement the Provisions of the Treaty of Amsterdam on the creation of an Area of Freedom, Security and Justice,* OJ C 19: 1.

———. 1999b. Financial Services: Implementing the Framework for Financial Services Action Plan. COM(1999) 232 final, 11 May.

———. 1999c. White Paper on Modernisation of the Rules Implementing Articles 85 and 86 of the EC Treaty, COM(99) 101 final.

———. 2000. *Green Paper: Legal Aid in Civil Matters—the Problems Confronting the Cross-Border Litigant.* COM (2000) 51 final. 9 February.

———. 2001a. *Proposal for a Council Regulation Establishing a General Framework for Community Activities to Facilitate the Implementation of a European Judicial Area in Civil Matters.* COM(2001) 221—C5•0254/2001—2001/0109(CNS).

———. 2001b. *White Paper on European Governance,* COM(2001) 428 final. 25 July.

———. 2002a. *Communication from the Commission: Action Plan "Simplifying and Improving the Regulatory Environment."* COM(2002) 278 final. 5 June.

———. 2002b. *Proposal for a Directive of the European Parliament and of the Council on Investment Services and Regulated Markets, and Amending Council Direc-*

tive 85/611/EEC, Council Directive 93/6/EEC and European Parliament and Council Directive 2000/12/EC (the MiFID Proposal), 19.11.2002, COM(2002) 625. 19 November.

———. 2002c. Green Paper on a European Order for Payment Procedure and on Measures to Simplify and Speed Up Small Claims Litigation. COM(2002) 746 final.

———. 2002d. Proposal for a Council Directive to Improve Access to Justice in Cross-border Disputes by Establishing Minimum Common Rules Relating to Legal Aid and Other Financial Aspects of Civil Proceedings, COM(2002) 13 final.

———. 2004a. *Facing the Challenge. The Lisbon Strategy for Growth and Employment: Report from the High Level Group Chaired by Wim Kok.* Luxembourg: EC.

———. 2004b. Commission Notice on Cooperation within the Network of Competition Authorities, OJ C 101 27 April, p.3.

———. 2005a. "Commission Defends Air Passenger Rights." Press Release IP/05/858, 6 July.

———. 2005b. *Communication from the Commission to the Council and the European Parliament: Better Regulation for Growth and Jobs in the European Union.* COM(2005) 97 final. 16 March.

———. 2005c. *Green Paper—Damages Actions for Breach of EC Anti-trust Rules, COM(2005) 672 final. 19 December.*

———. 2005d. "Internal Market: Commission Moves against 16 Member States for Failure to Implement EU Legislation on Financial Services." Press Release IP/05/1035, 3 August.

———. 2006. *Climate Change: Commission Takes Legal Action over Missing National Allocation Plans, Incomplete Emissions Reports.* Press Release IP/06/1763, 12 December.

———. 2007a. Communication pursuant to Article 17 of Regulation (EC) No. 261/04, COM (2007) 168 final, 4 April.

———. 2007b. "Commission Gives Airlines and Member States Six Months to Make the Air Passenger Rights Regulation Work." Press Release IP/07/471, 4 April.

———. 2007c. *EU Consumer Policy Strategy 2007–2013.* COM(2007) 99 final. 13 March.

———. 2007d. *Developing Anti-Discrimination Law in Europe: The 25 EU Member States Compared.* Prepared by Mark Bell, Isabelle Chopin and Fiona Palmer for the European Network of Independent Experts in the non-discrimination field. Directorate General for Employment, Social Affairs and Equal Opportunities, Unit G.2. Luxembourg: Office for Official Publications of the European Communities.

———. 2008a. "Commission Acts to Close Gaps in Employment Equality Rules." Press Release, IP/08/155 January 31.

———. 2008b. *Green Paper on Consumer Collective Redress.* COM(2008) 794 final, 27 Nov.

———. 2008c. "Proposal for a Council Directive on Implementing the Principle of Equal Treatment between Persons Irrespective of Religion or Belief, Disability, Age or Sexual Orientation." COM (2008) 426 final. 2 July.

———. 2008d. *White Paper on Damages Actions for Breach of EC Antitrust Rules.* COM(2008) 165 final. 2 April.

———. 2008e. Proposal for a Regulation on the Rights of Passengers in Bus and Coach Transport, COM(2008) 817 final, 4 December.

———.2008f. Proposal for a Regulation Concerning the Rights of Passengers when Travelling by Sea and Inland Waterway, COM(2008) 816 final, 4 December.

———. 2009a. "Employment Equality Rules: Case Closed for Estonia; Reasoned Opinions to Germany and Italy." Press Release IP/09/1620, 29 October.

———. 2009b. "Employment Equality Rules: Reasoned Opinion to the UK; Cases Closed for Slovakia and Malta." Press Release IP/09/1778, 20 November.

———. 2009c. *Proposal for a Regulation of the European Parliament and of the Council Establishing a European Securities and Markets Authority.* COM (2009) 503 final. 23 September.

———. 2009d. "Summary of the New Rail Passenger Rights." Press Release, 3 December. Available at http://ec.europa.eu/transport/passengers/rail/rail_en.htm (accessed 5 October 2010).

———. 2010. "Employment Equality Rules: Reasoned Opinion to Poland; Case Closed for Hungary" Press Release, IP/10/71 28 January.

Conant, Lisa. 2002. Justice Contained: Law and Politics in the European Union. Ithaca: Cornell University Press.

———. 2006. "Individuals, Courts, and the Development of European Social Rights." *Comparative Political Studies* 39(1): 76–100.

———. 2007. "Courts and the Americanization of Social Rights in Europe?" *American Political Science Association, European Politics and Society Section Newsletter* 6(1): 8–10.

Contini, Francesco, ed. 2000. *European Data Base on Judicial Systems.* Working Papers of the Istituto di Ricerca sui Sistemi Giudiziari, Consiglio Nazionale delle Ricerche. Bologna: Lo Scarabeo.

Cooper, Jeremy, ed. 2000. *Law, Rights and Disability.* London: Jessica Kingsley Publishers.

Cooter, Robert D., and Tom Ginsburg. 1996. "Comparative Judicial Discretion—an Empirical Test of Economic Models." *International Review of Law and Economics* 16: 295–313.

———. 2003. "Why the Same Laws Are Longer in Some Countries than Others." Law and Economic Research Paper no. LE03-012, University of Illinois. Available at http://ssrn.com/abstract=456520 (accessed 20 June 2010).

Coppedge, Michael. 1999. "Thickening Thin Concepts and Theories: Combining Large N and Small in Comparative Politics." *Comparative Politics* 31(4): 465–476.

Cornerstone Research. 2009. *Securities Class Action Filings: 2009 Mid-year Assessment.* Published in cooperation with Stanford Law School, Securities Class Action Clearinghouse. Available at http://securities.stanford.edu (accessed 20 Feb 2010).

Cotts, Cynthia. 2009. "Former Cohen Milstein Law Partner Hausfeld Opens New D.C. Firm." *Bloomberg News,* January 27. Available at http://www.bloomberg.com (accessed 21 June 2009).

Council of the European Union. 1998. "Presidency Conclusions – Cardiff European Council, 15 and 16 June 1998." SN 150/1/98 REV 1. Available at: http://www.consilium.europa.eu (accessed 4 October, 2010).

———. 1999. Presidency Conclusions – Tampere European Council, 15 and 16 October 1999. Available at http://ue.eu.int/ueDocs/cms_Data/docs/pressData/en/ec/00200-r1.en9.htm (accessed on 4 October, 2010).

Cousins, Mel. 1994. "The Politics of Legal Aid: A Solution in Search of a Problem?" *Civil Justice Quarterly* 13: 111–125.

Craig, Paul, and Gráinne de Búrca. 2008. *EU Law: Text, Cases, and Materials,* 4th ed. Oxford: Oxford University Press.

Cremona, Marise, and Bruno de Witte, eds. 2008. *EU Foreign Relations Law: Constitutional Fundamentals.* Oxford: Hart Publishing.

Cross, Frank B. 1992. "Law versus Economics?" *Law and Social Inquiry* 17(4): 653–658.

———. 2001. "Law and Economic Growth." *Texas Law Review* 80: 1737–1775.

Curtin, Deirdre, and Kamiel Mortelmans. 1994. "Application and Enforcement of Community Law by the Member States." In *Institutional Dynamics of European Integration,* pp. 423–466, ed. Deirdre Curtin and Ton Heukels. Dordrecht: M. Nijhoff.

Daalder, Hans. 1996. "The Netherlands: Opposition in a Segmented Society." In *Political Opposition in Western Democracies,* pp. 188–236, ed. Robert Dahl. New Haven: Yale University Press.

Damaska, Mirjan R. 1986. *The Faces of Justice and State Authority: A Comparative Approach to the Legal Process.* New Haven: Yale University Press.

Danglehant, Catherine. 1996. "Le nouveau statut des minoritaires dans les sociétés," *Revue des sociétés,* April–June, pp. 217–237.

Datamonitor. 2007a. "Legal Services in France." New York: Datamonitor.

———. 2007b. "Legal Services in Germany." New York: Datamonitor.

———. 2007c. "Legal Services in the United Kingdom." New York: Datamonitor.

———. 2009a. "Legal Services in France." New York: Datamonitor.

———. 2009b. "Legal Services in Germany." New York: Datamonitor.

———. 2009c. "Legal Services in the United Kingdom." New York: Datamonitor.

Daucourt, Thierry. 2009. "The Changing German Landscape." *Risk Management Magazine,* 56(5):60.

Davidow, J. 2002. "International Implications of US Antitrust in the George W. Bush Era." *World Competition* 25(4): 493–507.

Davies, Gareth. 2007. The Effect of Mrs. Watts Trip to France on the National Health Service. King's Law Journal 18(1): 158–167.

Davis, Neil, and Lesley Farrell. 2010. *United Kingdom: Private Enforcement; The European Antitrust Review 2010.* London: Law Business Research. Global Competition Review / SJ Berwin. Available at www.globalcompetitionreview.com (accessed 21 February 2010).

De Búrca, Gráinne. 1995. "The Language of Rights and European Integration." In *New Legal Dynamics of European Union,* pp. 24–54, ed. G. More and J. Shaw. Oxford: Clarendon Press.

———. 2001. "The Drafting of the European Union Charter of Fundamental Rights." *European Law Review* 26: 126–138.

De Búrca, Gráinne, and Bruno de Witte. 2005. *Social Rights in Europe.* Oxford: Oxford University Press.

Deeg, Richard, and Susanne Lütz. 2000. "Internationlization and Financial Federalism: The United States and Germany at the Crossroads?" *Comparative Political Studies* 33(3): 374–405.

Degener, Theresia, et al. 1995. "Disabled Persons' Status in the European Treaties: Invisible Citizens." European Parliament Doc. No. D/1995/7560/2.

Degener, Theresia, and Gerard Quinn. 2000. "A Survey of International, Comparative and Regional Disability Law Reform." Paper presented at the International Disability Law and Policy Symposium, sponsored by the US Social Security Administration and the Disability Rights Education and Defense Fund (DREDF), Washington, D.C., 22–26 October.

Dehousse, Renaud. 2000. "Integration through Law Revisited: Some Thoughts on the Juridification of the European Political Process." In *The*

Europeanisation of Law, pp. 15–29, ed. Francis Snyder. Oxford: Hart Publishing.

———. 2008. "The 'Community Method': Chronicle of a Death Too Early Foretold." In *Efficient and Democratic Governance in the European Union,* pp. 79–108, ed. Beale Kohler-Koch and Fabrice Larat. CONNEX Report Series No. 9, University of Mannheim. Available at http://www.connex-network.org/ (accessed 10 Oct 2010).

De Jong, Hendrik W. 1990. "Nederland: het kartelparadijs van Europa?" *Economisch Statistische Berichten,* 75: 244–248.

DeLisle, Jacques. 1999. "Lex Americana? United States Legal Assistance, American Legal Models and Legal Changes in the Post-Communist World and Beyond." *University of Pennsylvania Journal of International Economic Law* 20(2): 179–308.

Demetriou, Marie, and Margaret Gray. 2007. "Developments in EC Competition Law in 2006: An Overview." *Common Market Law Review* 44(5): 1429–1462.

Department of Constitutional Affairs. 2004. "Tackling the Compensation Culture-Government Response to the Better Regulation Task Force Report: Better Routes to Redress, 10 November." Available at http://www.dca.gov.uk/majrep/bettertaskforce/better-task-force.pdf (accessed on 4 October, 2010).

De Schutter, Olivier. 2006. "Group Litigation before the European Court of Justice." In *Civil Society and Legitimate Governance,* pp. 89–114, ed. S. Smismans. London: Elgar.

De Witte, Bruno. 2005. "The Trajectory of Fundamental Social Rights in the European Union." In *Social Rights in Europe,* pp. 153–168, ed. Gráinne de Búrca and Bruno de Witte. Oxford: Oxford University Press.

Dezalay, Yves. 1990. "The *Big Bang* and the Law: The Internationalization and Restructuration of the Legal Field." In *Global Culture: Nationalism, Globalization and Modernity,* pp. 279–294, ed. M. Featherstone. London: Sage.

———. 1996. "Between the State, Law, and the Market: The Social and Professional Stakes in the Construction and Definition of a Regulatory Arena." In *International Regulatory Competition and Coordination: Perspectives on Economic Regulation in Europe and the United States,* pp. 59–87, ed. William Bratton, Joseph McCahery, Sol Picciotto, and Colin Scott. Oxford: Clarendon Press.

Dezalay, Yves, and Bryant Garth. 1995. *Dealing in Virtue: International Commercial Arbitration and the Construction of a Transnational Legal Order.* Chicago: University of Chicago Press.

DG Employment and Social Affairs. 2006. Interview with author. European Commission, Brussels. 5 April.

Dickerson, Thomas. 1997. *Class Actions: The Law of 50 States*. New York: Law Journal Seminars Press.

Dietrich, Michael, Wolfgang Gruber, and Marco Hartmann-Rüppel. 2010. "Germany." In *The Private Competition Enforcement Review*, pp. 73–90, ed. Ilene Knable Gotts. London: Law Business Research.

Diller, Martin. 2007. "AGG-Hopping durch Schwerbehinderte." *Neue Zeitschrift für Arbeitsrecht* 23: 1321–1325.

Disability Policy Officer, Trade Union Congress. 2007. Interview. London. 11 July.

Disability Rights Commission (DCR). 2002. *50 Key Cases from the DRC*. London: DRC.

———. 2003. Strategic Plan Executive Summary, 2004–2007. London: DRC.

Disabled People's International Europe (DPI Europe). 2006. Interview. Paris, 20 December.

Discrimination Law Association. 2007. Telephone interview. 12 July.

Djelic, Marie-Laure. 1998. *Exporting the American Model*. Oxford: Oxford University Press.

———. 2002. "Does Europe Mean Americanization? The Case of Competition." *Competition and Change* 6(3): 233–250.

Dobbin, F., and J. Sutton. 1998. "The Strength of the Weak State." *American Journal of Sociology* 104: 441–476.

Doyle, Brian. 1993. "Employment Rights, Equal Opportunities and Disabled Persons: The Ingredients for Reform." *Industrial Law Journal* 22(2): 89–103.

———. 1995. *Disability, Discrimination, and Equal Opportunities: A Comparative Study of the Employment Rights of Disabled Persons*. New York: Mansell.

———. 1999. "From Welfare to Rights? Disability and Legal Challenges in the United Kingdom in the Late 1990s." In *Disability, Divers-ability, and Legal Change*, pp. 209–226, ed. M. Jones and L. A. Basser Marks. The Hague: Martinus Nijhoff.

Drahos, Michaela. 2001. *Convergence of Competition Laws and Policies in the European Community*. Deventer: Kluwer Law International.

Drezner, Daniel. 2001. "Globalization and Policy Convergence." *International Studies Review* 3: 53–78.

Driedger, D. 1989. *The Last Civil Rights Movement: Disabled Peoples' International*. London: C. Hurst.

Duchêne, Francois. 1994. *Jean Monnet: First Statesman of Interdependence*. New York: Norton.

Dumez, Hervé, and Alain Jeunemaître. 1996. "The Convergence of Competition Policies in Europe: Internal Dynamics and External Imposition."

In *National Diversity and Global Capitalism,* pp. 216–238, ed. S. Berger and R. Dore. Ithaca: Cornell University Press.

Durkheim, Emile. 1893/1984. *The Division of Labor in Society.* New York: Free Press.

Dyson, Richard. 2006. "Game's Up, Says Splits Lawyer." *Mail on Sunday,* 3 December. Available at http://www.dailymail.co.uk/ (accessed 4 October, 2010).

Eberlein, Burkhard, and Dieter Kerwer. 2004. "New Governance in the European Union: a Theoretical Perspective." *Journal of Common Market Studies* 42(1): 121–142.

Eckert, Daniel, and Holger Zschäpitz. 2004. "BGH statuiert ein Exempel an den Haffa-Brüdern." *Welt Online,* 17 December. Available at www.weltonline.de (accessed 10 March 2010).

Eckstein, Harry. 1975. "Case Study and Theory in Political Science." In *Handbook of Political Science,* pp. 94–137, ed. Fred Greenstein and Nelson Polsby. Reading, Mass.: Addison-Wesley.

Economist. 1988. "La Grande Boum." October 1, p.83.

———. 2008. "Deutsche Telekom in the Dock." 10 April.

Economist Intelligence Unit. 2007. *Collective Litigation in Europe: A survey from the Economist Intelligence Unit.* London: The Economist Intelligence Unit.

Eeckhout, Piet. 2002. "The EU Charter of Fundamental Rights and the Federal Question." *Common Market Law Review* 39: 945–994.

Ehlermann, Claus-Dieter. 1992. "The European Community, Its Law and Lawyers." *Common Market Law Review* 29: 213–227.

———. 1996. "Implementation of EC Competition Law by National Antitrust Authorities." *European Competition Law Review* 17(2): 88–96.

———. 2000. "The Modernization of EC Antitrust Policy: A Legal and Cultural Revolution." *Common Market Law Review* 37: 537–590.

EHRC (Equality and Human Rights Commission). 2008. "Legal Strategy 2008–9." Available at www.equalityhumanrights.com (accessed 10 February 2010).

Eilmansberger, Thomas. 2004. "The Relationship between Rights and Remedies in EC Law." *Common Market Law Review* 41: 1199–1246.

———. 2007. "The Green Paper on Damages Actions for Breach of the EC Antitrust Rules and Beyond." *Common Market Law Review* 44: 431–478.

Ellis, Evelyn. 2002. "The Principle of Non-discrimination in the Post-Nice Era." In *Accountability and Legitimacy in the European Union,* pp. 291–305, ed. A. Amull and D. Wincott. Oxford: Oxford University Press.

Employment Tribunals Service. 2000. *Annual Report and Accounts, 1999–2000.* London: HM Stationery Office.

———. 2001. *Annual Report and Accounts, 2000–2001.* London: HM Stationery Office.

———. 2002. *Annual Report and Accounts, 2001–2002.* London: HM Stationery Office.

———. 2003. *Annual Report and Accounts, 2002–2003.* London: HM Stationery Office.

———. 2005. *Annual Report and Accounts, 2004–2005.* London: HM Stationery Office.

———. 2006. *Annual Report and Accounts, 2005–2006.* London: HM Stationery Office.

———. 2007. *Employment Tribunal and EAT Statistics, 2006–07.* London: Ministry of Justice.

———. 2008. *Employment Tribunal and EAT Statistics, 2007–08.* London: Ministry of Justice.

———. 2009. *Employment Tribunal and EAT Statistics, 2008–09.* London: Ministry of Justice.

Engel, Christoph. 2001. "The European Charter of Fundamental Rights: A Changed Political Opportunity Structure and Its Normative Consequences." *European Law Journal* 7(2): 151–170.

Enriques, Luca, and Paola Volpin. 2007. "Corporate Governance Reforms in Continental Europe." *Journal of Economic Perspectives* 21(1): 117–140.

Epp, Charles. 1992. "Do Lawyers Impair Economic Growth?" *Law and Social Inquiry* 17(4): 585–623.

———. 1998. *The Rights Revolution.* Chicago: University of Chicago Press.

Eskridge, William, and John Ferejohn. 1996. "Virtual Logrolling: How the Court, Congress, and the States Multiply Rights." *Southern California Law Review* 68: 1545.

Euractiv. 2008. EU mulls collective redress for consumers. 28 November. Available at *www.euractiv.com* (accessed on 4 October, 2010).

European Disability Forum. 2006. Interview with author. Brussels, April 4.

European Disabled People's Parliament. 1993. Resolution of the European Disabled People's Parliament. 3 December. Available at www.leeds.ac.uk/disability-studies/archiveuk/DPI.

European Parliament. 1995. *Resolution on Racism, Xenophobia and Anti-Semitism.* C 308/104. October 26.

———. 1996. Report on (i) Parliament's opinion on the convening of the IGC (ii) evaluation of the work of the Reflection Group and definition of the political priorities of the European Parliament with a view to the Intergovernmental Conference. PE 216.237/fin. A4-0068/96.

———. 1999a. *Resolution on the Progress Made in 1998 in the Implementation of Cooperation in the Fields of Justice and Home Affairs Pursuant to Title VI of the Treaty on European Union,* B4–0111/99, 14 January.

———. 1999b. *Resolution on the Draft Action Plan of the Council and Commission on How to Best Implement the Provisions of the Treaty of Amsterdam on an Area of Freedom, Security, and Justice,* A4–0133/1999, 13 April.

———. 2001. Resolution on the Final Report of the Committee of Wise Men on the Regulation of European Securities Markets. B5-0173/2001.

———. 2003. *Report on Analysis of the Open Method of Coordination in the Field of Employment and Social Affairs, and Future Prospects.* 2002/2223 (INI), A5–0143/2003 Final, 30 April.

———. 2008. "Resolution on EU Consumer Policy Strategy 2007-2013." P6_TA(2008)0211.

———. 2010. "European Parliament Legislative Resolution of 22 September 2010 on the Proposal for a Regulation of the European Parliament and of the Council Establishing a European Securities and Markets Authority (COM(2009)0503 – C7-0167/2009 – 2009/0144(COD))." European Parliament, Document, P7_TA-PROV(2010)0339, 22 September.

Eurostat. 2001. *Disability and Social Participation in Europe.* Luxembourg: European Communities.

———. 2003. *Employment of Disabled People in Europe, Statistics in Focus, Theme 3-26/2003.* Luxembourg: European Communities.

Ewald, William. 1995. "Comparative Jurisprudence (II): The Logic of Legal Transplants." *American Journal of Comparative Law* 43(4): 489–510.

Ewing, Jack, Carol Matlack, Gail Edmondson, Stanley Reed, and Katharine Schmidt. 2001. "Europe's Shareholders: To the Barricades." *Businessweek Online,* 19 March.

Eyre, Sebastian, and Martin Lodge. 2000. "National Tunes and a European Melody? Competition Law Reform in the UK and Germany." *Journal of European Public Policy* 7(1): 63–79.

Falkner, Gerda. 1998. *EU Social Policy in the 1990s.* London: Routledge.

Falkner, Gerda, Oliver Treib, Miriam Hartlapp, and Simone Leiber. 2005. *Complying with Europe: EU Harmonisation and Soft Law in the Member States.* Cambridge: Cambridge University Press.

Farrow, Paul. 2002. "A Class Act? Does a Joint Suit Let Investors Win Compensation or Does It Just Line the Pockets of Opportunistic Lawyers." *Daily Telegraph,* 15 May. Available at www.telegraph.co.uk (accessed 20 March 2010).

Faull, J. 1991. "The Enforcement of Competition Policy in the European Community: A Mature System." *Fordham International Law Journal* 15: 219.

Fearnley, S., and T. Hines. 2003. "The Regulatory Framework for Financial Reporting and Auditing in the United Kingdom: The Present Position and Impending Changes." *International Journal of Accounting* 38(2): 215–233.

Featherstone, Mike, and Claudio Radaelli. 2003. *The Politics of Europeanization*. Oxford: Oxford University Press.

Ferejohn, John. 1995. "Law, Legislation and Positive Political Theory." In *Modern Political Economy,* pp. 191–215, ed. Jeffrey Banks and Eric Hanushek. New York: Cambridge University Press.

———. 2002. "Judicializing Politics, Politicizing Law." *Law and Contemporary Problems* 65(3): 41–68.

Ferguson, Nick. 1999. "Merger Fever Grips German Market." *International Financial Law Review* 26(9): 35–50.

Ferran, Eilís. 2004. *Building an EU Securities Market.* Cambridge: Cambridge University Press.

Ferrarini, Guido A. 2002. "Pan-European Securities Markets: Policy Issues and Regulatory Responses." *European Business Organization Law Review* 3: 249–292.

Financial Times. 1991. "Securities Firms Look across Borders." 7 January.

———. 2008. "Class Actions Enjoy a Revival among Investors." June 3.

Finnemore, Martha. 1996. *National Interests in International Society.* Ithaca: Cornell University Press.

FIN-USE (Forum of User Experts in the Area of Financial Services). 2004. "Financial Services, Consumers and Small Business: A User Perspective," 4 October. Available at http://ec.europa.eu/internal_market/fin-use_forum/docs/opinion1_en.pdf (accessed 10 February 2010).

Fisher, Jonathan, and Jane Bewsey. 1997. *The Law of Investment Protection.* London: Sweet and Maxwell.

Fishman, James. 1991. "Enforcement of Securities Laws Violations in the United Kingdom." *International Tax and Business Lawyer* 9:131–208.

Fleming, Charles. 2004. "Europe Learns Litigious Ways." *Wall Street Journal,* 24 February, A16.

Fligstein, Neil. 2001. "Social Skill and the Theory of Fields." *Sociological Theory* 19: 105–125.

Fligstein, Neil, and A. Stone Sweet. 2001. "Institutionalizing the Treaty of Rome." In *The Institutionalization of Europe,* pp. 29–55. ed. A. Stone Sweet, W. Sandholtz, and N. Fligstein. Oxford: Oxford University Press.

———. 2002. "Constructing Polities and Markets: An Institutionalist Account of European Integration." *American Journal of Sociology* 107: 1206–1243.

Flood, John. 1996. "Megalawyering in the global order." *International Journal of the Legal Profession* 3(1/2):169–214.

Flood, John, and Avis Whyte. 2006. "What's Wrong with Legal Aid? Lessons from Outside the UK." *Civil Justice Quarterly* 25: 80–98.

Flynn, Leo. 1999. "The Implications of Article 13 EC—after Amsterdam, Will Some Forms of Discrimination Be More Equal than Others?" *Common Market Law Review* 36 (6): 1127–1152.

Follesdal, Andreas, and Simon Hix. 2006. "Why There Is a Democratic Deficit in the EU: A Response to Majone and Moravcsik." *Journal of Common Market Studies* 44(3): 533–562.

Follesdal, Andreas, and Peter Koslowski. 1997. *Democracy and the European Union.* Berlin: Springer.

Fox, Eleanor. 1997. "US and EU Competition Law: A Comparison." In *Global Competition Policy,* pp. 339–354, ed. E. M. Graham and J. D. Richardson. Washington, D.C.: Institute for International Economics.

Franchino, Fabio. 2004. "Delegating Powers in the European Community." *British Journal of Political Science* 34: 449–476.

———. 2007. *The Powers of the Union: Delegation in the EU.* New York: Cambridge University Press.

Franks, Julian, and Colin Mayer. 1993. "European Capital Markets and Corporate Control." In *European Mergers and Merge Policy,* pp. 162–199, ed. M. Bishop and J. Kay. Oxford: Oxford University Press.

Fredman, Sandra 2002. *Discrimination Law.* Oxford: Oxford University Press.

———. 2005. "Disability Equality: A Challenge to the Existing Antidiscrimination Paradigm?" In *Disability Rights in Europe: From Theory to Practice,* pp. 199–218, ed. A. Lawson and C. Gooding. Oxford: Hart Publishing.

———. 2006. "Transformation or Dilution: Fundamental Rights in the EU Social Space." *European Law Journal* 12(1): 41–60.

Freedman, Michael. 2004. "Can You Say Tort?" *Forbes,* 27 December, 127.

Freshfields Bruckhaus Deringer. 2005. *Securities Litigation: A View from Germany.* Berlin: Freshfields Bruckhaus Deringer.

Fried Frank. 2006. France Adopts New Shareholder Disclosure Rules. Memorandum, Fried, Frank, Harris, Shriver and Jacobson LLP, Oct. 3. Available at: http://www.ffhsj.com/siteFiles/Publications/0EEDEC13448CA1AF767E3A1B8AE760D0.pdf (accessed 6 October, 2010).

Friedman Goldstein, Leslie. 2004. "Review Essay: From Democracy to Juristocracy." *Law and Society Review* 38(3): 611–629.

Frowein, Jochen, Stephen Schulhofer and Martin Shapiro. 1986. "Fundamental Human Rights as a Vehicle of Integration." In *Integration Through Law,* ed. M, Cappelletti, M. Secombe, and J. Weiler. Vol. 1, Book 3. New York: Walter de Gruyer.

FSA (Financial Services Authority). 2005. *Planning for MiFID*. London: FSA.

———. 2007. *Principles-Based Regulation: Focusing on the Outcomes That Matter.* London: FSA.

———. 2008. *Conduct of Business Sourcebook (COBS) Post-implementation Review: 2008 Statement of Interim Findings*. London: FSA.

———. 2009. *MiFID Supervisory Priorities—Results of a Wholesale Thematic Review*. London: FSA.

Furedi, Frank. 1999. *Courting Mistrust: The Hidden Growth of a Culture of Litigation in Britain*. London: Centre for Policy Studies.

Furse, Mark. 2000. *Competition Law of the UK and EC,* 2nd ed. London: Blackstone Press.

Galanter, Marc. 1974. "Why the Have Come out Ahead." *Law and Society* 9(1): 93–160.

———. 1983. "Mega-law and Mega-lawyering in the Contemporary United States." In *The Sociology of the Profession,* pp. 152–176, ed. R. Dingwall and P. Lewis. London: Macmillan.

———. 1992. "Law Abounding: Legalisation around the North Atlantic." *Modern Law Review* 55(1): 1–24.

———. 1996. "Lawyers in the Mist: The Golden Age of Legal Nostalgia." *Dickinson Law Review* 100: 549–562.

Galanter, Marc, and Thomas Palay. 1991. *Tournament of Lawyers: The Transformation of the Big Law Firm*. Chicago: University of Chicago Press.

Garamfalvi, Alexia. 2007. "US Firms Prepare for European Class Actions." *Legal Times,* June 25. Available at www.law.com/jsp/article.jsp?id=1182416759806 (accessed March 21, 2010).

Garrett, Geoffrey, R. Daniel Kelemen, and Heiner Schulz. 1998. "The European Court of Justice, National Governments and Legal Integration in the European Union." *International Organization* 52(1): 149–176.

Garth, Bryant. 2008. "The Globalization of the Law." In *The Oxford Handbook of Law and Politics,* pp. 245–264 ed. K. Whittington, R. D. Kelemen, and G. Calderia. Oxford: Oxford University Press.

Gatinois, Claire. 2010. "L'affaire Vivendi, jugée récemment aux États-Unis, pourra-t-elle relancer, en France, le débat sur le recours collectif en justice *(class action)*?" *Le Monde,* 3 February. Available at www.lemonde.fr (accessed 10 February 2010).

Geddes, Andrew. 1995. *Protection of Individual Rights under EC Law.* London: Butterworths.

General Council, OFT. 2007. Interview. London. 5 February.

George, Alexander L. 1979. "Case Studies and Theory Development: The Method of Structured, Focused Comparison." In *Diplomacy: New Ap-*

proaches in History, Theory and Policy, pp. 43–68, ed. P. G. Lauren. New York: Free Press.

George, Alexander L., and Andrew Bennett. 2005. *Case Studies and Theory Development in the Social Sciences.* Cambridge, Mass.: MIT Press.

George, Alexander L., and Timothy McKeown. 1985. "Case Studies and Theories of Organizational Decision Making." In *Advances in Information Processing in Organizations,* pp. 21–58, ed. R. F. Coulam and R. A. Smith. Greenwich, Conn.: JAI Press.

Gerber, David. 2001. *Law and Competition in Twentieth Century Europe: Protecting Prometheus.* Oxford: Clarendon Press.

Gerring, John. 1999. "What Makes a Concept Good?: An Integrated Framework for Understanding Concept Formation in the Social Sciences." *Polity* 31(3): 357–393.

Gerth, H. H. and C. Wright Mills. 1946. *From Max Weber: Essays in Sociology.* New York: Oxford University Press.

———. 1968. *From Max Weber: Essays in Sociology.* New York: Oxford University Press.

Ginsburg, T. 2003. *Judicial Review in New Democracies.* Cambridge: Cambridge University Press.

Girard, Carine. 2001. "Une typologie de l'activisme des actionnaires minoritaires en France." Revue Finance *Contrôle Stratégie* 4(3): 123–146.

———. 2009. "Comparative Study of Successful French and Anglo-Saxon Shareholder Activism." Paper presented at European Financial Management Association Meeting, Milan, Italy, June 24–27.

Glendon, Mary Ann. 1991. *Rights Talk.* New York: Free Press.

Goebel, Roger. 1991. "Lawyers in the European Community: Progress towards Community-Wide Rights of Practice." *Fordham International Law Journal* 15: 556.

———. 2002. "The Liberalization of Interstate Legal Practices in the EU: Lessons from the United States." In *Services and Free Movement in EU Law,* ed. Andenas and Roth. Oxford: Oxford University Press.

Goertz, Gary. 2006. "Assessing the Trivialness, Relevance, and Relative Importance of Necessary or Sufficient Conditions in Social Science." *Studies in Comparative International Development* 41(2): 88–109.

Goldhaber, Michael D. 2008. "'Shell Model' Opens Door to European Class Actions." *American Lawyer,* 7 January. Available at www.law.com (accessed 10 February 2010).

Goldman, Leslie. 1992. "The Modernization of the French Securities Markets: Making the EEC Connection." *Fordham Law Review* 60: 227–253.

Goldnagel, Jean-Marc. 2007. "Une réforme justifiée, de grave écueils à éviter." *Le Figaro,* 15 October. Available at www.lefigaro.fr (accessed 20 March 2010).

Goldthorpe, J. H., ed. 1984. *Order and Conflict in Contemporary Capitalism.* Oxford: Clarendon Press.

Gooding, C., and C. Behaviour. "Blackstone's Guide to the Disability Discrimination Act 1995." *British Journal of Learning Disabilities* 25(1): 997.

Gotanda, John Y. 2007. "Charting Developments Concerning Punitive Damages: Is the Tide Changing?" *Columbia Journal of Transnational Law* 45(2): 507–528.

Gow, David. 2006. "French Shareholders Launch Class Action Lawsuit against EADS." *Guardian,* July 11. Available at www.guardian.co.uk (accessed 21 March 2010).

Goyder, Daniel. 1998. *EC Competition Law,* 3rd ed. Oxford: Oxford University Press.

Goyder, Joanna. 2003. *EC Competition Law,* 4th ed. Oxford: Oxford University Press.

Graham, Cosmo. 2004. "The Enterprise Act of 2002 and Competition Law." *Modern Law Review* 67(2): 273–288.

Graham, George. 1989. "French Banking and Finance Investment: Buffetted by Winds of Change." *Financial Times,* November 2.

Gray, Alastair. 1994. "The Reform of Legal Aid." *Oxford Review of Economic Policy* 10(1): 51–67.

Green Cowles, Maria, James Caporaso, and Thomas Risse, eds. 2001. *Transforming Europe: Europeanization and Domestic Change.* Ithaca: Cornell University Press.

Greer, Scott L. 2006. "Uninvited Europeanization: Neofunctionalism, Health Services and the EU." *Journal of European Public Policy* 13(1): 134–152.

———. 2009a. *The Politics of European Union Health Policies.* Berkshire, England: Open University Press.

———. 2009b. Migration of Patients and Migration of Power: Politics and Policy Consequences of Patient Mobility in Europe. *Wisconsin International Law Journal* 26(3):909–934.

———. 2010. "On Thin Ice: EU Health Policy and its Futures." MS, University of Michigan, School of Public Health. Available at: http://papers.ssrn.com (accessed 25 October 2010).

Gross, Daniel, and Karel Lannoo. 2000. *The Euro Capital Market.* John Wiley and Sons.

Guarnieri, Carlo, and Patrizia Pederzoli. 2001. *The Power of Judges: A Comparative Study of Courts and Democracy.* New York: Oxford University Press.

Guersent, Olivier. 2004. "The Fight against Secret Horizontal Agreement in the EC Competition Policy." In *International Antitrust Law and Policy: Ford-*

ham Corporate Law Institute 2003, ed. B. Hawk. New York: Juris Publishing.

Gutiérrez de Cabiedes, Pablo. 2009. "Spain." *Annals of the American Academy of Political and Social Science* 622: 170–178.

Guy Carpenter (Guy Carpenter and Company). 2009. "Recent Legislative and Judicial Developments in Continental Europe Affecting the Casualty Insurance Industry." May. Available at www.gccapitalideas.com/wp-content/uploads/2009/06/conteuropeanlegalupdatefinal.pdf (accessed 10 February 2010).

Habermas, Jürgen. 1987. *The Theory of Communicative Action,* vol. 2. Boston: Beacon Press.

———. 1992. "Citizenship and National Identity: Some Reflections on the Future of Europe." *Praxis International* 12(1): 1–19.

HALDE (Haute autorité de lutte contre les discriminations et pour l'égalité). 2009. *Rapport Annuel 2008.* Paris: HALDE.

Hall, Peter, and Daniel Gingerich. 2004. "Varieties of Capitalism and Institutional Complementarities in the Macroeconomy: An Empirical Analysis." In Discussion Paper 04/5, Max Planck Institute for the Study of Societies, Cologne, Germany.

Hall, Peter, and David Soskice. 2001. *Varieties of Capitalism: The Institutional Foundations of Comparative Advantage.* Oxford University Press.

———. 2003. "Varieties of Capitalism and Institutional Change: A Response to Three Critics." *Comparative European Politics* 1: 241–250.

Hallstein, Walter. 1964. "Angleichung des Privat- und Prozessrechts in der Europäischen Wirtschaftsgemeinschaft." *Rabels Zeitschrift* 28: 211.

Haltom, William, and Michael McCann. 2004. *Distorting the Law: Politics, Media, and the Litigation Crisis.* Chicago: University of Chicago Press.

Handler, Joel. 1978. *Social Movements and the Legal System.* San Diego: Academic Press.

Hansen, J. L. 2004. "MAD in a Hurry: The Swift and Promising Adoption of the EU Market Abuse Directive." *European Business Law Review* 15: 183–221.

Harbour, Lawrence. 2003. "Representative Actions in Europe: Access to Justice?" *Class Action Litigation Report* (BNA) 4 (12): 474–477.

Hardach, K. 1980. *The Political Economy of Germany in the Twentieth Century.* Berkeley: University of California Press.

Harding, Christopher. 1980. "The Private Interest in Challenging Community Action." *European Law Review* 5: 354–361.

———. 1992. "Who Goes to Court in Europe?" *European Law Review* 2: 105–125.

Harding, Christopher, and Julian Joshua. 2003. *Regulating Cartels in Europe: A Study of Legal Control of Corporate Delinquency.* Oxford: Oxford University Press.

Harlow, Carol. 1998. "European Administrative Law and the Global Challenge." Working Paper 1998/23, Robert Schuman Center, European University Institute.

———. 1999. "Citizen Access to Political Power in the European Union." In EUI Working Paper RSC no. 99/2, European University Institute, San Domenico di Fiesole, Italy.

———. 2000. "A Common European Law of Remedies?" In *The Future of Remedies in Europe,* pp. 69–83, ed. Claire Kilpatrick, Tonia Novitz, and Paul Skidmore. Oxford: Hart Publishing.

———. 2002. "Public Law and Popular Justice." *Modern Law Review* 65(1): 1–18.

Harlow, Carol, and Richard Rawlings. 1992. *Pressure Through Law.* London: Routledge.

Hartnell, Helen E. 2002. "EUstitia: Institutionalizing Justice in the European Union." *Northwestern Journal of International Law and Business* 23: 65–138.

Harvey, Fiona. 2005. "Legal Action Threat over CO_2 Trading Limits." *Financial Times,* 7 January.

Hawkes, Steve. 2007. "Shell to Pay £180m to Settle Reserves Scandal. *Times Online,* April 11. Available at http://business.timesonline.co.uk/tol/business/industry_sectors/natural_resources/article1638892.ece (accessed 20 March 2010).

Hays, Daniel. 2009. "U.K. Firms Buy Big D&O Covers as Lawsuits Increase, RMs Reveal." *National Underwriter Online News Service,* June 23. Available at www.property-casualty.com/News/2009/6/Pages/UK-Firms-Buy-Big-DO-Covers-As-Lawsuits-Increase-RMs-Reveal.aspx (accessed 20 March 2010).

Hayward, J. E. S. 1982. "Mobilizing Private Interests in the Service of Public Ambitions: The Salient Element in the Dual French Policy Style." In *Policy Styles in Western Europe,* pp. 342–366, ed. Richardson. London: Allen and Unwin.

Head of Litigation Unit, OFT. 2007. Interview. London. 5 February

Head of Policy and Campaigns, Mencap. 2007. Interview. London. August 6.

Hempel, Rolf. 2002. *Privater Rechtschutz im Kartellrecht—eine Rechtsvergleichende Analyse.* Baden-Baden: Nomos Verlag.

———. 2004. Privater Rechtschutz im deutschen Kartellrecht nach der 7. GWB-Novelle. Wirtschaft und Wettbewerb. 54(4): 362–374.

Hendriks, Aart. 2005. "Promoting Disability Equality after the Treaty of Amsterdam." In *Disability Rights in Europe: From Theory to Practice,* pp. 187–196, ed. A. Lawson and C. Gooding. Oxford: Hart Publishing.

Henkin, Louis. 1990. *The Age of Rights.* New York: Columbia University Press.

Hensler, Deborah. 2000. *Class Action Dilemmas.* Santa Monica: RAND.

———. 2001. "Revisiting the Monster: New Myths and Realities of Class Action and Other Large Scale Litigation." *Duke Journal of International and Comparative Law* 11: 179-X.

Hensler, Deborah R., Christopher Hodges, and Magdalena Tulibacka, eds. 2009. *The Globalization of Class Actions.* Sage Publications.

Henssler, Martin, and Laurel S. Terry. 2001. "Lawyers Without Frontiers—a View From Germany." *Dickinson Journal of International Law* 19: 269–308.

Héritier, Adrienne. 2001. *New Modes of Governance in Europe.* Bonn: Max-Planck Project Group.

———. 2002. "New Modes of Governance in Europe: Policy-Making without Legislating?" In *Common Goods: Reinventing European and International Governance,* pp. 185-206, ed. A. Héritier. Lanham: Rowman and Littlefield.

Herman, Michael. 2008. "ECJ Tax Ruling Threatens London Stock Markets." *Times Online,* 14 May.

Hertig, Gerard, and Reuben Lee. 2003. "Four Predictions about the Future of EU Securities Regulation." *Journal of Corporate Legal Studies* 3: 359–377.

Hervey, Tamara K., and Jeff Kenner. 2003. *Economic and Social Rights under the EU Charter of Fundamental Rights.* Oxford: Hart Publishing.

Hervey, Tamara K., and Jean Vanessa McHale. 2004. *Health Law and the European Union.* New York: Cambridge University Press.

Heyer, Katharina C. 2002. "The ADA on the Road: Disability Rights in Germany." *Law and Social Inquiry* 27: 723, 725.

Hilson, Chris. 2002. "New Social Movements: The Role of Legal Opportunity." *Journal of European Public Policy* 9(2): 238–255.

———. 2004. "What's in a Right? The Relationship between Community, Fundamental and Citizenship Rights in EU Law." *European Law Review* 29(5): 636–651.

———. 2007. "Legitimacy and Rights in the EU." *Journal of European Public Policy* 14(4): 527–543.

Himsworth, Christopher. 1997. "Things Fall Apart: The Harmonization of Community Judicial Procedural Protection Revisted." *European Law Review* 22: 291–311.

Hirsch, Afua. 2008. "Woman Forced to Quit Job Wins New Rights for Carers." *Guardian,* 28 November.

Hirschl, R. 2004a. "The Political Origins of the New Constitutionalism." *Indiana Journal of Global Legal Studies* 11(1): 71–108.

———. 2004b. *Towards Juristocracy: The Origins and Consequences of the New Constitutionalism.* Cambridge, Mass.: Harvard University Press.

———. 2008a. "The Judicialization of Mega-politics." *Annual Review of Political Science* 11: 93–118.

———. 2008b. "The Judicialization of Politics." In *The Oxford Handbook of Law and Politics,* pp. 119–141, ed. K. Whittington and G. Calderia. Oxford: Oxford University Press.

HM Treasury, Financial Services Authority and Bank of England. 2003. *The EU Financial Services Action Plan: A Guide.* London: HM Treasury and FSA. Available at www.fsa.gov.uk/pubs/other/fsap_guide.pdf (accessed 5 October 2010).

———. 2004. The *EU Financial Services Action Plan: Delivering the FSAP in the UK.* London: HM Treasury and FSA. Available at www.fsa.gov.uk/pubs/other/deliver_fsap.pdf (accessed 5 October 2010).

HM Treasury and Financial Services Authority. 2004. *UK Implementation of the EU Market Abuse Directive—a Consultation Document.* London: HM Treasury and FSA. Available at www.hm-treasury.gov.uk/consult_market_index.htm (accessed 5 October 2010).

Hodges, Christopher. 2001. "Multi-party Actions: A European Approach" *Duke Journal of International and Comparative Law* 11: 321–354.

———. 2006. "Competition Enforcement, Regulation and Civil Justice: What Is the Case?" *Common Market Law Review* 43(5): 1381–1407.

———. 2007. "Europeanization of Civil Justice: Trends and Issues." *Civil Justice Quarterly* 26: 96–123.

———. 2008. *The Reform of Class and Representative Actions in European Legal Systems: A New Framework for Collective Redress in Europe.* Oxford: Hart Publishing.

———. 2009a. "England and Wales." Annals of the American Academy of Political and Social Science 622: 105–113.

———. 2009b. "European Union Legislation." *Annals of the American Academy of Political and Social Science* 622: 78–85.

———. 2009c. "From Class Actions to Collective Redress: A Revolution in Approach to Compensation." *Civil Justice Quarterly* 1: 41–66.

———. 2009d. "Europe: Part 1." In *Lawsuit! Reducing the Risk of Product Liability for Manufacturers,* pp.71–75, ed. R. Goodden. Hoboken, NJ: Wiley.

Hodson, D. 2004. "Macroeconomic Co-ordination in the Euro Area: The Scope and Open Limits of the Open Method." *Journal of European Public Policy* 11(2): 231–248.

Hoffmann, Dietrich, and Stefan Schaub. 1983. *The German Competition Law.* Deventer: Kluwer Law and Taxation Publishers.

Hofman, Herwig. 2006. "Negotiated and Non-negotiated Administrative Rule-Making: The Example of EC Competition Policy." *Common Market Law Review* 43(1): 153–178.

Holland, Kenneth, ed. 1991. *Judicial Activism in Comparative Perspective.* New York: St. Martin's Press.

Hollinger, Peggy. 2005. "France Mulls Allowing Class-Action Lawsuits." *Financial Times,* 7 January.

Holtmaat, Rikki. 2009. Report on Measures to Combat Discrimination—Directives 2000/43/EC and 2000/78/EC: Country Report 2008 The Netherlands. Prepared for European Network of Legal Experts in the Non-discrimination Field. Available at http://www.non-discrimination.net/

Holzinger, Katharina, Christoph Knill, and Andrea Lenschow. 2009. "Governance in EU Environmental Policy." In *Innovative Governance in the European Union,* pp. 45–62, ed. Ingeborg Tömmel and Amy Verdun. Boulder: Lynne Rienner.

Holzinger, Katharina, Christoph Knill, and Ansgar Schäfer. 2006. "Rhetoric or Reality? 'New Governance' in EU Environmental Policy." *European Law Journal* 12(3): 403–420.

Horn, Murray. 1995. *The Political Economy of Public Administration: Institutional Choice in the Public Sector.* Cambridge: Cambridge University Press.

House of Commons Constitutional Affairs Committee. 2006. *Compensation Culture, Third Report of Session 2005-2006.* London: The Stationery Office Limited.

Howell, Kerry. 2004. "Uploading, Downloading, and European Integration: Assessing the Europeanisation of UK Financial Services Regulation." *Journal of Banking Regulation* 6: 53–68.

Howlett, Michael, and M. Ramesh. 2003. *Studying Public Policy: Policy Cycles and Policy Subsystems,* 2nd ed. Toronto: Oxford University Press.

Human Rights Barrister, Matrix Chambers. 2007. Interview. London. 8 August.

Hvinden, Björn. 2003. "The Uncertain Convergence of Disability Policies in Western Europe." *Social Policy and Administration* 37(6): 609–624.

Idema, Timo, and R. Daniel Kelemen. 2006. "New Modes of Governance, the Open Method of Coordination and Other Fashionable Red Herring." *Perspectives on European Politics and Society* 7(1): 108–123.

Inter-institutional Monitoring Group. 2007. "Financial Report Monitoring the Lamfalussy Process." Brussels, October 15. Available at http://ec.europa.eu/internal_market/finances/docs/committees/071015_final_report_en.pdf. (accessed 11 February 2010).

Interrights. 2003. *Strategic Litigation of Race Discrimination in Europe: From Principles to Practice.* London: Interrights.

Interrights Legal Director. 2007. Interview. London, 6 July.

Jabko, Nicholas. 2006. *Playing the Market: A Political Strategy for Uniting Europe, 1985–2005.* Ithaca: Cornell University Press.

Jackson, Howell, and Eric Pan. 2001. "Regulatory Competition in International Securities Markets: Evidence from Europe in 1999—Part I." *Business Lawyer* 56: 653–695.

Jackson, Rupert. 2010. *Review of Civil Litigation Costs: Final Report ("The Jackson Costs Review"); Report Prepared for the Ministry of Justice.* London: HM Stationery Office.

Jacob, Herbert. 1997. "Introduction." In *Courts, Law, and Politics in Comparative Perspective,* pp. 1–15, ed. H. Jacob, E. Blankenburg, H. M. Kritzer, D. M. Provine, and J. Sanders. New Haven: Yale University Press.

Jacobs, Francis. 2007. "Citizenship of the European Union—a Legal Analysis." *European Law Journal* 13(5): 591–610.

Jacobsson, K. 2003. "Soft Regulation and the Subtle Transformation of States: The Case of EU Employment Policy." Paper presented at a seminar on the Open Method of Coordination, Minda de Gunzburg Center for European Studies, Harvard University, Cambridge, Mass.

———. 2004. "Soft Regulation and the Subtle Transformation of States: The Case of EU Employment Policy." *Journal of European Social Policy* 14(4): 355–370.

Jacoby, Mary. 2005. "Courting Abroad: For the Tort Bar, A New Client Base; European Investors." *Wall Street Journal,* 2 September.

Jahn, Joachim. 2007. "Furcht vor Sammelklagen und Erfolgshonoraren" [Fear of Group Actions and Success Fees]. *Frankfurter Allgemeine Zeitung,* June 19. Available at www.faz.net (accessed).

Jans, Jan. 2007. "The Effect in National Legal Systems of the Prohibition of Discrimination on the Ground of Age as a General Principle of Community Law." *Legal Issues of Economic Integration* 34(1): 53–66.

Jasanoff, Sheila. 1986. *Risk Management and Political Culture.* New York: Russell Sage Foundation.

Jennings, Richard, Harold Marsh, John C. Coffee, and Joel Seligman, eds. 1998. *Securities Regulation, Cases and Materials,* 8th ed. New York: Foundation Press.

Jenny, Frederic. 1990. "French Competition Policy in Perspective." In *Competition Policy in Europe and North America,* pp. 146–188, ed. W. S. Comanor. New York: Harwood Academic Publishers.

———. 1997. "France: 1987–94." In *Global Competition Policy,* pp. 87–114, ed. E. Graham and J. D. Richardson. Washington: Institute for International Economics.

Johnson, Justice Earl, Jr. 2000. "Equal Access to Justice: Comparing Access to

Justice in the United States and Other Industrial Democracies." *Fordham International Law Journal* 24: 83–110.

Jolivet, Annie. 2004. "Réformes en cours en faveur des personnes handicapées." Working Paper FR0403106F, European Industrial Relations Observatory 30 March. Available at http://eurofound.europa.eu/ (accessed 7 October 2010).

Jolowicz, Tony. 1994. Introduction to *Approximation of Judiciary Law in the European Union (The Storme Report),* ed. Maurice Storme. Dordrecht: K. Kluwer and Martinus Nijhoff.

Joshua, Julian. 2002. "A Sherman Act Bridgehead in Europe, or a Ghost Ship in Mid-Atlantic? A Close Look at the United Kingdom Proposals to Criminalise Hardcore Cartel Conduct." *European Competition Law Review* 23(5): 231–245.

Judicial Advisor, Equal Treatment Commission. 2006. Interview. Utrecht, the Netherlands. 13 December.

Jung, Peter. 2004. *Die Reform der Durchsetzung des Wettbewerbsrechts—Deutscher Landesbericht.* 21st Congress of the Fédération internationale de droit européen (hereafter, FIDE). Dublin, Ireland.

Jupille, Joseph. 2004. *Procedural Politics: Issues, Influence, and Institutional Choice in the European Union.* New York: Cambridge University Press.

Kaczorowska, Alina. 2006. "A Review of the Creation by the European Court of Justice of the Right to Effective and Speedy Medical Treatment and Its Outcomes." *European Law Journal* 12(3): 345–370.

Kagan, Robert. 1994. "Do Lawyers Cause Adversarial Legalism? A Preliminary Inquiry." *Law and Social Inquiry* 19(1): 1–62.

———. 1997. "Should Europe Worry about Adversarial Legalism?" *Oxford Journal of Legal Studies* 17(2): 165.

———. 2001. *Adversarial Legalism: The American Way of Law.* Cambridge, Mass.: Harvard University Press.

———. 2006. "American and European Ways of Law: Six Entrenched Differences." University of California, Berkeley, Institute of European Studies. Available at http://escholarship.org/uc/item/3Kt912b3 (accessed 7 October 2010).

———. 2007. "Globalization and legal change: The "Americanization of European law?" *Regulation & Governance* 1(2): 99–120.

———. 2008. "The 'Non-Americanization' of European Law." *European Political Science* 7: 21–31.

Kagan, Robert A., and Lee Axelrad, eds. 2000. *Regulatory Encounters: Multinational Corporations and American Adversarial Legalism.* Berkeley: University of California Press.

Kahn-Freund, Otto. 1974. "On the Uses and Misuses of Comparative Law." *Modern Law Review* 37(1): 1–27.

Karmel, Roberta S. 1982. *Regulation by Prosecution: The Securities and Exchange Commission versus Corporate America.* New York: Simon and Schuster.

———. 1999. "The Case for a European Securities Commission." *Columbia Journal of Transnational Law* 38: 9–43.

Karsten, Jens. 2007. "Passengers, Consumers and Travelers: The Rise of Passenger Rights in EC Transport Law and Its Repercussions for Community Consumer Law and Policy." *Journal of Consumer Policy* 30: 117–136.

Kassim, H. 2007. "Revisiting Competition Policy Reform: The European Commission and Policy Change." Paper given to a Competition Policy Workshop, University of Exeter, February.

Katz, Ellis, and G. Alan Tarr, eds. 1996. *Federalism and Rights.* Lanham, Md.: Rowman and Littlefield Publishers.

Kelemen, R. Daniel. 2002. "Survey of European Union Interest Groups." Results on file with Author and with Princeton University Survey Research Center.

———. 2003. "The EU Rights Revolution: Adversarial Legalism and European Integration." In *The State of the European Union,* vol. 6, *Law, Politics and Society,* pp. 221–234, ed. T. Börzel and R. Cichowski. Oxford: Oxford University Press.

———. 2004a. *The Rules of Federalism: Institutions and Regulatory Politics in the EU and Beyond.* Cambridge, Mass.: Harvard University Press.

———. 2004b. "The Politics of Environmental Policy in the US and EU: Coercive Federalism?" In *Trans-Atlantic Policymaking in an Age of Austerity,* pp. 203-223, ed. M. Levin, M. Landy and M. Shapiro. Washington DC: Georgetown University Press.

———. 2005. "The Politics of Eurocracy: Building a New European State?" In *The State of the European Union, (Vol. 7) With US or Against US?,* ed.,N. Jabko and C. Parsons. Oxford: Oxford University Press.

———. 2006. "Suing for Europe: Adversarial Legalism and European Governance." *Comparative Political Studies* 39(1): 101–127.

———. 2008. "The Americanisation of European Law? Adversarial Legalism *à La Européenne." European Political Science* 7: 32–42.

Kelemen, R. Daniel, and Anand Menon. 2007. "The Politics of EC Regulation." In *Better Regulation,* pp. 175–189, ed. S. Weatherill. Oxford: Hart Publishing.

Kelemen, R. Daniel, and Eric C. Sibbitt. 2004. "The Globalization of American Law." *International Organization* 58(1): 103–136.

———. 2005. "Lex Americana? A Response to Levi-Faur." *International Organization* 59(2): 463–472.

Kelman, Steven. 1981. *Regulating America, Regulating Sweden: A Comparative Study of Occupational Safety and Health Policy*. Cambridge, Mass.: MIT Press.

Kilian, Matthias. 2003. "Alternatives to Public Provision: The Role of Legal Expenses Insurance in Broadening Access to Justice: The German Experience." *Journal of Law and Society* 30: 31–48.

Kilian, Matthias, and Francis Regan. 2004. "Legal Aid and Legal Expenses Insurance: Two Sides of the Same Coin? The Experience from Germany and Sweden." *International Journal of the Legal Profession* 11: 233.

Kilpatrick, Claire. 2000. "The Future of Remedies in Europe." In *The Future of Remedies in Europe*, pp. 1–34, ed. Claire Kilpatrick, Tonia Novitz, and Paul Skidmore. Oxford: Hart Publishing.

Kilpatrick, Claire, Tonia Novitz, and Paul Skidmore. 2000. *The Future of Remedies in Europe*. Oxford: Hart Publishing.

Kissane, Mary. 1997. "Global Gadflies: Applications and Implications of US-style Corporate Governance Abroad." *New York Law Journal of International and Comparative Law* 17: 621–675.

Kitschelt, Herbert, Peter Lange, Gary Marks, and John D. Stephens, eds. 1999. *Continuity and Change in Contemporary Capitalism*. Cambridge: Cambridge University Press.

Klees, Andreas. 2006. "Breaking the Habits: The German Competition Law after the 7th Amendment to the Act against Restraints of Competition (GWB)." *German Law Journal* 7(4): 399–420.

Knill, Christoph. 1998. "Implementing European Policies: The Impact of National Administrative Traditions." *Journal of Public Policy* 18(1): 1–28.

Knill, Christoph, and Dirk Lehmkuhl. 2002. "The National Impact of European Union Regulatory Policy: Three Europeanization Mechanisms." *European Journal of Political Research* 41(2): 255–280.

Koch, Bernhard, and Helmut Koziol, eds. 2003. *Compensation for Personal Injury in a Comparative Perspective*. Vienna: Springer Verlag.

Kohler-Koch, Beate, and Rainer Eising, eds. 1999. *The Transformation of Governance in the European Union*. London: Routledge.

Kohler-Koch, Beate, and B. Rittberger. 2006. "Review Article: The 'Governance Turn' in EU Studies." Annual Review, *Journal of Common Market Studies* 44: 27–49.

Komninos, Assimakis. 2002. "New Prospects for Private Enforcement of EC Competition Law: *Courage v. Crehan* and the Community Right to Damages." *Common Market Law Review* 39: 447.

———. 2006. "Public and Private Antitrust Enforcement in Europe: Complement? Overlap?" *Competition Law Review* 3(1): 5–26.

———. 2007. "Effect of Commission Decisions on Private Antitrust Litigation: Setting the Story Straight." *Common Market Law Review* 44(5): 1387–1428.

Kritzer, Herbert M. 1990. *The Justice Broker.* Oxford: Oxford University Press.

———. 2001. "Litigation." In *International Encyclopedia of the Social and Behavior Sciences,* pp. 8989–8995. Amsterdam: Elgevier.

———. 2002a. "Lawyer Fees and Lawyer Behavior in Litigation." *Texas Law Review* 80: 1943–1983.

———. 2002b. "Seven Dogged Myths Concerning Contingency Fees." *Washington University Law Quarterly* 80: 739–794.

———. 2004. *Risks, Reputations and Rewards: Contingency Fee Legal Practice in the United States.* Stanford: Stanford University Press.

Kroes, N. 2005a. "Enhancing Actions for Damages for Breach of Competition Rules in Europe," Speech/05/533. Dinner speech at the Harvard Club, New York, September 22. Available at http://ec.europa.eu/competition/speeches/ (accessed 5, October 2010).

———. 2005b. "Taking Competition Seriously—Anti-Trust Reform in Europe." Speech 05/157. Paper presented at International Bar Association/European Commission Conference, Brussels, March 10. Available at http://ec.europa.eu/competition/speeches/ (accessed 5 October 2010).

Kruthaup, Kristen. 2009. "Formelsprache: Leider müssen wir Ihnen mitteilen. . . ." *Frankfurter Allgemeine Zeitung,* 30 January. Available at www.faz.net (accessed 20 February 2010).

Kuhr, Daniela. 2008. "Das Überforderte Recht." *Süddeutsche Zeitung,* 7 April. Available at www.sueddeutsche.de/wirtschaft/640/438384/text (accessed 20 February 2010).

Lamfulussy, Alexandre. 2001. "Final Report of the Committee of Wise Men on the Regulation of European Securities Markets February 2001—'the Lamfalussy Report.'" Brussels, 15 February.

Landfried, Christine. 1994. "The Judicialization of Politics in Germany." *International Political Science Review* 15: 113–124.

Langer, Maximo. 2004. "From Legal Transplants to Legal Translations: The Globalization of Plea Bargaining and the Americanization Thesis in Criminal Procedure." *Harvard International Law Journal* 45(1): 1–64.

Langevoort, Donald. 2005. "Structuring Securities Regulation in the European Union: Lessons from the US Experience." Law Working Paper no. 41/2005, European Corporate Governance Institute. Available at http://papers.ssrn.com/ (accessed 5 October 2010).

Lannoo, Karel. 2001. *Updating EU Securities Market Regulation: Adapting to the Needs of a Single Capital Market.* Financial Markets CEPS Task Force Reports. Brussels: Centre for European Policy Studies.

———. 2002. "Supervising the European Financial System." CEPS Policy Brief No. 21/May 2002. Brussels: Centre for European Policy Studies.

———. 2007. "MiFID: A Regulatory Doomsday?" CEPS Commentary 10 January 2007. Brussels: Centre for European Policy Studies.

Lannoo, Karel, and Matthias Levin. 2004. *Securities Market Regulation in the EU: Everything You Always Wanted to Know About the Lamfalussy Procedures.* Brussels: Centre for European Policy Studies.

La Porta, R., F. Lopez-de-Silanes, and A. Shleifer. 2006. "What Works in Securities Laws?" *Journal of Finance* 61(1): 1–32.

La Porta, R., F. Lopez-de-Silanes, A. Shleifer, and R. W. Vishny. 1997. "Legal Determinants of External Finance." *Journal of Finance* 52(3): 1131–1150.

———. 1998. "Law and Finance." *Journal of Political Economy* 106(6): 1113–1155.

Lasserre, Bruno. 2009. "The New French Competition Law Enforcement Regime." *Competition Law International* 5(3): 15–20.

Latraverse, Sophie. 2007. *Report on Measures to Combat Discrimination, Directives 2000/43/EC and 2000/78/EC, Country Report 2006 France.* Prepared for European Network of Legal Experts in the Non-discrimination Field. Available at http://www.non-discrimination.net (accessed Oct. 6, 2010).

———. 2008. Report on Measures to Combat Discrimination – Directives 2000/43/EC and 2000/78/EC: Country Report 2007 France. Prepared for European Network of Legal Experts in the Nondiscrimination Field. Available at http://www.non-discrimination.net/

Laudati, Laraine L. 1998. "Impact of Community Competition Policy on Member State Competition Law." In *Competition Policies in Europe,* pp. 381–410, ed. S. Martin. Amsterdam: Elsevier.

Laurance, Jeremy. 2006. "European Court Paves Way for Health Tourism," *Independent,* 17 May.

Laurence, Henry. 2001. *Money Rules: The New Politics of Finance in Britain and Japan.* Ithaca: Cornell University Press.

Law Society of England and Wales. 2005. *The Law Society of England and Wales' Response to the European Commission Green Paper on Financial Services Policy (2005–2010).* Brussels: European Commission, DG Internal Market.

Lawson, Anna. 2006. "The EU Rights-based Approach to Disability: Some Strategies for Shaping an Inclusive Society." GLADNET Collection Working Paper, Industrial and Labor Relations School, Cornell University,

Ithaca, N.Y. Available at http://digitalcommons.ilr.cornell.edu (accessed 10 March 2010).

Lawson, Anna, and Carole Gooding. 2005. *Disability Rights in Europe: From Theory to Practice.* Oxford: Hart Publishing.

Le Bris-Munch, Florence (associate of Classaction.fr). 2006. Interview. 19 December. Paris, France.

Legal Director FCU (Legal Director of the French Consumer's Union–UFC Que Choisir). 2006. Interview. Paris 18 December.

Legrand, P. 1996. "European Legal Systems Are Not Converging." *International and Comparative Law Quarterly* 45: 52–81.

Lehmbruch, Gerhard, and Philippe C. Schmitter. 1982. *Patterns of Corporatist Policy-Making.* London: Sage Publications.

Lehmkuhl, Dirk. 2008. "On Government, Governance and Judicial Review: The Case of European Competition Policy." Special Issue of *Journal of Public Policy* 28(1): 139–59.

———. 2009. "Cooperation and Hierarchy in EU Competition Policy." In *Innovative Governance in the European Union,* pp. 103–120, ed. I. Tömmel and A. Verdun. Boulder: Lynne Rienner.

Lenaerts, Koen. 2007. "The Rule of Law and the Coherence of the Judicial System of the European Union." *Common Market Law Review* 44(6): 1625–1659.

Lenaerts, Koen, and J. Vanhamme. 1997. "Procedural Rights of Private Parties in the Community Administrative Process." *Common Market Law Review* 34: 531.

Lester, Anthony. 1988. "The Overseas Trade in the American Bill of Rights." *Columbia Law Review* 88(3): 537–561.

Levi-Faur, David. 2005. "The Political Economy of Legal Globalization: Juridification, Adversarial Legalism and Responsive Regulation; A Comment." *International Organization* 59(2): 473–484.

Lévy, Marc, and Natasha Assadi-Tardif. 2009. "Cartel Regulation under French Law: A Pragmatic Approach." *European Antitrust Review.* London: Law Business Research. Global Competition Review / SJ Berwin. Available at www.globalcompetitionreview.com (accessed 20 February 2010).

———. 2010. "France." In *The International Comparative Legal Guide to Competition Litigation—2010,* London: Global Legal Group.

Lijphart, Arend. 1975. *The Politics of Accommodation.* Berkeley: University of California Press.

———. 1999. *Patterns of Democracy.* New Haven: Yale University Press

Lindblom, Per Henrik. 2009. "Sweden." *Annals of the American Academy of Political and Social Science* 622: 231–241.

Lipset, Seymour Martin. 1996. *American Excpeptionalism: A Double-Edged Sword.* New York: Norton.

Lloyd's (Lloyd's of London). 2008a. *Directors in the Dock: Report Prepared for Lloyd's by the Economist Intelligence Unit.* London: Lloyd's of London.

———. 2008b. *Litigation and Business: Transatlantic Trends; Report Prepared by Rand Europe for Lloyd's of London.* London: Lloyd's of London.

Longstreth, Andrew. 2009. "Extremely Rare F-Cubed Securities Class Action Trial to Start Against Vivendi." *American Lawyer,* 7 October. Available at www.law.com (accessed 20 March 2010).

Luhmann, Niklas. 1985. *A Sociological Theory of Law.* London: Routledge and Kegan Paul.

Luke, Antje. 2004. *Private Enforcement in the Field of Competition Law: French National Report.* 48th Congress of Competition Law Commission. Geneva, Switzerland, 1–5 September.

Lütz, Susanne. 1998. "The Revival of the Nation State? Stock Exchange Regulation in an Era of Globalized Financial Markets." *Journal of European Public Policy* 5(1): 153–168.

———. 2002. *Der Staat und die Globalisierung von Finanzmärkten: Regulative Politik in Deutschland, Großbritannien und den USA.* Frankfurt: Campus Verlag.

Maas, Willem. "The Genesis of European Rights." *Journal of Common Market Studies* 43(5): 1009–25.

Mabbett, Deborah. 2005. "The Development of Rights-Based Social Policy in the European Union." *Journal of Common Market Studies* 43(1): 97–120.

Macalister, Terry. 2004. "Trail of Emails Reveals Depths of Deceit at the Heart of Shell." *Guardian,* 20 April. Available at www.guardian.co.uk (accessed 21 March 2010).

Mace, Myles L. 1991. "The Take-over Directive." In *Law Society Standing Committee on Company Law Conference,* November, p. 2. Cited in Mads Andenas and Stephen Kenyon-Slade, eds. 1993. *EC Financial Market Regulation and Company Law.* London: Sweet and Maxwell. p. 149.

MacLachlan, D., and D. Swann. 1967. *Competition Policy in the European Community.* Oxford: Oxford University Press.

Magee, Stephen P. 1989. "The Optimum Number of Lawyers: Cross-National Estimates." *Law and Social Inquiry* 17(4): 667–693.

Magnier, Veronique. 2009. "France." *Annals of the American Academy of Political and Social Science* 622: 114–124.

Maher, Imelda. 1997. "Alignment of Competition Laws in the European Community." *Yearbook of European Law 1996* 16: 223–242.

Mahlmann, Matthias. 2008. Report on Measures to Combat Discrimination—Directives 2000/43/EC and 2000/78/EC: Country Report 2007 Germany.

Prepared for European Network of Legal Experts in the Nondiscrimination Field. Available at *http://www.non-discrimination.net/* (accessed Oct. 6 2010).

———. 2009. Report on Measures to Combat Discrimination—Directives 2000/43/EC and 2000/78/EC: Country Report 2008 Germany. Prepared for European Network of Legal Experts in the Nondiscrimination Field. Available at http://www.non-discrimination.net/ (accessed Oct. 6 2010).

Mahoney, James, and Kathleen Thelen, eds. 2010. *Explaining Institutional Change: Ambiguity, Agency, and Power.* Cambridge: Cambridge University Press.

Majone, Giandomenico. 1991. "Cross-National Sources of Regulatory Policymaking in Europe and the United States." *Journal of Public Policy* 2(1): 79–106.

———. 1993. "The European Community between Social Policy and Social Regulation." *Journal of Common Market Studies* 31(2): 153–170.

———. 1994. "The Rise of the Regulatory State in Europe." *West European Politics* 17(3): 78–102.

———. 1995. "Mutual Trust, Credible Commitments, and the Evolution of Rules for a Single European Market." EUI Working Paper RSC 95/1. European University Institute, Florence, Italy.

———. 1996. *Regulating Europe.* London: Routledge Press.

———. 1998. "Europe's 'Democratic Deficit': The Question of Standards." *European Law Journal* 4(1): 5–28.

———. 2008. "The European Community between Social Policy and Social Regulation." *Journal of Common Market Studies* 31(2): 153–170.

Malisoff, Harry. 1952. "The British Disabled Persons (Employment) Act." *Industrial and Labor Relations Review* 5(2): 249–257.

Mancini, Federico, and David Keeling. 1994. "Democracy and the European Court of Justice." *Modern Law Review* 57(2): 175–190.

Manfredi, Christopher. 2001. *Judicial Power and the Charter: Canada and the Paradox of Liberal Constitutionalism,* 2nd ed. Toronto: Oxford University Press.

Manzano, J. P. 2007. "La UE concluye que una empresa puede jubilar de manera forzosa a los 65 años" [The EU Concludes That a Business Can Force 65-Year-Olds to Retire]. *El Mundo* 17 October.

Martin, Eric. 2007. "Liberalization and Cravathism: How Liberalization Triggered the Reorganization of the Legal Profession in Germany and Japan." *Stanford Journal of International Law* 43: 169–199.

Martin, Lisa. 1992. "Interests, Power, and Multilateralism." *International Organization* 46(4): 765–792.

Martin, Stephen, ed. 1998. *Competition Policies in Europe.* Amsterdam: Elsevier.

Mass, Willem. 2005. "The Genesis of European Rights." *Journal of Common Market Studies* 43(5): 1009–1025.

Mattei, Ugo. 1994. "Why the Wind Changed: Intellectual Leadership in Western Law." *American Journal of Comparative Law* 42(1): 195–218.

Mattli, Walter, and Anne-Marie Slaughter. 1995. "Law and Politics in the European Union: A Reply to Garrett." *International Organization,* 49(1): 183–190.

———. 1998. "Revisiting the European Court of Justice." *International Organization,* 52(1): 177–209.

McCann, Michael. 2006. "Law and Social Movements: Contemporary Perspectives." *Annual Review of Law and Social Science* 2: 17–38.

McCrudden, Christopher. 2001. "The Future of the EU Charter of Fundamental Rights." Jean Monnet Working Paper no. 10/01, Jean Monnet Center, New York University School of Law..

McCubbins, Matthew D., Roger G. Noll, and Barry R. Weingast. 1987. "Administrative Procedures as Instruments of Political Control. *Journal of Law, Economics, and Organization* 3(2): 243–277.

———. 1999. "The Political Origins of the Administrative Procedure Act. *Journal of Law, Economics, and Organization* 15(1): 180–217.

McGowan, Lee. 2000. "Competition Policy: The Limits of the European Regulatory State." In *Policy-Making in the European Union,* pp. 115–197. ed. H. Wallace and W. Wallace.

———. 2005. "Europeanization Unleashed and Rebounding: Assessing the Modernization of EU Cartel Policy." *Journal of European Public Policy* 12(6): 986–1004.

McGowan, Lee, and Michelle Cini. 1999. "Discretion and Politicization in EU Competition Policy: The Case of Merger Control." *Governance* 12(2): 175–200.

McGowan, Lee, and Stephen Wilks. 1995. "The First Supranational Policy in the European Union: Competition Policy." *European Journal of Political Research* 28(2): 141–169.

McGuinness, Christine. 1988. "Toward the Unification of European Capital Markets: The EEC's Proposed Directive on Insider Trading." *Fordham International Law Journal* 11: 432–452.

McIntosh, David, and Marjorie Holmes, eds. 2003. *Personal Injury Awards in EU and EFTA Countries.* Deventer: Kluwer Law International.

McLachlan, D., and D. Swan. 1963. "Competition Policy in the Common Market." *Economist Journal* 73(289): 54–79.

MEDEF (Mouvement des Entreprises de France). 2008. Telephone interview. Paris 9 October.

Melnick, R. Shep. 1996. "Federalism and the New Rights." *Yale Law and Policy Review* 14: 325–354.

Menéndez, Agustín José. 2002. "Chartering Europe: Legal Status and Policy Implications of the Charter of Fundamental Rights of the European Union." *Journal of Common Market Studies* 40(3): 471–490.

Mercer, Helen. 1995. *Constructing a Competitive Order: The Hidden History of British Antitrust Policies.* Cambridge: Cambridge University Press.

Merle, Philippe. 2005. *Droit des Sociétés,* 10th ed. Paris: Hachette.

Meyer, John, John Boli, George Thomas, and Francisco Ramirez. 1997. "World Society and the Nation-State." *American Journal of Sociology* 103(1): 144–181.

Mezey, Susan G. 2005. *Disabling Interpretations: The Americans with Disabilities Act in Federal Court.* Pittsburgh: University of Pittsburgh Press.

Mill, John Stuart. 1843/2002. *A System of Logic.* Rpt., Honolulu, Hawaii: University Press of the Pacific.

Milne, Richard. 2008. "Deutsche Telekom Sued in Class Action for €80m." *Financial Times,* April 8. Available at www.ft.com (accessed 10 February 2010).

Milward, Alan S. 1992. *The European Rescue of the Nation State.* Berkeley: University of California Press.

Minder, Raphael. 2005a. "EU Airlines Counts the Cost of Compensation Confusion." *Financial Times,* 13 July.

———. 2005b. "France Fined €20million over Fish Stocks" *Financial Times,* 13 July.

———. 2006. "EU Court Dismisses Airline Challenge over Compensation." *Financial Times,* 10 January.

Mistral, Jacques. 2004. "Les défauts et les risques du système américain des 'class actions' devraient inciter à une action prevéntive pour en éviter la prolifération en Europe," Working Paper Ambassade de France aux États-Unis, Washington, DC, 3 November.

Moe, Terry. 1990. "Political Institutions: The Neglected Side of the Story." *Journal of Law, Economics, and Organization* 6: 213–254.

Moe, Terry, and Michael Caldwell. 1994. "The Institutional Foundations of Democratic Government: A Comparison of Presidential and Parliamentary Systems." *Journal of Institutional and Theoretical Economics* 150(1): 171–195.

Moloney, Niamh. 2002. *EC Securities Regulation.* Oxford: Oxford University Press.

———. 2005. "Building a Retail Investment Culture through Law: The 2004 Markets in Financial Instruments Directive." *European Business Organization Law Review* 6: 341–421.

———. 2007. "Innovation and Risk in EC Financial Market Regulation after the Financial Services Action Plan: New Instruments of Financial Market Intervention and the Committee of European Securities Regulation." *European Law Review* 32(5): 627–663.

———. 2008. *EC Securities Regulation*. Second Edition. Oxford: Oxford University Press.

Momège, Chantal, and Nicolas Bessot. 2005. *National Report: France; Ashurst Study on the Conditions of Claims for Damages in Case of Infringement of EC Competition Rules*. Brussels: DG Competition, European Commission.

Le Monde. 2007. "Les consommateurs favorables à l 'action de groupe' à la française" [Consumers in Favor of Class Actions à la *française*], 29 September.

Monti, Mario. 2001. "Effective Private Enforcement of EC Antitrust Law." Speech by Mr. Mario Monti, European Commissioner for Competition Policy, at the Sixth EU Competition Law and Policy Workshop, Florence, Italy, June 1–2. Available at http://europa.eu/competition/speeches/ (accessed 7 October 2010).

———. 2004a. "The EU Gets New Competition Powers for the 21st Century: Interview with Mario Monti, Commissioner Responsible for Competition." Special issue of *Competition Policy Newsletter*, no. 1, p.1. Available at http://ec.europa.eu/competition/publications/cpn/2004_special_edition.pdf (accessed 7 October 2010).

———. 2004b. "Private Litigation as a Key Complement to Public Enforcement of Competition Rules and the First Conclusions on the Implementation of the New Merger Regulation," Speech 04/403. Paper presented at IBA 8th Annual Competition Conference, Fiesole, Italy, 14 September. Available at http://ec.europa.eu/competition/speeches/ (accessed 7 October 2010).

Morag-Levine, N. 2003. "Partners No More: Relational Transformation and the Turn to Litigation in Two Conservationist Organizations." *Law and Society Review* 372: 457–509.

Moran, Michael. 1991. *The Politics of the Financial Services Revolution: The USA, UK, and Japan*. Basingstoke: Palgrave Macmillan.

Moravcsik, Andrew. 2002. "In Defence of the 'Democratic Deficit': Reassessing Legitimacy in the European Union." *Journal of Common Market Studies* 40(4): 603–624.

Morgan, E. J. 2001. "A Decade of Merger Control." *International Journal of the Economics of Business* 8(3): 451–473.

Morgan, E., and S. McGuire. 2004. "Transatlantic Divergence: GE-Honeywell and the EU's Merger Policy." *Journal of European Public Policy* 11(1): 39–56.

Morgan, Glenn, and Sigrid Quack. 2005. "Institutional Legacies and Firm Dynamics: The Growth and Internationalization of UK and German Law Firms." *Organization Studies* 26(12): 1765–1785.

Morris, Ben. 2005. "Competition Regulation in the United Kingdom: The Move from Administrative Flexibility to Juridification." *Revue Française d'Administration Publique* 114(2): 309–322.

Mügge, Daniel. 2006. "Reordering the Marketplace: Competition Politics in European Finance." *Journal of Common Market Studies* 44(5): 991–1022.

Mühlbach, Tatjana, and Alexander Rinne. 2010. "Germany: Private Antitrust Litigation." In *European Antitrust Review 2010,* pp. 130–134. London: Law Business Research.

National Law Journal. 1985. "The NLJ 250," September 30, pp.S4-S18.

———. 1990. "The NLJ 250," September 24, pp.S4-S22.

———. 1995. "The NLJ 250," October 9, pp.C6-C26.

———. 2000. "The NLJ 250," December 4, pp.C20-22.

———. 2005. "The NLJ 250," November 14, available at www.law.com, (accessed 15 October 2009).

Neven, Damien J., Penelope Papandropoulos, and Paul Seabright. 1998. *Trawling for Minnows: European Competition Policy and Agreements between Firms.* London: Centre for Economic Policy Research.

New York Times. 2005. "Lawyers Want to Bring Class-Action Suits to France." *New York Times,* 11 November. Available at www.nyt.com (accessed 20 June 2010).

Nicol, Danny. 2001. *EC Membership and the Judicialization of British Politics.* Oxford: Oxford University Press.

Nivola, Pietro. 1997. *Comparative Disadvantages? Social Regulations and the Global Economy.* Washington D.C.: Brookings Institution Press.

OECD (Organization for Economic Cooperation and Development). 2003. *Transforming Disability into Ability: Policies to Promote Work and Income Security for Disabled People.* Paris: OECD.

Ohlendorf, Bernd, and Michael Schreier. 2008. "AGG-konformes Einstellungsverfahren—Handlungsanleitung und Praxistipps." *Betriebs Berater* 63: 2458–2565.

O'Keeffe, Siún. 2001. "First Among Equals: The Commission and the National Courts as Enforcers of EC Competition Law." *European Law Review* 26(3): 301–311.

Oliver, Michael. 1983. *Social Work with Disabled People.* Tavistock: Macmillan.

———. 1990. *The Politics of Disablement: A Sociological Approach.* New York: St. Martin's Press.

———. 1996. *Understanding Disability: From Theory to Practice.* Basingstoke: Macmillan.

ORGECO (Organisation générale des consommateurs). 2006. Interview. 19 December.

Orr, Robert. 2004. "FSA Chairman Warns against Embracing 'Litigious Society.'" *Financial Times,* 22 September.

Osborne, Alistair. 2008. "Euro Court Throws out £300m Claim by Thomas Cook." *Daily Telegraph,* Sept. 10. Available at http://www.telegraph.co.uk/ (accessed on 5 October, 2010).

Pan, Eric. 2003. "Harmonization of US-EU Securities Regulation: The Case for a Single European Securities Regulator." *Law and Policy in International Business* 34(2): 499–537.

Parker, George. 2007. "EU Considers Consumer Class Action." *Financial Times,* 4 March.

Parker, George, Tobias Buck, and Nikki Tait. 2007. "Business Warns EU against Class Actions." *Financial Times,* 13 March.

Paulis, Emil, and Eddy de Smijter. 2005. "Enhanced Enforcement of the EC Competition Rules since 1 May 2004 by the Commission and the NCAs: The Commission's View." Paper presented at the IBA Conference on the Antitrust Reform in Europe, Brussels, Belgium, 9–11 March.

Peel, Michael. 2007. "Class Action Lawsuits Could Take Root." *Financial Times,* 29 October.

Pelkmans, Jacques, and Jeane-Mey Sun. 1995. "Regulatory Competition in the Single Market." *Journal of Common Market Studies* 33(1): 67–89.

Peltzer, Martin, and Paul Scesniak. 1995. *German Securities Trade Act / Wertpapierhandelsgesetz.* Cologne: Dr. Otto Schmidt Verlag.

Petit, Nicolas, and Louise Rabeux. 2008. "Judicial Review in French Competition Law and Economic Regulation—A Post–*Commission v. Tetra Laval* Assessment." Working Paper, University of Liege. Available at SSRN: http://ssrn.com/abstract=1290143 (accessed).

Pierson, Paul. 1993. "When Effect Becomes Cause: Policy Feedback and Political Change." *World Politics* 45(4): 595–628.

———. 2004. *Politics in Time: History, Institutions, and Social Analysis.* Princeton: Princeton University Press.

Pollack, Mark. 1997. "Delegation, Agency, and Agenda Setting in the European Community." *International Organization* 51: 99–134.

———. 2008. "Discussion: The Community Method and New Modes of Governance." In *Efficient Democratic Governance in the European Union,* pp. 151–162. ed. B. Kohler-Koch and F. Larat. CONNEX Report series No. 9, University of Mannheim. Available at http://www.connex-network.org/ (Accessed 7 October 2010).

Posner, Elliot. 2009. *The Origins of Europe's New Stock Markets.* Cambridge, Mass.: Harvard University Press.

Prechal, Sacha. 1995. *Directives in EC Law.* Oxford: Oxford University Press.

———. 2005. *Directives in EC Law,* 2nd Ed. Oxford: Oxford University Press.

PricewaterhouseCoopers. 2009. *2008 Securities Litigation Study.* New York: PricewaterhouseCoopers.

Pritchard, John. 1997. *The Legal 500—Europe, Middle East, and Africa 1997.* London: Legalese.

———. 2000. The Legal 500- Europe, Middle East, and Africa 2000. London: Legalese.

———. 2004. The Legal 500- Europe, Middle East, and Africa 2004. London: Legalese.

Przeworski, Adam, and Henry Teune. 1970. *The Logic of Comparative Social Inquiry.* New York: Wiley-Interscience, Wiley and Sons.

Putnam, Robert. 1992. *Making Democracy Work.* Princeton: Princeton University Press.

Quack, Sigrid, and Marie-Laure Djelic. 2005. "Adaptation, Recombination and Reinforcement: The Story of Antitrust and Competition Law in Germany and Europe." In *Beyond Continuity: Institutional Change in Advanced Political Economies,* pp. 255–281, ed. W. Streeck and K. Thelen. Oxford: Oxford University Press.

Quaglia, L. 2007. "The Politics of Financial Services Regulation and Supervision Reform in the European Union." *European Journal of Political Research* 46(2): 269–290.

Que Choisir. 2008. *Réponse au livre blanc sur les actions en dommages et interêts pour infraction aux règles communautaires sur les ententes et les abus de position dominante.* Paris: UFC–Que Choisir.

Quinn, Gerard. 2001. "The European Union and the Council of Europe on the Issue of Human Rights: Twins Separated at Birth?" *McGill Law Journal* 46: 849–874.

Radaelli, Claudio. 2000. "Whither Europeanization? Concept Stretching and Substantive Change." European Integration Online Papers no. 8. Available at www.eiop.or.at/eiop/pdf/2000–008.pdf (accessed 20 February 2010).

———. 2003. "The Europeanization of Public Policy." In *The Politics of Europeanization,* pp. 27–56, ed. K. Featherstone and C. M. Radaelli. Oxford: Oxford University Press.

Ramseyer, J. Mark, and Frances M. Rosenbluth. 1993. *Japan's Political Marketplace.* Cambridge, Mass.: Harvard University Press.

Rasmussen, Hjalte. 2007. "Present and Future European Judicial Problems after Enlargement and the Post-2005 Ideological Revolt." *Common Market Law Review* 44(6): 1661–1687.

Rasmussen, Morten. 2008. "The Origins of a Legal Revolution—the Early History of the European Court of Justice." *Journal of European Integration History* 14(2): 77–98.

Rawlings, Richard. 1993. "The Eurolaw Game: Some Deductions from a Saga." *Journal of Law and Society* 20(3): 309–339.

Reding, John, Edward Han, and Jason Sonoda. 2009. "Approval of Class Action Settlement by the Amsterdam Court of Appeals Closes Chapter on One 'F-Cubed' Securities Litigation, but the Future of Such Actions Remains Uncertain." Paul Hastings Client Alert, June. Available at www.paulhastings.com (accessed 20 March 2010).

Regan, Francis. 1999. "Why Do Legal Aid Services Vary between Societies?" In *The Transformation of Legal Aid*, pp. 179–201, ed. F. Regan, A. Paterson, and T. Goriely. Oxford: Oxford University Press.

Regan, Francis, Alan Paterson, and Tamara Goriely, eds. 1999. *The Transformation of Legal Aid.* Oxford: Oxford University Press.

Rehder, Britta. 2007. "What Is Political about Jurisprudence? Courts, Politics and Political Science in Europe and the United States." In Discussion Paper 07/5, Max Planck Institute for the Study of Societies, Cologne, Germany.

———. 2009. "Adversarial Legalism in the German System of Industrial Relations?" *Regulation and Governance* 3(3): 217–234.

Reich, Norbert. 2005. "The 'Courage' Doctrine: Encouraging or Discouraging Compensation for Antitrust Injuries?" *Common Market Law Review* 42: 35–66.

———. 2007. "Horizontal Liability in EC Law: Hybridization of Remedies for Compensation in Case of Breaches of EC Rights." *Journal of Common Market Studies* 44(3): 705–742.

Rennie, David. 2005. "European Student Had Right to UK Loan." *Daily Telegraph,* 16 March.

Reuters Deutschland. 2009. "Rechtsstreit mit Haffas bringt Constantin 48 Mio Euro." 21 October. Available at http://de.reuters.com (accessed 7 October 2010).

Richardson, J., ed. 1982. *Policy Styles in Western Europe.* London: George Allen and Unwin.

Rickman, Neil, Paul Fenn, and Alastair Gray. 1999. "The Reform of Legal Aid in England and Wales." *Fiscal Studies* 20 (3): 261–286.

Riley, Alan. 2002. "Cartel Whistleblowing: Toward an American Model?" *Maastricht Journal of European and Comparative Law* 9: 67–102.

———. 2003. "EC Antitrust Modernisation: The Commission Does Very Nicely—Thank You! Part 1: Regulation 1 and the Notification Burden; Part 2: Between the Idea and the Reality: Decentralisation under Regulation 1." *European Competition Law Review* 24: 604–615, 657–672.

Riley, Alan, and John Peysner. 2006. "Damages in EC Antitrust Actions: Who Pays the Piper?" *European Law Review* 5: 748–761.

Roach, Kent, and Michael Trebilcock. 1996. "Private Enforcement of Competition Laws." *Osgoode Hall Law Journal* 34 (3): 461–508.

Robins, Jon. 2005. "Michael Hausfield Brings Class Actions to the UK." *Lawyer,* 24 October. Available at www.thelawyer.com (accessed 20 March 2010).

Romano, Roberta. 1998. "Empowering Investors: A Market Approach to Securities Regulation." *Yale Law Journal* 107: 2359–2679.

———. 2001. "The Need for Competition in International Securities Regulation." *Theoretical Inquiries in Law* 2: 387–562.

Roquette, A. J. 1993. "New Developments Relating to the Internationalization of the Capital Markets: A Comparison of Legislative Reforms in the United States, the European Community, and Germany." *University of Pennsylvania Journal of International Business Law* 14: 565.

Rosch, J. Thomas. 2008. "Striking a Balance? Some Reflections on Private Enforcement in Europe and the United States." Paper presented at *International Chamber of Commerce Annual Meeting.* New York, 24 September.

Rose-Ackerman, Susan. 1995. *Controlling Environmental Policy: The Limits of Public Law in Germany and the United States.* New Haven: Yale University Press.

Rouhette, Thomas. 2007. "The Availability of Punitive Damages in Europe: Growing Trend or Nonexistent Concept?" *Defense Counsel Journal* 74(4): 320–342.

Ryan, Patrick S. 2003. "Understanding Director & Officer Liability in Germany for Dissemination of False Information: Perspectives from an Outsider." *German Law Journal* 4(5): 439–475.

Sabalot, Deborah A., and Richard J. C. Everett. 2004. *The Financial Services and Markets Act.* London: LexisNexis.

Sandholtz, W., and John Zysman. 1989. "1992: Recasting the European Bargain." *World Politics* 42 (1): 95–128.

Sartori, Giovanni. 1970. "Concept Misinformation in Comparative Politics." *American Political Science Review* 64 (4): 1033–53.

Scharpf, Fritz W. 1996. "Negative and Positive Integration in the Political Economy of European Welfare States." In *Governance in the European Union,* pp. 17–39, ed. G. Marks, F. Scharpf, P. Schmitter, and W. Streeck. London: Sage.

———. 2003."Problem-solving Effectiveness and Democratic Accountability in the EU." MPIfG Working Paper 031. Cologne, Germany: Max Planck Institute for the Study of Societies.

Scheingold, Stuart. 1974. *The Politics of Rights: Lawyers, Public Policy and Political Change.* New Haven: Yale University Press.

Schepel, Harm, and Erhard Blankenburg. 2001. "Mobilizing the European Court of Justice." In *The European Court of Justice,* pp. 9–42, ed. Gráinne de Búrca and J. H. H. Weiler. Oxford: Oxford University Press.

Schickler, Eric. 2001. *Disjointed Pluralisms.* Princeton: Princeton University Press.

Schiek, Dagmar, Lisa Waddington, and Mark Bell. 2007. *Cases, Materials and Text on National, Supranational and International Non-discrimination Law.* Ius Commune Casebooks for the Common Law of Europe. Oxford: Hart Publishing.

Schimmelfennig, Frank. 2006. "Competition and Community: Constitutional Courts, Rhetorical Action, and the Institutionalization of Human Rights in the European Union." *Journal of European Public Policy* 13(8): 1247–1264.

Schlozman, Kay, and John Tierney. 1983. "More of the Same: Washington Pressure Group Activity in a Decade of Change." *Journal of Politics* 45: 351–377.

Schwarze, Hans-Joachim. 1991. "The European Insider Dealing Directive and Its Impact on the Member States, Particularly Germany." In *European Insider Dealing,* ed. Klaus Hopt and Eddy Wymeersch. London: Butterworths.

Schwarze, Jürgen. 2000. "The Convergence of the Administrative Laws of the EU Member States." In *The Europeanisation of Law,* pp. 163–182, ed. Francis Snyder.

Scott, J., and David M. Trubek. 2002. "Mind the Gap: Law and New Approaches to Governance in the European Union." *European Law Journal* 8(1): 1–18.

Scott, Peter. 2009. "A New Model for Private Damages." *Global Competition Review,* 13 October. Available at www.globalcompetitionreview.com (accessed February 20 2010).

Sellers, Jeffrey M. 1995. "Litigation as a Local Political Resource: Courts in Controversies over Land Use in France, Germany, and the United States." *Law and Society Review* 29: 475.

Senden, Linda. 2004. *Soft Law in European Community Law.* Oxford: Hart Publishing.

Senior Judicial Advisor, General Employers Organization of the Netherlands *(Algemene Werkgeversvereniging Nederland).* 2006. Interview. The Hague, the Netherlands. 15 December.

Senior Legal Policy Officer, CG-Raad. 2009. Interview. Utrecht, the Netherlands. 9 December.

Shapiro, Martin. 1981. *Courts: A Comparative and Political Analysis.* Chicago: University of Chicago Press.

———. 1993. "The Globalization of Law." *Indiana Journal of Global Studies* 1(1): 37–64.

———. 1998. "Globalization of Freedom of Contract." In *The State and the Freedom of Contract,* pp. 269–363, ed. H. Scheiber. Stanford: Stanford University Press.

———. 2001. "The Institutionalization of the European Administrative Space." In *The Institutionalization of Europe,* pp. 94–112. ed. A. Stone Sweet, W. Sandholtz, and N. Fligstein. Oxford: Oxford University Press.

———. 2004. The Institutionalization of European Administrative Space. University of California at Berkeley, Center for Culture, Organizations and Politics, Working Paper, November 10. Available at http://www.escholarship.org/uc/item/4b839871 (accessed 3 October, 2010).

———. 2005. "Rights in the European Union: Convergent with the USA?" In *State of the European Union,* vol. 7, *With US or Against US?* pp. 371–390, ed. N. Jabko and C. Parsons. Oxford: Oxford University Press.

———. 2006. "The US Supreme Court and the European Court of Justice Compared," in *Comparative Federalism,* pp. 195–220, ed. A Menon and M. Schain. Oxford: Oxford University Press.

Shapiro, Martin, and Alec Stone. 1994. "The New Constitutional Politics of Europe." *Comparative Political Studies* 26 (4): 397–420.

Shapiro, Martin, and Alec Stone Sweet. 2002. *On Law, Politics, and Judicialization.* Oxford: Oxford University Press.

Shaw, Jo. 1998. "The Interpretation of European Union Citizenship." *Modern Law Review* 61(3): 293–317.

———. 2000. *Social Law and Policy in an Evolving European Union.* Oxford: Hart Publishing.

Sherwood, Bob. 2003. "Onward and Upward: March of the New Litigation." *Financial Times,* 19 July.

———. 2005. "No Win, No Fee Deals to Be Simplified." *Financial Times,* 11 August.

Siebel, Ulf, Michael Prinz zu Löwenstein, and Robert Finney. 1995. *German Capital Market Law.* Munich: C. H. Beck Verlag.

Siedenbiedel, Christian. 2007. "Dann eben die drei Monatsgehälter." *Frankfurter Allgemeine Zeitung,* 31 January. Available at www.faz.net (accessed 20 February 2010).

Silver, Carole. 2000. "Globalization and the U.S. Market in Legal Service—Shifting Identities." *Law and Policy in International Business* 31(4): 1093–1150.

———. 2005. "Winners and Losers in the Globalization of Legal Services: Situating the Market for Foreign Lawyers." *Virginia Journal of International Law.* 45(4): 847–934.

Silvestri, Elisabetta. 2007. "Local Matters: Internationalizing Strategies of U.S. Law Firms." *Indiana Journal of Global Legal Studies* 14(1): 67–94.

———. 2009. "Italy." *Annals of the American Academy of Political and Social Science* 622: 138–148.

Simmons, Beth. 2001. "The International Politics of Harmonization: The Case of Capital Market Regulation." *International Organization* 55(3): 589–620.

Simmons, Beth, Frank Dobbin, and Geoffrey Garrett, eds. 2008. *The Global Diffusion of Markets and Democracy.* New York: Cambridge University Press.

Simmons, Beth, and Zachary Elkins. 2004. "The Globalization of Liberalization: Policy Diffusion in the International Political Economy." *American Political Science Review* 98(1): 171–189.

Skidmore, Paul. 2001. "EC Framework Directive on Equal Treatment in Employment: Towards a Comprehensive Community Anti-discrimination Policy?" *Industrial Law Journal* 30: 126–132.

Skowronek, Stephen. 1982. *Building a New American State: The Expansion of National Administrative Capacities, 1877–1920.* New York: Cambridge University Press.

Slepcevic, Reinhard. 2009. "The Judicial Enforcement of EU Law through National Courts: Possibilities and Limits." *Journal of European Public Policy* 16(3): 378–394.

Smismans, Stijn. 2008. "New Modes of Governance and the Participatory Myth." *West European Politics* 31(5): 874–895.

Smith-Hillman, A. V. 2006. "EC Approach to Governance as Applied to the Modernisation of Competition Policy." *European Business Review* 18(1): 33–49.

Snow, David, and Robert Benford. 1988. "Ideology, Frame Resonance, and Participant Mobilization." In *From Structure to Action: Social Movement Participation Across Cultures,* pp. 197–217, ed. B. Klandermans, H. Kriesi, and S. Tarrow. Greenwich, Conn.: JAI Press.

Snyder, Edward, and Thomas Kauper. 1991. "Misuse of the Antitrust Laws: The Competitor Plaintiff." *Michigan Law Review* 90(3): 551–603.

Snyder, Francis, ed. 2000. *The Europeanisation of Law: The Legal Effects of European Integration.* Oxford: Hart Publishing.

Sorge, Nils-Viktor. 2008. "Angry Shareholders Take on Deutsche Telekomin Court Showdown." *Spiegel Online,* 7 April. Available at www.spiegel.de/international/business (accessed 20 June 2010).

Souam, Saïd. 1998. "French Competition Policy." In *Competition Policies in Europe,* pp. 205–227, ed. Stephen Martin. Amsterdam: Elsevier.

Spar, Debora. 1997. "Lawyers Abroad." *California Management Review* 39(3): 8–28.

Stein, Eric. 1981. "Lawyers, Judges, and the Making of a Transnational Constitution." *American Journal of International Law* 75: 1–27.

Stichting Shell Reserves Compensation Foundation. 2009. "Amsterdam Court of Appeals Declares Shell Settlement Binding." Press Release, 29 May. Available at www.shellsettlement.com (accessed 20 June 2010).

Stone, Alec. 1992. *The Birth of Judicial Politics in France.* Oxford: Oxford University Press.

Stone Sweet, Alec. 2000. *Governing with Judges.* Oxford: Oxford University Press.

———. 2004. *The Judicial Construction of Europe.* Oxford: Oxford University Press.

Stone Sweet, Alec, and T. Brunell. 1998. "Constructing a Supranational Constitution." *American Political Science Review* 92(1): 63–81.

Storme, Marcel. 1994. *Approximation of Judiciary Law in the European Union.* Dordrecht: M. Nijhoff.

Story, Jonathan, and Ingo Walter. 1997. *Political Economy of Financial Integration in Europe: The Battle of the Systems.* Cambridge, Mass.: MIT Press.

Stout, Lynn. 2002. "The Investor Confidence Game." Research Paper no. 02–18, UCLA School of Law, Los Angeles.

Streeck, Wolfgang. 1997. "German Capitalism: Does It Exist? Can It Survive?" In *Political Economy of Modern Capitalism: Mapping Convergence and Diversity,* pp. 33–54, ed. C. Crouch and W. Streeck. London: Sage.

Streeck, Wolfgang, and Kathleen Thelen. 2005. *Beyond Continuity: Institutional Change in Advanced Political Economies.* Oxford: Oxford University Press.

Stulz, René. 2009. "Securities Laws, Disclosure, and National Capital Markets in the Age of Financial Globalization." *Journal of Accounting Research* 47(2): 349–390.

Stuyck, J., E. Terryn, and T. Van Dyck. 2006. "Confidence through Fairness? The New Directive on Unfair Business-to-Consumer Commercial Practices in the Internal Market." *Common Market Law Review* 43(1): 107–152.

Stuyck, Jules, et al. 2007. *An Analysis and Evaluation of Alternative Means of Consumer Redress Other than through Ordinary Judicial Proceedings: Final Report; A Study of the European Commission, Health and Consumer Protection Directorate-General, Directorate B–Consumer Affairs.* Louvain: Study Center for Consumer Law, Katholieke Universiteit Leuven.

Sugarman, Stephen D. 2006. "A Comparative Law Look at Pain and Suffering Awards." *DePaul Law Review* 55: 399–434.

Suleiman, Erza N. 1978. *Elites in French Society: The Politics of Survival.* Princeton: Princeton University Press.

Sun, Jeanne-Mey, and Jacques Pelkmans. 1995. "Regulatory Competition in the Single Market." *Journal of Common Market Studies* 33(1): 67–89.

Sunstein, Cass. 1990. *After the Rights Revolution: Reconceiving the Regulatory State.* Cambridge, Mass.: Harvard University Press.

Swann, D. 1983. *Competition and Industrial Policy in the European Community.* London: Methuen.

Swidler, Anne. 1986. "Culture in Action: Symbols and Strategies." *American Sociological Review* 51(2): 273–286.

Swire, Peter. 1996. "The Race to Laxity and the Race to Undesirability." *Yale Law and Policy Review / Yale Journal of Regulation Symposium Issue* 14: 67–110.

Switzer, Jacqueline Vaughn. 2003. *Disabled Rights: American Disability Policy and the Fight for Equality.* Georgetown: Georgetown University Press.

Szyszczak, Erika. 1996. "Making Europe More Relevant to Its Citizens: Effective Judicial Process." *European Law Review* 21: 351–364.

Tait, Nikki. 2008a. "Brussels Enters Fray over Class Actions." *Financial Times,* 26 March.

———. 2008b. "Microsoft to Appeal against €900m Penalty." *Financial Times,* 10 May.

———. 2008c. "Cartel Fine Doubled for Repeat Offender." *Financial Times,* 11 June. Available at http://www.ft.com (accessed 20 March 2010).

Tait, Nikki, and Bob Sherwood. 2005. "Class Actions across the Atlantic." *Financial Times,* 16 June.

Tarrow, Sidney. 1993. "Cycles of Collective Action: Between Moments of Madness and the Repertoire of Contention." *Social Science History* 17(2): 281–307.

Tate, C. Neal, and Torbjorn Vallinder, eds. 1995. *The Global Expansion of Judicial Power.* New York: NYU Press.

Taub, Stephen. 2007. "Royal Dutch Shell to Pay $350 M." *CFO.com,* 11 April.

Taylor, Simon. 2007. "UK Main Obstacle to Treaty Reforms." *The European Voice,* 31 May. Available at http://www.europeanvoice.com (accessed 4 October 2010).

TEEC (The European Evaluation Consortium). 2005. *Evaluation of the Functioning of the European Judicial Network in Civil and Commercial Matters: Final Report to the European Commission, Directorate General Justice Freedom and Security.* Brussels: TEEC.

Teubner, Gunthur, ed. 1987. *Juridification of Social Spheres.* Berlin. Walter de Gruyter.

Thelen, Kathleen. 2003. "How Institutions Evolve." In *Comparative Historical*

Analysis in the Social Sciences, ed. James Mahoney and Dietrich Rueschemeyer. Cambridge: Cambridge University Press.

Thill-Tayara, Mélanie, and Marta Giner Asins. 2008. "France." *PLC Cross-Border Competition Handbook 2007/2008,* pp. 171–183. London: Practical Law Company.

Thornhill, John. 2005. "US warns France on Class Actions." *Financial Times,* 26 January.

Thornton, Patricia. 1998. *Employment Quotas, Levies, and National Rehabilitation Funds for Persons with Disabilities: Pointers for Policy and Practice.* Geneva: International Labour Office.

Thornton, Patricia, and Neil Lunt. 1997. *Employment Policies for Disabled People in Eighteen Countries—a Review.* York: University of York Social Policy Research Unit.

Tilly, Charles. 1978. *From Mobilization to Revolution.* Reading, Mass.: Addison-Wesley.

Tiratsoo, N., and J. Tomlinson. 1997. "Exporting the Gospel of Productivity: United States Technical Assistance and British Industry, 1945–1960." *Business History Review* 71(1): 41–81.

Tobler, Christa. 2005. *Remedies and Sanctions in EC Non-discrimination Law.* Report from European Network of Legal Experts in the Non-discrimination Field, Prepared for European Commission, Directorate General for Employment, Social Affairs, and Equal Opportunities, Unit D.3. Luxembourg: Office for Official Publications of the European Communities.

Tolmein, Oliver. 2010. (Partner at Kanzlei Menschen und Rechte, Hamburg, Germany.) Personal correspondence, 22 February.

Toube, David. 2001. "Background to U.K. Regulation." In *The Financial Services and Markets Act: A Practical Legal Guide,* ed. J. Perry. London: Sweet and Maxwell.

Trade Union Disability Alliance. 2007. Interview. London. 11 July.

Traynor, Ian. 2007. "Germany sets collision course with UK on rights." *The Guardian,* 21 June, available at http://www.guardian.co.uk (accessed 4 October 2010).

Trebilcock, M. J., and E. M. Iacobucci. 2002. "Designing Competition Law Institutions." *World Competition* 25(3): 361–394.

Tridimas, Takis. 2000. "Enforcing Community Rights in National Courts: Some Recent Developments." In *The Future of Remedies in Europe,* pp. 35–50, ed. Claire Kilpatrick, Tonia Novitz, and Paul Skimore. Oxford: Hart Publishing.

Trubek, David. 1994. "Global Restructuring and the Law." *Case Western Law Review* 44: 407–498.

Trubek, David, Yves Dezalay, Ruth Buchanan and John Davis. 1994. "Global Restructuring and the Law. *Case Western Law Review* 44:407–98.

Trubeck, David, and J. S. Mosher. 2003. "New Governance, Employment Policy, and the European Social Model." In *Governing Work and Welfare in a New Economy: European and American Experiments,* pp. 33–58, ed. J. Zeitlin and David M. Trubek. Oxford: Oxford University Press.

Trubek, David, and Louise Trubek. 2005. "Hard and Soft Law in the Construction of Social Europe: The Role of the Open Method of Co-ordination." *European Law Journal,* 11(3): 343–364.

———. 2007. "New Governance and Legal Regulation." New Modes of Governance Project working paper, reference number LTFIa/D5f. Available at http://www.eu-newgov.org (accessed on 20 June, 2010).

Tsebelis, George. 2002. *Veto Players: How Political Institutions Work.* Princeton: Princeton University Press.

Tsoukalis, Loukas. 1993. *The New European Economy.* Oxford: Oxford University Press.

Turner, David. 2005. "Watchdog Calls in Lawyers over Equality Directive." *Financial Times,* 11 March.

Tzankova, Ianika, and Daan Lunsingh Scheurleer. 2009. "The Netherlands." In *The Globalization of Class Actions,* ed. Deborah R. Hensler, Christopher Hodges, and Magadalena Tulibacka. *Annals of the American Academy of Political and Social Science* 622: 149–161.

UPIAS/Disability Alliance. 1976. *Statement of "Fundamental Principles of Disability."* London: UPIAS/Disability Alliance. Quoted in Lawson, Anna. 2006. "The EU Rights-based Approach to Disability: Some Strategies for Shaping an Inclusive Society." GLADNET Collection Working Paper, Industrial and Labor Relations School, Cornell University, Ithaca, N.Y. Available at http://digitalcommons.ilr.cornell.edu (accessed 10 February 2010).

Vallindas, G. 2006. "New Directions in EC Competition Policy: The Case of Merger Control." *European Law Journal* 12(2): 616–660.

Vanberg, Georg. 2001. "Legislative-Judicial Relations: A Game-Theoretic Approach to Constitutional Review." *American Journal of Political Science* 45: 346–361.

———. 2008. "Establishing and Maintaining Judicial Independence." In *The Oxford Handbook of Law and Politics,* pp.99-118, ed., K. Whittington, R.D. Kelemen, G. Caldeira. Oxford: Oxford University Press.

Vanberg, Georg, and James R. Rogers. 2007. "Resurrecting Lochner: A Contingent Defense of Judicial Activism." *Journal of Law, Economics, and Organization.* 32: 442–468.

Van Boom, Willem. 2009. "Collective Settlement of Mass Claims in the Netherlands." In *Auf dem Weg zu einer europäischen Sammelklage?* pp. 171–192, ed. Matthias Casper, André Janssen, Petra Pohlmann, and Reiner Schulze. Munich: Sellier.

Van Dam, Cees. 2006. *European Tort Law.* Oxford: Oxford University Press.

Van de Vijver, Niels R. 2000. *Securities Regulation in the Netherlands.* Amsterdam: Allen and Overy Legal Practice.

Van Gerven, Walter. 1995. "Bridging the Gap Between Community and National Laws: Towards a Principle of Homogeneity in the Field of Legal Remedies?" *Common Market Law Review* 32: 679–702.

———. 2005. "Private Enforcement of EC Competition Rules." Paper prepared for Joint EU Commission/IBA Conference on Antitrust Reform in Europe: A Year in Practice, Brussels, Belgium, 10–11 March.

Vanhala, Lisa. 2006. "Fighting Discrimination through Litigation in the UK: The Social Model of Disability and the EU Anti-discrimination Directive." *Disability and Society* 21(5): 551–565.

———. 2009a. "Anti-discrimination Policy Actors and Their Use of Litigation Strategies: The Influence of Identity Politics." *Journal of European Public Policy* 16(5): 738–754.

———. 2009b. "Making Rights a Reality? Disability Rights Activists and Legal Mobilization in Canada and the United Kingdom." PhD diss., Oxford University.

Van Koppen, Peter. 1992. "Judicial Policymaking in the Netherlands." *West European Politics* 15(3): 80–92.

Van Miert, Karel. 1994. Speech reported in *International Bar News,* January/February.

Van Oorschot, W., and B. Hvinden. 2000. "Introduction: Towards Convergence?: Disability Policies in Europe." *European Journal of Social Security* 2(4): 293–302

Van Waarden, Frans. 1992. "Emergence and Development of Business Interest Associations: An Example from the Netherlands." *Organization Studies* 13(4): 521–561.

———. 1995. "Persistence of National Policy Styles: A Study of their Institutional Foundations." In *Convergence or Diversity? Internationalization and Economic Policy Response,* pp. 333–372, eds. B. Unger and F. Van Waarden. Aldershot: Avebury.

———. 2002a. "Courts and (Epistemic) Communities in the Convergence of Competition Policies." *Journal of European Public Policy* 9(6): 913–934.

———. 2002b. "Dutch Consociationalism and Corporatism: A Case of Institutional Persistence." *Acta Politica.* 37(1–2): 44–67.

———. 2003. "The Societal and Historical Embeddedness of Dutch Corporatism." In *Renegotiating the Welfare State,* ed. F. Van Waarden and G. Lehmbruch. London: Routledge.

———. 2009. "Power to the Legal Professionals: Is there an Americanization of European Law?" *Regulation and Governance* 3(3): pp. 197–216.

Van Waarden, Frans, and M. Drahos. 2002. "Courts and (Epistemic) Communities in the Convergence of Competition Policies." *Journal of European Public Policy* 9(6): 913–934.

Van Waarden, Frans, and Youri Hildebrand. 2009. "From Corporatism to Lawyocracy? On Liberalization and Juridification." *Regulation and Governance* 3(3): 259–286.

Vauchez, Antoine. 2008. "The Force of a Weak Field: Law and Lawyers in the Governance of the European Union." *International Political Sociology* 2(2): 128–144.

Velthuyse, H. E. M., and F. M. Schlingmann. 1995. "Prospectus Liability in the Netherlands." *Journal of International Banking Law* 6: 229–236.

Verloren van Themaat, Weyer, and Johannes Hettema. 2004. *National Report: The Netherlands—Ashurst Study on the Conditions of Claims for Damages in Case of Infringement of EC Competition Rules.* Brussels: DG Competition, European Commission.

Verougstraete, Ivan. 1992. "Judicial Politics in Belgium." *West European Politics* 15(3): 93–107.

Viscusi, Kip, ed. 2002. *Regulation through Litigation.* Washington, D.C.: Brookings Institution Press.

Vogel, David. 1986. *National Styles of Regulation.* Ithaca: Cornell University Press.

———. 1995. *Trading Up: Consumer and Environmental Regulation in a Global Economy.* Cambridge, Mass.: Harvard University Press.

———. 2003. "The Hare and the Tortoise Revisited: The New Politics of Consumer and Environmental Regulation in Europe. *British Journal of Political Science* 33: 557–580.

Vogel, Joseph. 2009. "France: Overview." *The Handbook of Competition Enforcement Agencies—2009: Global Competition Review.* London: Law Business Research.

Vogel, Steven. 1996. *Freer Markets, More Rules: Regulatory Reform in Advanced Industrialized Countries.* Ithaca: Cornell University Press.

———. 2007. Why Freer Markets Need More Rules. In *Creating Competitive Markets: The Politics of Regulatory Reform,* pp.25-42, ed., Mark Landy, Martin Levin and Martin Shapiro. Washington, DC: Brookings Institution Press.

Volcansek, Mary. 1992. "Judicial Politics and Policy-Making in Western Europe." Special Issue of *West European Politics* 15(3).

Völcker, Sven. 2007. "Rough Justice? An Analysis of the European Commission's New Fining Guidelines." *Common Market Law Review* 44(5): 1285–1320.

Volkskrant. 2005. "Megaclaims in Holland: 'Hebzucht is toch prima?'" [Megaclaims in Holland: "Greed Is Good, Isn't It?"], 3 November. Available at www.volkrant.nl (accessed 10 February 2010).

Wach, Karl, Manja Epping, Ute Zinsmeister, and Eva Bonacker. 2004. *National Report: Germany-Ashurst Study on the Conditions of Claims for Damages in Case of Infringement of EC Competition Rules.* Brussels: DG Competition, European Commission.

Waddington, Lisa. 1995. *Disability, Employment and the European Community.* London: Blackstone.

———. 1996. "Reassessing the Employment of People with Disabilities in Europe: From Quotas to Anti-discrimination Laws." *Comparative Labor Law Journal* 18: 62–101.

———. 2006a. *From Rome to Nice in a Wheelchair: The Development of a European Disability Policy.* Groningen: Europa Law Publishing.

———. 2006b. "Legislating to Employ People with Disabilities: The European and American Way." *Maastricht Journal of European and Comparative Law* 1(4): 367–395.

Waddington, Lisa, and Mark Bell. 2001. "More Equal than Others: Distinguishing European Union Equality Directives?" *Common Market Law Review* 38: 587–611.

Waddington, Lisa, and Matthew Diller. 2002. "Tensions and Coherence in Disability Policy: The Uneasy Relationship between Social Welfare and Civil Rights Models of the Disability in American, European and International Employments Law." In *Disability Rights Law and Policy, International and National Perspectives,* pp. 241–282, ed. M. L. Breslin and S. Yee. Ardsley, N.Y.: Transnational Publishers.

Waddington, Lisa, and Marianne Gijzen. 2004. "Dutch Report on the Implementation of the Disability Provisions of the Framework Employment Directive." Brussels: European Commission.

Waelbroeck, Denis, and Donald Slater. 2006. "The Commission's Green Paper on Private Enforcement: Americanization of EC Competition Law Enforcement?" 2006 EU Competition Law and Policy Workshop Proceedings, Robert Schuman Centre for Advanced Studies, Florence, Italy, European Studies Institute.

Waelbroeck, Denis, Donald Slater, and Gil Even-Shoshan. 2004. *Study on the Conditions of Claims for Damages in Case of Infringement of EC Competition Rules.* Brussels: Ashurst.

Wallace, David. 2007. "The Perfect Storm? International Trade in American-style Tort Litigation." Working Paper, Chadbourne and Parke. Available at http://works.bepress.com/david_wallace/1 (accessed 10 February 2010).

Ward, Angela. 2000. "The Limits of the Uniform Application of Community Law and Effective Judicial Review: A Look Post-Amsterdam." In *The Future of Remedies in Europe,* pp. 213–229, ed. Claire Kilpatrick, Tonia Novitz, and Paul Skidmore. Oxford: Hart Publishing.

———. 2007. *Judicial Review and the Rights of Private Parties in EU Law,* 2nd ed. Oxford: Oxford University Press.

Warren, Manning Gilbert. 1990. "Global Harmonization of Securities Laws: The Achievements of the European Communities." *Harvard International Law Journal* 31(1): 185.

———. 1994. "The European Union's Investment Services Directive." *University of Pennsylvania Journal of International Business Law* 15: 181–200.

———. 2003. *European Securities Regulation.* The Hague: Kluwer Law International.

Watson, Alan. 1978. "Comparative Law and Legal Change." *Cambridge Law Journal* 37: 313, 313–314, and 321.

———. 1993. *Legal Transplants: An Approach to Comparative Law,* 2nd ed. Athens: University of Georgia Press.

———. 2003. *Legal Origins and Legal Change.* London: Hambledon Press.

Watt, Nicholas. 2005. "Brussels Wins Right to Force EU Countries to Jail Polluters." *Guardian,* 14 September.

Weatherill, S. 2005. *EU Consumer Law and Policy.* Cheltenham: Elgar European Law.

Weatherill, S., and U. Bernitz. 2007. *The Regulation of Unfair Commercial Practices under EC Directive 2005/29.* Oxford: Hart Publishing.

Weaver, R. Kent, and Bert A. Rockman, eds. 1993. *Do Institutions Matter? Government Capabilities in the U.S. and Abroad.* Washington D.C.: Brookings Institution Press.

Weber, Martin. 1994. "Deutsches Kapitalmarktsrecht im Umbruch—das Zweite Finanzmarkförderungsgesetz." *Neue Juristische Wochenzeitschrift* 44: 2849–2860.

Weber, Max. 1914/1978. *Economy and Society.* Berkeley: University of California Press.

———. 1918/1958. "Politics as a Vocation." Reprinted in *From Max Weber: Essays in Sociology,* pp. 77-128, ed. H.H. Gerth and C. W. Mills. Oxford: Oxford University Press.

Weiler, Joseph H. H. 1986. "Eurocracy and Distrust: Some Questions Concerning the Role of the European Court of Justice in the Protection of Fundamental Human Rights within the Legal Order of the European Communities." *Washington Law Review* 61: 1103–1142.

———. 1991. "The Transformation of Europe." *Yale Law Journal* 100: 2403–2483.

———. 1994. "A Quiet Revolution: The ECJ and Its Interlocutors." *Comparative Political Studies* 26(4): 510–534.

———. 1996. "European Neo-constitutionalism: In Search of Foundations for the European Constitutional Order." In *Constitutionalism in Transformation,* pp. 105–121, ed. R. Bellamy and D. Catiglione. Oxford: Blackwell.

———. 1999. *The Constitution of Europe.* Cambridge: Cambridge University Press.

———. 2006. "The Essential (and Would-Be Essential) Jurisprudence of the Court of Justice: Lights and Shadows Too." In *The Future of the European Judicial System in Comparative Perspective.* pp. 117–127, ed. I. Pernice, J. Kolcott, C. Saunders. Baden-Baden: Nomos Verlag.

Weiler, Joseph H. H., and N. J. S. Lockhart. 1995. "'Taking Rights Seriously' Seriously: The European Court and Its Fundamental Rights Jurisprudence." *Common Market Law Review* 32: 51–94, 579–627.

Weisbrod, Burton, Joel Handler, and Neil Komesar. 1978. *Public Interest Law: An Economic and Institutional Analysis.* Berkeley: University of California Press.

Wells, Katie. 2003. "The Impact of the Framework Employment Directive on UK Disability Discrimination Law." *Industrial Law Journal* 32 (4): 253–273.

Werdigier, Julia. 2007. "Europe Braces for Waves of US-Style Class Action." *International Herald Tribune,* 31 October.

Wesseling, Rein. 1997. "The Commission Notices on Decentralisation of EC Antitrust Law: In for a Penny, Not for a Pound." *European Competition Law Review* 18: 94–97.

———. 2008. *National Report for the Netherlands.* 23rd Congress of FIDE, Linz, Austria.

Westendorp, Carlos. 1995. *Report by the Reflection Group: A Strategy for Europe.* Brussels: European Parliament (5 December).

Whish, Richard. 2001. *Competition Law,* 4th ed. London: Butterworths.

Whittington, Keith E. 2003. "Legislative Sanctions and the Strategic Environment of Judicial Review." *I-Con: The International Journal of Constitutional Law* 1(3): 446–474.

Whittle, Richard. 2002. "The Framework Directive for Equal Treatment in Employment and Occupation: An Analysis from a Disability Rights Perspective." *European Law Review* 27(3): 303–326.

Wiegand, W. 1991. "The Reception of American Law in Europe." *American Journal of Comparative Law* 39(2): 229–249.

Wiesmann, Gerrit. 2008. "D Telekom Dotcoms Star Retakes Limelight." *Financial Times,* April 13.

Wigger, Angela. 2007. "Towards a Market-Based Approach: The Privatization and Micro-Economization of EU Antitrust Law Enforcement." In *The Transnational Politics of Corporate Governance Regulation,* pp. 98–118, ed. H. Overbeck, B. van Apeldoorn, A. Nölke. London: Routledge.

Wigger, Angela, and Andreas Nölke. 2007. "Enhanced Roles of Private Actors in the EU Business Regulation and the Erosion of the Rhenish Model of Capitalism: The Case of Antitrust Enforcement." *Journal of Common Market Studies* 45(2): 487–513.

Wilks, Stephen. 1999. *In the Public Interest: Competition Policy and the Monopolies and Mergers Commission.* Manchester: Manchester University Press.

———. 2005a. "Agency Escape: Decentralization or Dominance of the European Commission in the Modernization of Competition Policy?" *Governance* 18(3): 431–452.

———. 2005b. "Competition Policy: Challenge and Reform." In *Policy-Making in the European Union,* pp. 113–139, ed. H. Wallace, W. Wallace, and M. Pollack. Oxford: Oxford University Press.

———. 2007. "The European Competition Network: What Has Changed?" Paper presented at the European Union Studies Association Biennial Conference, Montreal, Canada, 17–19 May.

Wilks, Stephen, and Lee McGowan. 1995. "Disarming the Commission: The Debate over a European Cartel Office." *Journal of Common Market Studies* 32(2): 259–273.

Willett, Linda. 2005. *U.S.-Style Class Action in Europe: A Growing Threat?* Washington, D.C.: National Legal Center for the Public Interest.

Williams, Kevin. 2005. "State of Fear: Britain's 'Compensation Culture' Reviewed." *Legal Studies* 25(3): 499–514.

Wils, Wouter. 2003. "Should Private Antitrust Enforcement Be Encouraged in Europe?" *World Competition* 26(3): 473–488.

———. 2007. "The European Commission's 2006 Guidelines on Antitrust Fines: A Legal and Economic Analysis." *World Competition* 30(2): 197–229.

Wittgenstein, Ludwig. 1953/1973. *Philosophical Investigations.* Trans. G. Anscombe, 3rd Ed., New York: Prentice Hall.

Wollschläger, Christian. 1998. "Exploring the Global Landscapes of Litigation Rates." In *Soziologie des Rechts: Festschrift für Erhard Blankenburg zum 60,* pp. 587–588, ed. J. Brand and D. Strempel. Baden Baden: Nomos.

Woods, Donncadh, Ailsa Sinclair, and David Ashton. 2004. "Private Enforcement of Community Competition Law." *Competition Policy Newsletter,* no. 2, pp. 31–37.

Woolfe, Jeremy. 2007. "Use of US Class Action Gathers Apace." *Financial Times,* 26 November.

Wurmnest, Wolfgang. 2005. "A New Era for Private Antitrust Litigation in Germany?" *German Law Journal* 6(8): 1173–1190.

Wymeersch, Eddy. 1998. "The Implementation of the ISD and CAD in National Legal Systems." In *European Securities Markets: The Investment Services Directive and Beyond,* pp. 3–45, ed. G. Ferrarini. London: Kluwer Law International.

———. 2005. "The Future of Financial Regulation in Europe." *Common Market Law Review* 42: 987–1010.

Yeung, Karen. 1998. "Privatizing Competition Regulation." *Oxford Journal of Legal Studies* 18(4): 581–615.

Zander, Michael. 2002. "Will the Revolution in the Funding of Civil Litigation in England Eventually Lead to Contingency Fees?" *DePaul Law Review* 52: 259–298.

Zeitlin, Jonathan. 2005. "Conclusion." In *The Open Method of Co-ordination in Action: The European Employment and Social Inclusion Strategies,* pp. 447–503, ed., J. Zeitlin and P. Pochet. Brussels: P.I.E.–Peter Lang.

Zeitlin, Jonathan, and Philippe Pochet. 2005. *The Open Method of Coordination in Action: The European Employment and Social Inclusion Strategies.* Brussels: P.I.E.–Peter Lang.

Zimmermann, Reinhard. 1995. "The 'Europeanization' of Private Law within the European Community and the Re-Emergence of a European Legal Science." *Columbia Journal of European Law* 1: 63–105.

Zolberg, Aristide. 1972. "Moments of Madness." *Politics and Society* 2(2): 183–207.

Zuckerman, A. 1999. *Civil Justice in Crisis.* Oxford: Oxford University Press.

Zysman, John. 1983. *Governments, Markets and Growth: Finance and the Politics of Industrial Change.* Ithaca: Cornell University Press.

Acknowledgments

This book has been years in the making, and many students, colleagues, and friends have helped me with it along the way. I am deeply grateful to all of them.

I could not have completed this book without the help of a group of dedicated and extremely talented research assistants, who helped me with various aspects of the project over the past few years. My team included Anne Gèniets, Timo Idema, Esther Herlin-Karnel, Tim Knievel, Gabrielle Krapels, Tobias Lenz, Jeff Miller, Oliver Munn, Parina Patel, Philip Streich, Terence Teo, Ed Turner, Lisa Vanhala, Juri Viehoff, Stefan Vollmerding, Nicolas Wilhelm, and Samuel Zeidman. I thank them all for their hard work and their good humor.

For research funding, I thank the Economic and Social Research Council of the United Kingdom. Also, for funding and institutional support, I thank the School of Social Science at the Institute for Advanced Study, where I was a member during the 2007–2008 academic year. I wrote more than half of the manuscript during my year at the Institute. I could not have asked for a better environment in which to work or a more supportive and inspiring group of colleagues.

I thank the many colleagues and friends who provided insights and helpful comments on my earlier work on adversarial legalism in the European Union or on sections of the book manuscript: Karen Alter, Francesca Bignami, Giovanni Capoccia, James Caporaso, Rachel Cichowski, Lisa Conant, Paul Craig, Eric Feldman, Orfeo Fioretos, Elizabeth Fisher, Milt Heumann, Lisa Hilbink, Chris Hodges, Walter Mattli, Chris McCrudden, Anand Menon, Lisa Miller, Mark Pollack, Ralf Poscher, Jeremy Richardson, Fritz Scharpf, Philippe Schmitter, Alec Stone Sweet, Brian Tamanaha, Andrew Tarrant, Frans van Waarden, Angela Wigger, Bruno de Witte, and Antoine Vauchez. I owe a particular debt of gratitude to three giants at the University of California, Berkeley—Robert Kagan, Martin Shapiro, and David Vogel—who provided much of the intellectual inspiration for the book and shared their sage advice with me as I worked on it. I also owe special thanks to my dear old friend, Eric Sibbitt, who collaborated with me on some of my earliest work on the issues explored in the book and profoundly shaped my thinking.

Finally, I thank my wife, Tasha, and our daughter, Zara, whose love and support make everything possible for me.

Index

Harvard University Press is a member of Green Press Initiative (greenpressinitiative.org), a nonprofit organization working to help publishers and printers increase their use of recycled paper and decrease their use of fiber derived from endangered forests. This book was printed on recycled paper containing 30% post-consumer waste and processed chlorine free.